Music in English Children's Drama of the Later Renaissance

Originally published in 1992, *Music in English Children's Drama of the Later Renaissance* is the first book-length study to examine the Elizabethan and Jacobean children's drama, not only from a musicological perspective, but also drawing on the histories of literature, culture, and the theater. It gives the children's companies new historical significance, showing that they were an integral and ultimately influential part of the London theatrical world. These companies originated important features of later drama, such as music before and between acts, and the exploitation of different timbres for specific effects.

Those interested in music history, English literature, theater history, and cultural history will find this a comprehensive and fascinating study. Of special note are the appendices, which offer a unique and important reference source by providing the only definitive list of the plays and songs used by the children.

Music in English Children's Drama of the Later Renaissance

Linda Phyllis Austern

Routledge
Taylor & Francis Group

First published in 1992
by Gordon and Breach

This edition first published in 2024 by Routledge
4 Park Square, Milton Park, Abingdon, Oxon, OX14 4RN

and by Routledge
605 Third Avenue, New York, NY 10017

Routledge is an imprint of the Taylor & Francis Group, an informa business

© 1992 Linda Phyllis Austern

Publisher's Note
The publisher has gone to great lengths to ensure the quality of this reprint but points out that some imperfections in the original copies may be apparent.

Disclaimer
The publisher has made every effort to trace copyright holders and welcomes correspondence from those they have been unable to contact.

A Library of Congress record exists under LCCN: 92014000

ISBN: 978-1-032-83178-7 (hbk)
ISBN: 978-1-003-50816-8 (ebk)
ISBN: 978-1-032-83179-4 (pbk)

Book DOI 10.4324/9781003508168

Music in English Children's Drama of the Later Renaissance

Linda Phyllis Austern

University of Notre Dame
Indiana, USA

Gordon and Breach
USA Switzerland Australia Belgium France Germany Great Britain
India Japan Malaysia Netherlands Russia Singapore

Gordon and Breach Science Publishers

5301 Tacony Street, Drawer 330
Philadelphia, Pennsylvania 19137
United States of America

Parc Scientifique et Technologique
Chemin de la Sallaz
1400 Yverdon, Switzerland

Private Bag 8
Camberwell, Victoria 3124
Australia

58, rue Lhomond
75005 Paris
France

Glinkastrasse 13–15
O–1086 Berlin
Germany

Post Office Box 90
Reading, Berkshire RG1 8JL
Great Britain

3-14-9, Okubo
Shinjuku-ku, Tokyo 169
Japan

Emmaplein 5
1075 AW Amsterdam
Netherlands

Library of Congress Cataloging-in-Publication Data

Austern, Linda Phyllis, 1957–
    Music in English children's drama of the later Renaissance / Linda
Phyllis Austern.
        p.   cm. -- (Musicology ; v. 13)
    Originally presented as the author's thesis (Ph. D.--University of
Chicago, 1984).
    Includes bibliographical references (p.   ) and indexes.
    ISBN 2–88124–558–7 (France : hard)
    1. Incidental music--17th century--History and criticism.
2. Music--England--17th century--History and criticism.
3. Children's plays, English.   I. Title.   II. Series: Musicology
(New York, N.Y.) ; v. 13.
ML173.A95   1992
781.5′52′0830942--dc20   92–14000
                                                 CIP

CONTENTS

CONTENTS

ILLUSTRATIONS

INTRODUCTION TO THE SERIES

The Gordon and Breach Musicology series, a companion to the *Journal of Musicological Research*, covers a creative range of musical topics, from historical and theoretical subjects to social and philosophical studies. Volumes thus far published show the extent of this broad spectrum, from *Music, Film and Art; The Trombone: Its History and Music, 1697–1811;* and *Musical Life in Poland: The Postwar Years 1945–1977* to *The Early Works of Felix Mendelssohn: A Study in the Romantic Sonata Style.* The editors also welcome interdisciplinary studies, ethnomusicological works and performances analyses. With this series, it is our aim to expand the field and definition of musical exploration and research.

ACKNOWLEDGEMENTS

Each stage of this work has been both a joy and a learning experience, made more so by the generosity of the many who assisted me along the way. Thanks are due first to my advisors from the University of Chicago, Howard Mayer Brown and David M. Bevington, who taught me scholarship in two disciplines and originally encouraged me to work on this topic; to Hans Lenneberg, who offered practical library advice; to Ellen T. Harris, who first suggested that what began as a doctoral dissertation should be rewritten as a book.

I owe a great deal to the helpful and knowledgeable staffs of the following libraries in Great Britain and the United States, who allowed me access to restricted materials, provided the answers to many questions, provided microfilms when I needed them, and cheerfully let me go about my research: the Bodleian Library of Oxford University, the British Library, the Department of Special Collections of Cornell University Libraries, Edinburgh University Library, the Guildhall Library, Houghton Library of Harvard University, King's College Library of Cambridge University, Lambeth Palace Library, the Library of Congress, the Newberry Library, the New York Public Library, the Public Record Office in London, the Perry Room Library of the Royal College of Music, Trinity College Library in Dublin, and the Department of Special Collections of the University of Chicago Libraries. The Reverend Richard Fenwick of St. Paul's Cathedral in London was kind enough to allow me access to such uncatalogued documents as are still under the jurisdiction of the cathedral, and to arrange an interview with the current principal of the St. Paul's Cathedral choir school. Mr. Colin Scull, the Serjeant of the Vestry and unofficial historian of the Chapel Royal, was kind enough to share a wealth of information relating to the choirboys of that establishment. I also wish to thank the many individuals who assisted in preparing this book for publication: Carmelo Comberiati, Ellen T. Harris, Ralph Locke, Michael Shapiro (whom I later learned had been a reader for the press, and who provided many useful suggestions), Matt Steel, and the two individuals who prepared the camera-ready musical examples, Michael Fallon and Michael Molloy.

I would like to thank Cambridge University Press and Rutgers University Press for their permission to reprint material from their publications. Figures 1 and 2, which appear in chapter 2, originally appeared in K. Muir and S. Schoenbaum's *A New Companion to Shakespeare Studies* (Cambridge University Press, 1971). Examples 1 and 16, which appear in chapters 7 and 10 respectively, are reprinted from Claude Simpson's *The British Broadside Ballad and Its Music* (copyright © 1966 by Rutgers University, The State University of New Jersey).

Thanks are also due to the many friends, colleagues, and students who sometimes stood behind me and sometimes distracted me terribly from the writing of this book, especially Stuart Kisilinsky, who was with me all the way, and my husband, Anthony Elmendorf, who is at this point probably the world's most musicologically literate mathematician. This book is made possible in part by support from the Institute for Scholarship in the Liberal Arts, College of Arts and Letters, University of Notre Dame.

Linda Phyllis Austern

INTRODUCTION

Musicke dothe comprehende al disciplines, as Plato saithe in the first booke of his laws, as *Musicke* cannot be entreated without al disciplines.

Henry Cornelius Agrippa von Nettesheim,
Of the Vanitie and Uncertaintie of Artes and Sciences (c.1530)

Although this work is principally concerned with the music from one small English dramatic repertory, it also discusses sixteenth- and early seventeenth-century music, musicians, literature, theater, and society at large. Late Renaissance thinkers did not completely sever music from poetry, rhetoric, drama, medicine, astronomy, or natural philosophy. In tracing these earlier intellectual patterns, *Music in English Children's Drama of the Later Renaissance* draws on a wider range of material than many of today's specialized academic studies. Such interdisciplinary scholarship may be frustrating to the modern reader and writer, who generally have a comprehensive background in only one field. For this reason, I include elementary details that may be obvious to specialists. If I tend toward overdocumentation in fields outside of music, it is only because I am primarily a musicologist.

Elizabethan and Jacobean England have come to be known as the Golden Age of English drama. The earliest permanent English theaters and professional drama companies were founded during this period, and brilliant literary figures such as William Shakespeare and Ben Jonson dominated the dramatic landscape. Two distinct but mutually influential types of theater and drama companies developed during these years. The first type of theater, known as "public," descended from the animal-baiting arena or inn yard where troupes of itinerant actors had traditionally performed for whatever audience would gather to watch them. Public theaters were relatively large, open-roofed, and constructed on circular or polygonal plans. Costly seats were available in sheltered galleries, but admission to stand in the yard was not expensive. The audience, therefore, came from diverse social backgrounds, and plays written for them tended to have a broad appeal. Public theater actors were men who trained from boyhood for their stage careers through the apprenticeship system.

The other theatrical tradition had a slightly different derivation, contemporary status, and audience appeal. Generally known by the more exclusive term "private," it descended from the banquet hall of a court or manor house where the nobility had long been entertained. Private theaters were small, rectangular, completely enclosed, and provided seats for the entire audience. The price of admission was generally higher than for the public theaters and, consequently, excluded more people. Plays written for the private theaters often focused on the economic, social, political, and intellectual concerns of a self-conscious, self-styled elite. The actors originally employed in the private theaters further recalled aristocratic diversions, for they were at first the choirboys of St. Paul's Cathedral and the Chapel Royal, who had traditionally played before the Tudor court. Even when these boys were joined or supplanted by non-chorister actors and their court performances had all but ceased, the mystique of royal entertainment was carefully maintained.

Where modern scholarship has compared these two theatrical traditions, the role of music has been especially important. Music was a distinct, vital component of English Renaissance drama regardless of the theater or acting company. However, previous studies have tended to emphasize the children's intensive musical training, their connections with prestigious musical establishments, the stylistic contrast between the polyphonic art songs for which the children's theaters were famous, and the unaccompanied ditties and simple trumpet signals associated with the popular stages. Plays written for the boys are frequently cited for their unusually rich musical directions, and the private theater has been regarded as the equal province of musicians and dramatists. However, a careful reexamination of the children's dramatic repertoire and contemporary documents relating to the stage shows this dichotomy to be exaggerated. In fact, children's plays make selective use of all sorts of contemporary secular music and rely more strongly on nondramatic late Renaissance English attitudes toward music than on the special musical training available to some of their actors.

Since the most inclusive and reliable sources of information about music in the Elizabethan and Jacobean theaters are the plays themselves, I began this study by reviewing all extant plays acted by children's companies between the late 1590s and 1613, the final and most professional phase of their history. English dramatic imprints and manuscripts from this period include four sorts of musical reference: (1) stage directions that call for music, (2) song lyrics or musical titles interspersed with spoken dialogue as part of the action of the play, (3) musical performances implied by spoken dialogue, and (4) discussions of the art or science of music. Because of slight variations between all sources of the same work from this era, I collated all extant sixteenth- and seventeenth-century editions of the plays for variant musical information.

A careful reading of this body of plays reveals more historical continuity and less of a manifest musical contrast between children's and adults' drama than previous emphasis had implied. For example, children's plays certainly tend to use more music than adults'; the most musical plays of the era belong to the children's repertoire; and the most elaborate extant theatrical songs belong to children's plays. However, a number of plays written for boy actors fail to include any music whatsoever, and less than half of the children's music is the polyphonic art song for which they have gained modern fame. In fact, the same lyrics familiar from the adult stage or to any student of Elizabethan and Jacobean popular music—such ballads as "Fortune my Foe" and "Walsingham," and such widely circulating ayres as John Dowland's "Now O Now I Needs Must Part" and Robert Jones's "Farewell Dear Love"—appear repeatedly in children's drama. The vast majority of texted songs in children's plays are the sort of unaccompanied, preexistent pieces associated more strongly with the public theaters. Furthermore, as the popularity of children's drama waned and adult troupes took over the private theaters in the early seventeenth century, adult drama began to include a high proportion of specially composed polyphonic art song. A careful study of extant archival and historical documents reveals that, in its final years, children's drama became dissociated from the great musical establishments of London, and some of its star performers went on to win fame as adult actors in popular companies.

As I began to see the strong musical cross-influence between the children's and adults' dramatic companies, I read all extant plays written for London performance between c.1575 and 1625. Again I found literary and dramatic continuities that scholars who had limited themselves to specific playwrights or repertories had overlooked. Regardless of dramatic company, year of first performance, or theater, certain dramatic situations were more likely to require music than others, and certain types of characters were more likely to perform. The sort of music used at any given moment clearly arose from dramatic requirements rather than from the mass availability of specially trained musicians or an acoustically favorable performance space.

Children's plays include a slightly higher average number of songs than adults' plays acted during the same years, because most children's plays are comedies or romances, and these are the genre that include the most music. During the reign of Elizabeth I, children's plays required more accompanied art songs and courtly dances because of an emphasis on wealthy or exotic settings. However, with the accession of James I, literary interest began to shift toward London and the common citizen, so stage music instead evoked these more familiar things with quotations from popular ballads and well-known lute ayres. There are, however, three significant differences between the use of music in children's and adults' plays: (1) when music is integrated into the action, children's plays are more likely to call for multiple musicians; (2) children's plays require a greater variety of musical instruments and musical styles (before 1609); and (3) performances of children's plays routinely include pre- and inter-act music. It is quite significant that when adult drama companies began to appear in the private theaters in 1609, they absorbed most of the musical features of children's performances. Therefore it was the children's musical innovations that paved the way for the musical conventions of the Caroline and Restoration stages.

It became apparent that the musical conventions of Elizabethan and Jacobean drama owed their origins to nondramatic ideas and practices, not to the special training of specific troupes of actors. Therefore, I turned to nondrama discussions of music published in England between 1550 and 1650. The magnitude and diversity of these discussions are astounding, for it seems that writers on nearly every topic known to sixteenth- and seventeenth-century England had something to say about music. And many of these observations are reflected in the theater. It has long been assumed that music in Elizabethan and Jacobean drama was but an echo of music in contemporary life and thought. But every specific use of music in children's plays between 1597 and 1613 has an established antecedent outside the theater that would have been familiar to playwright and audience alike, and most of the children's playwrights connect dramatic music to contemporary thought in the texts of their plays. The present study has, therefore, effectively become an examination of the way in which one small compendium of literature represents contemporary attitudes toward the theory and practice of music.

Nonetheless, the importance of the music itself to a study such as this can scarcely be overestimated. The relevant music belonged to a living, multifaceted theater that has been reduced to bare bones by the editions of plays that have come down to us. Elizabethan and Jacobean plays were not printed with musical notation or detailed descriptions of visual display; therefore, the modern scholar must seek these particulars elsewhere. Fortunately, the excellent work of such scholars as Philip Brett, Mary Chan, John. P. Cutts, John H. Long, and Andrew Sabol has shown that contemporary settings of theatrical music can be recovered. I used every extant manuscript I could locate and every publication of English secular music between c. 1575 and c.1700 in my search for settings and lyrics from children's plays, for many theatrical pieces are older than the plays in which they appear, and later manuscripts and publications often preserve earlier material whose other sources have been lost. I discovered that there are no extant manuscripts that seem to have belonged to children's dramatic companies, and that all extant manuscripts and publications of specifically theatrical music belong to subsequent eras. Slightly fewer than half of the lyrics and titles from these plays can be found in extant settings, and only about half of the musical performances indicated in the plays include text or title. Therefore, only a fraction of what was actually heard during a performance can be reconstructed. But the sources of the extant music from children's plays are as varied and widespread as the lyrics and titles. They range from broadside ballads to elegant manuscript partbooks for voices and viols, and from theoretical treatises to dance collections. The music itself is a diminutive mirror of contemporary musical taste, for it includes madrigals and Morris dances, courtly lute ayres and common drinking songs.

I have chosen to quote directly from a variety of Elizabethan, Jacobean, and Caroline sources, for summaries in modern language cannot do justice to most sixteenth- and seventeenth-century thinkers. I have retained the original spellings and punctuation, but have modernized the shape of the long "s" of contemporary usage and have interchanged the complementary pairs of letters "i"/"j", "u"/"v", and "w"/"vv" to accord with modern usage. I have added in square brackets letters that were indicated but not written out or printed, and have shown where a signature appears in manuscript documents. For the sake of consistency, I have uniformly spelled play titles to accord with the principal sixteenth- and seventeenth-century editions cited and quoted. In my musical transcriptions, I have indicated the original clef, key signature, and mensuration signature at the beginning of each voice, and have noted subsequent changes where they occur. I have retained the original note values but added bar lines that were originally absent. Textual underlay reproduces the original musical source as faithfully as possible, and textual repetition that was indicated but not written out is supplied in square brackets. With the exception of Appendix B, in which song titles and incipits are uniformly given as they are in the printed play texts, the titles of musical pieces are presented to accord with the specific source under discussion at that point in the narrative.

CHAPTER 1

THE CHILDREN'S DRAMA COMPANIES

The supinity of elder days hath left so much in silence, or time hath so martyred the Records, that the most industrious heads do find no easie work to erect a new *Britannia*.

Thomas Browne, *Hydrothapia* (1658)

The histories of the children's drama companies of the English Renaissance remain quite fragmentary since few original records relating to them have survived. The scattered scraps of evidence suggest the ephemeral qualities of youth and novelty with occasional flashes of literary and dramatic brilliance, tempered by humor, pathos, melodrama, and intrigue. These elements have inspired many to reconstruct these elusive histories, which deserve a summary here because the musical nature of children's drama is inexorably linked to its description and changing fortune.[1]

The use of children as actors in elite entertainment was not the exclusive product of the English Renaissance, but was an ancient and widespread European custom. Since the birth of liturgical drama, the singing boys of chapels and cathedrals had taken part in lavish dramatic entertainment on holy days and to celebrate such solemn events as weddings and coronations. Later, grammar school students also became part of this tradition. These boys bore only superficial resemblance to the young apprentice actors of the Renaissance, for acting was merely peripheral for them. England witnessed a unique development in the practice of children's drama, which ultimately led to unprecedented commercial status for companies consisting entirely of youths. An increase in the popularity of children's drama at the court of Elizabeth I coincided with the birth of professional theater in England, and led to regular paid performances in permanent theaters by the boy choristers of the Chapel Royal and St. Paul's Cathedral. A brief history of drama from the later seventeenth century reminds us that English authority grew increasingly dubious of the complete transformation of sacred choirboy into profane actor until children's drama vanished entirely:

Playes (which so flourisht amongst the Greeks and afterward among the Romans) were almost wholly abolisht when their Empire was first converted to Christianity . . . from which time to the last Age, they Acted nothing here [in England], but Playes of the holy Scripture, or Saints Lives; and that without any certain Theaters or Companies, till about the beginning of Queen Elizabeths Reign, they began here to assemble into Companies, and set up Theaters. . . . In which time, Playes were so little incompatible with Religion, and the Theater, and the Theater with the Church, as on week-dayes after Vespers, both the Children of the Chappel and St. Paul's, Acted Playes, the one in white-Friers, and the other behinde the Convocation-house in Pauls, till people growing more precise, and plays more licentious, the Theater of Pauls was quite supprest, and that of the Children of the Chappel, converted to the use of the Children of the Revels.[2]

The continuously documented history of English children's drama belongs entirely to the sixteenth and seventeenth centuries and is most easily divided into two periods. The first extends from 1516 to 1590 and is characterized by the performance of plays at court by choirboys and select grammar school students.[3] These court appearances led to rehearsals before elite groups of paying spectators as entrepreneurs realized that a profit could be made from the occasion. The second period extends from approximately 1597 to 1613 and is characterized by commercialization and competition. At this point, children's drama meant theatrical performances by companies composed predominantly of choristers who were occasionally invited to play at court. These companies competed directly with the adult troupes of the day. In spite of weakened connections with their parent choirs and the increasing rarity of court appearances, the two principal children's companies continued to emphasize their royal patronage and by calling themselves the Children of the Chapel (meaning the boy choristers of the sovereigns own chapel) and the Children of Paul's (meaning the boy choristers of St. Paul's Cathedral). These companies met with such commercial success that shortly after the beginning of the seventeenth century an independent professional boy company was founded with royal patronage as the Children of the King's Revels. During their heyday, the children's companies enjoyed widespread fame and attracted some of the most talented young playwrights and musicians of the era. The three children's companies that enjoyed commercial success had separate but parallel histories which affected their personnel, repertoire, and critical reception.

THE CHILDREN OF THE CHAPEL BEFORE 1600

The Children of the Chapel were the first troupe of English boy actors to leave a continuous record. Their history begins with the performance of a play written by their Master and Gentleman of the Chapel Royal, William Cornish, at Eltham on Twelfth Night 1516. From then until the accession of Elizabeth in 1558, they remained relatively inactive according to the scanty records that have survived.[4] However, Elizabeth apparently encouraged the presentation of plays by choristers and grammar school students, and the Children of the Chapel were not infrequently invited to play before her court during the early years of her reign. These Children achieved eminence under the guidance of Richard Edwards, who was appointed their Master in 1561. Edwards's standpoint patent of impressment permitted him to take "as manye well singing children as he or his deputie shall think mete" for the purpose of furnishing Her Majesty's Chapel Royal.[5] These were the children whom he brought to Court in special dramatic entertainments. According to a domestic dialogue of 1573, Edwards was revered after his death in 1566 as much for plays as for music:

[1.]   There is a good song: I do marvell who hath made it.
[2.]   It is the master of the children of the Queenes chapell.
[1.]   What is his name?
[2.]   Maister Edwards. [1.] Is he a live?
[2.]   I heard that he was dead.
[3.]   It is alreadi a good while a go: there are at least five yeers and a half.
[2.]   Truelie it is a pitie: he was a man of good wit, and a good poete: and a great player of playes.[6]

The Children of the Chapel continued to act at court under the direction of Edwards's successors. In 1576, perhaps inspired by the simultaneous construction of London's first public playhouse, the acting Master of the Children leased some rooms in a former Dominican priory known as the Blackfriars and converted them into a small theater. The acquisition of this Blackfriars theater marked the first step toward commercialization, for it offered a regular forum for paying spectators to watch rehearsals for court performances. A second step toward professional status came during the season of 1582–83, when the lease of the Blackfriars property was transferred to an opportunistic entrepreneur named Henry Evans. Evans was a remarkably shrewd and unscrupulous businessman whose association with the Children of the Chapel covered more than two decades, and under whom they reached their zenith. But their history was interrupted in 1584 when the owner of the Blackfriars property resumed possession and evicted his histrionic tenants. The Children of the Chapel did not resume playing in London until 1600.

THE CHILDREN OF PAUL'S BEFORE 1597

It is somewhat more difficult to document the early history of the Children of Paul's.[7] Their initial dramatic activity in the sixteenth century cannot be dated precisely, but, like the Children of the Chapel, they rose to prominence during the early years of the Elizabethan era. They quickly became the Queen's favorite boy actors and appeared at Court more frequently than their Chapel rivals. The principal figure in the company's early development was Sebastian Westcott, who assumed Mastership of the St. Paul's Cathedral choristers in 1547.[8] Under his guidance, the boys not only performed regularly at Court but acquired their own theater.

The Paul's playhouse was in operation on an indeterminate part of Cathedral property by the mid-1570s.[9] Its precise opening date is unknown, but by December of 1575 it had become London's first private theater.[10] Like the nearby Blackfriars, it was a convenient place to hold rehearsals for Court performances before eager paying spectators. By the time the Children of Paul's theater had opened, their choir was considered the finest in England. An expatriated Frenchman writes in a dialogue between two gentlemen at St. Paul's Cathedral:

[1.]   Hearken, I do heare a sweet musicke: I never heard the like.
[2.]   See wheather wee may get to the quier, and wee shall hear the fearest voyces of all cathedral churches in England.[11]

Westcott died in 1582, and two years later the Children of Paul's merged briefly with the Children of the Chapel and performed as a composite company at Court and the Blackfriars.[12] When the Blackfriars theater closed later that year, the Children of the Chapel temporarily ceased giving plays, but the Children of Paul's were in greater demand than ever before. Thomas Gyles was appointed Master of the Children of St. Paul's in 1584, and the Queen showed her favor by granting him a special commission "to take up singing children" in the manner usually reserved for the Masters of the Children of the Chapel Royal or the Windsor Chapel:

By the Queene
[signed] Elizabeth R

Whereas we have authorysed our servaunte Thomas Gyles M[r] of the Children of the cathedrall churche of St. Paules within our cittie of London to take upp suche apte and meete Children as are most fitt to be instructed in the arte and science of musicke and singinge as may be had and found out witnin anie place of this our realme of England and Wales to be by his education and bringing up made meete and hable to serve us in that behalf when our pleasure is to call for them.[13]

However, the company did not enjoy this favor long. During the season of 1589–90, they fell from grace for literally serving as mouthpieces for the extremist exchange of religious and political satire known as the Marprelate controversy. Martin Marprelate was the pseudonym of a Puritan writer or writers who published a series of caustic pamphlets during 1588–89 that attacked the validity of the Anglican episcopacy. The Anglican authorities secured a number of young writers for a counterattack, including John Lyly, the leading playwright for the Children of Paul's. The questionable play or plays are no longer extant, but it appears that the anti-Martinist position articulated by the Children of Paul's did more harm than good to the theocracy and state. Consequently, the Children of Paul's were banished from court and theater for nearly a decade. During this time there was no children's drama in London.

THE CHILDREN OF PAUL'S, 1597–1607

While the children's dramatic companies remained dormant, the young English drama industry grew at a rapid pace. By the mid-1590s, greater London boasted several public playhouses and professional dramatic companies. The first Englishmen to earn fame as actors, including Edward Alleyn, Richard Burbage, and William Kempe, rose to distinction during the 1590s, and William Shakespeare emerged as England's preeminent playwright. Plays that belong to the period between the two phases of children's drama include Shakespeare's *A Midsummer Night's Dream*, *Richard III*, *Romeo and Juliet*, and Marlowe's *Dr. Faustus*. When the children's troupes were revived at the end of the century, they faced stronger competition than ever before, and their orientation was far more commercial.

The Children of Paul's were resuscitated as early as 1597.[14] But they did not become fully competitive until 1600 when Edward Pearce "yealded up his place [as a Gentleman of the Chapel Royal] for the mastership of the Children of Poules."[15] Under Pearce's guidance, these Children regained the Queen's favor and reached their dramatic zenith. One of them later recalled his Master with nothing but the highest praise:

Maister Edward Pearce ... sometime Maister of the Children of Saint Paules in London, and there my Maister, a man of singular eminency in his profession, both in the Educating of Children for the ordering of the Voyce so, as the Quality might afterward credit him and preferre them: and also in those his compositions to the Lute, whereof, the world enjoyes many, (as from the Maister of that instrument) together with his skillful Instructions for other instruments too, as his fruits can beare him witness.[16]

Pearce not only oversaw the musical training of these boys but managed their playhouse.[17] His company was the most musical in contemporary London, and its playhouse attracted the most fashionable element of society, as John Marston reminds us in a play he wrote for the Children of Paul's:

Sir Edward Fortune.   I saw the Children of Pauls last night.
                          And troth they pleased me pretty, pretty well.

Ned Planet.   I' faith I like the audience that frequenteth there
                   With much applause: a man shall not be choked
                   With the stench of garlic, nor be pasted
                   To the barmy jacket of a beer-brewer.[18]

Many sources give insight into the lives of these boys. The Bishop of London describes them as being "well instructed and fitt for their places and they doe diligentlie keepe theire accustomed howers in repayring unto divine service, they come to Church in decent order."[19] At the same time, the unknown author of *The Maydes Metamorphosis* comments in mock horror on the profane disorder that occasionally crept into their plays: "Well, you have wicked Maisters that teach such little Boyes as you are to sweare so young."[20] Thomas Dekker, who also wrote for the company, describes, in his sarcastic advice to a would-be gallant, a distraction available to the same children during the sacred service:

Never be seen to mount the steppes into the quire, but upon a high Festivall day, to preferre the fashion of your doublet, and especially if the singing boyes seeme to take note of you: for they are able to buzze your praises, above their Anthems if their Voyces have not lost their maidenheads; be sure your silver spurres dogge your heeles, and then the Boyes will swarm about you like so many white butter-flyes when you in the open Quire shall draw forth a perfumd embrodered purse . . . and quoyt Silver into the Boyes hands, that it may be heard above the first lesson.[21]

In another play, Marston shows us an image of high-spirited, mischievous boys whose activities also included basic grammar education:

Enter a Schole-maister, draws the curtains behind, with BATTUS, NOWS, SLIP, NATHANIELL, and HOLOFERNES PIPPO, schole-boyes, sitting, with bookes in their hands.

        All.   Salve, magister.
        Pedant.   Salvete pueri estote salvi, vos salvere exopto. Vobis salu-
                      tem, Batte, mi fili, mi batte!

Battus.	Quid vis.
Pedant.	Stand forth: repeat your lesson without booke.
Battus.	A nowne is the name of a thing that may be seene, felt, heard, or understood.
Pedant.	Good boy: on, on.
Battus.	Of nownes some bee substantives and some be substantives [sic].

❖ ❖ ❖ ❖ ❖ ❖

Pedant.	.... Holla! holla! holla! you Holifernes Pippo, put him downe! Wipe your nose: fie, on your sleeve! where's your muckender your grandmother gave you? Well, say on: say on.[22]

Some of the ambitious plays presented by the company after 1600 required more actors than the choir maintained. There is little doubt that these extra actors were provided by the grammar school at St. Paul's, which not only had its own history of performing plays, but whose students learned music from the Master of the Choristers, and whose own Masters taught grammar to the choristers.[23] Richard Mulcaster, appointed headmaster of the school in 1597, came to St. Paul's with interest and experience in children's drama.[24] However, the revived drama company did not last very long. In 1607 the Paul's playhouse closed forever, and for unknown reasons the company ceased giving plays.

THE CHILDREN OF THE CHAPEL 1600–1613

The most brilliant and fantastical chapter in the history of English children's drama belongs to the Children of the Chapel between 1600 and 1613. This company provided serious competition for the most famous adult troupes of the day and launched the careers of such eminent dramatists as John Fletcher and Ben Jonson. But the final phase of its history is marred by the abuse of power and repeated offenses against royalty and the policies of state. In 1600, Henry Evans leased a new theater in the Blackfriars for the Children of the Chapel, and shortly thereafter the company returned to Court for the first time in sixteen years. Under the managerial guidance of Evans and the direction of Nathaniel Giles, Master of the Children of the Chapel Royal, the company quickly rose to stellar status. However, Evans, Giles, and other members of the syndicate were overenthusiastic at the start, and had the first of many brushes with authority not long after the revival when they kidnapped a gentleman's son to serve as an actor.

Unlike the Children of Paul's, the Children of the Chapel had no convenient institution from which to recruit extra actors for their increasingly ambitious plays. Nathaniel Giles therefore interpreted his patent of impressment for Chapel services quite liberally, and used it to obtain extra boys specifically for the theater. On or about 13 December 1600, one of his deputies made the mistake of abducting the only son and heir of a gentleman for use in the theater, which resulted in a vigorous complaint by the boy's father to the Star Chamber. This complaint is still extant, and offers a fascinating glimpse into the offstage conduct of a contemporary drama establishment.[25] It covers one side of a large folio with bombastic language that any contemporary dramatist might envy:

To the Queenes moste excellent ma^{tie}
[5 December 1601]

In all humblenes complayning, sheweth and informeth your moste excellent ma^{tie}, your highnes true, loyall and faythful subjecte Henry Clifton, of Toftres in your highnes countie of Norff[olk], esquire, That whereas your excellent ma^{tie}, for the better furnishing of your Chappell Royall wth well singing childeren, by your ma^{ties} letters patents under the greate seale of England, bearing date at Westminster the XVth date of July, in the nyne and thirtieth yere of your highnes raigne, aucthorized your highnes servant Nathaniell Gyles, master of your Highnes said Chapell, by himself, or his deputie, to take such childeren as he or his said deputie should thinke meete ... for your ma^{ties} said better service, But soe yt is, moste excellent Soveraigne, that the said Nathaniell Gyles, confederating himself wth one James Robinson, Henry Evans, & others ... committed, endevouring, conspiring & complotting howe to oppresse divers of your ma^{ties} humble & faythful subjects, & therby to make unto themselves an unlawfull gayne and benefitt, they the said confederates devysed, conspired & concluded, for theire owne corrupte gayne & lucre, to erecte, sett upp, furnish and maynteyne a play house or place in the Blackefryers wthin your ma^{ties} Cytie of London, & to the end they might better furnish theire said playes, they ... [have] moste wrongfully, unduly & unjustly taken divers & severall childeren from divers & sondry scholes of learning and other places, & apprentices to men of trade from theire masters, noe way fiting for your ma^{ties} service in or for your Chappell Royall, but the childeren have [been] soe taken & employed in acting ...

The document proceeds to explain that Thomas Clifton, about thirteen years of age, had been seized by James Robinson on his way to school from his home in Great St. Bartholomew's, and carried off to the Blackfriars "wth greate force and vyolence," where he was kept "amongste a company of lewde & dissolute mercenary players." Clifton Senior demanded the immediate release of his son, for playing was not a fitting occupation for a gentleman's heir. But the confederates cited Giles's patent of impressment and kept the boy.

Young Thomas was rescued not long after, but his irate father investigated the company and concluded that "John Chappell, a gramer scholler of Mr Spykes schole neetre Criplegate, London; John Motteram, a gramer scholler in the free schole at Westminster; Nathan Field, a scholler of a gramer schole in London, kepte by one Mr Monkaster; Alvery Trussel, an apprentice to one Thomas Gyles; one Phillip Pykman and Thomas Grymes, apprentices to Richard & Georg Chambers; [and] Salmon Pavy, apprentice to one Peerce" had all been impressed for use in "playes & enterluds" and not even taught to sing. As a result of Clifton's suit, Henry Evans was censured for "unorderlie carriage and behavior in taking up of gentlemens childeren against theire wills and to ymploy them for players and for other misdemeanors" and was ordered to have nothing further to do with the Blackfriars establishment.[26] Instead, he left town for a few years until the episode was forgotten.

The Clifton indiscretion ultimately failed to hurt the company's continued success. The boys still occasionally performed at Court, and their Blackfriars theater became the most fashionable in London. They were enough of a national treasure that distinguished foreign visitors came to see them; and Thomas Middleton, who wrote for both principal children's troupes, facetiously instructed a would-be gallant to meet all the right people and be seen in all the right places, which included the Blackfriars:

he must acquaint himself with many gallants of the Innes of Court, keep rank with those that spend most . . . and then after dinner . . . (if his humor so serve him) to call in at the Black-fryers, where he should see a neast of Boyes able to ravish a man.[27]

However, the company's star was quickly eclipsed after the accession of James I. James was never as enthusiastic about children's drama as Elizabeth had been. Not long after he came to the throne he withdrew his direct patronage from the company and officially dissociated them from his Chapel Royal by entitling them to the new name of Children of the Queen's Revels.[28] Shortly thereafter, these Children began to perform satiric plays that mocked His Majesty almost to the point of treason. In 1606, following a series of particularly libelous plays, the King decreed that his Chapel choristers should have no more part in such blasphemous exercises. He issued a new patent of impressment to Nathaniel Giles that stipulated that none of the boys taken for service in the Chapel Royal could appear in plays:

Provided alwayes and wee doe straightlie charge and commaunde that none of the said choristers or children of the chappell so to be taken by force of this commission shalbe used or imployed as Comedians or Stage players, or to exercise or acte any stage playes[,] Interludes[,] Comedies or Tragedies, for that it is not fitt or decent that such as shoulde sing the praises of God Almightie shoulde be traynned upp or imployed in suche lascivious and prophane exercises.[29]

The company then acting at the Blackfriars began to call itself simply the Children of the Revels, but continued to provoke the King with scathing satiric drama. In 1608, the company so strongly "offended in ye matter of y^e

Mynes and other lewd words" that James "vowed they should never play more but should first begg their bred and he wold have his vow performed."[30] This time his vow was performed, for later that year Henry Evans dissolved the syndicate, and the lease to the Blackfriars theater was transferred to the leading adult company of the day, the King's Men.

However, the infamous Chapel company was reorganized the following year by goldsmith Robert Keysar and King's Musician Philip Rosseter. Keysar and Rosseter found a theater in the nearby Whitefriars, and the resurrected company turned away from offensive political satire. In 1610, Rosseter and fellow musician Robert Jones were among those granted a new patent, which restored the patronage of the Queen and the title of children of the Queen's Revels.[31] But the time for children's drama had passed, and this final incarnation of the venerable company did not last long. In March of 1613, the last remnant of what had once been the Children of the Chapel was absorbed by the Lady Elizabeth's Men. In spite of the rapid changes of title and fortune the company experienced between 1600 and 1613, there was a great deal of continuity among its personnel and playwrights.

THE CHILDREN OF THE KING'S REVELS

For a very short time, a mysterious third children's company played in Jacobean London. It was known as the Children of the King's Revels and lacked even the nominal connection to any school, chapel, or cathedral that had been the hallmark of previous children's troupes. Its purpose was to cash in on the great success enjoyed by the Children of Paul's and the Children of the Chapel. Not many documents relating to the company have survived, but it was organized by an entrepreneur who had previously been connected to the Children of Paul's, its director was an actor and not a musician, and it played at the Whitefriars theater only during 1607 and 1608.[32] The Children of the King's Revels were clearly not a successful experiment, and they had completely vacated the Whitefriars long before Rosseter's reorganized company moved in.

THE CHILD ACTORS

A number of features helped to make children's drama distinctive. The exclusive theaters of the Blackfriars, Whitefriars, and St. Paul's were not only smaller, more luxurious, and more costly than the public theaters, but were closer to the central scenes of aristocratic London life. They were places to see and be seen. Their actors hinted at courtly splendor, for the Children of Paul's and the Children of the Chapel were among Queen Elizabeth's favorite entertainers and continued to delight King James's court for several years.

The very names of the companies, with their emphasis on "children," suggested precocious talent, and, until the final years, conjured up images of exquisite musical ability and an ecclesiastical discipline that was amusingly incongruous with the bold plays and bawdiness for which they were famous. The actors were young, and they were selected by virtue of their beauty, grace, and, in most cases, their musical talent.

The attraction and abilities of the boy actors were fundamentally distinct from those of their adult rivals, and became even more so during the final phase of their history. English dramatic art changed rapidly during the last quarter of the sixteenth century, and children's drama came to occupy a specific niche in the theatrical landscape. Harold Newcomb Hillebrand emphasizes an increase in the critical faculties of an audience that had come to know the power of professional adult acting, and therefore began to regard children's drama as something separate:

Even admitting that the Jacobean spectators were as the Elizabethans had been, surely they found no illusion when boys impersonated men, they who knew Burbage and Alleyne. Boys on the stage must have seemed to them largely what boys on stage seem to us—masqueraders. They had charm, of course, the charm of piquant strangeness, and the genuine charm of delightful music, nimble dancing, the vivacity of rattling comedy, often precocious skill. . . . But granting all that, and making allowances for the perpetuating of an old tradition, I cannot help feeling that the fundamental attraction of the boy actors for the Jacobean public was the whimsical charm of a masquerade.[33]

But the Elizabethans and Jacobeans elevated this "masquerade" to high art. The children used unique styles of acting that helped to distinguish them from the men of the public theaters, and their dramatists and directors helped to emphasize the unmanly qualities that belong to boys.

The acting styles used by the children were more limited than those used by their adult rivals.[34] They relied heavily on a dual consciousness of actor as actor and character, and maintained a distance between the audience and the action.[35] Dual consciousness was especially easy to maintain, for boys generally between the ages of eight and fifteen were cast in the roles of adult men, and a combination of self-reference and incongruous bawdry drew attention to the immaturity of the actors. Furthermore, references to musical ability were not uncommon in children's plays before c.1607, serving to remind the audience that some of the actors had been conscripted to sing the divine service.

Michael Shapiro has recognized three basic styles of acting used by boy companies: natural, declamatory, and parodic.[36] The first of these was essentially a mimicry of adult mannerisms that could be transformed by the phenomenon of dual consciousness into ritualized mockery of the adult world.

By reducing the behavior of adults to child size, the entire adult world and the very principle of authority became correspondingly petty and childish. This style of acting had to maintain sufficient distance from the spectators to avoid pernicious insult. The fine line between amusement and travesty that the children crossed is clearly related to this style of acting.

The declamatory style was a highly formalized combination of gesture, elocution, and vocal inflection that was closely allied with formal oration. It was a grandiloquent, moving, metaphorical style far removed from mockery. The declamatory style was, therefore, suitable for the serious portrayal of heroic or authoritarian characters and could project genuine pathos. The affect of this starkly artificial style was not infrequently augmented by music. Contemporary rhetoricians and poets believed music to be a higher form of expression than language, capable of expressing the same ideas with greater eloquence and power:

Yea, in my opinion, no Rhetoricke more perswadeth, or hath greater power over the mind; nay, hath not Musicke her figures, the same with Rhetorique? What is a *Revert* but her *Antistrophe*? her reports, but sweet *Anaphoras*? her counterchange of points, *Antimetaboles*? her passionate Aires but *Prosopoeas*? With infinite other of the same nature.[37]

The parodic style of acting, like the natural, used mimicry to achieve miniature caricature. In this case, the target of the attack was the theatrical behavior and dramatic techniques used by adult actors; young boys could reduce the passions of mature acting to a humorously absurd level by imitating or exaggerating the nuances and gestures associated with their grown-up rivals. The common use of verbal parody in children's drama, and the reappropriation of famous lines or entire plays from the adult repertoire, suggests an appropriately mocking style of acting. This style, too, has a musical analogue in the form of derisive imitation of well-known songs from other plays and printed song books.[38]

Another distinctive feature of children's plays was the greater emphasis on female characters and femininity. Englishmen of the Elizabethan and Jacobean eras believed boyhood and womanhood to have many common characteristics, as William Shakespeare reminds us:

Rosalind [disguised as Ganymede]. . . . Hee was to imagine me his Love, his Mistris: and I set him every day to woe me. At which time would I, being but a moonish youth, greeve, be effeminate, changeable, longing, and liking, proud, fantastical, apish, shallow, inconstant, ful of teares, full of smiles; for every passion something, and for no passion truly any thing, as boyes and women are for the most part, cattle of this colour[39].

The public theaters, of course, had young apprentice actors and perhaps even older specialists to play the female parts, but all the actors of the children's stage were cattle of this color. Numerous self-referential passages in children's plays remind us that the convincingly feminine beauties involved in the action were really pretty boys:

> And women will ensue
> Which I must tell you true
> No women are indeed
> But pages made for need
> To fill up womens places
> By vertue of their faces
> And other hidden graces
> A hall, a hall; whist, still, be mum,
> For now with silver song they come.[40]

Gordon Lell has pointed out that such references also implied the fashionably forbidden fruit of homosexuality to an audience familiar with the erotic works of classical authors.[41] Certainly the most infamous detractors from the theater from Gosson to Prynne stressed the shameful use of artifice that required boys "to put one the attyre, the gestures, the passions of a woman."

The final distinctive feature of children's plays was their music. Not every play written for the children required music, but their theatrical music was deemed especially noteworthy by numerous commentators. Perhaps the most famous description of children's theatrical music was written by Frederic Gershow, a German who visited the Blackfriars theater in 1602. He was particularly impressed by the musical ability of the boy actors, and describes an hour-long concert before the featured play:

Von dannen sind wir auf Kinder-comoediam gangen. . . . Es hat aber mit dieser Kinder-comoedia die Gelegenheit: die Königin hält viel junger Knaben, die sich der Singkunst mit Ernst befleissigen mussen und auf allen Instrumenten lernen, auch dabenbenst studieren. Diese Knaben haben ihre besondere praeceptores in allen Kunsten, insonderheit sehr gute musicos.
. . . Eine ganze Stunde voher [eine comoedia] höret man eine köstliche musicam instrumentalem von Orgeln, Lauten, Pandoren, Mandoren, Geigen und Pfeiffen, wie denn damahlen ein Knabe cum voce tremela in einer Basgeigen so lieblich gesungen, dass wo es die Nonnen zu Mailand ihnen nicht vorgethan, wir seines Gleichen auf der Reise nicht gehöret hatten.[43]

Playwrights often commented on the children's musical ability and exquisite performances, especially in self-referential passages such as this sarcastic enumeration of the features that made children's plays noteworthy:

I wonder that any man is so mad, to come and see these rascally tits play here [at the Blackfriars] —they acts like so many wrens or pismires—not the fift part of a good face amonst them all—and their music is abominable—able to stretch a mans eares worse than tenne-pillories, and their ditties—most lamentable things like the fellowes that made them—poets.[44]

But even during the brightest moments of children's drama, many Englishmen objected to its artificial charm. Long before the revival of the 1590s, antitheatrical writers such as Anthony Munday reserved special criticism for boy actors:

When I see by them yong boies, inclining of themselves unto wickednes, trained up in filthie speeches; unnatural and unseemlie gestures, to be brought up by these Schoole masters in bawdrie, and idlenes, I cannot chuse but with teares and griefe of hart lament[45].

Long before Henry Evans and Nathaniel Giles's profit motives brought them before the law, John Northbrooke condemned the use of children's drama "publilely for profit and gaine of mony."[46] William Shakespeare, one of the few playwrights of stature to write only for adult companies, disdained the custom of children's drama and its undue mockery of the public theater:

Rosincrantz. . . . But there is Sir an ayrie of Children, little Yases, that crye out on top of the question: and are most tyranically clap't for't: these are now the fashion, and so be-rattle the common Stages (so they call them) that many wearing Rapiers, are affraide of Goosequils, and dare scarce come thither.

Hamlet. What are they Children? Who maintains 'em? How are they escoted? Will they pursue the Quality [of acting] no longer than they can sing? Will they not say afterwards if they should grow themselves to common Players (as is most like if their meanes are not better) their Writers do them wrong, to make them exclaim against their owne succession.[47]

As Shakespeare reminds us, the boys who delighted audiences for a few years had uncertain futures. Some, as he wisely prophesied, grew to common players and succeeded to adult dramatic companies. A few others attended university and won fame as musicians and composers. But the majority of names to appear on the scanty actor and chorister lists connected with the children's companies are never seen again.

As the Jacobean court masque became the most fashionable form of entertainment for the nobility, children's drama lost its mystique. And when the leading adult troupes moved into private theaters, they quickly overshadowed the waning art of children's drama. After less than a century of continuous existence, the phenomenon of English children's drama reached its conclusion. Except for a brief experiment during the 1630s, no more companies of boy actors played the English stages.

CHAPTER 2

THE PERFORMERS AND THEIR THEATERS

There [in the theater] set they abroche straunge consortes of melody, to tickle the eare; costly apparel, to flatter the sight; effeminate gesture, to ravish the sence; and wanton speache, to whet desire too [sic] inordinate lust.

Stephen Gosson, *The Schoole of Abuse* (1579)

The Elizabethan and Jacobean theater was a place of sensory delight whose focal point was its versatile actors, for it lacked painted scenery and front drop curtains. As Jacobean thinker Thomas Gainesford explains in an anthology of his era's knowledge,

Player hath many times, many excellent qualities: as dancing, activitie, musicke, song, elloqution, ability of body, memory, vigilancy, skill of weapon, pregnancy of wit, and such like: in all which hee resembleth an excellent spring of water, which growes the more sweeter, and the more plentiful by the often drawing out of it: so are all these the more perfect and plausible by the often practise.[1]

Since each member of each acting company had more experience in some of these qualities than others, each troupe placed slightly different emphasis on all of them. Members of the children's companies obviously had great ability in dancing, music, song, and, because of the emphasis placed on rhetoric in Elizabethan and Jacobean education, possessed ability of body, elocution, and memory. But the dramatic perfection and plausibility that come only from years of constant practice do not belong to youth, nor do pregnancy of wit, skill of weapon, or mature vigilance. Therefore, these latter qualities were less important in most plays written for the children.

15

THE PLAYERS

At the end of the sixteenth century, when the children's companies resumed playing in London, the profession of player was just beginning its long ascent from vagabond status to respectability.[2] Most men regarded professional actors with disdain. Detractors from the theater emphasized their slothful, untrustworthy qualities, and often pointed out that these rogues had chosen the stage over honest vocations:

Most of the Players have bene eyther men of occupations, which they have forsaken to lyve by playing, or common minstrels, or trayned up from theire childehoode to this abominable exercise & now have no other way to gete theire livinge.[3]

The boys of the private theaters were different. They were not paid for acting, nor did they serve as lowly actor's apprentices. They were principally angelic choirboys and privileged schoolboys pressed into occasional playing by certain of their masters. The theater required and therefore strengthened their budding musical, grammatical, and rhetorical skills, "For as Poetrie & Piping are Cosen germans; so piping, and playing are of great affinity, and all three chayned [together]."[4] Indeed, these skills served some of them quite well in later life.

Some of the Children of the Chapel and of Paul's from the period between 1597 and 1613 can be identified. The principal actors of the Children of the Chapel are named in the first folio of Ben Jonson's *Workes*, under the plays which the poet wrote for the company. (See Table 1.)

Unfortunately, contemporary personnel lists for the Chapel Royal do not include the names of individual Children, so the complete company composition cannot be determined.[8] But it is clear from company patents and the Clif-

Table 1.   The principal actors of the Children of the Chapel as given in Jonson's folio *Workes* (1616).

Cynthias Revels (1600)	*The Poetaster* (1601)	*Epicoene* (1609)
Nat. Field	Nat. Field	Nat. Field
Sal. Pavy	Sal. Pavy	Gil Carie
Tho. Day	Joh. Underwood	Hug. Attawel
Joh. Underwood	Will. Ostler	Joh. Smith
Rob. Baxter	Tho. Marton[6]	Will. Barkstead
Joh. Frost[5]		Will. Pen
		Ric. Allin
		Joh. Blaney[7]

ton suit that, in spite of previous claims to the contrary, the Children who acted at Blackfriars were a mixture of chorister and nonchorister actors until at least 1606.[9] Cuthbert and William Burbage, who later inherited the Blackfriars property, tell us that as the boys grew to manhood, some were taken into the company of the King's Men as professional actors, and that as young men left, the company dwindled in size, presumably because the King had forbidden his new choristers from appearing in plays:

Now for the Blackfriers, that is our inheritance; our father purchased it at extreame rates, and made it into a playhouse with great charge and trouble; which after was leased out to one Evans that first sett up the boyes commonly called the Queenes Majesties Children of the Chappell. In process of time, the boyes growing up to bee men, which were Underwood, Field, Ostler, and were taken to strengthen the Kings service; and the more to strengthen the service, the boyes dayly wearing out, it was considered that house would bee as fitt for ourselves [the King's Men], and soe purchased the lease remaining from Evans with our money, and placed men players, which were Hemings, Condall, Shakespeare, &c.[10]

Certainly Underwood, Field, and Ostler later distinguished themselves as "Principall Actors" with the King's Men.[11]

Other biographical information survives for several Children of the Chapel. William Barkstead published two lengthy poems during his tenure with the company, and may have assisted John Marston with *The Insatiate Countesse*, which was written for the Children between 1609 and 1611.[12] A uniquely annotated copy of Jonson's *Workes* assigns Barkstead the role of Morose in *Epicoene* of 1609.[13] He was probably well into his teens by the time the company dissolved in 1613, and his fate after that is unknown.

On the other hand, a considerable amount of information survives about Nathan Field, who became a legend in his own time. He was born in 1587 to the Reverend John Field, author of a violent attack on the theater, who did not live to see his son grow into the despised profession of player.[14] Young Nathan was inducted into the Children of the Chapel at the age of thirteen, and was still with the company an unprecedented ten years later. The only role that may be assigned to him with any certainty is the title character of George Chapman's tragedy, *Bussy D'Ambois*.[15]

During the second decade of the seventeenth century, Field became one of the most celebrated professional actors in England as a member of the King's Men. He also earned a considerable reputation for success with women.[16] Ben Jonson, who wrote for him in both companies, pays tribute to his outstanding ability as an actor, and reminds us in a scene from *Bartholomew Fair* that handsome leading men have always been well-loved by ladies:

    Cokes.   [examining puppets]. . . which is your Burbage now?
    Leatherhead.   What meane you by that, Sir?

Cokes.	Your best Actor. Your Field?
Little-Wit.	Good ifaith! You are even with me, Sir.
Leatherhead.	This is he, that acts young Leander, Sir. He is extreamly belov'd of the womenkind, they doe so affect his action.[17]

His reputation for excellence continued after his death in 1633, as a Restoration writer tells us:

It was hapines of the Actors of those Times to have such Poets as [Shakespeare, Jonson, Beaumont, and Fletcher] to instruct them, and write for them; and no less of those Poets to have such docile and excellent Actors to Act their Playes as a Field and a Burbage.[18]

Like many actors of his era, Field tried his hand at writing plays, and completed *A Woman is a Weather-Cocke* and *Amends for Ladies* for the Children of the Chapel before he left them.[19] He later coauthored *The Fatall Dowry* with Philip Massinger for the King's Men.[20]

William Ostler, too, became an applauded actor with the King's Men. Tradition associates his name with Ophelia, Desdemona, and Rosalind in the adult company, but there are no roles that may be assigned to him with any certainty.[21] Sir John Davies paid him the highest compliment by calling him the "King of Actors" in a witty epigram:

To the Roscius of these Times, Mr. W. Ostler.
epig[ram] 205

Ostler thou tookst a knock, thou would'st have giv'n
    Neere sent thee to thy latest home: but O!
Where was thine Action when thy Crowne was riv'n
Sole King of Actors, then, wast idle? No:
Thou hadst it, for thou wouldst bee doing; Thus
Good Actors Deeds are oft most dangerous;
        But if thou plaiest thy dying Part as well
        As thy Stage parts, thou hast no Part in hell.[22]

Salmon Pavy gained immortality by dying in 1603, young, talented, and admired by Ben Jonson. Jonson wrote him a touching epitaph, which tells us that Pavy had been famous at the age of thirteen for portraying old men on stage and had joined the Children of the Chapel at the age of ten:

Epigram CXX

Epitaph on S[almon] P[avy] a child of Q[een]
    E[lizabeth's] Chappel
Weep with me all you that read

This little storie:
And know, for whom a teare you shed,
   Death's selfe is sorry.
'Twas a child, that so did thrive
   In grace, and feature,
As heaven and nature seem'd to strive
   Which own'd the creature,
Yeeres he numbred scarce thirteene
   When fates turn's cruell,
Yet three fill'd zodiackes had he beene
   The stages jewell;
And did act (what now we mone)
   Old men so duely
As sooth, the parcae thought him one
   He plai'd so truely.
So, by error, to his fate
   They all consented;
But viewing him since (alas, too late)
   They have repented
And have sought (to give new birth)
   In bathes to steepe him;
But, being so much to good for earth,
   Heaven vows to keepe him.[23]

The situation with the Children of Paul's is different, for there are no extant lists of the principal actors. However, the Visitation Books of two successive Bishops of London include the names of the choristers from St. Paul's Cathedral from the beginning and end of the final phase of the company's dramatic activity. (See Table 2.)

Table 2. St. Paul's Cathedral choristers from the Bishop of London's Visitations Books of 1598 and 1607.

1598	1607
John Taylor	Henry Burnett
William Thaire	Richard Kenede
Richard Brackenbury	John Mansell
John Norwood	Thomas Peers
Robert Coles	Richard Patrick
John Thomkins	Nicholas Crosse
Samuel Marcupp	Thomas Waters
Thomas Rainescrofte	John Dawson
Russell Gyrdler	Thomas Codbolt
Carolus Pytcher	Lightfoot Codbolt[25]
Charles Pendry[24]	

The first quarto of John Marston's *Antonio and Mellida* is the only source of actor names for the company. The play was presented in 1599 or 1600, and a stage direction in Act IV, scene i reads "Enter Andrugio, Lucio, Cole and Norwood."[26] Only Andrugio and Lucio are characters in the play, and only they join in the action. Robert Cole[s] and John Norwood, who presumably play the two characters, were choirboys at St. Paul's Cathedral. Presumably their chorister colleagues also appeared in plays along with grammar school students from the St. Paul's Cathedral school. As with the Children of the Chapel, it is impossible to determine company composition.

Biographical details have survived for two Children of Paul's, both of whom became eminent musicians. Thomas Ravenscroft, the "Rainescrofte" of the 1598 chorister list, is the only contemporary Child of Paul's to refer later to his time at the cathedral.[27] He is also uniquely responsible for preserving a number of songs from plays produced by the Children of Paul's during his tenure in the choir.[28] He was born no later than 1590, and was therefore at least eight when listed as a Cathedral chorister in 1598.[29] He left St. Paul's for Cambridge in 1604, and was made a Bachelor of Music at Cambridge University not later than 1607.[30] In 1609, the first two of his five musical publications appeared in London.[31] He is best known today as the collector and editor of popular English songs both sacred and secular, but in his own time he won praise from the likes of Thomas Campion, John Dowland, Nathaniel Giles, and Martin Peerson as a composer and music theorist.[32] However, he faded into obscurity shortly after the publication of his final and most important collection in 1621.[33]

John T[h]omkins was born in 1586, younger half brother to the more famous Thomas Thomkins, about twelve years old when the 1598 list of St. Paul's choristers was compiled. He probably left the cathedral as an older teenager around 1605, for he was appointed organist of King's College Chapel at Cambridge in 1606, and was awarded the degree of Bachelor of Music by Cambridge University in 1608.[34] He later returned to St. Paul's Cathedral as organist, and from there moved on to become a Gentleman and Organist of the Chapel Royal, and a highly respected performer and composer. After his death in 1638, his friend and colleague William Lawes immortalized him with an exquisite musical tribute whose text pays homage to his outstanding musical ability:

An elegie on the death of his very worthy Friend and
Fellow-servant, M. John Tomkins, Organist of
his Majesties Chappell Royall.

Musick, the Master of thy Art is dead,
And with him all thy ravisht sweets are fled;
Then beare a part in thine own Tragedy:

Lets celebrate strange griefe with Harmony.
Lets howle sad notes stolne from his owne pure verse,
In stead of teares shed on his mournfull Herse.[35]

No names of any Children of the King's Revels have survived.

THE ROLES

The specific skills and training of individual actors clearly influenced the dramatic roles created for all permanent theater companies of later Renaissance England. It is possible to arrive at some conclusions about training and casting in the children's companies by examining the roles devised for the boy players, which demand varying degrees of musical and dramatic skill. There are minor roles that require little more than singing and dancing, major roles that require as wide a range of declamatory and gestural ability as any conceived for the adult stage, and roles of various degrees of importance that require an impressive combination of vocal, instrumental, and physical competence. It seems that most of the young actors first acquired and perfected purely musical skills, graduating to more demanding dramatic roles as their continued training and capabilities permitted.

Recent scholarship has emphasized the vital connection between the lost art of rhetoric and the craft of the Elizabethan and Jacobean actor, for each combined speech and gesture to bring words to life.[36] But music belongs to the continuum, for it was a preparative to rhetoric and therefore to acting. In rhetoric, vocal modulation and specific formal gesture united endlessly "according to the varietie of passions that are to be expressed."[37] The same expressive vocal and visual ability belonged to rhetoricians and "the makers of Tragedies, stage plaiers, and Poetes."[38] Indeed, the rhetorical exercises practiced by schoolboys differed only in degree from the precise science of stage players:

The [rhetorical] gesture must followe the change and varietie of the voyce, answering thereunto in everie respect: yet not parasiticallie as stage plaiers use, but gravelie and decentlie as becommeth men of greater calling.[39]

The actor's combination of conventional gesture and vocal modulation was far more important than his physical presence in the creation of character. He was defined by his use of rhetorical gesture, for his was

the Arte of *Imitation* and *Demonstration*, expressinge the tinges conceaved in the minde with a seemly gesture: so plainely and lively representinge mens manners and affections: that the very beholder plainly perceaveth him to be a stage player by infinite gestures and movinges, although he saie nothinge. This Arte dothe so much excell, that there neede [be] no interpretours, for it doth so aptly represent with pleasaunt gesture an olde man, a boye, a woman, a servaunt, a handmaide, a drunkarde, an angrie person, and the differences and passions of all persons, that also the beholder standinge aloofe of, not hearinge the Enterlude maie perceave the argument thereof by the onely motions of the Plaier.[40]

The combination of speech and gesture was so powerful and so familiar to the Renaissance that one sage remarked, "*Rhetoricke* is nothing els, but an Arte of perswading and moving the affections."[41]

However, rhetoric was not the only art of passion and persuasion known to the Renaissance, since

The scie[n]ce [of music] itself hath naturally a verie forcible strength to trie and tuch the inclination of the minde, to this or that affection.[42]

Through sound alone, music could accomplish all that rhetoric could do through the combination of discourse and movement:

As *Mercurie* by his eloquence reclaymed men from their barbarousnesse and crueltie: so *Orpheus* by his Musick subdued fierce beasts, and wild birds.[43]

Therefore, music and rhetoric could express similar passions in the theater. Furthermore, since the art of song used only the voice and did not require the simultaneous use of voice and action, it was an ideal preparative for the art of rhetoric. William Byrd clearly spoke for his entire era when he proclaimed that everyone should learn to sing because "it is the best meanes to procure a perfect pronounciation, and to make a good Orator."[44] Henry Peacham the younger, son of the most famous Elizabethan rhetorician, tells us that

the exercise of singing openeth the breast and pipes [and] it is a most ready helpe for a bad pronunciation, and distinct speaking which I have heard confirmed by many divines: yea, I my selfe have knowne many Children to have bin holpen of their stammering in speech, onely by it.[45]

The children of the private theaters, who were talented musicians and grammar scholars, could therefore prepare naturally and easily for the intricacies of serious acting through the study of singing, which would easily lead to all of the other components of rhetoric and the arts of the stage player. Even musical skills were taught gradually, for instrumental music requires coordination and concentration that singing does not:

Musicke . . . is devided into two partes, the voice and the instrument . . . both the two in this age [of childhood] best be begon, while both the voice and the jointe be pliable to the traine. The voice craveth lesse coste to execute her part. . . The instrument seemeth more costly, and claimes both more care in keping, and more charge in compassing.[46]

The briefest, simplest roles in the children's plays, which probably went most often to the youngest and least experienced boys, are clearly designed for singers whose acting skills have yet to be developed. These are the singing choruses of pages, shepherds, fairies, and "boys" who appear only briefly on stage, who are rarely given individual names, and whose designations often imply comparative youth or diminutive stature.

Related to these anonymous aggregate roles are the individual boy or servant characters, such as Doyt, Pilcher, and Dandiprat of the anonymous *Blurt, Master-Constable* and Audrey of Middleton's *A Trick to Catch the Old-One* who sing in conjunction with roles that require mime, limited dialogue, and an undoubtedly natural style of acting. There are also other minor musical roles clearly designed for those with more musical than dramatic ability. Important noble characters often have pages to carry regalia or armor who may be asked to sing, and not infrequently a "boy" is introduced solely to provide a song. And in several plays, most notably those with common London or tavern scenes such as Beaumont and Fletcher's *The Scornful Lady* and Dekker and Webster's *Westward Ho*, groups of instrumentalists appear on stage to lend atmosphere to the scene. These are scarcely more than living stage properties, since they rarely speak and could easily have been backstage musicians brought forward in appropriate costume.

At the other end of the spectrum are major dramatic roles which generally exclude musical performance. These include leading characters like Byron of Chapman's *Conspiracy and Tragedy of Charles, Duke of Byron* and major supporting roles like Andrugio of Marston's *Antonio and Mellida*. These roles undoubtedly went to the oldest, most talented members of the companies, boys who already had training in rhetoric and/or considerable experience on stage; one such role, the title character of Chapman's *Bussy D'Ambois*, is known to have been played by a seventeen-year-old Nathan Field. Many of the leading roles in children's drama require poise, a wide range of emotional response, swordsmanship, and the memorization of one lengthy formal speech after another. Most of these characters are mature adults and many are dukes and kings. It is not inconceivable that some of these roles went to veteran actors whose singing voices had broken; a number of leading characters request songs from companions but do not sing themselves even when it would be appropriate to do so.

Most of the roles that require combined musical and dramatic experience are clearly written with an emphasis on either a musical or an acting skill, and these roles were probably played by boys whose primary ability lay in one or the other area. Old Merrithought of Beaumont's *Knight of the Burning Pestle* and Quicksilver of Chapman, Jonson, and Marston's *Eastward Ho*, for example, are each assigned a large number of simple unaccompanied songs that, according to dialogue and context, need not be sung with extraordinary beauty or virtuosity. On the other hand, Hedon and Amorphus of Jonson's *Cynthia's Revels* and Balurdo of Marston's *Antonio* plays apparently require real skill as viol players and singers, but the characters are extremely affected and therefore require only a limited range of dramatic expression. There are a few roles that seem to require equal ability in both areas, most notably Franceschina of Marston's *The Dutch Courtesan*, who must sing and play the lute well enough to cause Malheureux to fall in love with her, express a full range of womanly emotions, and speak her substantive part in a Dutch accent. Because puberty often came much later in the sixteenth and seventeenth centuries than it does now, even demanding female roles like Franceschina or Eurimine of the anonymous *Maydes Metamorphosis* could have been convincingly played by older members of the companies with considerable training in music and rhetoric behind them.[47] The children's troupes were repertory companies, and each role was probably created with the talents of a specific individual in mind.

OFF-STAGE MUSICIANS

Most of the instrumental music that accompanied the children's plays was performed by off-stage musicians. All three companies made use of a wide variety of musical instruments, but the two principal ones used almost every sort of instrument known in contemporary England. The plays are full of directions for music to sound from above, below, or within; to accompany mimed action, song, dance; to set the atmosphere; and to emphasize important speeches. These hidden performers included individuals with competence on keyboards, plucked and bowed strings, woodwinds, brass, and percussion instruments. The great musical forces necessary to play all of these instruments were not required by every dramatic work, for some plays use little off-stage music while others almost literally resound from beginning to end with a wide variety of instruments.

It is quite clear that these instrumentalists were obtained by all companies on a play-by-play basis, but their precise identities are uncertain. St. Paul's Cathedral and the Chapel Royal were musical centers in contemporary London, and the many adult musicians associated with both could have been paid occasionally to accompany their younger colleague's dramatic exercises. Older choristers whose skills were not required for a particular play or ex-choristers who could no longer sing but had great instrumental skill could have been recruited to play for specific works. The adult companies of the era sometimes hired the King's Musicke or the official London City Waits to provide music for their plays.[48] It is probable that the Children of the Chapel turned to the King's Musicke after King's Musician Philip Rosseter helped to reorganize their company in 1609, and that the Children of the King's Revels, who were not connected to a great London musical establishment, relied on the City Waits for their instrumental music.

THE THEATERS

Elizabethan and Jacobean plays in performance included an interplay between sight and sound, word and action, and physical and symbolic realities. The theater itself was constructed to facilitate unity between the literal and the allegorical. The contemporary stage, a seemingly simple set of interlocking multidimensional platforms, was of the utmost importance in bringing diverse elements together. As David Bevington has said,

The [Elizabethan] theater is anything but the bare plain platform sometimes supposed. It can offer a symbolic locale for the action it encompasses. Within its facade lies that which is to be concealed and discovered; the facade itself can at times signify the fortifications of a city or castle, with a place above for actors to appear as though into a city or tower or inner room. The architecture of the stage is an appropriate background for exterior or interior scenes. The open stage, with heavens above and hell beneath, is an essential part 'of the vision of man's central place in a cosmos of dignity and order.'[49]

All that was needed to create a multitude of imaginary landscapes were actors, dialogue, and an audience accustomed to these theatrical conventions.

All Elizabethan and Jacobean theaters had certain features in common, but each was as unique as its resident acting company. Playwrights not only wrote with company personnel in mind, but with an eye and ear toward the theater in which the story was to unfold. The smaller, enclosed private theaters permitted greater auditory and visual detail than the larger, semi-outdoor public theaters; after all, minute details, sparing gestures, or the soft strains of plucked string instruments do not carry very far. Many sights and sounds were effectively different in both sorts of theater, for the sight of a violent murder or the piercing sound of a trumpet have different impact on nearby and distant viewers. While a natural daylight or a close approximation was the normal illumination for all Elizabethan and Jacobean theaters, some evidence suggests that private playhouses may have occasionally altered light and darkness artificially to meet the emotional requirements of specific plays.[50] Most public theaters could accommodate around three thousand spectators, but a capacity of seven hundred was large for a private theater.

Little is known specifically about the stages at the private theaters except that they were smaller than their public counterparts and that members of the audience could pay extra to be seated on stools on the main platform.[51]

Elizabethan and Jacobean stages generally consisted of a main stage in the form of a raised platform with a trap door that led to a substage area and conventional doors that led backstage, an inner discovery space, a multipurpose upper area, and a two-story tiring-house that served principally as the backstage area but which opened onto the stage at both levels. The discovery space was most often an open tiring-house doorway inside which curtains had been hung, or to whose front hangings had been fastened. The space was quite shallow and permitted little internal movement.[52] The upper area consisted of a gallery or galleries that fronted the tiring-house at the second story and overlooked the main stage. It was variously used by actors, musicians, and spectators according to circumstance or occasion.[53] In the private theater, a portion of this upper area served as a music room whose origin lay in the musicians' gallery of the great hall or banqueting house of the Tudor nobility.[54] The stage facade was typically decorated with rich architectural detail that could suggest both indoor and outdoor locations according to the contemporary conventions of the visual arts.[55]

Modern knowledge of the Children of Paul's playhouse is quite scanty, based primarily on vague contemporary descriptions and references.[56] Its indeterminate location was so close to the Cathedral that most contemporary references simply discuss plays presented "at Paul's." There is no evidence that the Children obtained a new theater when they resumed playing in the later 1590s, so they probably used the same stage from the time of Westcott until their final dissolution in 1607.

The building that housed the theater was evidently quite small, polygonal in shape, and the theater may have seated fewer than a hundred spectators.[57] However, the main platform of the stage was large enough to accommodate at least seventeen actors at once and to allow groups of dancers to perform a wide variety of social and theatrical dances. The complete stage had the capacity for a banqueting scene that included a march of servants to bring in the meal to the accompaniment of an organ and mixed consort.[858] There were evidently two music rooms, for a stage direction in Marston's *Antonio's Revenge* calls for the ghost of Andrugio to appear "betxist the music houses."[59] These music rooms were probably located on the second story, for more directions indicate music from "above" than any other location, but the musicians were mobile enough to provide music from "within" and beneath the stage. The music rooms were probably hidden from view under normal circumstances, for many scenes include verbal directions for music to begin.[60] (See Figure 1.)

A great deal has been written about the structure and location of the Second Blackfriars theater, the playhouse used by the Children of the Chapel from 1600 until 1660, for numerous seventeenth-century documents concerning it

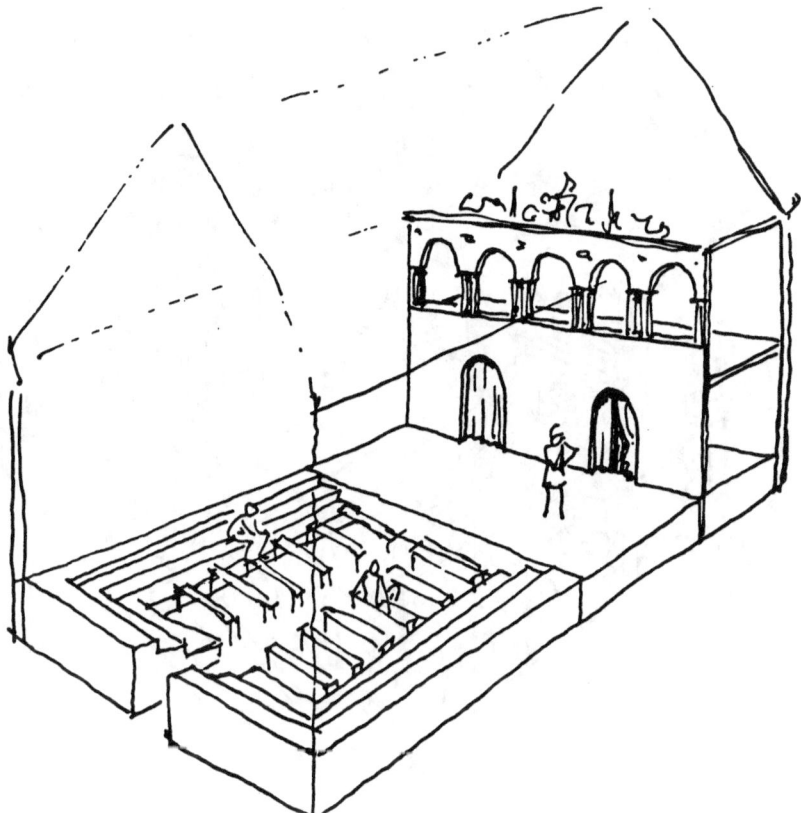

Figure 1.   A reconstruction of a small private playhouse such as Paul's.

have remained extant. This Blackfriars theater, not to be confused with the First Blackfriars which had been used before the revival, was located in the Upper Frater of the dissolved Dominican priory of the Blackfriars. The lease granted to Henry Evans in 1600 was only for the parliament chamber, "a great hall or roome, with roomes over the same," that occupied the top story of the building.[61] The theater had the capacity to seat several hundred spectators, and it measured sixty-six feet from north to south by forty-six feet from east to west. The entrance was on the north side, and the floor was paved. The Blackfriars included galleries, boxes, and a pit for spectators; and the stage of unknown dimensions ran from east to west at one end of the hall.[62] (See Fig-

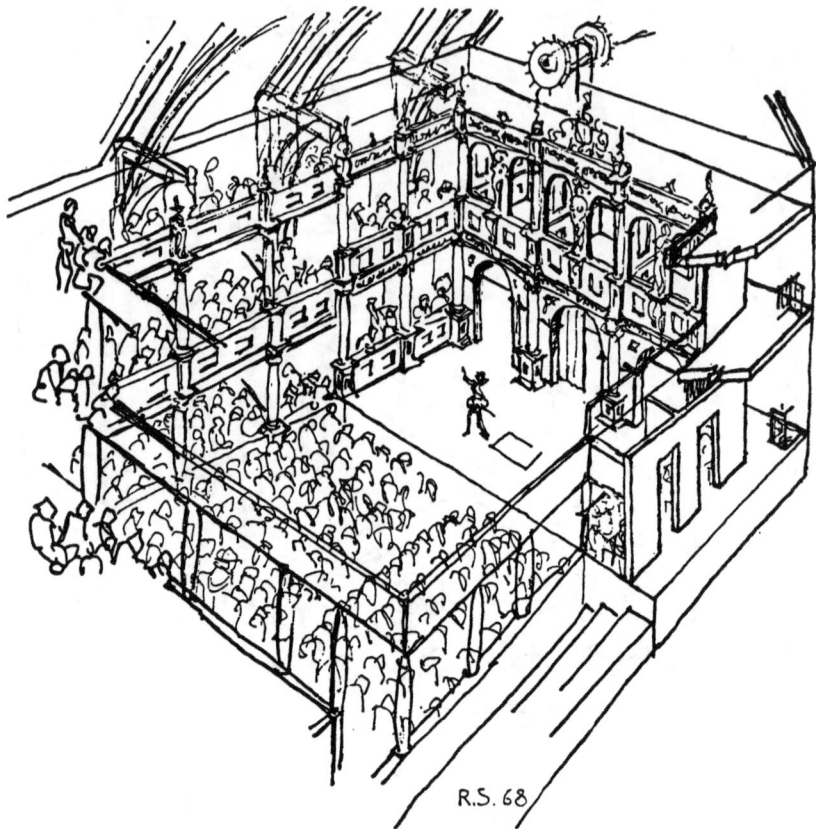

Figure 2.   A reconstruction of the second Blackfriars.

ure 2) It is assumed that the two-story tiring-house behind the stage ran the full width of the hall and opened onto the main stage at the upper level in three boxes that might have been used variously as a Lord's room, a music room, and an upper station for the performance of action "above."[63]

As with the Paul's theater, more stage directions for Blackfriars plays call for music from "above" than from any other location, but music also sounded from within, below, and afar off. The music room was large enough to accommodate an organ, a consort of viols, and a chorus of singers at one time.[64] As at Paul's, the Blackfriars music room was clearly hidden from the view of actors and spectators, requiring verbal cues between actors and musicians.[65]

The music room was undoubtedly located behind a curtain that could be pulled aside when the musicians were to be made visible.

Very little is known about the Whitefriars playhouse, where the Children of the Chapel concluded their history and where the Children of the King's Revels presented all of their plays. The property had originally been "a messuage or mansion howse parcell of the late dissolved monastery called the Whitefriars, in Fleete Streete, in the suburbs of London."[66] Like the Blackfriars, it was therefore part of a medieval conventual building and was analogous to a courtly hall. The auditorium was constructed from the monks' refectory.[67] Joseph Quincy Adams has estimated the dimensions of the theater at approximately thirty-five feet by eighty-five feet, based on an undocumented survey of the Whitefriars property taken in the early seventeenth century.[68] These measurements would make it the largest children's theater. Not coincidentally, it is the only children's theater in which the loud outdoor hautbois and trumpet were used. The main stage was large enough to accommodate huge crowd scenes and groups of dancers. There was undoubtedly a music room, since most Whitefriars plays call for off-stage music.

CHAPTER 3

THE PLAYS AND PLAYWRIGHTS

Of all the Arts, that of the Dramatick Poet is the most difficult and most
subject to censure; for in all others, they write onely of some particular
subject, as the Mathematician of Mathematicks, or the Philosopher of
Philosophy; but in that, the Poet must write of every thing, and every
one undertakes to judge of it.

Richard Flecknoe, *A Short Treatise of the English Stage* (1664)

The Elizabethan and Jacobean playwright was at once poet, philosopher, historian, propagandist, moralist, social commentator, and literary critic. His art
required intellectual breadth, an ear for linguistic subtlety, and an understanding of the changing tastes of his audience. His work was literally on public
display, and was therefore open to public criticism. "Children's drama" is not
a discrete body of literature, for all dramatic works of the later English Renaissance share common stylistic and thematic features, and many playwrights wrote for both children's and adults' troupes. However, children's
plays tend toward the experimental, toward literary and dramatic artifice, and
toward a sense of exclusiveness. Ejner Jensen has perceived the common
bond among the diverse works acted by the children's companies after 1597
to be a unique impulse that

held certain contraries in a remarkably creative balance: an Elizabethan enthusiasm
for the act or writing joined to a disenchantment with the world that was its subject, a
mastery of dramatic conventions joined to a willingness to exploit and even parody
them, a sly mocking of the boy actors coupled with a sometimes dazzling use of their
powers.[1]

It was a brave new drama that tempered prescription with novelty, and whose finest playwrights were willing to risk censure. The musical and satiric aspects of children's drama have been considered especially noteworthy, but they are simply the most brilliant hues in an iridescent picture.

MUSIC AND ENGLISH RENAISSANCE DRAMA

Children's drama has often been distinguished from adult drama by its seemingly regular use of large quantities of music.[2] Michael Shapiro has shown that between c. 1597 and 1613, 76% of the plays acted by the Children of Paul's include an average of 5 songs each, 72% of the plays acted by the Children of the Chapel include an average of 2.4 songs each, and 49% of the plays acted by the King's Men, the most musical adult company, include an average of 1.4 songs each.[3] However, children's drama was by no means uniformly musical. A re-evaluation of extant material sheds new light on the traditional view that children's and adults' drama were entirely musically distinct. First, it must be recognized that children's plays were conceived primarily as dramatic, not musical, entertainment. Dramatic requirements governed the use of music in English Renaissance drama, not the other way around. Some children's plays from the period between 1597 and 1613, such as Samuel Daniel's *Tragedy of Philotas* and the anonymous *The Puritan*, include absolutely no music whatsoever; while some adults' plays from the same period, such as William Shakespeare's *As You Like It* and *The Tempest*, include extraordinary amounts of music. Furthermore, music was partly a matter of the playwright's taste. Some dramatists, such as William Shakespeare, clearly loved music and recognized its dramatic power; while others, such as John Webster, apparently had no special fondness for it.

Second, music had a definite place in the Elizabethan and Jacobean theater, public or private, no matter who served as actors. Contemporary thinkers regarded music and poetry as twin arts, and believed drama to have been born of their union:

The matters whereof verses were first made, were eyther exhortations to vertue, dehortationds from vices, or the prayses of some laudable thing. From thence they beganne to use them in exercises of immitating some vertuous wise man at their feastes; where as some one should be appointed to represent an other mans person of high estimation, and he sang fine ditties and wittie sentences, tunably to their Musick notes. Of thys sprang the first kynd of Comedyes, when they beganne to bring into these exercises, more persons than one.[4]

The exquisite combination of music and poetry only continued to delight theater audiences through the ages, as playwright John Marston reminds us in a discussion of dramatic entertainment:

Musicke and poetry were first approv'd
By common scence; and that which pleased most
Held most allowed passe.[5]

Music was such a standard feature of English drama by the seventeenth century that William Prynne, author of the infamous antitheatrical tract *Histrio-Mastix*, not only describes playhouses as "resounding always with such voluptuous Melody,"[6] but elevates music to one of the principal vices of the theater:

The third unlawfull Concomitant of Stage-Playes *is effeminate delicate, lust-provoking Musicke. . .*
That which is always accompanied with effeminate lust-provoking Musicke, is doubtlesse inexpedient and unlawfull unto Christians.
But Stage-playes are alwayes accompanied with such Musicke.[7]

However, certain dramatic genres called for more music than others. Comedy, including romance and pastoral, was inherently musical. Not only did literary theorist William Webbe specify that it was comedy that had evolved from song at ancient feasts, but the Puritan writer Stephen Gosson believed music an inseparable part of comedy.[8] Vocal music especially had a place of honor in comedies, no matter what company performed. Tragedy and its close relative chronicle history were far less musical, especially in terms of texted song. As Thomas Rymer, a later seventeenth-century analyst of Shakespeare-era drama, reminds us, the most common excuses for song and musical spectacles were incongruous with the aims of tragedy:

Therefore a distinction is to be made between what *pleases naturally* in it self, and what *pleases* upon account of *machines, actors, dances,* and circumstances which are meerly *accidental* to *tragedy.*[9]

A statistical examination of the dramatic repertoires of certain companies is illuminating. The Children of Paul's made the most regular use of song of any London company between 1597 and their demise in 1607, and 84.2% of their plays were comedies. From 1600 until they were absorbed into the Lady Elizabeth's Men in 1613, 74.2% of the plays acted by the Children of the Chapel were comedies; but for the same time period, only 38% of the plays acted by the King's Men were comedies. Children's plays often used a greater variety and larger amount of music than similar adults' plays, but the same sorts of situations and same sorts of characters are associated with music in all contemporary plays.

THE AUDIENCE

The literary tastes of the audience had a great impact on the plays produced at the children's theaters after the revival of the late 1590s. The children's companies, for whom royal patronage and court performance had become peripheral, followed suit and began to compete directly with London's adult companies for audiences. The traditional view that the public and private theater audiences were completely separate groups of people has recently been called into question.[10] As Ann Jennalie Cook has said,

> Speculation concerning those long-dead theatergoers must rest precariously upon such fragmentary data as remain undestroyed by the harsh effects of time. A wide assortment of sermons, official complaints, regulatory documents, diaries, letters, and foreign travellers' accounts, as well as passages from plays and other works of literature, all refer to audiences. For in his own day, the Renaissance playgoer occasioned criticism, controversy, contempt, and curiosity. Reports of his nature varied widely. . . . Modern accounts of the audience suffer from the bias of the writer fully as much as did the contemporary accounts.[11]

One current view holds that only the wealthy had the leisure time and money to attend the theater on a regular basis in Shakespeare's day, and truly dedicated theatergoers undoubtedly went wherever the entertainment was thought to be best, public or private playhouse.[12] However, it has also been shown that the common citizenry, apprentices , and members of the lower classes were also among the playgoing audiences of the era, occasionally finding their way even into the more expensive, self-styled elite private theaters.[13] The choice of theater and drama company was clearly influenced by many factors, of which cost of admission, reputation, and sort of drama and performance were three of the most important. The first quarto of *Hamlet* makes it abundantly clear that, shortly after the turn of the century, the fare offered at the private theaters lured many attendees away from the public theaters, for Gilderstone explains to Hamlet that his favorite city tragedians have been forced to go on tour because

> [N]oveltie carried it away,
> For the principall publicke audience that
> Came to them are turned to private playes,
> And to the humour of children.[14]

What made the humor of the children so popular with this audience? For one thing, the expensive indoor performances literally shut out the common folk with the garlic aroma and barmy jackets who could occasionally find the means to attend a public play. The mystique of courtly entertainment still hung in the air at the Blackfriars and Paul's theaters, so that those not invited to Court performances could still feel that they were participating in a form of entertainment intended for royalty.[15] The private theater was a place to reinforce actual or strived-for social status, probably patronized by "courtiers [who] could see the plays as often as they pleased, joined by that host of lesser gentlemen and would-be gallants, upstart merchants' sons and fashionable ladies who could only dream of attending a glittering performance before royalty or nobility."[16]

The privileged playgoers who helped to catapult the private theaters to competitive status were apparently a diverse lot from the remarkably heterogeneous upper ranks of what has been characterized as a "violent, hierarchically organized society."[17] Some were probably hereditary gentry, others newly come to lands or titles, and still others drawn from among "those whome their race and bloud, or at least their vertues make noble and knowne."[18] Some were doubtless successful merchants, others prosperous lawyers, and still others university men of assorted origins, all of whom were recognized as gentlemen by the status-conscious society of the time.[19] How different they really were from most of those who attended the public playhouses hardly matters, for the private playwrights continually flatter and lampoon an audience that believes itself elite.

The private theater audience clearly admired the sort of innovation the playwrights provided. A Venetian diplomat to Elizabethan England remarked, "The English are universally partial to novelty,"[20] and, as Gilderstone implies to Hamlet, this partiality is especially well reflected in the boys' plays. Part of this novelty was probably the young actors, but the plays in which they appeared brought innovation to the stage. New dramatic genres were continually devised, and old ones altered, sometimes later evolving into standard fare in the adults' theaters. The children's playwrights had a talent for transferring the latest ideas from nondramatic literature to the stage. Alfred Harbage perhaps overstates the case, when he argues that the children's playwrights began to channel the new literary fashion for eroticism and satire of the 1590s into their drama shortly after the revival;[21] but at least later, popular jestbooks, coney-catching pamphlets, current politics, and recent Continental literary arrivals did influence the continually-changing fare at the children's theaters. The children's plays catered to their audience by reinforcing smug feelings of upper-class status and responding to cravings for artistic novelty, which kept them well-attended until they ceased to be the latest rage among the fickle playgoers of Jacobean London.

TYPES OF DRAMA

Children's drama after 1597 was characterized by the rapidly changing literary and dramatic taste of its inconstant era. Before 1590, most of the plays acted by the children's troupes were inspired either by the works of classical dramatists, or by the highly musical, semidramatic entertainments of the early Tudor court in which choirboy-actors had originally performed.[22] Most of these plays are fanciful comedies or moralities, and their favorite themes are the many forms of love and honor. When the children's companies resumed playing at the close of the sixteenth century, at first they began with the sorts of plays that had brought them earlier fame, most notably the quasi-mythological romances that had dominated their productions in the 1580s. But literary taste and the children's companies' audience and position in the theatrical world had changed during a decade of dormancy, and their plays, too, had to change to bring them continued success. As their writers experimented with new modes of expression, the plays came to retain the broad hallmark of earlier children's drama: a tendency toward comedy. The predominance of comedy may help account for the great success of the children's companies at their zenith, for contemporary writers, such as Stephen Gosson, describe the main attractions of comedy as being those things at which the child actors apparently excelled:

So in Comedies delight being moved with varietie of shews, of eventes, of musicke, the longer we gaze, the more we crave, yea so forcible are they, y^t afterwards being but thought upo[n], they make use seeke for the like an other time.[23]

After the revival of the late sixteenth century, children's drama, taking a cue from nondramatic literature, quickly became dominated by satire and the comedy of manners. Alfred Harbage has observed,

The most striking thing about the list [of plays] is the overwhelming preponderance of satirical comedies, all but a dozen of the total being classifiable as such. Most of the rest are tragedies or tragicomedies. . . . In all but a few of the plays, the theme is sexual transgression, coupled in tragedy with trechery and murder, and in comedy with cupidity and fraud. It is a body of drama preoccupied with lust and murder or lust and money, and with the exhibition of the foolish and the foul.[24]

Scathing satiric drama, social criticism, and an obsession with the darker aspects of human nature ultimately moved to the adult theater and profoundly influenced Jacobean drama. This literary movement, first seen in drama in the form of satiric comedy in the children's theaters, was born of the same social and psychological disorder that ultimately led to civil war.[25] No institution or public figure in contemporary London was immune from the satiric barbs of children's drama. Poets, courtiers, merchants, usurers, royalty, religion, politics, music, and even the drama were mocked repeatedly and without mercy on the children's stage, clearly part of a general trend by which the arts became vehicles for cloaked political expression.[26] Both the final popularity and the demise of children's drama were apparently tied to its political daring, for no adult companies took such great risks or so offended His Majesty.[27] The same tender years of the actors that allowed them to reduce issues and people to miniaturized mockeries also gave them a fancied immunity from rebuttal and censorship. The type of play that permitted such liberties was deplored even as it flourished:

Now to speake of some abuse lately crept into the quality, as an inveighing against the State, the Court, the Law, the Citty, and their governments, with the particularizing of private mens humors (yet alive) Noblemen, and others. I knoew it distastes many; neither do I any way approve it, nor dare I by any means excuse it. The liberty which some arrogate to themselves, committing all their biternesse, and liberall invectives against all estates, to the mouthes of Children, supposing their juniority to be a priviledge for any rayling, be it never so violent, I could advise all such, to curbe and limit this presumed liberty within the bands of discretion and government.[28]

In his sarcastic advice to would-be gallants, Thomas Dekker gives us an idea of how some of the targets of this invective behaved in the playhouse:

Now, sir, if the writer be a fellow that hath either epigramd you, or hath had a flirt at your mistris, or hath brought either your feather or your red beard, or your little legs, &c on the stage, you shall disgrace him worse then by tossing him in a blancket, or giving him the bastinado in a Taverne, if in the middle of his play (bee it Pastorall or Comedy, Morall or Tragedie) if you rise with a screud and discontented face from your stoole to be gone: no matter whether the Scenes be good or no, the better they are, the worse do you distaste them: and beeing on your feete, sneake not away like a coward, but salute all your gentle acquaintance, that are spred either on the rushes, or in the stools about you, and draw what troope you can from the stage after you.[29]

Contemporary writers tended not to label their works any more specifically than "comedy" or "tragedy," so it has fallen to modern scholars to create discrete categories for the purposes of discussion. Several have considered the classification of "satiric comedy" far too broad for accurate description of the children's repertoire after 1597.[30] Michael Shapiro has proposed the clearest system of classification of the children's comedies in the form of four roughly chronological categories, each with increasingly satirical content: Lylyesque comedy, new romantic comedy, "comicall satire" and humors satire, and city comedy.[31] I can also be demonstrated that the first and last of these are associated with specific kinds of music.

The Lylyesque comedy with which the children's troupes resumed playing inherited its conventions from the quasi-mythological, quasi-pastoral dramas of John Lyly and his contemporaries from the prerevival period. These conventions include a forest or pastoral setting, characters or situations borrowed from classical mythology, symmetrical groups of allegorical characters who belong to the Arcadian or wooded landscape, and subplots consisting of satirical episodes involving witty servants who could have stepped straight from the comedies of Terence or Plautus. Lylyesque drama belonged more to the literary and dramatic climate of the 1580s than the 1600s, and it quickly gave way to more novel sorts of drama after a few brief attempts at resurrection.

But even these brief experiments tend to exert independence from classic example of the genre; stock characters and situations begin to approach the parodic, and the larger-than-life heroes take on more human traits. However, in its original or brave new form, this sort of drama invariably includes elaborate musical spectacle and multiple large-scale musical numbers. Lylyesque comedy and the related pastoral are the only genres presented by the children after 1597 that regularly involve most of the cast in such musical displays as elaborate theatrical dances, large celebratory choruses, and superlative scenes that combine stage machinery, fantastic costume, and multiple musical numbers. Few musical events in Lylyesque comedy are drawn from daily life in Renaissance England, for it is the music of magic and fantasy. By 1600, elaborate musical scenes and a constant tendency toward music had become a stock indication of the world beyond mortal beings, conjuring up images of a golden age of innocence and a forgotten place where mankind danced hand in hand with greater beings on forever verdant ground.

The glittering attraction of such Arcadian fables paled quickly as the new century dawned, as the dismal failure of John Fletcher's 1608 pastoral, *The Faithful Shepherdess*, attests. As early as 1600, the more forward-looking of the children's dramatists recognized that new plays that walked in the shadows of old would not meet with commercial success:

They say, the *umbrae*, or ghosts of some three or four plays, departed a dozen years since, have been seen walking on your stage here: take heed, boy, if your house be haunted with such *hobgoblins*, 'twill fright away all your spectators quickly.[32]

These playwrights sought new ideas for children's plays not in the antiquated allegories of Lyly and Peele, but in the more recent romances of Shakespeare and Greene. Certain aspects of these adult plays of the 1590s proved quite suitable for the children's particular talents, and were summarily adapted into what Shapiro has labeled new romantic comedy.[33] Several of these plays, most notably the anonymous *Blurt, Master-Constable or the Spaniards Night Walk* and *The Wisdom of Dr. Dodypoll*, include familiar elements from Lylyesque comedy, but most completely dispense with the distinctive features of that earlier drama. Speech becomes less formal and more prosaic, short satiric servant scenes develop into farcical subplots, the supernatural element has all but vanished, and the mythic green habitat has been transformed into remote medieval England or some exotic Continental dukedom. With the shift from unearthly to the more human, the special excuse for musical spectacle is gone, but some of these plays remain quite musical. Romance itself whispers of the exotic and mysterious, and these things were always musical in the Elizabethan and Jacobean imagination. The action of these plays may be removed from the mythic world of the Golden Age, but it hardly becomes mundane. In new romantic comedy, the music of the magical joins the music of daily life as the more human kings and dukes combine fantasticadventure- with more commonplace activities, such as feasting and social dancing, that require music on stage as they did in life.

Shortly after the turn of the century, several playwrights with a more satiric turn of mind devised humors satire from a combination of recent trends in drama and nondramatic poetry. This was a dramatic genre that combined the action of the latest romantic comedy with a satiric plot, and owed as much to fashionable satiric poetry as to dramatic romance. The plots are normally built around an elaborate intrigue designed to discomfit or expose one or more "humors" characters, individuals driven by a single ruling passion or neurotic compulsion, whose ridiculous self-imposed behavior has become predictable. These characters belong to the pallid flip side of allegory and serve as unidimensional sham heroes. From the same impetus that led to humors satire, Ben Jonson derived "comicall satire," a self-selected label for his specific contribution to the genre. Like formal satire, humors satire and comicall satire conform to a structural principal whereby a blunt, plain-speaking adherent to old-fashioned values encounters a series of unidimensional fools and proceeds to describe and denounce them; but like romance, these plays tend to maintain a sense of geniality and good will beneath their explicit moralizing. These plays are not musically distinct as a genre, but music, especially appropriately texted songs, often helps to illustrate the ruling passions of the humors characters.

The final comic genre devised by the children's playwrights was the most satiric, the most scathing, and the one with the greatest impact on the Jacobean theater. The genre is known today as city comedy, distinguished principally by its clearly defined contemporary London setting, recognizable character types from the social milieu between manual laborers and prosperous merchants, colloquial diction, and biting satire.[34] City comedy grew from the sense of social unrest and dissatisfaction that dominated the Jacobean era, and its life span is almost precisely that of Jacobean rule. It dominated the children's stages during the first decade of the Jacobean era, and was quickly adopted by the adult actors. Inspiration for the genre, especially as written for the children, did not come from an apocalyptic vision as much as a particular, local, critical observation of vice and folly by bitter jesters and the more academic writers of the same satiric verse of the 1590s that gave rise to other forms of drama.[35]

At the dawn of the seventeenth century, when such works were first devised, English civilization was largely based on local pieties, local traditions, and local knowledge.[36] Contemporary life was marked by rapid change and violence,[37] and this overtly critical body of plays could present such in the most familiar urban locations:

> Our scene is London, cause we would make it knowne,
> No countries mirth is better then our owne.
> No clime breeds better matter, for your Whore,
> Baud, Squire, Imposter, many persons more,
> Whose manners, now call'd humors, feede the stage:
> And which have still beene subject, to the rage,
> Or spleene, of *comick* writers.[38]

The children's brand of city comedy was inspired as much by written sources such as coney-catching pamphlets and ancient Roman verse satire as by personal observation of London and her people. These plays adopted a wry and sardonic wit, and became racy comedies with prevalent elements of sex, financial intrigue, and biting satire—the very elements which Harbage has considered most titillating to the private theater audiences.[39] The children's city comedies were not so much realistic portraits of contemporary London life as caricatures diminished to child-size and reflected from a slightly distorted mirror. Plays from this category, especially Chapman, Jonson, and Marston's infamous *Eastward Ho*, were deemed offensive by the powers of censorship and the King himself. These plays turned the world of the common Londoner upside down, and were thus all the more amusing to the self-styled elite who patronized the private theaters: the honest tradesman became simply stupid or gullible, his wife became ready to cuckold him with the first adventurer to come along, servants bested their masters, children scorned their parents, and only a few sly rogues or courtly gallants ever emerged unscathed at the conclusion of the play.

City comedy must now be recognized as one of the most important and most neglected musical dramatic genres of early seventeenth-century England.[40] The plays are not consistently musical, but their music is that of contemporary London and its varied denizens. These works are populated not only by lawyers, laborers, apprentices, dandies, and merchants clearly recognizable by their behavior and dialogue, but also by many sorts of amateur and professional musician, no more immune from mockery than the others. And the critical tone that finds fault with every other aspect of London life pokes fun at a broad spectrum of contemporary musical taste, the musical canon, and familiar musical styles.

Only a few tragedies or tragicomedies were presented by children's companies during their fully commercial phase. Tragedy requires mature dramatic skills that come only after years of careful training and practice, which made the genre less attractive to companies composed of younger actors. As Stephen Gosson tells us, "The argume[n]t of Tragedies is wrath, crueltie, incest, injurye, murther eyther violent by sworde, or voluntary by poyson."[41] These qualities belong more to corrupt maturity than to youth, and may seem less convincing when approached by child actors. However, boy tragedians could permit the spectator a detachment from material that might otherwise threaten his social identity.[42] Furthermore, the boys probably played extremely convincing women, and women constitute the majority of pathetic victims in early seventeenth-century English tragedy. Thus, the audience could identify more with the hapless victims than with monstrous perpetrators who are almost invariably mature men, giving children's drama a potentially unique perspective on the gender-separate patriarchal world of the later Renaissance.

The tragedies performed by the children follow a fairly even distribution from the late 1590s until the early 1610s. Their styles vary as much as those of comedy, and no single mode of expression dominates. R. A. Foakes has perceived a parallel course of development between the styles of children's comedy and tragedy.[43] As with comedy, the children's tragedy was highly innovative and had a lasting impact on Jacobean drama. Indeed, the children were the leaders in the tragedy of sex and violence that came to dominate the Jacobean stage.[44] Like the parallel developments in comedy, four phases of children's tragedy can be distinguished after 1597. The first is marked by the same satirical self-mocking inventiveness that permeates humors satire and "comicall satire," and is represented by John Marston's highly innovative *Antonio's Revenge* and his tragicomic *The Malcontent*. Shortly after the accession of James, parallel to the rise of city comedy and as the younger boys had grown in size and skill, an attempt was made at serious tragedy that exploited sex, violence, and clashing ideologies on a grand scale in Marston's *The Wonder of Women or the Tragedy of Sophonisba* and George Chapman's *Bussy D'Ambois*. Foakes considers Chapman's *The Conspiracy and Tragedy of Charles, Duke of Byron* as the sole effort to bring this development to a logical conclusion and produce a fully-fledged tragedy of ideas.[45] The final phase of children's tragedy belongs to the waning years of the last company, shortly before its actors were absorbed into the adult company of the Lady Elizabeth's Men. These plays, which include Beaumont and Fletcher's *Cupid's Revenge* and Marston and Barkstead's *The Insatiate Countesse*, belong almost fully to the new genre of Jacobean tragi-comedy.

Tragedy is far less musical than comedy, but most of the children's tragedies, like most of the adults', do require some music. The musical limitations of tragedy apply far more to song than to instrumental music, and many songless tragedies resound with military or stateroom sennets and tuckets. The children's tragedies often make innovative use of comparatively large amounts of instrumental music. Marston's *Sophonisba*, with its almost continuous music of the battlefield and its audible harmony of magic at work, is the most musical play of the era. And *Antonio's Revenge* uses music to accompany ingenious dumbshows to open each act in a wordless summary of the increasing horror. Perhaps most importantly from a historical perspective, *Antonio's Revenge* and *The Malcontent* are the first tragedy and tragicomedy to feature masques at the climax, a fairly standard device in later adult tragedy and tragicomedy. Songs, too, were used effectively, if less frequently, in children's tragedy as in adults', for song can capture and express inner feelings far better than simple speech; and song, as a harmless, innocent pastime, can be used as a jarring contrast to successive or simultaneous deeds of violence.

THE PLAYWRIGHTS

Volumes have been written about the greater of the children's playwrights, and few facts have survived concerning most of the lesser. However, it is the playwrights' separate visions of the world and their art that ultimately give shape to that nebulous body of works labeled "children's drama," and it was they, too, who chose what sort of plays to write and whether to incorporate music into the action. It is not without significance that five of the six most musical playwrights of the era wrote the majority of children's plays.

Before the revival at the end of the sixteenth century, most of the children's plays had been written by their directors or managers, men such as William Cornish, Richard Edwards, and Sebastian Westcott. Only as the acquisition of playhouses hinted at commercial possibilities were outside dramatists brought in with regularity, and only after the revival, when the companies became fully competitive, did professional playwrights become completely responsible for the repertoire. Playwrights were scarcely more respectable than players in contemporary England, but, as with players, if they were of high enough social standing to write as amateurs, they remained immune from the stigma of the profession;[46] and the nominally amateur children's companies were most acceptable for the talents of gentlemen playwrights. However, it was the play itself and not its creator that was the more important. In fact, a significant percentage of contemporary plays were printed without an author's name on the title page, and many plays were collaborative ventures. Drama companies engaged the exclusive services of playwrights just as they engaged the exclusive services of actors.

Most of the children's playwrights, like the actors they wrote for, were exceptional in their profession for one reason or another. Most were young, and several transferred to the King's Men in their maturity as did some of their actors. Some children's playwrights, like Edward Sharpham and Lording Barry, were gently-born amateurs. Others, like Ben Jonson and George Chapman, were scholars. Nearly all were extremely well educated at Oxford, Cambridge, and/or the Inns of Court. Nearly all had claims to the same privileged status as their audiences. Their work ranges from first-rate to third-rate, their productivity from prolific to only one or two plays in a lifetime, and most also wrote nondramatic works. Some, like Ben Jonson, rank among the finest writers to ever use the English language, while others, such as Edward Sharpham, remain only of historical interest.

When both companies resumed playing around the turn of the century, "a group of writers, antagonistic to popular literature and restive in the employ of actors—self-made scholars like Chapman and Jonson, and new recruits among the Inns of Court and university wits like Marston and Middleton— were ready to secede to the elite theaters and supply a new repertory."[47] Paul's at first secured John Marston as their major new dramatist, while the Chapel company found in Ben Jonson another young, though more experienced, playwright. Thomas Middleton later joined and succeeded Marston, and George Chapman, already famous as a poet and dramatist, soon became associated with the Children of the Chapel. John Marston soon switched over to the Chapel company, and shortly thereafter the same company attracted novice playwrights Francis Beaumont and John Fletcher.

These six men wrote over two thirds of the children's plays after 1597, and all stand among the most outstanding dramatists of their age. They were all highly educated men in an era when education implied thorough training in the classics and philosophy, and when theoretical and speculative music were inseparable parts of philosophy and the mathematical sciences.[48] These erudite playwrights moved in a cultured society that admired fine writing and poetry, and the few major libraries of which we have record give proof of the broad intellectual interests characteristic of this unspecialized age.[49] The other men who wrote for the children's companies also came mostly from similar intellectual backgrounds. Knowledge of the classics, of Renaissance literary theory, and of philosophy colors nearly all of their works. It is, therefore, not surprising that many of the children's playwrights speak knowledgeably of theoretical and speculative music, or use practical music to striking effect, in their dramatic works.

Any discussion of the major playwrights who wrote for the children after 1597 must begin with John Lyly, for though it is doubtful that he wrote more than one work for them during this period, his influence is apparent in several early postrevival plays. Lyly (1554?–1606) was the gently-born grandson of William, High Master of St. Paul's grammar school, and son of Peter, a diocesan official at Canterbury where John was born. John Lyly was made a Bachelor of Arts at Oxford University in 1573, and a Master of Arts at the same university two years later. By the middle of the following decade, he had become the principal playwright for the Children of Paul's, and probably helped them damagingly into the Marprelate controversy a few years later. His plays exploit the most outstanding talents of the children; they are light comedies full of high-blown rhetorical devices and brilliant musical spectacle. His mythological/pastoral settings, pert and witty dialogue, and larger-than-life allegorical characters made his plays quite popular during the 1580s, but his style had become antiquated by the late 1590s.

John Marston (1576–1634) became Lyly's first major successor with the Children of Paul's. He was the son of a prosperous Coventry lawyer and distinguished member of the Middle Temple who hoped that young John would follow in his footsteps. But, although young Marston took up residence at the Middle Temple after receiving his baccalaureate degree from Oxford in 1594, he severely disappointed his father by choosing a literary career. His entire opus is the work of a young man, for by 1608 he had completely given up writing and was ordained a priest of the Anglican church a year later. However, during his brief literary career he earned the wrath of King James, the remonstrance of the Bishop of London and the Archbishop of Canterbury, and the highest praise from his contemporaries. Marston began his literary career as a poet during the late 1590s, and by 1598, shortly before he tried his hand at writing plays, he was already considered by Francis Meres as one of England's finest satirists.[50] His plays, all written for either the Children of Paul's or the Children of the Chapel, are dominated by elements of sex, violence, and music. His dark, cynical vision of human nature, racy dialogue, and twisted wit have continued to divide modern critics into those who dismiss him as prurient sensationalist and those who consider him an unjustly maligned genius.[51]

David G. O'Neill has demonstrated that it was impossible to earn a degree from Oxford or reside at the Inns of Court in Marston's day without gaining a thorough knowledge of theoretical and practical music.[52] Marston himself clearly loved music and knew well its limitless dramatic potential—his dramatic dialogue often turn to musical metaphor, and every one of his plays calls for unusually large amounts of music. He must be considered the most musically innovative dramatist of his day, and has previously been considered the most musical in general.[53] His greatest musical strength lies in the superimposition of music and action, which often borders on the melodramatic, and he sometimes blends the use of music with elements of sex or violence to produce striking, unforgettable effects. He was clearly quite sensitive to instrumental timbres, for his work calls for a greater variety of musical instruments under more circumstances than that of any of his dramatic contemporaries. He generally integrates song flawlessly into the dramatic action, but the few lyrics for which he seems responsible are surprisingly crude and clumsy. He was obviously more concerned with the dramatic use of song than with the choice of any particular song or song style.

Ben Jonson (1572–1637), one of the greatest English men of letters and perhaps the leading dramatist of his age, was the first major playwright associated with the Children of the Chapel after their revival in 1600. His father had been a minister of Scottish origin, but he was expected to follow the trade of his bricklaying stepfather. Like Marston, he thwarted the older man's hopes. Unlike Marston, he spent his entire adult life writing plays, poems, and prose works. Jonson was a literary trendsetter for his entire career, and was as much concerned with his society and the artist's position in it as with his art. His plays exhibit wit, erudition, and an understanding of the philosophical side of music although he never received a university degree. By 1600, he had already written plays for the Lord Chamberlain's Men, and later tried to create the impression that he was then a novice catapulted to sudden fame with *Every Man in his Humour*.[54] It was with the Children of the Chapel that he first began to incorporate music into his works.[55]

Jonson was as much a scholar as a poet. His wide and deliberate choices of reading matter greatly affected the style and content of his writing. His eclectic library included works that touched on ancient and contemporary ideas about music and related disciplines.[56] Not all of Jonson's plays, even for the Children of the Chapel, include an exceptional amount of music. But he obviously took contemporary ideas about music and the other arts quite seriously, and with the greatest of care chose what sort of music to include where in his plays. His later great success as a masque writer has been attributed to his early experiments in the combination of music and drama, which were written for the Children of the Chapel.[57] And the use of music in his mature plays, written for the King's Men, is almost flawless.

As with the works of Lyly, some of the plays Jonson wrote for boy actors exemplify a nearly perfect relationship between the aims of the dramatist and the talents of his actors. He focuses on the imitative, rhetorical, and musical abilities of the children. Standing opposite his occasional friend and one-time collaborator, John Marston, Jonson's particular musical strength is his use of song. He normally wrote his own lyrics, which demonstrate the same wide range of style and affect as the scenes in which they appear; and some of them were so elegant that they were later separated from their dramatic contexts to stand on their own as song or poetry. Nearly all of his songs contribute greatly to the plot, setting, and characterizations of the plays for which they were written, serving as minute reinforcements for the straight dramatic texts. Jonson rarely specifies the names of the musical instruments to be used in the plays, but generally simply calls for "musicke." Elements of song, dance, and drama blend almost perfectly when they are used together, demonstrating a great desire on the part of the dramatist to unite his art forms as completely as possible. But the drama itself is always dominant.

It is not surprising that Francis Beaumont (c. 1584–1616) and John Fletcher (1579–1625) wrote their first plays for the children's companies, for they were gently-born aspirants to literary careers. They kept their fashionable spectators and youthful performers in mind as they wrote individual and collaborative works for the children.[58] Like Ben Jonson, they are known for their elegant lyrics and the ingenious combinations of music that pervade their work for both children and adults. Also like Jonson, they began to write for the King's Men after they left the Children of the Chapel. The integration of masques and masquelike scenarios into the action of the play seems to be a particular strength of both dramatists, but none of their children's plays include formal masques.

The entire corpus of their dramatic work includes highly varied musical requirements. Beaumont and Fletcher were clearly unaffected by the musical reputations or strengths of the companies for whom they wrote; the use of music in their plays for adults and children ranges from minimal to extreme. Their most musical collaboration, The Maid's Tragedy, was written for the King's Men; and their least, The Scornful Lady, for the Children of the Chapel. Fletcher appears to have been the more musically sensitive of the two, but Beaumont's solo work varies more widely in amount of music than Fletcher's; Beaumont's Philaster, written for the King's Men, requires no music, but his Knight of the Burning Pestle, written for the Children of the Chapel, calls for thirty-four song fragments, seven complete songs, and assorted instrumental pieces. None of Fletcher's works is without music, but none requires the sheer quantity of The Knight of the Burning Pestle.

George Chapman (c. 1560–1634) remains a fairly enigmatic figure. He was no longer a young man when he first began writing plays and poetry in the mid-1590s, and, though it is usually assumed that he spent time at both Oxford and Cambridge, neither residence can be verified. Like his colleague and one-time collaborator, Ben Jonson, Chapman was very much an intellectual. He knew Greek and Latin extremely well and had an obvious familiarity with classical thought and writing. Platonic ideas, including those of the fifteenth-century Florentine neo-Platonist, Marsilio Ficino, permeate his work, and his poems and plays are suffused with Platonic and humanistic ideas about music. His first plays were written for the Lord Admiral's Man, and, even before he left them for the Children of the Chapel, he was considered one of England's finest dramatists.[59] Like Ben Jonson, he apparently learned how to integrate music into his plays when he began to write for children, and like Jonson, his music always serves the drama. Most of the works he wrote after he left the Children of the Chapel are nondramatic poems and translations of classical authors.

Thomas Middleton (1580–1627) is the one major children's playwright from the post-1597 period who is not generally considered outstandingly musical or highly innovative, but many of his plays include music and nearly all bear his stamp of individuality. He was born to the sort of nouveau gentleman popularized in the satiric literature of the day, a London bricklayer who accumulated a significant estate and received a grant of arms. Thomas matriculated at Queen's College, Oxford, in 1598, but left without a degree some time later and began to earn his living as a writer. In time he became a prolific, versatile writer, whose opus included poems, pageants, pamphlets, and longer prose works as well as plays. Middleton began his dramatic career with the Children of Paul's, and after the demise he went onto the Lady Elizabeth's Men and later the King's Men. His works for the children are not musically distinct from those he wrote for adults, and all integrate such music as they use quite well into the action. But nearly all of Middleton's musical situations are more typical of the dramatic conventions of the age than of one individual's art.

CHAPTER 4

PRACTICAL MUSIC AND THE DRAMATIC TEXT

If Musique and sweet Poetry agree,
As they must needes (the Sister and the Brother)
Then must the Love be great, twixt thee and mee,
Because thou lov'st the one, and I the other

> Richard Barnfield, Sonnet I, to his friend Maister R.L.
> In Praise of Musique and Poetrie (1598)

Elizabethan and Jacobean drama was a living art that united music, language, gesture, color, and visual objects in performance. Neither playwrights, composers, nor company managers considered later publication as they collaborated on their productions. However, many plays were set in print after closing on stage, with varying degrees of textual accuracy, with or without the dramatist's cooperation, with very few stage directions, and with no musical notation. Sometimes the results were quite random and disorderly.[1] But many printers and publishers left just enough information in the dialogue and sketchy stage directions that other aspects of the original performances can be reconstructed. In particular, it is possible to arrive at an idea of what sorts of music were used in which plays through careful attention to the given song lyrics, calls for "musicke," and the names of musical instruments included in stage directions and dialogue.

English Renaissance drama was predominantly a verbal-visual form of entertainment, and dramatists were primarily regarded as poets. But a play relied on many sorts of sound for its full auditory effect, from carefully conceived silences to the artificial sounds of birds and gunfire, from formal or colloquial speech to many kinds of music. Each of these became part of the theatrical poetry. English Renaissance literary and musical theorists continually stress the close affinity between poetry and music; one of the former explains that

poets were the first. . . musitiens of the world, [for] they did altogether endevor the[m]selves to reduce the life of man to a certain method of good maners, and make the first difference betweene vertue and vice, and then tempered all these knowledges and skilles with the exercise of a delectable Musicke by melodious instruments, which withall served to delight their hearers, & to call the people together by admiration, to a plausible and vertuous conversation.[2]

In a similar manner, Elizabethan and Jacobean theatrical music helped to set certain ideas or situations apart from others and give them greater significance or dramatic effect. English thinkers of the era, influenced by the ideas of Renaissance neo-Platonism, believed music to be the most powerful and immediate striker of the senses:

It hath beene anciently held, and observed, that the *Sense of Hearing* and the *Kindes of Musicke*, have most Operation upon manners. . . . The Cause is, for the *Sense of Hearing* striketh the *Spirits* more immediately than the other *Senses*: and more incorporeally than *Smelling*: for the *Sight, Taste,* and *Feeling*, have their Organs, not of so present and immediate Access to the Spirites, as the hearing hath. . . but Harmony, entering easily and mingling not at all, and Comming with a manifest Motion: doth by custome of often Affecting the *Spirits*, and Putting them into one kind of Posture, alter not a little the nature of the *Spirits* even when the Object is removed.[3]

In the children's theater, where actors and playwrights were especially inclined toward music, and where most musical sounds would carry well, many kinds of song and musical instruments were used for all of these reasons to augment the lesser affects of speech and gesture.

SONG

To the Elizabethans and Jacobeans, song was a peerless art which drew singular eloquence and power from the balanced union of music and poetry. Many of the era's finest poets and music theorists discuss this perfect unity, and many more modern scholars have studied all aspects of sixteenth- and early seventeenth-century English song.[4] The classical writers so beloved by Elizabethan thinkers praised song in the highest terms and reminded readers of the ancient miracles wrought by the powerful combination of words and melody. Though the twin arts of music and poetry had their separate practitioners, separate rules, and often went separate ways, by the close of the sixteenth century the two had become mutually influential in England. Sir Philip Sidney reminds us that many poets routinely wrote with an ear toward music:

> Hee [the poet] beginneth not with obscure definitions . . . but hee commeth to you with words set in delightful proportion, either accompanied with or prepared for the well enchanting skills of *Musicke*.[5]

And Thomas Ravenscroft points out that certain rhythmic patterns in music had been influenced by poetic feet.[6]

Many scholars have noted that song texts tend to be simpler and more direct than poems not specifically written for music.[7] In the theater, where only brief segments of the larger dramatic poem were accompanied by music, songs especially tend to emphasize a single idea or underscore a specific situation. By virtue of possessing music, a dramatic song is set apart from the rest of the text, making it an ideal vehicle to draw attention to an important aspect of the dramatic whole. Furthermore, accompanied song, with its repetitions and vocal rests, often provides a calm contrast to rapid dialogue and frenzied action. As Bertrand H. Bronson has pointed out, English speech is rhythmned by its natural accent, and impassioned speech naturally approaches chant.[8] In Elizabethan and Jacobean drama, song was thus used most frequently to stand for specific passions, or to intensify the most passionate points of the play. Indeed, by Prynne's day, such passionate song had become "the second unlawfull Concomitant of Stage-Plays,"[9] for the drama was *"always fraught with adulterous, obscene, lascivious Songs and wanton Pastorals, which adde strength and fuell to mens lusts."*[10]

In spite of the emotionally intense, static quality of most dramatic songs, the type of song used in Elizabethan and Jacobean drama was generally appropriate to the singer, situation, and setting of the play. Song topics tend toward aspects of love and loss, though drink, divinity, despair, exultation, and descriptions of nature are well represented. Children's drama included all sorts of characters, settings, and situations, and thus made use of all sorts of contemporary songs. However, most scholars, by seeking to present children's and adults' drama as polar opposites, have tended to minimize the importance of less formal types of song.[11] The public adult stage relied most heavily on unaccompanied popular song, and this sort of song accounts for about two-thirds of the identifiable children's repertoire. The remaining third is the sort of accompanied or choral song which has become associated with the children, and which the adult companies increasingly adopted as they appeared in private theaters.

Unaccompanied Song

The unaccompanied songs in children's plays include ballads, rounds and catches, drinking songs, nonsense songs, and snatches of well-known ayres and madrigals. The unaccompanied repertoire is predominantly pre-existent and popular, or conceived by playwright and composer in popular style. Unaccompanied popular songs add verisimilitude to the London street, shop, and tavern scenes of such city comedies as Dekker and Webster's *Northward Ho*, and help to characterize such urban rogues as Quicksilver of Chapman, Jonson, and Marston's *Eastward Ho*. These songs also help to identify common laborers such as Juniper of Jonson's *His Case is Altered*, rustics like Mopso and Frisco of the anonymous *The Maydes Metamorphosis*, and merry old fools like Merrythought from Beaumont's *The Knight of the Burning Pestle*. They are mostly the simple songs of common folk, and their familiar, easily recognizable nature permitted playwrights great freedom to use them earnestly, humorously, or ironically. They range in length from complete multistanza ballads to single lines quoted from familiar songs. They are often introduced into surrounding dialogue and action so carefully as to seem spontaneous to both the audience and other characters, and may flow quickly from one into another.

A special sort of unaccompanied song, far more common in children's drama than in adults', is the ayre or madrigal that has become severed from its polyphonic setting. The ayre and the native English art of the madrigal came of age and grew to maturity with the second phase of children's drama, so it is not surprising that they found their way into these plays. One tends not to associate either genre with the singers of common ballads, but many such characters mix previously published ayres and madrigals with ballads and catches in a variety of contemporary plays. Indeed, once the polyphonic accompaniment is removed, many ayres and the most melodic lines of a few madrigals become tuneful songs with limited vocal range, not musically unlike ballads. Some songs, such as John Dowland's "Now O Now I Needs Must Part" or "Sorrow Stay," clearly became popular with the sort of privileged Englishman who purchased music books or maintained music manuscripts, even if they did not actually become part of the oral tradition to which they are connected in certain contemporary plays.

One subspecies of such unaccompanied ayres that is unique to the children's plays is the parody of a previously published lute ayre. This is clearly a musical equivalent of the literary penchant for satiric wit that marks so many of the children's plays. Songs selected for parodic treatment come from the most widely circulating musical publications of the time, such as John Dowland's *First Booke of Songs or Ayres*, which went through four printings between 1597 and 1613; or such landmark music books as Robert Jones's *Second Booke of Songs and Ayres* (1601), which was the first English publication to include tablature for the lyra-viol. It may, therefore, be assumed that the original songs were familiar to the cultured sophisticates who patronized the children's theaters, thus giving the parodies added entertainment value.

The texts of the ayres are twisted in various manners and for various purposes, but always with enough semblance to the original wording that the audience would have had little difficulty recognizing the clever alteration of a well-known song. Indeed, parody is ineffective if the original words and their close association with the tune cannot be easily recalled. The parodic songs in children's plays are always cleverly adjusted to the specific dramatic situation, and are often meant to emphasize the great wit of the character who sings them. The complete song is not always used in a parody, but there is always enough for the listener to recognize the tune and recall the original words. For example, in Act V, scene i of Chapman's *The Widdowes Teares*, the clever Tharsalio believes that he has finally caught Cynthia proving unfaithful to Lysander. In glee, he bursts into a parody of the refrain of "Say Love If Ever Thou Didst Find" from John Dowland's *Third and Last Booke of Songs and Ayres*, which had been published two years before the premier of the play: "She, she, she, and none but she,/ She onely queene of love and chastitie." The audience would not only recall the original refrain of "She, she, she and only she,/She onely queene of love and beautie" through Tharsalio's witty and seemingly appropriate alteration, but also the entire song about the uniquely chaste woman who is never touched by Love's arrow and who "from heaven her vertues she doth borrow." To recall the original text is to increase the comical irony of the situation, for the audience knows, at the expense of the overly zealous Tharsalio, that things are not what they seem to be, and Cynthia remains the paragon of heavenly virtue.

The simple unaccompanied songs on the children's stage were by no means limited to solos, but also included rounds and catches. Since these popular songs could be sung by one or more individuals, dialogue or stage directions always indicate when such a simple monody is to be sung canonically by several participants, such as

> **Old Merrythought.**   . . . Let's have a catch. Boy, follow me; come.
> Ho, ho, nobody at home,
> Meate, nor drinke, nor money ha wee none,
> Fill the pot Eedy,
> Never more need I.

(Beaumont, *The Knight of the Burning Pestle*, Act IV, scene iv)

or

> **Phylautus.**   Can ye part in a Song?
> **Graccus.**   Verie tolerably.
> **Phylautus.**   Weele have a catch then, if with sol, sol la.

(*Everie Woman in her Humour*, Act II, scene ii)

The texts of such songs are always quite simple and not infrequently nonsensical, for each line has to fit with each other when sung in canon. And such simple rounds are as much a game as a piece of music.

The final kind of unaccompanied children's song, also choral, more closely resembles accompanied song in textual and musical style, and should thus be considered below.

Accompanied and Polyphonic Song

The accompanied songs and stylistically similar part-songs used in children's plays include consort songs, madrigalian compositions, and ayres. This repertoire appears to be specifically written for use in the plays and includes the latest stylistic developments in contemporary nondramatic art song. These songs are primarily used in works with courtly, foreign, or pastoral settings, and help to bring the cultured or the exotic into the drama. They are also used in plays set closer to the streets of contemporary London to add extra entertainment value, as in Audrey's mocking spinning song from Act IV, scene v of Middleton's *A Tricke to Catch the Old-One*; or to draw special attention to the extraordinary musical ability of a particular character, such as Franceschina in Marston's *The Dutch Courtesan*. These are the intricate songs for which the children's companies are best known, and they provide the greatest contrast to the songs in contemporary adults' plays. Until the King's Men took over the Blackfriars theater in 1609, accompanied song was a great rarity on the adult stage; and never did the adults display as much stylistic versatility as the children, for madrigals and consort songs are completely absent from their plays.

Unlike most unaccompanied songs, accompanied or polyphonic choral songs are clearly set apart from spoken dialogue as special events within the action of the plays. Most were obviously written for the works in which they appear, and many were intended as stunning set pieces. They were not drawn from the oral tradition or previously published sources, and it was therefore necessary to provide complete text if the text itself was relevant to the action. Accompanied song texts are set apart from spoken dialogue, are often labelled "song," and are normally printed in a contrasting typeface. Stage directions generally indicate the beginning of the song, and often call for the accompaniment or an instrumental introduction:

Scudmore. Nevill my friend, well I must something do;
Oh, why should Musicke, which joyes everie part,
Strike such sharpe killing discords to my hart?

*Musicke. Enter Sir John Worldly, who meets the Parson & entertains him. Count,
Bellafront, Strange, Kath., Lucida, with willow. Pendant, Sir Inne: Ninnie, My Lady
Ninnie, Mrs. Wagtayle, S. Abraham melancholy, [and] W.I. walk gravely afore all
softly on. Scudmorestands before, and a Boy singes to the tun'd Musicke.*

SONG

(Field, *A Woman is a Weather-Cocke*, Act II)

Furthermore, introductory dialogue often cues hidden instrumentalists and
serves as a preface to formal song, such as:

Mercury. Begin, and (more to gracy thy cunning voice)
The humorous aire shall mixe her solemne tunes,
With thy sad words: strike musicque from the spheares,
And with your golden raptures swell our eares.

SONG

(Jonson, *Cynthia's Revels*, Act I, scene ii)

The meters and rhyme schemes of the accompanied song lyrics vary as
widely as do those of similar contemporary non dramatic songs. The last two
decades of the sixteenth century were a time of great experimentation and
change in English verse, and many of these changes were reflected in poetry
for music. Italian verse had the greatest impact, bringing seven- and eleven-
syllable lines, trochaic rhythms, and feminine rhyme wholeheartedly into
English poetry.[12] The influence of Italian lyric poetry is, of course, quite evident in children's dramatic song, in such examples as:

Queene, and Huntresse, chaste, and faire,
Now the Sunne is laid to sleepe,
Seated, in thy silver chaire,
State in wonted manner keepe:
Hesperus intreats thy light,
Goddesse, excellently bright.

(Jonson, *Cynthia's Revels*, Act V, scene vi)

and

Lovers rejoice, your pains shall be rewarded,
The god of love himelfe grieves at your crying:

> No more shall frozen honour be regarded,
> Nor the coy faces of a maid denying.
> No more shall Virgins sigh, and say we dare not,
> For men are false, and what they do they care not.
> All hall be well againe, then doe not greeve,
> Men shall be true, and women shall beleeve.

(Beaumont and Fletcher, *Cupid's Revenge*, Act I, scene i)

However, as is clear from even these few examples, slavish imitation of Italian verse was exceedingly rare. Elizabethan nationalists admired the achievements of Italian civilization, but wished to earn equal approbation for English things, as Richard Mulcater reminds us:

I love *Rome*, but *London* better, I favor *Italie*, but *England* more, I honor the *Latin* but I worship the *English*. I wish all were in ours, which theie had from others.[13]

As children's drama sought new inspiration from home and incorporated a greater number of unaccompanied songs from the streets of London, its accompanied lyrics drew continuing inspiration from native poetry. The characteristic six- and eight-syllable iambic lines, simple rhyme scheme, and strong masculine endings that had marked English poetry for years are quite evident in this repertoire:

> Since painful sorrowes date hath end
> And time hath coupled friend with friend,
> Rejoyce we all, rejoyce and sing,
> Let all these groaves of *Phoebus* ring:
> Hope having wonne, depaire is banisht:
> Then trip we all this Roundelay,
> And still be mindful of the bay.

(*The Maydes Metamorphois*, Act V)

> Chaunt birds on everie bush
> The Blackbird and the Thrush
> The chirping Nightingale,
> The Mavis and Wagtaile,
> The Linnet and the Larke
> Oh how they begin, harke, harke!

(*Everie Woman in her Humour*, Act V, scene i)

The native "fourteener," so well loved by earlier Tudor poets, is also used in the repertoire (here split at the eighth syllable, but with the AABB rhyme scheme intact):

> Amidst the mountaine Ida groves,
> Where *Paris* kept his Heard,

Before the other Ladies all
He would have thee prefer'd.
Pallas, for all her painting, than
Her face would seeme but pale,
Then *Juno* would have blush't for shame
And *Venus* looked stale.
Eurimine, thy selfe alone
houldst beare the golden ball;
So far would thy most heavenly forme
Excell the others all;
O happie *Phoebus*! happie then,
Most happie should I bee
If faire *Eurymine* would please
To joyne in love with mee.

(*The Maydes Metamorphosis*, Act III)

And the classical influence of quantitative verse, which inspired some of England's most daring poets right before the resurrection of the children's companies, is equally evident in some of these lyrics:

Slow, slow fresh fount, keepe time with my salt teares;
Yet slower yet, o faintly gentle springs:
List to the heavy part the musicque beares,
Woe weepes out her division when she sings.
Droupe hearbs, and flowres;
Fall griefe in showres;
Our beauties are not ours:
O, I could still
(Like melting snow upon some craggie hill,)
Drop, drop, drop, drop,
Since natures pride is, now, a whither'd daffodil.

(Jonson, *Cynthia's Revels*, Act I, scene ii)

Rhyme scheme and meters sometimes exhibit sophisticated variance from standard patterns, and clearly demand correspondingly unique musical settings:

Come sleepe, and with thy sweet deceiving,
Locke me in delight a while,
Let some pleasing Dreames beguile
All my fancies that from thence
I may feele an influence,
All my power of care bereaving.

(Beaumont and Fletcher, *The Woman Hater*, Act III, scene i)

O that joy so soone should waste!
Or so sweet a blisse

> As a kisse,
> Might not for ever last!
> So sugred, so melting, so soft, so delicious,
> The dew that lyres on roses,
> When the morn herself discloses,
> Is not so precious.
> Or rather then I would it smother,
> Were I to taste such another;
> It would be my wishing
> That I might dye, kissing.

(Jonson, *Cynthia's Revels*, Act IV, scene iii)

Accompanied songs and those others intended for polyphonic performance that grace the children's plays include choruses and dialogue songs.
Choruses are always labelled as such in the original imprints, or are prefaced
by stage directions that call for a group to sing, such as "Enter the Faieries,
singing and dancing" (*The Maydes Metamorphosis*, Act II), "Chorus. Io to
Hymen" (Marston, *Sophonisba*, Act I, scene ii), and "They rise and sing in
praise of Pan" (Fletcher, *The Faithful Shepherdess*, Act I, scene ii). Dialogue
songs are divided line by line in the manner of spoken dialogue:

Ovid.   . . . Apollo, command us louder musicke, and let
          Mercury, and Momus contend to please and re-
          vive our senses.

SONG

Hermogenes.	Then, in a free and lofty straine,
	Our Broken tunes we thus repaire;
Crispinus.	And we answere them againe,
	Running divisions to the panting aire:
Ambo.	To celebrate this feast of sense,
	As free from scandall as offence.
Hermogenes.	Here is *beautie*, for the eye;
Crispinus.	For the eare, sweet *melodie*;
Hermogenes.	*Ambrosiak* odours, for the smell;
Cripinus.	Delicious *nectar*, for the taste;
Ambo.	For the touch, *a ladies waste*;
	Which doth all the rest excell.

(Johnson, *The Poetaster*, Act IV, scene v)

Accompaniment for these varied songs is most often specified as "musicke," but lute, viol, harp, organ, recorder, and cornett are also specified as
accompanying instruments, alone or in consort. Some songs are sung by principal characters, a few of whom provide their own accompaniment on lute or

viol; and others are sung by minor characters apparently introduced for the sole purpose of providing a song or two. Nearly all songs called for in children's plays, accompanied or unaccompanied, are sung on stage as part of the action, but a few belong to the inter-act entertainment for which the private theaters were known.

"MUSICKE"

Since music was one of the aspects of the drama that was sacrificed when Elizabethan and Jacobean plays were committed to print, the musical directions that remain often hover somewhere between the vague and the cryptic. However, by following dialogic clues and patterns in stage directions and dialogic clues, it is possible to refine even the frustrating catchall term "musicke" that appears so often in these plays and clearly refers specifically to the instrumental variety.

Stringed instruments are given the principal place of honor in contemporary manuscripts and publications of instrumental music, and in paintings depicting musical instruments. The preference for strings is reflected in many of those scenes that simply call for "musicke" in children's drama. More often than not, dialogue describing nonspecific music refers to stringed instruments. And the majority of extant contemporary settings of the accompanied songs that are introduced in children's drama with directions for "musicke" require lute or viols to support the voice. However, "musicke" clearly does not always imply strings or strings alone. In Jonson's *Epicoene* (Act III, scene vii), "musique of all sorts" apparently includes drum, trumpets, and a consort of viols or violins. Day's *Isle of Gulls* (Act III, scene iii) calls for "Musicke of Bels &c." And the versatile cornett is used so frequently in children's drama that it is difficult to believe that it, too, did not occasionally provide "musicke," especially in scenes of courtly revelry and religious devotion.

"Loud" is the adjective most often applied to the simple word "musicke" in stage directions, and is apparently meant to describe the sound of cornetts, trumpets, or other powerful wind instruments. Loud music most often ushers titled or otherwise important characters onto the stage, such as:

Enter Mercurie with lowde musicke.

(Marston, *The Malcontent*, Act V, scene iv)

Lowde musique, and enter Byron.

(Chapman, *The Tragedy of Byron*, Act I, scene ii)

Loud musicke, in which time, enter Sir John Worldly, Sir Innocent, Bellafront,
Lucida

(Field, *A Woman is a Weather-cocke*, Act V).

The same sort of music sometimes ushers characters off the stage at the conclusions of acts, as in Marston's *Antonio's Revenge* (Act IV, scene iii). Loud
music is also associated, to a lesser extent, with ritual and celebration, as in
the wedding scenes in Marston's *Sophonisba* (Act I, scene ii) and Field's *A
Woman is a Weather-cocke* (Act II). Dialogue and further stage directions let
us know that "Loud Musicke" is played by cornetts in *A Woman is a Weather-
cocke* (Act II) and trumpets in Dekker and Marston's *Satiromastix*. "Lowdest
Musicke" is the music of cornetts in *Antonio's Revenge* (Act IV, scene iii), and
"Loud, full musicke" refers to cornetts and organs at the conclusion of the
first act of *Sophonisba*.

"Soft Musicke" is called for in several plays, but there are few clues as to its
composition. It accompanies stately entries in Marston's *The Fawne* and
Dekker and Marston's *Satiromastix*. It is used melodramatically to emphasize important dialogue in *A Woman is a Weather-Cocke* (Act V), *Sophonisba*
(Act V, scene ii), and *Antonio's Revenge* (Act I, scene ii). It represents the
supernatural and the completion of an evil spell in *Sophonisba* (Act IV, scene
i). In all instances except *The Fawne* (Act IV), it plays beneath dialogue,
which makes its softness a practical necessity. The only instance in which
such soft music is described in greater detail is in *Sophonisba* (Act IV, scene
iii), in which case it is played by a bass lute and a treble viol.

"Infernall musicke" is specified in only one scene of children's drama,
where it represents demonic power and the dark working of witchcraft. In Act
IV, scene i of *Sophonisba*, such music is required to play softly as the evil sor-
ceress Erictho works her hellish magic. Nowhere is its composition indicated, but dialogue informs us that, softened as it may be, it is louder than the
music of the treble viol and bass lute used for contrast in the same scene. The
contemporary Italian infernal orchestra, a combination of viols and trombones, with or without organ,[14] would have provided just the right sort of
contrast. Furthermore, all of these instruments are used at other points in the
same play.

"Solemnpe [sic] Musique" is also specified once in the children's repertoire, to accompany a funeral song and march in Act V of John Day's *Law
Tricks*. Again, there is no indication in the play as to what produced this music, but funeral scenes in other children's plays call for flutes, recorders, cornetts, or trumpets. It is unlikely that the trumpet would have provided
accompaniment for a singer, but the other three instruments are good candi-

dates for the solemn funeral music in Day's play. Finally, "The vilest, out-of-tune musicke" opens Marston's *The Malcontent* to set the stage for vile political corruption. This discordant music could have been anything that contemporary musicians and auditors found jarring, dissonant, and thoroughly unpleasant to hear. The same play later calls for a variety of stringed and wind instruments to perform diverse specific musical functions, and any or all of them could have contributed to the introductory cacophony.

MUSICAL INSTRUMENTS

In spite of the haphazard, general nature of extant dramatic musical directions, it is quite clear that the children's companies made use of a wide variety of musical instruments for many purposes. However, it is impossible to conclude with complete certainty what instruments were used when, by whom, and how often, because not only are most stage directions irretrievably vague, but Renaissance taxonomy, especially as applied to music, was an imprecise science. As early as 1586, the growing proliferation of musical instruments that marked the twilight of the Renaissance, and the attendant terminological problems, were deemed noteworthy in England:

[W]e be nowe adaies fallen into a kind of intemperance and wantonnese, especially in the framing of [musical] instruments, in so much that the devising of them is not so great a trouble as their naming.[15]

Furthermore, England had no theorist or historian of music like Adriano Banchieri, Marin Mersenne, or Michael Praetorius to catalogue and describe her instruments and their uses. Thus, the description of musical instruments fell to poets and philosophers, many of whom clearly had not the vaguest notion of how to play them. Not a single comprehensive work devoted to musical instruments emerged from the considerable scholastic efforts of Elizabethan and Jacobean thinkers. But many and diverse were the writers who mentioned instruments in their works. Several poems purport to list the instruments played in England, but none claims to be comprehensive, and all derive their final authority from artistic fancy. Michael Drayton's list of instruments, from his whimsical history of Great Britain, is one of the most detailed:

> The trembling Lute some touch, some Straine the Violl best
> In sets which there were seene, the Musick wondrous choice:
> Some likewise there affect the Gamba with the voice,
> To shew that *England* could varietie afford.
> Some that delight to touch the sterner wyerie Chord,

> The Cythron and the Kit the wandring Fidlers like.
> So were there some againe, in this their learned strike
> Loud Instruments that lov'd: the Cornet and the Phife,
> The Hoboy, Sagbut deepe, Recorder, and the Flute:
> Even from the shrillest Shawme unto the Cornamute.
> Some blow the Bagpipe up, that plaies the Country-round:
> The Taber and the Pipe, some take delight to sound.[16]

The art of the English dictionary was born with the accession of James I, but the first few exemplars avoid most musical terms. English-foreign language dictionaries are of somewhat greater antiquity and tend to be loaded with musical terminology, but must be used skeptically and wisely. For instance, Claude Desainlien's *Dictionarie of French and English* tells us that viols and violins are identical, and generates new confusion about how to tell a cornett from a horn from a trumpet.[17] All of these sources help to indicate how late Renaissance Englishmen thought about musical instruments, although a few of the more careful scholars, such as Francis Bacon, are indeed enlightening. And since contemporary English discussions of musical instruments are so incomplete and imprecise, the information gleaned from the stage contributes greatly to our knowledge.

Not all instruments were used equally by all three children's companies. (See Table 3.) According to extant stage directions and dialogue, all three companies relied principally on cornetts, lutes, viols, and violins to play during the action. Beyond this core, other instruments make only sporadic appearances. The Children of the King's Revels, the only company formed independently of a contemporary musical establishment, apparently used the least variety of instruments, and the Children of the Chapel used the greatest. Beyond dramatic requirements based on contemporary nontheatrical usage and ancient convention, the specific choice of instrument may have related to practical factors. For example, only the company that clearly relied on outside professional musicians, the Children of the King's Revels, uses the hoboy, an instrument associated with the professional waits who were often hired by adult companies. Only the two companies associated with liturgical establishments use the organ in their plays. And the company with the smallest theater, the Children of Paul's, is apparently the only one to have used the comparatively soft harp. The following discussion of the instruments used in the children's drama is only an approximation of contemporary practices in the Blackfriars, Whitefriars, and Paul's theaters. The sporadic printed stage directions are not always specific, and must be considered representative or approximate rather than complete.

Table 3 A comparative list of musical instruments called for in the children's plays.

Instruments	Children of Paul's	Children of the Chapel	Children of the King's Revels
Bell	x	x	x
"Consort"	x	x	
Cornett*	x	x	x
Drum		x	
Flute	x		
Harp	x		
Hoboy			x
Horn		x	
Lute	x	x	x
(Lute, Bass)		x	
Lyra		x	
Organ	x	x	
Pipe & Tabor	x		
Recorder	x	x	
Theorbo		x	
Trumpet	x**	x	
Viol	x	x	x
Violin ["fiddle"]	x	x	x

*Presumably used with trombones in most instances.
**The only play acted by the Children of Paul's to call for trumpet in stage directions was printed only "As it hath bin presented publikely, by the Right Honorable, the Lord Chamberlaine his Servants; and privately by the Children of Pauls."

The Loud Instruments: Cornetts, Hoboyes, Trumpets, etc.

The cornett

The versatile cornett was apparently used more frequently than any other instrument in the children's theaters, where it was used in the divine service, processions, and chamber music as in life. It also had several specifically theatrical uses, in which it was substituted for other loud instruments, ancient and Renaissance. The exquisite sound of this adaptable instrument, whose compass was like that of the contemporary violin and which could resemble the clarity of the human voice or the shrill blast of the hunting horn, earned great praise in its heyday:

Quant à la propriété du son qu'il rend, il est semblable à l'esclat d'un rayon de Soliel, qui paroist dans l'ombre ou dans les tenebres, lors qu'on l'etend parmy les voix dans les Eglises Cathedrales, ou dans les Chapelles.[18]

The brilliant sound of this instrument had a dynamic range that went from the softness of a recorder to the strident sonority of a trumpet, making it eminently suitable for rapid divisions,[19] which made it ideal for adding continual interest to the lengthy dance and masque scenes in which it was often used. Like other contemporary consorts of instruments, not all sizes of cornett were equally well regarded. The bass cornett lacked the brilliant sweetness of the others, and, in consort, was generally replaced by the trombone, which substitution was highly commended by Michael Praetorius: "Über weil der resonanc gar unlieblich und hornhasstig/ so halt ich mehr darvon/ das man eine pasaun an dessen stad gebrauche."[20] The replacement of the bass cornett with the trombone was so standard that it may be assumed that the consorts of cornetts used in the children's theaters were ordinarily a mixture of cornetts and trombones.

Cornetts were played both on stage and off in children's drama, though they most frequently play behind the scenes. Since they were among the standard church instruments of the day, the principal children's companies had regular access to expert cornettists, at least until the Children of the Chapel were officially severed from the Chapel Royal. Some of the cornettists may have been the older members of the dramatic troupes; a "boy" who serves as a "page" to the title character plays one on stage in Act I, scene ii of Marston's *Antonio's Revenge*, disabusing us of the notion that young musicians were incapable of mastering the technique of this demanding instrument.[21] The most frequent function of the cornett in children's plays is to herald the formal entry of noble characters. Trumpets generally provide this service in the public theater, but the gentler sounds of the cornett was more suitable for the smaller spaces of the private theaters.

The next most frequent use of the cornett in this body of plays is to indicate a battle in progress. This is a theater-specific use of the instrument, and, in children's plays, a function unique to the cornett. Again, the traditional trumpet may have been overpowering in the private theaters for the constant, continuous performance that supports most stage battles. The bellicose music of cornetts not only helps to provide background for pantomimed armed confrontations, but also helps to create the illusion of an infinite battlefield or tournament ground in a small theater lacking perspective scenery.

The best example of the auditory illusion of warfare produced by cornetts is Act V, scene ii of *Sophonisba*, in which the cornetts scarcely cease playing from beginning to end. The scene takes place on a huge battlefield outside of ancient Carthage, and, as the audience knows from the preceeding action, it is a major struggle between two massive armies. No more than seven characters are required on stage at any time, but through dialogue, frenzied pacing, and music one gets the impression of an intense fight between many soldiers. The musical stage directions, most of which appear in rapid succession, accompany military action. They are specified from within, at a distance, and at close range to give the impression of greater space than the tiny stage afforded. All directions are for cornetts. From the opening direction of

Enter two pages, with targets and javelins; Laelius and Jugurth, with halberds, Scipio and Massinissa armed; cornets sounding a march

through the climax of

Cornets sound a charge, Massinissa and Syphax combat. Syphax falls, Massinissa unclasps Syphax caske, and as ready to kill him, speakes Syphax

to the final "Exeunt, cornetts flourishing" that clears the stage, such directions as "cornets a flourish," "Cornetts, a march far off," and "Cornets sound a charge" help transform the barren stage and its youthful actors into a distant battlefield where two superior military multitudes are locked in mortal combat.

Similar to the use of the cornett to conjure up images of war is its function to help dramatize the hunt. In Act III, scene iv of Marston's *The Malcontent*, cornetts add auditory verisimilitude to a hunt and help the audience imagine that the very limited scene before them is only part of a larger, outdoor exercise with all the trappings of the hunting ritual:

Ferrando.   the dogs are at fault.
Cornets like hornes within.

The musical signals of the contemporary hunt, and probably also of the dramatized battle, were rhythmic rather than melodic or harmonic, meant to guide the movements of hunters or soldiers. The higher members of the cornett family are most suitable for this function, but even the less elegant, hornlike bass would not be particularly inappropriate for the short sennets, flourishes, marches, and other brief outbursts of these boisterous outdoor maneuvers. Therefore, in these instances, trombone support would have been unnecessary.

Cornetts, presumably with bass trombones, are also used to accompany more peaceful pastimes such as masques, dances, and dumb shows. Presumably, the music for these events went beyond simple rhythmic signalling:

A dumbe show. the cornets sounding for the Act. Enter Castilio and Forobosco, Alberto and Balurdo, with poleaxes; Piero, talking with Strotzo, seemeth to send him out; exit Strotzo. Re-enter Strotzo with Maria, Nutriche, and Lucio. Piero passeth through his guard, and talks with Maria with seeming amorousness; she seemeth to reject his suit, flies to the tomb, kneels, and kisseth it. Piero bribes Nutriche and Lucio; they go to her, seeming to solicit his suit. She riseth, offers to go out; Piero stayeth her, tears open his breast, embraceth and kisseth her; and so they go out in state.

(Marston, *Antonio's Revenge*, Act III, scene i)

Cornets playing. Drunkenness, Sloth, Pride, and Plenty lead Cupid to his state, who is followed by Folly, Warre, Beggary, and Slaughter.

(Marston, *The Fawne*, Act V, scene i; the start of a masque)

Enter Foure boyes antiquely attiered with bows and quivers dauncing to the Cornets, a phantastique measure, Massinissa in his night gowne led by Asdruball and Hanno followed by Bytheas and Jugurth. The boyes draw the curtaines discovering Sophonisba to whom Massinissa speakes.

(Marston, *Sophonisba*, Act I, scene ii)

Cornetts accompany a sacrifice in Act III, scene ii of *Sophonisba*, and a wedding in Act I, scene ii of the same play. The sacrifice and wedding are in this play the ancient pagan equivalents of contemporary church services for which cornetts were used routinely. In both episodes, the cornetts are accompanied by organ as in English churches of the author's day; and for the wedding, a choir of singers joins them to bless the happy couple.

Cornetts sound for quite a few stately exits in children's plays, especially at the end of acts or completed plays:

Cornets a flourish. Exeunt Omnes.
Finis.

(Marston, *The Malcontent*, end of play)

[Piero.]   Let's all turn sighers. Come, despite of fate,
             Sound lowdest musicke, lets passe out in state.
The cornets sound. Exeunt.
(Marston, Antonio's Revenge, Act III, scene i)

Cornetts are nearly always used in consort, specified in the plural, but solo cornetts are required in Act I, scene ii of *Antonio's Revenge*, and in Act V, scene i of Marston's *What You Will*. They are generally not directed to play with other sorts of instruments, but they are accompanied by organs in the above examples from *Sophonisba*, and they accompany a group of singers in Act V, scene iv of *The Malcontent*.

The clear reliance on cornetts indicated by stage directions in the children's plays has led to the frequent speculation that these versatile, elegant instruments took the place of the loud instruments of the public adult theater, the hoboy, horn, and trumpet. Cornetts indeed often took over the signaling capacity of these three instruments, and, as indicated above, could be called upon to imitate the sound of the more raucous members of the Renaissance "loud band." However, hoboy, horn, and trumpet were all used by the children. These three instruments, louder and less capable of expression than the cornett, were clearly favored less by the boy companies, and the latter two were seemingly reserved for special effects.

The hoboy

Hoboys were apparently used only by the Children of the King's Revels, which company made the least use of cornetts. They are called for only in wedding celebrations in Armin, Robert's *The Two Maids of More-Clacke* (Act I, scene i) and the anonymous *Everie Woman in her Humour* (Act V, scene i), in which they accompany dancing after the ceremony. Stage directions inform us that the Waits of London play in the first instance, and since it is well known that these musicians often accepted theatrical engagements, there is no reason to assume that a different group played the same instruments in a work acted by the same company in the same season. Michael Praetorius reminds us that the instrument which England called an hoboy was more widely known as a shawm;[22] and, like cornetts, complete consorts of these instruments often included a bass trombone.[23]

The horn

The "horne" is called for only in Act II, scene i of Jonson's *Epicoene*, where it signals the arrival of "a post from the court." In this instance, art clearly imitates life, for the late Renaissance horn was a rather primitive instrument with limited melodic capabilities whose principal function was loud, brief proclamation.[24]

The trumpet

The trumpet is generally associated with the public theater, where, presumably, its loud and penetrating blast would travel further than the sound of a cornett. But it is also called for in plays first produced by the principal children's companies.[25] Trumpets and drums were a fixed combination for scenes with military overtones in the contemporary theater, as the Citizen's Wife from Beaumont's *The Knight of the Burning Pestle* reminds us:

Call *Rafe* againe *George*, call *Rafe* again, I prethee sweet heart let him come and fight before me, and let's ha some drums, and some trumpets, and let him kill all comes neere him, and thou lov'st me *George*.

(Beaumont, *The Knight of the Burning Pestle*, Act II, scene ii)

But since the private theater audience sat nearer the stage than their public theater counterparts, and since the entire space was roofed, the trumpet's loud blare was unnecessary if not uncomfortable to auditors. Thus, the cornett generally took its place in military or state scenes. But when a particularly loud sound was desirable, the trumpet, most often with drum, was brought in for the task. In Act III, scene i of Chapman's *The Revenge of Bussy D'Ambois*, drums and trumpets inform Maillard and Chalon--and the audience--that their final troupes have arrived on the scene and the battle can begin. And in Act III, scene vii of Jonson's *Epicoene*, several characters have arranged to punish Morose with extended pandemonium, the climax of which features drum and trumpet:

> [Truewit.] . . . — Captain Otter! what news?
> Otter.   I have brought my bull, beare, and horse in private, and yonder are the trumpetters without, and the drum, gentlemen. *The drum, and trumpets sound.*
> Morose.   Ô, ô, ô.
> Otter.   And we will have a rouse in each of 'hem, anon, for bold Britons, yfaith.
>   *The drum, and trumpets sound.*
> Morose.   Ô, ô, ô.
>   *Exit hastily.*

later in the same play (Act IV, scene ii), trumpets alone accomplish a similar deed. Contemporary English classicists inform us that the trumpet had ancient funereal associations;[26] trumpets accompany a double funeral procession to bring Beaumont and Fletcher's *Cupid's Revenge* to a louder-than-life conclusion. Like the horn, the contemporary trumpet had limited melodic capabilities and was, therefore, not used for extended performances.

The Softer Wind Instruments: Flutes, Pipes, and Recorders

The flute

"Still Flutes" are called for only twice in the children's repertoire, both times in plays written for the Children of Paul's. In Act V, scene i of *Antonio and Mellida*, "The Still Flutes sound a mournefull cynet" before the entry of a funeral procession. In Act IV, scene iii of *Antonio's Revenge*, "The still flutes sound softly" as the innocent Mellida is brought on stage to hear her death sentence unjustly proclaimed. The association of the flute with death and mourning shown in these scenarios was quite ancient and widespread throughout the Western world.[27]

It is far easier to associate the flute symbolically with death in these two plays than to ascertain exactly what instrument was signified by the term "still flute." Elizabethan and Jacobean scholarship suffer from a general lack of distinction between assorted whistles, pipes, and flutes, which has caused no end of confusion among modern scholars about which were transverse and which had fipples, and which had what sort of sound or compass. However, it is possible to identify the instrument used in Marston's plays. The term "still," the only direct clue to its identity, was used by a contemporary poet in a musical context to mean the opposite of "loud."[28] More recently, it is said to have referred to low, subdued music.[29] Michael Praetorius tells us that "dolk-flotten" (gentle, or "still," flutes) are a special kind of "querflotten" (transverse flutes) that share several distinctive characteristics with "plockflotten" (recorders):

Die querpfeiffen. . . haben sornen sechs höcher/ hinten keins: geben Naturalich 15. Stimmen öder Thon. . . .
    Eben solch gelegenheit hat es mit Dolkflotten (welche sonsten Querflotten gennent) nur dass dieselbige gleich einer Plockflotten intonieret und geblasen werden.[30]

This somewhat imprecise description nonetheless helps to establish that the still flute of the English stage was a transverse flute with certain technical similarities to the recorder, including its sweeter tone and slightly larger compass.

The pipe

The only pipe named in stage directions in children's drama is called for in Act I, scene i of John Marston's *Jacke Drum's Entertainment*, another play written for the Children of Paul's. It is played along with the percussive tabor by the rustic Timothy Tweedle to accompany a Whitsuntide Morris dance. Pipe and tabor were inseparable from each other, and were associated with such common folk as Timothy Tweedle and such rustic dances as the venerable Morris. The pipe in this case was a whistle flute similar to the recorder, but possessing only four holes so that it could be played by the left hand alone. The right hand was therefore left free to beat the small tabor that invariably hung from the left arm or shoulder.

The recorder

Recorders are used by both principal children's companies, in one play each. In Act IV of the anonymous *The Maydes Metamorphosis*, they accompany a duet sung by a forester and a shepherd, where they represent the sweet pipes of Pan. Fipple flutes or pipes of any sort have an ancient association with the simple folk of field or forest, and with the sort of mythic pastoral elements that dominate *The Maydes Metamorphosis*. The other work to require the recorder uses it in a very different manner. Between Acts II and III of Marston's *Sophonisba*, a consort of recorders plays with organ to help set the mood for the solemn religious rite of Act III. Later in the same play (Act V, scene iii), the same combination of instruments plays "to a single voice" as Massinissa presents the body of the title character in "mournefull solemnity" to the conquering Romans.

The recorder is used in scenes of great solemnity and otherworldly purity in other contemporary plays as it is used before the divine ritual in *Sophonisba*.[31] And contemporary Englishmen believed the "pipe" to have been a normal part of ancient Roman funerals, as the recorder plays for Sophonisba's funeral.[32] The Children of the Chapel were famed recorder players as early as the reign of Henry VIII,[33] and most sizes of the instrument are technically within the reach of even the smallest musician. However, the recorder was surprisingly little used in children's drama, probably because of its strong negative literary and iconographic connotations. *The Praise of Musicke*, taking a cue from classical writers, tells us that "playing on a Recorder doth neither avail the mind, nor help knowledge any thing at all," and certainly the instrument cast off by the goddess of wisdom and damned by the god of music could not be given general usage in the highly allegorical drama of a symbol-conscious age.[34]

Bowed String Instruments: Fiddles, Lyras, and Viols

The fiddle

The violin, used in quite a number of children's plays and by all companies, is always referred to in stage directions and dialogue as a "fiddle" or "fidle." And, to add a little taxonomic confusion where none apparently exists, "fiddle" was obviously London slang for any instrument at all during the late Elizabethan and Jacoban eras, and "fiddlers" signified the lowest sort of common musician, no matter what he played. Randle Cotgrave reminds us of the dual usage of the term by his translation of the French "violier" as "A Fidler, or common Musition, that playes on a violin."[35] The fiddles in children's plays are clearly most often violins, for their performers and auditors constantly refer to scraping bows across cat's guts and to the *da braccio* position of playing.

The fiddles are most often played by musician characters as part of the action in plays with contemporary urban English settings. They are especially associated with the streets and taverns of London, where their players, as in life, are scarcely a step above vagabonds. By the Restoration, theatrical "fiddlers" were those musicians who were costumed and often given a few lines of dialogue,[36] and it is clear that this custom dates back to the time of children's drama. "Fiddles" in the children's plays include the viol (*Antonio's Revenge*, Act III, scene iv), the lute (John Day, *Law Trickes*, Act III, scene i), and unspecified wind instruments (Dekker and Webster, *Westward Ho*, Act IV, scene i) as well as the more usual violin. And "fiddlers" are a downtrodden, unruly lot who often serve as the butt of jokes or deception.

The lyra

The lyra is specified in only one play, performed by the Children of the Chapel. In Act IV, scene iii of Jonson's *Cynthia's Revels*, Hedon and Amorphus each perform a solo song to their own accompaniment on "that most affected instrument, the lyra." It is a scene of courtly entertainment, of artistic rivalry and self-inflation, in which both characters perform pretensious songs of their own composition to demonstrate their refined taste and considerable skill. The early seventeenth-century English term "lyra" or "lyra viol" referred to a viola da gamba, most often a small bass, that was tuned to facilitate chordal playing and whose music was notated in tablature for ease of performance.[37] There are no essential differences between the contemporary repertoires for lyra and for plucked strings.[38] The lyra viol attained new popularity in courtly circles around 1600, the year in which Jonson's satiric comedy of courtly manners was performed, when Daniel Farrant introduced to Court a viol with a set of sympathetic metal strings beneath the fingerboard.[39] The following year saw the first publication to include tablature for the lyra viol.[40] Ben Jonson thus chose an instrument that represented the latest musical novelty for his pair of fashionably avant-garde sophisticates to play.

The lyra or lyra viol of English usage is not to be confused with the older lira (lirone, lironi perfetto, lira da gamba) of Continental usage. But both were often used to provide rich accompaniment for solo song, and Mary Chan believes that the similarity between the names is not coincidental.[41] Both instruments were regarded as unusually expressive, and what Jonson's effete courtier Amorphus says of his lyra is quite similar to what Marin Mersenne said of the very different Continental lyra:

> **Amorphus.**   . . . but here is an instrument that (alone) is able to infuse soule into the most melancholique, and dull disposde creature upon earth.
>
> (Jonson, *Cynthia's Revels*, Act IV, scene iii)

Or le son de la lyra est fort languissant et propre pour exiter à la devotion, et pour faire rentrer l'esprit en soi- meme.[42]

The viol

Viols are among the instruments most frequently used in children's drama, and plays written for all three companies demand them. They are played by characters on stage in all companies, and by off-stage musicians for the Children of Paul's and the Children of the Chapel. The Children of Paul's were renowned for their viol playing as early as the 1540s,[43] and after the revival of the later 1590s, they apparently relied more on the viol than did the other children's companies. Viols are used in consort and as solo instruments, and they most often accompany song. Solo singers accompany themselves on viols in *Antonio's Revenge* (Act III, scene iv) and John Day's *Humour Out of Breath* (Act IV). These actors may have played their viols "lyra way" to fill out the harmonies. Solo song is accompanied by consorts of viols in Marston's *Jacke Drum's Entertainment* (Act IV), and Chapman's *Sir Gyles Goose-Cappe* (Act I, scene iv). Viols play with voices and organ between Acts III and IV of *Sophonisba*. The most common dramatic function of these instruments is to provide entertainment by and for characters in the drama, similar to their normal function outside of the theater.

Stage directions and dialogue rarely specify which size of viol is used in the plays, but it may be assumed that the bass was the favorite solo instrument as it was outside of the theater. Bass viols are called for specifically in Act III, scene iv of *Antonio's Revenge* and Act IV of *Humour Out of Breath*, where they accompany solo singers. A treble viol is named in Acts IV and V of *Sophonisba*, where it is accompanied by a bass lute. Stage directions normally call for "viols" in the plural, presumably meaning a consort of three to six. A number of play texts do not specify what instruments accompany lyrics for which contemporary settings for voices and viols have been identified. This suggests that viols were used more frequently in the children's theaters than the scanty stage directions suggest.

Plucked String Instruments: Harps, Lutes, and Theorboes

The harp

The harp is named in only two children's plays, both of which were presented by the Children of Paul's shortly after their revival. "A boy" accompanies solo entrants in a singing contest in Act V, scene i of Marston's *Antonio and Mellida*, and Phoebus accompanies the final song and dance of *The Maydes Metamorphosis* on his harp to close the play. Francis Bacon indicates that two types of harp were in current usage in contemporary England, the "Welche-Harpe" and the "Irish-Harpe." These two clearly possessed very different sonorities, for Bacon tells us that, if played together, their sounds "agree not so well."[44] Both instruments were fairly small though more massively built than their Continental counterparts, and both were played with two hands. Either was therefore capable of complete harmonic support for a solo singer or even a chorus.[45] The Irish harp had thirty to fifty metal strings plucked with long fingernails; its Welsh counterpart was strung with gut, had brays, and was limited to about thirty strings.[46] Both instruments had relatively soft sounds, which may explain why the harp was used only in the smallest children's theater. The greater resonance of the Irish harp was more likely to have carried above the sound of voices in the theater, and it was known for an unusual sweetness of sound that would have been most suitable for the divinity of Phoebus in *The Maydes Metamorphosis*.[47]

The lute

The standard "lute" is called for in one play for each of the three children's companies, and is played each time by a named character as part of the action. In Marston's *The Dutch Courtesan*, Franceschina accompanies herself with the instrument almost every time she sings (Act I, scene ii; Act II, scene i; and Act V, scene i). In the same author's *What You Will*, Phylus plays and sings a serenade to Celia at Jacomo's bidding. And in John Day's *Law Trickes*, Count Lurdo plays a dance on his lute to woo the scornful Emilia (Act III, scene i). The lute was, of course, used frequently to accompany songs and dances in late Renaissance England, as a large number of manuscripts, publications for the instrument, and discussions in word books indicate. It is quite possible that, like the viol, the instrument was used far more frequently than the scanty stage directions show, and that it may have contributed to the "musicke" that accompanied so many songs and dances.

The bass lute and treble viol are played together by off-stage musicians during and between Acts IV and V of Marston's *Sophonisba*. Here the lute is far removed from normal social usage, for it is a component of the "soft musicke" of powerful magic at work. The sweet combination of bass lute and treble viol provides enchanting strains of music repeatedly against a dramatic background of infernal sorcery, deception, and unnatural lust. Its sound comes to represent the unfathomable workings of the supernatural apparatus to both the audience and the characters who command and describe it. Nowhere else in children's drama is the bass lute named.

The theorbo

In Act II, scene i of Chapman's *All Fooles*, Valerio is gulled into playing the theorbo and singing before an assembly of mocking courtiers. Nowhere else in the children's repertoire is the instrument called for. The theorbo is a large member of the lute family, possessing longer stopped courses and a separate nut and pegbox for an additional set of long, unstopped bass strings. It was invented in northern Italy circa 1589, where it became an immediate favorite continuo instrument for solo singing.[48] And its rich, sonorous contrabass tones gave it lasting appeal for the purpose.[49] The theorbo is generally supposed to have been introduced into England by Inigo Jones around 1605.[50] The innovative Children of the Chapel, who were also the first company to use the lyra, presented *All Fooles* in 1604, clearly the first use of the instrument in English drama.

Other Instruments

The organ

The organ is the only keyboard instrument called for in children's drama. It is used in two plays, one presented by the Children of Paul's and the other by the Children of the Chapel. In Act II, scene i of Middleton's *A Mad World My Masters*, "The organs play, and covered dishes march over the stage," and there is later "a song to the organs." The scene itself is a banquet at the home of a wealthy man, who has been showing off his treasures to his guests. Sir Bounteous Progress, the host, is especially proud of the musicians he maintains, and among them are the organist. The organist and his instrument are visible to the other characters and the audience at this point in the action, since Sir Bounteous gestures toward him before he plays and acknowledges him as "my organist." Presumably, the curtains of the music room have been drawn back so that it becomes the musicians' gallery of a banqueting hall.

The organ is used several times in Marston's *Sophonisba*, but never as a solo instrument. In Act I, scene ii it plays along with cornetts and voices for a wedding ceremony; between Acts II and III it accompanies recorders to precede a scene of religious ritual and contrasting domestic strife; in Act III, scene i, it accompanies cornetts and a solo singer during a sacrifice to Mercury and Phoebe; and in Act V, scene iii, it joins recorders to accompany a funeral. Each of these rites is a pagan equivalent of contemporary English ecclesiastical ceremonies that would surely have used the organ; "because dey were used in de service of God [organs] are elsewhere called de Instruments of God."[51]

It may be assumed that both instruments were small chamber organs. In the first case, the dramatic occasion calls for a chamber organ--the setting is a gentleman's private house and the stage at Paul's was notoriously tiny. In the second case, the Blackfriars music room had to accommodate at one time not just an organ but also a chorus and consort of cornetts. Thomas Mace refers later in the seventeenth century to an advantage such an instrument might have had in dramatic productions where it accompanied voices or other instruments:

But this Device of a Table Organ, sends forth its Notes so Equally alike, that All, both performers, and Auditors, receive their just, and due Satisfaction, without the least Impediment; the Organ in this Service not being Eminently to be Heard, but only Equal with the other Musick.[52]

There would have been no shortage of competent organists among the Children of Paul's or the Children of the Chapel, but it is also possible that adult organists from St. Paul's Cathedral or the Chapel Royal were called in to play for their young colleagues.

Percussion instruments

Most of the references to percussion instruments in children's plays are to fixed combinations of percussion and nonpercussion instruments: pipe and tabor, drum and trumpet. But the bell alone is used as a signaling device in John Day's *Isle of Gulls* (Act III), Fletcher's *Faithful Shepherdess* (Act II, scene i) and Marston's *Histrio-Mastix* (Act II). In each instance, it is used to attract attention to an important announcement or event. In Armin's *The Two Maids of More-Clacke* (sig. B4ᵛ) and in Middleton's *Michaelmas Term* (Act IV), a bell tolls to signify death. A solo drum is used in Beaumont's *The Knight of the Burning Pestle* (Act V, scene i) to signify the militarism normally reserved for drum and trumpet together, as a company of soldiers arrives on the scene.

Consort

Although it is clear that assorted consorts of instruments are used throughout the children's repertoire, only two plays call for music under the rubric of "consort." One of these plays was acted by the Children of Paul's, the other by the Children of the Chapel. In Act I, scene ii of Marston's *The Fawne*, a stage direction calls for the "consort of musique" to play. Immediately afterward, we are told that "the musicke gives us notice that the Prince is hard at hand." Since this annunciation is a dramatic function normally reserved for cornetts in children's drama, it is likely that the assembled consort was composed of cornetts, or cornetts and trombones.

The other instance in which a consort is called for is Act II, scene i of Middleton's *A Mad World My Masters*, in which the audience is shown a group of musicians such as were maintained as part of wealthy households. As Charles Butler tells us, contemporary consorts could be made up of groups of like or unrelated instruments:

Consort. De several kindes of Instruments are commonly used severally by dem selvs: as a set of Viols, a set of Waits [i.e., hoboys], or de like: but soomtime, upon soom special occasion, many of bode Sortes [string and wind] are most sweetly joined in Consort.[53]

Francis Bacon tells us that some instruments agree in consort better than others:

All *Concords* and *Discords* of *Musicke* are (no doubt) *Sympathies* and *Antipathies* of Sounds. And so (likewise) in that *Musicke*, which we call *Broken Musicke* or *Consort Musicke*; some *Consortes* of *Instruments* are sweeter than others; (a Thing not sufficiently yet observed;) as the *Irish Harpe*, and *Bass Viall* agree well: the *Recorder* and *Stringed Musicke* agree well: *Organs* and the *Voice* agree well, & c. But the *Virginalls* and the *Lute*; or, not of the *Welche-Harpe*, and *Irish-Harpe*, or the *Voice* and *Pipes* alone, agree not so well.[54]

Because the scene is intended to dazzle the guests of Sir Bounteous Progress with their host's wealth and good taste, it is doubtful that a combination of instruments that "agrees not so well" was used here. Since the organ and voices are specified separately and additionally to the consort, the "consort" probably does not refer to them. This household consort probably consisted of the instruments of the English "mixed consort": lute, treble viol or violin, bass viol, bandora, cittern, and flute. These are the instruments for which at least one contemporary collection intended for household musicians was written.[55] Furthermore, these are among the instruments associated with one of the children's theaters by Frederick Gershow and not terribly unlike the instruments we have already seen in connection with other plays.

Sound Effects

Certain artificial sounds that can hardly be classified as instrumental or even musical are called for in these plays. But these sounds belong to the complete compendium of auditory effects of the children's dramas and must therefore be considered here. Like some of the music, their function is atmospheric.

Like all of the music, they add a great deal to the plays produced in the Elizabethan and Jacobean private theaters. Like the directions for musical instruments, directions for sound effects are quite sporadic and probably indicate only a fraction of their actual usage. These sound effects include "chambers shot off" (Chapman, *The Revenge of Bussy D'Ambois*, Act IV, scene i), a "peale of shot" (Marston, *Antonio and Mellida*, Act I, scene i), the sound of birds (*Blurt, Master-Constable*, Act IV, scene iii); and Marston, *The Dutch Courtesan*, Act II, scene i), and thunder (Chapman, *Bussy D'Ambois*, Act IV, scene ii). It may be assumed that the more militant sound effects were produced with guns and gunpowder, but the others are somewhat more mysterious. Francis Bacon refers to water-filled pipes in organs that imitate the sound of birds with "a continuall Trembling."[56] It is also possible for large drums with deep timbre to imitate thunder, though there are no references to such a custom in the contemporary theater.

The list of instruments called for in plays first acted by the children's companies is necessarily incomplete. Background music is most often referred to simply as "musicke," when indicated at all, and these works abound with such cryptic musical directions as "alarum," "flourish," and "sennet" with no instrument named in the direction. Contemporary settings of songs from these plays sometimes include instrumental accompaniment when none is indicated in the play imprints, or require instruments not named in the plays. Such song texts as

> Sound Lute, Bandora, Gittern,
>   Violl, Virginalls, and Sithron!
> Voices spring and lift alowde,
> Her name that makes the Musicke proud:
>   This night perfection
>   Makes her election:
> Follow, follow, follow, follow round,
> Looke you to that, nay you to that, any you to that:
> Anon you will be found, anon you will be found, anon you
>   will be found[57]

imply that instruments are playing that are not named in that--or any other extant--children's play. It is possible, even probable, that the list of instruments that can be made from extant versions of the plays is grossly incomplete. However, stage directions and dialogue are all we have from which to learn what instruments were used how in the children's theater; and from even the random indications that survive, certain patterns can be seen.

CHAPTER 5

PRELIMINARY, INTER-ACT AND FINALE MUSIC

Musick for a while
Shall your cares beguile

John Dryden and Nathaniel Lee, *Oedipus* (1678), Act III, scene i

According to a number of eyewitness accounts, sixteenth- and seventeenth-century discussions of dramatic practice and sporadic stage directions and dialogue in the extant copies of children's plays, a complete performance at any of the children's theaters included music before, between, and at the end of the acts of the plays. This music permitted the more musical members of the companies to display their skills even when the featured play was not particularly musical, and helped to distinguish the children's performances from the adults'. Furthermore, the children's use of inter-act music is of great historical significance, because at the opening of the seventeenth century it was unique to their theaters, but by the Restoration it had become a standard part of London dramatic entertainment.[1] However, because preliminary, inter-act, and finale music may or may not have related to the featured play, descriptions of them remain highly varied and widely scattered. And the phenomenon of extra-dramatic music in the private theaters still remains to be completely characterized and put into context by modern scholars.

The children's great reputation for musical entertainment undoubtedly came more from this extra-dramatic music than from incidental songs and instrumental pieces. All children's performances seem to have included pre- and inter-act music, whereas some of their featured plays apparently required

no music within the action. In addition, if Frederick Gershow is to be believed, these extra-dramatic musical diversions were as memorable as the
plays themselves. A unique pair of play imprints shows dramatists' attitudes
toward this musical custom, and makes it clear that the musical entertainment
that separated the children's performances from the adults' was extra-dramatic. John Marston's *The Malcontent* was written for the Children of the
Chapel around 1603, but was stolen by the King's Men in revenge for the earlier theft of one of their plays. Both companies presented *The Malcontent* at
around the same time, and it was published in two versions. The adults' version differs from the children's most significantly by the addition of an Induction by John Webster that explains why the Men stole the play and how it was
altered for them:

> **Sly.** . . . I would know how you came by this play?
>
> **Condell.** Faith, sir, the book was lost; and because 'twas pittie so
> great a play should be lost, we found it and play it.
>
> **Sly.** I wonder you would play it, another company having inter-
> est in it.
>
> **Condell.** Why not Malevole in folio with us, as well as Ieronimo in
> *decimo sexto* with them? They taught us a name for our
> play, we call it *One for Another.*
>
> **Sly.** What are your additions?
>
> **Burbage.** 'Sooth, not greatly needful; only as your sallet to your
> great feast, to entertain a little more time, and to abridge
> the not-received custome of musicke in our theater.[2]

The musical abridgements clearly do not include anything within the play, for
not one single song, dance, or musical direction from the alternate version has
been cut.[3] And the musical custom that did not transfer between the children's and adults' theaters was not music for the action but extended music
before or between the acts. Therefore, what must have been cut was extra-
dramatic and not vital enough to the plot or theme to have been committed to
print even in the children's version.

The other imprint that apparently refers to extra-dramatic music is the first
quarto of John Marston's *The Wonder of Women or the Tragedy of Sophonisba*. On the bottom of the final page, beneath the epilogue, the following apology is printed in a contrasting typeface:

After all, let me intreat my Reader not to taxe me, for the fashion of the Entrances and
Musique of this Tragidy, for know it is printed onely as it was presented by youths, &
after the fashion of the private stage. Nor let soe easily amended errors in the Printing
afflict thee since thy own discourse will easily set upright any such unevenness.[4]

None of the musical directions within the acts of the play differ significantly
from those of Marston's other plays except in those details that make them

specifically part of *Sophonisba*. The play calls for musical instruments used virtually nowhere else in the repertoire, but the same may be said of several of Marston's other plays. It is quite clear that the carefully prepared effect made by the music on the action in *Sophonisba* is Marston's.[5] However, the play is the only one of its era to include precise descriptions of inter-act music at the end of each act. These uniquely valuable directions must be what so disturbed Marston, and they certainly represent the fashion of the private stage. It is equally clear from Marston's apology that the music to which he refers was not under the jurisdiction of the playwright.

PRELIMINARY MUSIC

The only contemporary reference to a full-length concert before the featured play at any of the children's theaters is the one in Gershow's diary. But there is ample evidence that two other sorts of music regularly preceeded the children's plays: trumpet blasts or "soundings" to signal the start of the play, as used at all Elizabethan and Jacobean theaters;[6] and music of varied sorts to introduce the first Act, which was principally associated with the children's theaters. William Rankins reminds us that the primary purpose of the trumpet's shrill voice at the opening was "to cal menne to plays,"[7] but Thomas Dekker reminds us sarcastically that in the private theaters this sound also drew attention to the most fashionable spectators purposefully taking their coveted seats upon the stage at the last possible moment:

Present not yourself on the stage, especially at a new play, until the quaking Prologue hath by rubbing got colour into his cheeks, and is ready to give the trumpets their cue that he's upon point to enter.[8]

The trumpet soundings also served to call the same gallants' attention away from other distractions and to the play that was about to begin:

Before the play begins, a fall to cards; you may win or lose, as fencers do in a prize, and beat one another by confederacy, yet share the money when you meat at supper: notwithstanding, to gull the ragamuffins that stand aloof gaping at you, throw the cards, having first torn four or five of them, round the stage, just upon the third sound.[9]

Several children's plays call for preliminary action during and between the three soundings. One gets the distinct impression that the period just before the actual beginning of the play was filled with all sorts of activity from both audience and players. Jonson's *Cynthia's Revels* calls for the entry of "three of the Children, struggling" to open the Induction just after the "second sounding." The entire Induction takes place between the second and third soundings, the latter of which heralds the entry of the Prologue. Immediately after the second sounding for Jonson's *Poetaster*, the audience is meant to see Envie "arising in the midst of the stage," where she stays and speaks until driven back by "The third sounding" and the inevitable entry of the Prologue. A list of corrections printed as part of the 1602 quarto of Dekker and Marston's *Satiro-Mastix* reminds the reader that the three soundings of standard theatrical practice were part of a living theater and did not transfer successfully to the printed page, which may explain why they are not indicated in most dramatic texts.

Ad Lectorum.

Instead of the trumpets sounding thrice, before the play begin: it should not be amisse (for him that will read) first to behold this short comedy of errors, and where the greatest enter, to give in stead of a hisse, a gentle correction.[10]

There are a number of indications that music of other sorts may have played just before the opening action of most children's plays, perhaps serving the function of an overture. This music clearly varied from play to play, was sometimes related to the opening action or theme of the play, and presumably followed the three loud soundings. Chapman's festive *May Day* opens with:

> Actus prima, scaene prima.
> Chorus juvenum cantates & saltantes.
> *Exeunt saltan.*
> *Interim, intrat Lorenzo*, papers in his hand.[11]

The opening dialogue of *Satiro-Mastix* implies that music is playing when two nameless women enter to strew flowers about the stage. Further dialogue tells us that this music, which continues as they go about their task, signals the preparation for a wedding. Thus, *Satiro-Mastix* opens with music that literally sets the stage for the action. Marston's tragicomic *The Malcontent*, with its theme of corruption and disorder, opens with "The vilest out-of-tune musicke being heard" as the first characters enter the scene and discuss the unpleasant noise and rank smell that has invaded the Genoese court and surrounded them. And in the same author's *Sophonisba*, the major characters accompany the Prologue onto the stage as the military cornetts that dominate the play sound a march. The characters enter from opposite doors in two groups, one armed for battle and the other presumably dressed for court, one composed of epic villains and the other of extraordinary heroes. As they stand in symbolic tableau of the play's central conflict, the Prologue speaks. The majority of children's plays do not indicate music at their openings, just as the majority do not specify trumpet soundings. It is probable that opening music was a standard feature of the children's plays, but was recorded only randomly in the copies of the text that were ultimately printed.

INTER-ACT MUSIC

Inter-act music appears to have been a normal feature of performances in all three children's theaters, but few specific details about it have survived. Like other musical directions in these plays, inter-act music is mentioned sporadically and nonchalantly, and is sometimes linked to specific action or discussed in dialogue. In the play publications, it is sometimes appended to the previous act, sometimes to the following act, and sometimes extremely difficult to separate from musical action that belongs to the play proper. The tantalizing tidbits relating to inter-act music that remain scattered throughout the repertoire imply extreme variety and many degrees of relationship to the main drama. Inter-act music seems to have sometimes been instrumental, sometimes vocal, and sometimes a mixture of both. Inter-act music occasionally accompanied dance, occasionally mimed action, and occasionally neither. Sometimes there may have been short dramatic scenarios mixing music and spoken dialogue between the acts of the play. Sometimes inter-act music set the stage for the action to follow, sometimes it reinforced previous action, sometimes it followed the antics of minor characters that had little bearing on the main plot, and sometimes it was not at all related to the play. It may have been constant, it may have been intermittant; it may have connected acts to each other, or it may have divided them further than a silent pause. As Frederick Sternfeld has pointed out, inter-act music provided an excellent opportunity to add music to dramatic entertainment that was primarily verbal.[12] The impact of these musical interludes, then, may well have varied according to the character of the play and the sorts or amounts of music included within its acts.

The regular use of inter-act music in the private theaters probably dates from their inception. Like so many aspects of private theater performance, inter-act music was also a feature of plays acted at Court, the Inns of Court, and the universities.[13] By Prynne's time, inter-act music was common, and by Dryden's time, it was expected of all theatrical performances. As Dryden tells us, it provided a pleasant contrast to spoken dialogue:

A scene of mirth, mixed with tragedy, has the same effect on us as our music has between the acts; which we find a relief to us from the best plots and languages of the stage, if the discourses have been long.[14]

Undoubtedly, this relief, this contrast with the action of the play, was equally important at the beginning of the seventeenth century when the use of inter-acts was young. Inter-act music was not only practical, but had the revered backing of "ancient authority" from long before the revival of children's drama at the end of the sixteenth century. *The Arte of English Poesy* tells us that in ancient times, music helped refresh the theater audience between the acts of plays:

Also there was place appointed for their musicians to sing and play upon their instruments at the end of every scene, or to the intent that the people might be refreshed and kept occupied.[15]

The only indication we have of how long inter-act breaks lasted in the sixteenth or early seventeenth century is Cockledemoy's statement at the close of Act IV of Marston's *The Dutch Courtesan*:

> Tis time to take a nap, untill halfe an houre hence:
> God give your Worships Musicke, content, and rest.

Most often, inter-act music is indicated only as "music for the act" or simply "act"; sometimes it is only written down as "musicke" after the conclusion of an act proper, such as:

Quadratus.   I come hotte blouds, those that their state would swell,
Must bear a counter-face: the divell and hell
Confound them all, that's all my prayers exact,
So ends our chat, sound musick for the act. *Exeunt.*
(Marston, *What You Will*, end of Act II)

Whilest the Act is playing, Hercules and Tiberio enters.
(Marston, *The Fawne*, opening line of Act II)

Musicke. Finit Actus Tertius.
(Middleton, *Michaelmas Term*, end of Act III)

When greater detail is provided, it becomes clear that this inter-act music sometimes continued the closing sentiment of one act into, or perhaps through, the break. The first act of Marston's *Antonio's Revenge* ends with Pandulpho's lengthy soliloquoy about the gory murder of his son, Feliche. At the end of his impassioned speech, Pandulpho calls for sad music to sound for the act to reinforce the dominant mood of the drama:

Pandulpho.   Wouldst have me cry, run raving up and down:
For my sonnes losse? Wouldst have me turne ranke mad:
Or wring my face with mimick action:
Stampe, curse, weep, rage, and then my bosom strike?
Anyway, tis apish action: player-like,
If he is guiltlesse, why should teares be spent?

Thrice blessed soule that dyeth innocent.

This heart in valor even Jove out-goes;
Jove is without, but this 'bove sense of woes;
And such a one eternity. Behold,
Good morrow sonn: thou bidst a fig for cold,
Sound lowder musicke, let my breath exact,
You strike sad Tones unto this dismall act.

A similar sort of gloomy music is requested under very different circumstances at the close of Act III of Marston's *The Dutch Courtesan*. The comical vintner, Mulligrub, has just been the unwilling victim of yet another prank that has confused and upset him. To close the Act, he says to his wife:

Come lets goe heare some musicke, I will never more say my praiers. Lets go heare some dolefull musicke.

But unlike Act I of *Antonio's Revenge*, this Act does not end on a tragic note, for Mulligrub is a gullible figure who serves as the source of much mirth for the other characters and the audience. The tragic music he calls for need not be as severe or serious as that which Pandulpho requests at a moment of genuine pathos and high tragedy; indeed, if mirthful music were played after Mulligrub's request, the comedy would be all the greater. But in both instances, the author, through his characters, exerts a small amount of control over the impact of the inter-act music that is not generally thought of as an organic part of his play.

Inter-act music may also be appropriate to the setting of the play, or to the action that it preceeds or follows. The third act of Chapman's *May Day* ends in a tavern, and the fourth act opens with the main characters from the tavern scene a little bit drunker at home. To bridge the two acts, Quintiliano has the tapster call in some "tavern musicians" to accompany him home—and provide appropriate inter-act music. The same musicians appear again at the start of Act IV, as if they had done as bidden:

Quintiliano.   . . . Come honorable Clarissimo, lets retire to our strength, taste a fresh carouse or two, and then march home with musicke. Tapster, call us in some musicke.

Drawer.   I will sir.

Finis Actus Tertii

ACTUS QUARTUS

Enter Quintiliano, Leonoro, Innocentio, Lionell, Fannio, with Musicians.

The music called for at the close of Act III not only provides entertainment during the break, but helps the audience imagine the action between tavern and home. Undoubtedly, the "musicke" was appropriate to the tavern milieu in which it was requested, and in which the act closed.

The common London setting of Marston's *The Dutch Courtesan* receives support and reinforcement from the music between Acts II and III in which "fiddlers" play at Mulligrub's request. The vintner asks his wife whether there are any "Fidlers in the house," and is told that "M. *Creakes* noyse" fits the description. So he asks the jolly band to "play, laugh, [and] make merry." In this way, the theatrical musicians who provide the inter-act entertainment are put into the context of the drama.

Only two children's plays describe multiple inter-act entertainments, and only one of these describes what sorts of instruments play each time or what effects are desired. The plays, Beaumont's *Knight of the Burning Pestle* and Marston's *Sophonisba* were both acted by the Children of the Chapel during the same phase of their history, but could hardly be more different. The former is a wickedly witty burlesque romance, combining elements drawn from farce, romance, satire, city comedy, and social and dramatic criticism into a single ingenious whole. The latter is a somber Roman tragedy, based on a careful reading of historical sources, and an equally careful plan "to inlarge every thing as a poet"[16] into an epic drama of clashing ideas and superhuman courage and treachery. Both plays are extraordinarily musical, and both use very different sorts of inter-act music to very different ends.

The Knight of the Burning Pestle, acted in 1607, is an extremely parodic play, and it is therefore difficult to judge just how representative its inter-acts may be. Its inter-act music is accompanied by commentary from the Citizen and his Wife, who sit among, and pretend to be, members of the Blackfriars audience. But they are caricatures of common London playgoers even as the play to which they belong is a burlesque of popular dramatic romance. They are simple folk who think themselves more cultured than they are, who would like to see a simple romantic comedy in which an ordinary man becomes a hero. And, between the acts of a play which they mercilessly try to reshape to their own desires, they call for popular music and loudly wish that each inter-act would end so that they could get back to the main business of the drama. Their commentaries are punctuated with irrelevant misinformation, and they do not hesitate to speak to the performers. The first inter-act features a solo dancer:

[all characters] *Exeunt.*

Boy daunceth. Musicke. Finis Actus Primi.

Wife.	. . . Harke, harke husband, harke, fiddles, fiddles; now surely they go finely. They say 'tis present death for those fidlers to tune their Rebeckes before the great Turkes grace, is't not *George*? But looke, looke, here's a youth dances: now good youth doe a turn a'th toe, sweet heart, I'faith Ile have *Rafe* come and do some of his Gambols; hee'l ride the wild mare Gentlemen, 'twould do your hearts good to see him. I thanke you kinde youth, pray bid *Rafe* come.
Citizen.	Peace Cunnie. Sirrah, you scurvy boy, bid the plaiers send *Rafe*, or by Gods—and they do not, Il'e teare some of their periwigs beside their heads; this is all Riffe Raffe.

Such solo dancing is believed to have been customary between the acts of children's drama, but only this play shows the custom in action.[17] However, Beaumont himself refers to solo dancing between the acts as if it was the norm in his commendatory verse on John Fletcher's *Faithful Shepherdess*:

> Nor want there those, who as the Boy doth dance
> Between the Acts, will censure the whole Play;
> Some if the Wax-lights be not new that day;
> But multitudes there are whose judgement goes
> Headlong according to the Actors cloathes.[18]

From the wife's commentary in *The Knight of the Buring Pestle*, especially the reference to "rebeckes," it may be assumed that violins were among the instruments that played for the boy; but, as we have seen, "fiddle" was a generic term for instruments of music, and the Citizen's Wife is an unreliable witness of almost anything.

Between Acts II and III, there is only instrumental entertainment, which the Citizen and his Wife do not find entirely to their liking. He has apparently requested the Waits of Southwark, the sort of professional musicians who were often hired for the adults' theaters, and feels deceived that another group is playing. Both he and his wife call to the musicians to play their favorite tunes, well known as popular music of the time. Even so, at least one of the couple is incapable of recognizing the famous Lachrimae tune whether or not it is actually sounding, a sly comment on the differences in taste, knowledge, and aesthetic judgment between the citizen class and the higher-born:

Wife.	How do'st thou like this *George*?
Citizen.	Why this is well coney: but if Raph were hot once, thou shouldst see more.
Wife.	The Fidlers go againe husband.

> **Citizen.** I Nell, but this is scurvy musicke: I gave the whores on gal-
> lowes money, and I think hee has not got me the waits of
> South-warke, if I heare 'em not anan, Il'e twinge him by the
> eares. You Musicians, play *Baloo*.
>
> **Wife.** No good George, lets ha *Lachrimae*.
>
> **Citizen.** Why, this is it, cony.

It is impossible to judge whether the musicians followed these requests, or how far removed from these very popular tunes their music was.

At the end of Act III, there is a performance similar to that between Acts I and II. If the Wife's reaction is at all representative of real playgoers, it may be that solo dancers were tipped by near and generous members of the audience:

> *Musicke. Boy daunceth.*
>
> **Wife.** Looke *George*, the little boy's come againe, mee thinkes he
> lookes something like the prince of *Orange* in his long stock-
> ings, if hee had a harnesse about his necke. *George* I will have
> him dance *Fading*: Fading is a fine Jigge Il'e assure you
> Gentlemen: being brother, now a capers sweet heart, now a turn
> a'th toe, then tumble: cannot you tumble youth?
>
> **Boy.** No indeed forsooth.
>
> **Wife.** Nor eat fire?
>
> **Boy.** Neither.
>
> **Wife.** Why then I thanke you heartily, there's two pence to buy you
> points withall.

There is no inter-act printed for the end of Act IV. The complete entertain-ment between the acts of *The Knight of the Burning Pestle*, then, included instrumental music, dance, and dialogue that parody popular taste and incor-porate typical features of private theater inter-acts. One can get little idea of what was actually played from George and Nell's amusing commentary; nor can one tell whether additional music may have been performed before or af-ter their own part in the inter-acts.

Sophonisba's inter-acts stand in stark contrast to the merriment of *The Knight's*. The first Act closes with the interruption of the wedding between the title character and Massinissa, at which point all the men, including the bridegroom, are hastily called off to war. The second Act opens in the military camp where several of Massinissa's supposed allies plot against him, his bride, and the Carthaginian state. The inter-act music is orchestrated with the organ and cornetts that had accompanied the wedding, which sound ironic notes as the scene shifts from the unfulfilled nuptials to mimed action in which the traitors hatch their plot during the inter-act:

The ladies draw the curtains about *Sophonisba*, the rest accompany *Massinissa* forth, the Cornetts and Organs playing loud full Musicke for the Act.

Actus Primi.

FINIS

Actus Secundi.

Scena Prima.

Whil'st the Musicke for the first *Act* soundes *Hanno, Carthalo, Bytheas, Gelosso* enter: they place themselves to Counsell, *Gisco* th'impoisoner waiting on them, *Hanno, Carthalo,* and *Bytheas,* setting their hands to writing, which being offer'd to Gelosso, he denies his hand, and as much offended impatiently starts up and speakes.

This action helps explain to the audience what has gone on after the broken wedding but before the next scene opens. The description implies that inter-act music was most often considered to belong to the preceding, rather than the following, Act; but sometimes, as here, it helps to link them.

The second Act ends with extreme treachery and great intrigue in the military camp, and the third opens in Suyphax's palace shortly before Sophonisba offers a sacrifice to Mercury and Phoebe. The inter-act, "Organ mixt with recorders," in this case sets the scene for coming action rather than echoing preceding deeds. Not long after the inter-act, the organ, first associated with the sacred rite of marriage, accompanies the sacred rite of sacrifice. Acts III and IV are separated by the music of "Organs, Violls and Voices," which does not relate to preceding or following action but is by no means out of place between the acts of a somber, melodramatic tragedy.

The music between Acts IV and V not only connects the two Acts perfectly, but, like the example from Chapman's *May Day*, it helps the audience imagine implicit action between them. By the fourth Act of the play, the depraved villain Syphax has tried everything within his power to bring Sophonisba to his bed, willing or unwilling. At last, he decides to seek supernatural assistance to fulfill his burning lust. With quaking steps, he descends into the dark abode of the loathsome witch Erictho, and she promises him a charm that will force the chaste Sophonisba to his bed. But what the evil king does not know is that Erictho has long desired his embrace, and plans to deceive him. As she casts her powerful spell, "infernall musique" plays, but as it begins to take effect the softer strains of a treble viol and bass lute fill the air of her haunted cavern. These instruments later accompany two songs as the spell becomes final, and they become the inter-act music that serves at once as sexual metaphor and prolongation of audience suspense:

A treble Violl and a base Lute play softlyd [sic] within the Canopy.

[**Syphax.**]   Harke harke, now softer melody strikes mute
Disquiet nature: O thou power of sound
How thou dost melt me. Harke, now even Heaven
Gives up his soule amongst us: Now's the time
When gready expectation strains mine eyes
Prepare my appetite for loves strict gripes
O you dear sounds of Bloud and Beauty
Rayse active Venus worth fruition
Of such provoking sweetnesse. Harke: she comes.

A short song to the soft Musique above.

Now nuptiall Hymes inforced Spirits sing
Harke, *Syphax* harke:

Cantant.

Now Hell and Heaven ringes
With Musique spight of *Phoebus*: Peace:

*Enter Erictho in the shape of Sophonisba, her face vailed and hasteth to
the bed of Syphax.*

Shee coms:
Fury of blouds impatient: *Erictho*
Bove thunder sit; and to thee egregious soule
Let all flesh bend. Sophonisba thy flame
But equal mine, and weele joy such delight
That Gods shall not admire, but even spight.

Syphax hasteneth within the Canopy as to Sophonisbas bed.

Actus Quarti

FINIS

A Base Lute and a Treble Violl
play for the Act

Actus Quinti Scena Prima.

Syphax drawes the curtaines and discovers Erichtho lying with him.

Erictho.   Ha, ha, ha.
Syphax.   Light, light.
Erictho.   Ha, ha.
Syphax.   Thou rotten scum of Hell --
O my abhorred heat! O loathed delusion!
They leape out of bed and Syphax takes him to his sword.
Erictho.   Why foole of kings, could thy weake soule imagin
That t'is within the graspe of Heaven or Hell
To inforce love?

The music leads from Syphax's mood of wild elation to absolute horror with
unparalleled theatrical effectiveness. The audience awaits only the discovery

of the demonic treachery brought about by Erictho, while imagining their sexual fulfillment to the strains of the music between the acts. The complete entertainment between the acts of *Sophonisba*, then, included a variety of instrumental and vocal music as well as pantomime, some of which related to preceding or following action and some of which did not.

The scattered stage directions and dialogue that refer to inter-act music elsewhere in the repertoire show the above examples to be representative of most sorts: inter-act music was sometimes vocal and sometimes instrumental, it sometimes related to the action or setting of the play, and it sometimes accompanied mimed action that hinted at what was to come. Mimed inter-acts are of great dramaturgical importance, because they are almost inseparable from the main body of the play and add greatly to the outcome of the drama. As between the first and second Acts of *Sophonisba*, they generally let the audience in on some small action that helps explain events between those that ended one act and those that begin another, and that anticipates what is to follow immediately, such as:

Toward the close of the [inter-act] musick, the justices three men prepare for a robberie.

(Middleton, *The Phoenix*, between Acts II and III)

Whilst the Act is a-playing, *Hercules* and *Tiberio* enters; *Tiberio* climbs a tree, and is received above by *Dulcimel*, *Philocalia*, and a Priest: Hercules stays beneath.

(Marston, *The Fawne*, between Acts IV and V)

A special sort of pantomime to music between the acts is a dumb show, one of the most controversial aspects of Elizabethan drama. Theoretically, there is little difference between the pantomime and dumb show, for both are action without dialogue.[19] But the dumb show goes beyond simple silent action and becomes a visual emblem of the sort so important to Elizabethan drama.[20] Dumb shows most often symbolize important action to come by reducing the theme or outcome of the next act into a few brief gestures. They die out with the reign of Elizabeth, they are principally associated with Senecan tragedy, and, perhaps most importantly, they are almost consistently labeled "The Dumb Show" in dramatic imprints. George Kernodle has said of these brief musical spectacles:

Most dumb shows had the purpose of symbolizing by mood or theme the main action. But some later dramatists in England. . . made a different use of the separate pantomimed show—they compacted part of the main story into the briefer form of action without speech, still using the musical accompaniment and striving for a more picturesque arranged effect than was possible in the spoken scenes.[21]

But unlike simple pantomime, the dumb show is absolutely vital to the impact of the complete play. And one gets the distinct impression that the playwright himself cared greatly about the dumb shows that belonged to his plays. The dumb show has been considered a descendant of the Italian *intermedio*,[22] but may also trace its ancestry to the chorus of Greek drama and the pantomimes of street festivals.[23] The dumb show is particularly effective as a symbol of theme and action because the spoken word was replaced by music and gesture, which speak differently to the senses and the intellect.

A typical dumb show occurs between Acts IV and V of Marston's very Senecan but highly original *Antonio's Revenge*. Like all dumb shows, it symbolizes coming action and depicts pure passion to the incessant accompaniment of music. This short piece is extremely effective as theater, and serves as a very affective summary of the final act and climax of the play in which the evil Piero is murdered by the survivors and friends of his own victims:

The Cornets sound for the Act.

The dumb show.

Enter at one dore *Castilio* and *Forobosco* with halberds, four pages with torches, *Lucio* bare, *Piero*, *Maria*, and *Alberto* talking. *Alberto* draws out his dagger, *Maria* her knife, aiming to menace the Duke [Piero]. Then *Galeatzo* betwixt two Senators, reading a paper to them; at which they all make semblance of loathing *Piero*, and knit their fists at him; two Ladies and *Nutriche*. All these go softly over the stage, whilest at the other dore enters the Ghost of *Andrugio*, who passeth by them tossing his torch about his head in triumph. All forsake the stage, saving *Andrugio*, who, speaking, begins the Act.

A number of plays, principally comedies from the early years of the revival, open or close acts with brief musical scenarios that bear little or no relationship to the rest of the play. These have been considered inter-acts that have been printed as part of the play.[24] The music in these scenes is often spectacular. At the end of Act II of *The Maydes Metamorphosis* there are several songs and two dances done by a group in fantastic costumes; and at the end of *Blurt, Master-Constable*, a group of pert serving boys sings a dialogue to the accompaniment of a consort of viols as they continue their boyish mischief. A typical scenario of this sort is printed as a preface to Act II of Marston's *Antonio and Mellida*. Seemingly by chance, as they go about mundane tasks for their masters, a trio of mischievous servants, Catzo, Dildo, and Flavia, meet. Their meeting is not at all related to the plot of the drama, and features irrelevant, bawdy dialogue. The climax of their brief meeting is a song in which all participate, before they return hastily and guiltily to the routine life of servants.

FINALE MUSIC

The final distinctive extra-dramatic musical custom of the children's theaters is finale music. Like pre- and inter-act music, finale music is indicated only randomly in dramatic imprints and appears to have varied widely. Sometimes it was vocal, sometimes instrumental; sometimes a lengthy production, and sometimes apparently just enough music to usher the cast from the stage in grace and splendor. Final songs are associated most strongly with the period before 1590, though a fair number of later plays require them. Final songs seem to be an exclusive virtue of comedy, but instrumental conclusions belong to both comedy and tragedy.

Nine comedies, roughly spanning the years of the revival period, have survived with concluding songs, and seven include complete text. If these are representative, concluding songs enable the play to end on a note of merriment by summarizing the happy outcome of the play, reinforcing its pleasing theme, or inviting audience applause, such as:

> Now each one drie his weeping eyes,
> And to the well of knowledge haste;
> Where purged of your maladies,
>> You may of sweeter waters taste:
>> And, with refined voice, report
> The grace of *CYNTHIA*, and her court.

> (Jonson, *Cynthia's Revels*)

> Better Musicke nere was knowne,
> Then a quire of hearts in one.
> Let each other that hath beene,
> Troubled with the gall or spleene:
> Learne of us to keep his brow
> Smoth and plaine as ours are now.
> Sing though before the hour of dying
> He shall rise and then by crying,
> Hay oh, 'tis nought but mirth,
> That keepes the body from the earth.

> (Beaumont, *The Knight of the Burning Pestle*)

> Oares, oares, oares, oares,
> To London hay, to London hay
> Hoist up sayles and lets away
> For the safest bay
> For us to land is London shores.
> Oares, oares, oares, oares:
> Quickly shall we get to Land,
> If you, if you, if you

> Lend us but halfe a hand.
> O lend us half a hand.

(Dekker and Webster, *Westward Ho*)

A final dance is combined with the closing songs in *The Maydes Metamorphosis* and George Chapman's *Sir Gyles Goosecappe*.

A gentle good-natured speech that expresses sentiments similar to those found in these valedictory songs ends *Blurt, Master-Constable*, but at the close of the speech, the Duke calls for music:

> **Duke.**   And since this heate of furie is all spent,
> And tragicke shapes meete comicall event:
> Let this bright morning merrily be crown'd
> With daunces, banquets, and choyce musickes sound.

Likewise, the final speech of *Antonio and Mellida* calls for the music of "lydian wires" to close the play; and the final speech of Middleton's *The Phoenix* is apparently accompanied by music. All of these plays are witty comedies which end quite literally on harmonious notes.

The case of tragedy is quite different. *Sophonisba* ends with a very dignified flourish of cornetts, and Beaumont and Fletcher's *Cupid's Revenge* concludes with a trumpet march as all leave the stage in a funeral procession. Even the tragicomic *Malcontent* finishes with a simple flourish of cornetts. It would seem that extended harmony was deemed inappropriate to plays that closed in tragic discord, but the simple instrumental signals would alert the audience that the play was done and provide a sonorous background for the exit of the actors.

CHAPTER 6

MUSIC FOR CEREMONY, SPECTACLE AND SOCIAL OCCASION

All representations, especially those of this nature in court, public spectacles, either have been or ought to be the mirrors of man's life.

Ben Jonson, *Love's Triumph through Callipolis* (1631)

In Elizabethan and Jacobean England, formal ceremony and spectacle gave shape and legitimacy to many aspects of daily life. It was an era in which monumental events and rites of passage were shrouded with both symbolic and literal meaning, and a culture in which many persons played both practical and allegorical roles. As David Bevington has so perceptively observed, ceremony was omnipresent in English Renaissance life because it gave overt form to the social roles through which members of society found their place and identity.[1] The very theatrical nature of public spectacle and private ceremony made them quite attractive to many playwrights, among whom were those who wrote both children's plays and spectacular presentations such as masques and pageants. The ceremonies of the stage, mostly patterned after those of life, offered a natural pretext for dramatic conflict, an ideal cover for forbidden deeds, and, especially in the private theaters, an opportunity for brilliant spectacle. Ceremony was used literally and ironically, both to reinforce and undermine dialogue and action.

It is often forgotten that both on stage and off, most Renaissance ceremonies were accompanied by music that united otherwise disparate elements. In the theater, it is often the music itself that binds together vital scenes that take place against the background of a great occasion. It is also often the music itself that motivates characters to action that alters the course of the play. Scenes woven around musical ceremony, spectacle, and social occasion account for a significant part of the music in children's plays. These scenes are not without dramatic and historical consequence. They contribute a dimension of contemporary realism to plays by representing actual musical customs on the stage. They serve as a convenient excuse for the playwright to assemble the entire cast on stage at once to ravel or unravel complex threads of plot, or serve as the basis for a wide variety of dramatic effects that often require the music itself for their completion. They provide extra entertainment for an audience that relished music and spectacle to the point that the contemporary stage frequently took on the atmosphere of a festival.[2] And they allowed the more innovative, musically oriented playwrights the opportunity to develop musical dramatic effects that became stock parts of later plays or influenced later masque writing.

Music is integral to many spectacular or otherwise formal scenes in children's drama. But not all English Renaissance dramatists regarded such scenes as essential to successful plays; indeed, some felt that conspicuous musical additions would only provide irrelevant distraction from the plot and spoken dialogue. In the words of Thomas Heywood, there should be

> no drum, nor trumpet, nor dumb show;
> No combat, marriage, not so much today,
> As song, dance, masque, to bumbaste out a play.[3]

Attitudes such as this clearly influenced even the most musical of the children's playwrights, for combat, marriage, song, dance, and masque never overpower the play in which they appear. But in those scenes built around ceremony, spectacle, and social occasion in which music plays a part, that music often becomes central to the development of the drama. Musical ceremony on stage varies widely, ranging from state occasions to private events, and from comical to tragical in outcome. But in nearly every case, it serves as a turning point for the plot of the play, or to buttress a subplot scenario.

MASQUES

The grandest, most lavish, and consistently most central of the musical spectacles in children's drama are its very varied masques. The masque itself is a form far richer than the play in the language of symbolism, and often becomes a more compact and effective method than simple dialogue or action for drawing attention to an official state of affairs or to an active conflict between order and disorder. The majority of masques in children's plays form a backdrop to a climactic scene, in which a major conflict is resolved by the masque or in spite of it, within the presentation of the masque itself or beneath its layers of arcane emblem and disguise. As in life, masques within plays are celebratory affairs, most often held to commemorate the nuptials of the nobility, to mark an important event in the life of a ruler, or to entertain distinguished visitors. And nearly always the intent of a masque is to reinforce the richness and power of a court and its reigning head of state. Also, unfortunately true to life outside the theater, the masque is cut drastically when committed to print within the barren play text, and its two most vital components—music and visual imagery—are completely sacrificed. This inevitable reduction of living splendor to a few stage directions and fragments of dialogue has led to a great deal of debate as to what does and does not represent a masque in contemporary drama.

The English masque and children's drama went through infancy and youth side by side, though children's drama matured more rapidly and died before the masque reached its prime. The masque became part of English courtly entertainment in early Tudor times, and was associated with children's drama from the very first presentations by the Children of the Chapel before the Tudor Court to the absorption of the same company into the Lady Elizabeth's Men nearly a century later. As the masque became more elaborate and moved closer to the drama during the early years of the seventeenth century, masque influence on plays increased greatly. And it was Ben Jonson, who, after the death of children's drama, became the pre-eminent writer of masques and brought the form to unparalleled literary heights. But, though distantly related and sometimes mutually influential, masque and drama always remained distinct, in some respects almost at odds with each other, throughout their histories in England.

It must be emphasized that the essence of the English masque is the masked dance. Indeed, the form itself is a direct descendant of the early Tudor disguising, which had already included the three dances that comprise the core of the masque: an entry dance of disguised individuals, followed by a main dance, and finally an exit dance. But the mature masque form of the later sixteenth century also includes a revels or taking-out dance before the exit dance, in which spectators are led into the dance by the masked figures. This combination of audience participation and the mystery of disguise contains great dramatic potential that was by no means overlooked by the later children's playwrights. But it is not the only aspect of the masque that appealed to dramatists.

The literary nature of the masque is of only secondary importance. Meaning in the masque is expressed through costume, movement, properties, song, and instrumental music; spoken dialogue only reinforces these things and points to the allegory that loosely binds the masque together. Drama, on the

other hand, uses all of these elements differently. Everything in the play revolves around the dialogue, and its other aspects relate directly to its literary
content. Both are living forms, but both deliver different messages. Ian Spink
has perceived the use of music in masque and drama to be at variance:

> In the masque, music was a means of magnifying the theme.... Through it reality was
> suspended and a world of symbolism conjured up. Everything became possible,
> except (paradoxically) those particular effects which song could produce within the
> context of spoken drama. Thus in this magical world, its power to create atmosphere,
> to delineate character and to express feeling was diminished simply because song, as
> such, was no longer used as a special effect. But in the play its role was to deepen, not
> suspend reality; to make certain things more credible within the human situation.[4]

Music is the essence of the one, the poignant finishing touch of the other. But
the masque within the play took on the meanings of both, and afforded the
dramatist a greater vocabulary of musical effect. He could at once invert the
reality affected by the rest of the play and strengthen it. The seeming contra-
diction between the two forms led to unparalleled effects, in which reality became a dream and dream became reality, controlled by the magic of
continuous music. Only at the end of many dramatic masques, when the participants shed their masks and the world of the play returns to focus, does the
audience fully understand what has transpired while the masque progressed.

A number of children's plays from the reign of Elizabeth include masques,
for they were written with an eye toward the Court of a Queen who loved music, dance, and spectacle. But as the masque developed rapidly under her successor and rose to become the favored form of entertainment of the Jacobean
Court, it became central to a greater number of plays. Masques were by no
means limited to children's plays, for they quickly became an established part
of dramatic fashion after the accession of James; but between 1599 and 1611,
the majority of plays to include masques were written for the children.[5] The
boys, who had for so long been associated with courtly revelry and who themselves possessed the graces of music and charm that are so necessary to the
masque, served as a link between fashionable courtly entertainment and the
popular London stage. Furthermore, their principal postrevival playwrights
were also important figures in the development of the Jacobean masque.

As the masque changed and was used more widely outside of the theater,
its form in the drama changed as well. But rarely was an entire masque, consisting of an entry dance, main dance, revels, and exit dance, included within
a play. In Elizabethan drama, an entry of disguised individuals who dance
normally functions as a masque. It literally takes center stage, and other action is all but suspended while the masque is presented. Under James, when
speech and song became more central to the masque, one or both are often
integrated into theatrical masques. But the basic Jacobean dramatized

masque consists of an entry and dance by masked persons followed by a revels section in which they dance with the remaining characters. And, perhaps most importantly, the Jacobean dramatic masque tends to be punctuated with dialogue or action that relates to the main part of the play. These truncated masques, barely sufficient to let the audience know that what they see before them is a masque, often differ little from other dance scenes or extended celebrations of noble characters, which has led to great scholarly confusion over just what is or is not to be considered a masque.[6]

For the present purpose, a masque will be defined as anything so labeled in a play imprint or so called in dramatic dialogue, since in the children's repertoire, few other episodes take on the complete aspect of a masque. But what remains in the play imprints as masque varies widely and is sometimes of little help in reconstructing the author's or director's intent. Stage directions such as "Enter Maister Correction, Cupid, and the maskers dauncing" (Sharpham, *Cupid's Whirligig*, Act V) or "Enter the maskers they dance" (Marston, *The Dutch Courtesan*, Act IV, scene i) give us little idea of what the theater audience heard or saw. But other masques are clearly delineated in the play imprints and include more complex directions, such as that from the climax of Marston's *The Malcontent*, which indicates action, costumes, musical instrumentation, and changes in the dance.

An excellent example of the use of masque in Elizabethan children's comedy is found in Act V, scenes vii-xi of Ben Jonson's anti-Court satire, *Cynthia's Revels*. This masque-within-a-play, which predates the author's earliest court masques, the *Masque of Blackness*, some four to six years, becomes absolutely central to the plot and outcome of the play. It actually consists of two simple masked entries with descriptive speech, each considered a separate masque, which join together for a final spectacular dance before the participants unmask. As each fantastic figure emerges to join the masque, his costume and properties are explained to the audience by a similarly disguised presenter, without whom the arcane allegorical meaning of each component part would be less clear. And the final dramatic effect of this masque is entirely dependent on the precise understanding of each symbol.

In Act V, scene v of the play, the virtuous scholar Crites is asked to "provide strait for a masque" for the pleasure of the wise goddess Cynthia. At first he is hesitant, for Cynthia's court lacks the harmony that would be elevated to a symbolic level in a masque, and her effete courtiers lack the virtue to play its exalted roles. But Crites plans a masque that will expose the folly and superficiality of the courtiers to Cynthia herself, and so teach them true nobility. In the two-part masque, eight masked virtues appear, four at a time; and before they dance, each is introduced in a speech that describes in great detail his fantastical appearance and attributes of goodness:

Cupid. . . . the third, in the discoloured Mantle spangled all over, is Euphantaste, a well-conceived Wittinesse, and employed in honouring the Court with the riches of her pure inventions. Her device, upon a Petasus or Mercurial hat, a crescent; the word, sic laus ingenii; inferring that the praise and glory of witte doth ever increase as doth thy growing moon

The fourth, in white, is Aphelia, a nymph as pure and simple as the soule, or as an abrase table, and is therefore called Simplicitie; without folds, without pleights, without colour, without counterfiet; and (to speake plainly) plainnesse itself. Her device is no device. The word under her silver shield, omnis abest focus: alluding to thy spotlesse selfe, who art as far from impuritie as from mortalitie

Myself, celestial Goddesse, more fit for the court of Cynthia than the arbours of Cytherea, am called Anteros, or Love's enemy; the more welcome therefore to thy court, and the fitter to conduct this quaternion, who as they are thy professed votaries, and for that cause adversaries to Love, yet thee (perpetuall Virgin) they both love, and vow to love eternally.

After they have all been presented, these fantastics dance before Cynthia and the rest of her court, the great virtues of that court made flesh and brought to move in graceful harmony against a continuous background of music. But like all masques, this one moves toward the climactic moment when myth and reality merge in the disclosure of the faces beneath the masks as the fantasy dissolves. At the end of this masque, it is not Cynthia's votaries and the chief virtues of her court who stand exposed, but the most foolish, self-loving courtiers who had dared to fancy themselves the chief worthies of her court. But the wise goddess brings them to repentance of their ways, and at last restores her court to the harmony and order that lay only on the surface of the masque.

A representative example of the uses of masque in Jacobean children's comedy is found in Act V, scenes i and ii of Field's *A Woman is a Weather-Cocke*. Unlike the masque in *Cynthia's Revels*, which does not include a taking-out dance, it is the dance between the masked men and the lady spectators that becomes the focus of the episode. Also unlike *Cynthia's Revels*, the symbolism of the devices is not of central importance, and so the costumes and underlying fable of the masque are not explained. And these masquers speak to each other as they prepare for the spectacle and as they dance, so that the crossed intrigues of crossed lives come in and out of audience focus as the dancers weave past each other. The masque is planned as the pinnacle of the double wedding celebration of the eldest and youngest daughters of Sir John Worldly, and it also becomes the pinnacle of the play. The very complicated plot revolves around these two unhappy planned marriages and the many love affairs they interrupt. As the central conflict is resolved against the harmonious background of the masque's music, so too can the other tangled threads unwind and bring the play to an ordered conclusion. And as the masks of the participants are lifted, so too can other, more longstanding deceptions be laid aside. The masque, then, takes on a three-fold significance: it represents a contemporary social custom, it provides a central focus for the resolution of conflict, and it foreshadows the harmonious outcome of climactic tension. One by one, difficulties are resolved after the masked Scudmore takes his beloved Bellafront to dance, and daringly leads her from under the nose of her supposed new husband, Count Fredericke, to marry her himself:

After one straine of the Musicke, Scudmore takes Bellafront, who seemes unwilling to dance, Count [Fredericke] takes Lucida, Pendant Kate, Sir Abraham Mistris Wagtaile; Scudmore as they stand, the other Courting too, whispers as followes.

Scudmore.	I am your *Scudmore. Soft Musicke.*
Bellafront.	Ha?
Scudmore.	By heaven I am.
	Be rul'd by me in all things.
Bellafront.	Even to death.

❖ ❖ ❖ ❖ ❖

Musicke, & they dance, the second straine; in which Scudm: goes away with her.

Omnes Spectator.	Good verie good.
	The other foure dance, another strain, honor and end.
Count.	But where's the Bride and Nevill?

❖ ❖ ❖ ❖ ❖

Enter Scudmore unvizarded, Bellafront with Pistols, and the right Parson.

Count.	This *Nevill*, this is *Scudmore.*
Omnes.	How?
Count.	But heere's my Ladie.
Scudmore.	No my Gentlewoman.
Abraham.	Zoones Treason, I smell power.
Bellafront.	In short know,
	That I am married to this Gentleman,
	To whom I was contracted long ago:
	This Priest the inviolable knot hath ty'de,
	What ease I find being un-Ladifyed.
Count.	What riddle's this?
Innocent.	Ware the Statue of two Husbands.
Scudmore.	
Bellafront.	Pish.
Count.	This is the verye Priest that married me,
	Is it not Sister?
Neville.	No.

Enter Nevill like the Parson too.

Thus, at the very moment when masks should be removed and the masque allowed to finish, new elements of disguise and deception take center stage. But one by one, disguises are removed, deception confessed, and it becomes clear that the unhappy double wedding ceremony was invalid so that all are free to marry whom they choose—with a bona fide priest on hand to perform the multiple ceremony. The fantastic world of the masque has provided an opportunity to alter reality, and, with its conclusion, the world of the play will never be the same again.

In life, masques were emblematic of harmony and were thus associated with such joyous events as weddings and ceremonious occasions of state. And where they approached the drama, it was on the side of comedy.[7] But seventeenth-century dramatists, beginning with John Marston, saw within these joyous connotations the means to bring masque to tragic drama as a powerful tool, an often ironic note of concord in a disordered state. The music that must be present for a masque easily becomes the background for a series of horrifying actions that could not be described in, or accompanied by, spoken words and retain their full effect; so moving and so perfectly formed are such scenes that Restoration tragicomedy with inserted masques, descended from the children's earlier experiments, has been classified as semiopera.[8]

The earliest use of masque in tragedy, and one of the most effective in the entire repertoire, is found in Act V, scene iii of Marston's *Antonio's Revenge*. Like the masque in *A Woman is a Weather-Cocke*, it occurs at the climax of a wedding celebration and of the play. Also like that in *A Woman is a Weather-Cocke*, it alters the outcome of the play and the lives of its major characters. In this case, however, the masque covers not the triumph of true love but brutal revenge for tyranny and murder. It is planned to celebrate the wedding of the evil Piero, Duke of Venice, and Maria, widow of the rival Duke of Genoa who was murdered by Piero. Piero is in excellent spirits, for all his treachery has made him secure in his rule. But each of the masquers, with whom the bride is in full cooperation, harbors beneath his disguise a personal vendetta against the villainous Duke and a weapon with which to dispatch him. Even the ghost of Andrugio, Maria's late husband, has given his blessing to the plot, for until he is avenged he cannot rest. The expectation of dark vengeance creates suspense for the audience, who knows what is to come. But Piero, the unsuspecting but deserving target of the gory plan, is in the mood for merriment:

> **Piero.**   Why then, Io to Hymen! Mount a lofty note,
> Fill red-cheek'd *Bacchus*, let *Lyaeus* float
> In burnish'd goblets! Force the plump-lipp'd god
> Skip light lavoltos in your full-sapp'd veins!

. . . [T]he cornets sound a sennet.

Enter Antonio, Pandulpho, and Alberto in maskery, Balurdo and a torch-bearer.

Piero.   Call *Julio* hither; where's the little soule?
I saw him not to day. Here's sport alone
For him i'faith; for babes and fooles I know
Relish not substance, but applaud the show.

To the conspirators as they stand in ranke for the measure.

To Antonio.

Galeatzo.   All blessed fortune crowne your brave attempt.

To Pandulpho.

I have a troupe to second your attempt.

To Alberto.

The Venice States joyne hearts unto your hands.

Piero.   By the delights in contemplation
Of coming joyes, 'tis magnificent.
You grace my marriage eve with sumptuous
pomp.
Sound still, loud musick. O your breath gives
grace
To curious feete that in proud measure pace.

Antonio [to Maria].   Mother, is Julio's body—

Maria [to Antonio].   Speake not, doubt not, all is above hope.

Antonio.   Then will I daunce and whirle about the ayre.
Me thinkes I am all soule, all heart, all spirit.
Now murder shall receive his ample merite.

The Measure

*Whilst the measure is dancing, Andrugio's ghost is placed betwixt
the musicke houses.*

Piero.   Bring hither suckets, candied delicates.
Wee'll taste some sweetmeates, gallants, with
tart sour sauce.

Ghost of Andrugio.   Here will I sit, spectator of revenge,
And glad my ghost in anguish of my foe.

But Piero tastes no sweetness, for the conspirators unmask prematurely and serve him more cruelly than he has served others. They bind him, cut out his tongue, and present him not with candied delicates but with the body of his small son, Julio, arranged on a platter. Finally, they stab him repeatedly until he dies. This savage murder becomes the main body of a masque that was to have paid tribute to the corrupt Duke, and its costumed figures are metamorphosed from obsequity to Vengeance personified at the moment of unmasking. The final discordant act of brutality is prepared ironically by a dance, the ancient symbol of harmony and concord, whose music apparently continues beyond the premature unmasking. The sound of that music must remain mysterious to us, for there are no indications in the stage directions or dialogue as to its nature. But the "measure" which the conspirators dance as they approach the moment of their triumph was probably "solemne, grave, and sloe,"[9] most likely a pavan or almain matched to unique, elaborate choreography.[10] The stately sound and steps of such a dance would not only prolong audience suspense before the violent conclusion of the masque, but provide a shocking contrast to the rapid disorder that follows. Indeed, it is possible that the same stately strains of music continue obliviously through the savage murder of the Duke.

NON-MASQUE DANCES

The dances included in the masque are far from the only ones used in children's drama after 1597. A wide variety of independent dances belong to these plays, ranging from formal courtly dances by the nobility to country dances by rustic folk, from spectacular theatrical dances to simple solo caperings. As in the masque, the type of dance is more often left unspecified, and there are few hints as to music or choreography. Like the masque within the drama, dances are held to celebrate a variety of occasions and often become central to the plot. But dance, being a broader and less rigid category than masque, ranges far more widely in its presentation and its impact on the play. Sometimes it is included for purely atmospheric reasons, sometimes only to entertain. It belongs not just to the nobility, but to all sorts of characters who grace the stages, from riff-raff to supernatural beings. Some dances are an end in themselves, and others belong to more extended celebrations such as weddings and religious ceremonies. Like the masque, the dance was often used to emphasize an important occasion or a confrontation between characters. But, quite central to its presentation, the dance of course held no element of surprise, no central moment of truth when the faces beneath masques were to be revealed.

Both Elizabeth and James loved the dance, and during their time many of their subjects practiced this graceful art. Dancing was considered "an elegant thing, which cheareth up the minde, exerciseth the body, delights the spectators, which teacheth many comely gestures, equally affecting the eares, eyes, and soule it selfe."[11] On classical authority, dance was seen to symbolize harmony and concord.[12] This association made it suitable for many solemn occasions and quite attractive to contemporary dramatists. But, of course, the sensual aspect of the art was loudly condemned, and not just by England's Puritan extremists:

Therefore it must needes be, that dau[n]sing is the vilest vice of al: and truely it cannot easely be saide what mischiefes the sight, and the hiring [sic] doo receave hereby, which afterwarde be the causes of communication and embracinge. They daunce with disordinate gestures, and with monstrous thumpinge of the feete, to pleasaunt soundes, to wanton songes, to dishonest verses: Maidens and Matrons are groped and handled with unchaste hands, & kissed, and dishonestly embraced: and the things which nature hath hidden, modestie covered, are then oftentimes by meanes of lasciviousnes made naked, and ribaldrie under the colour of pastime is dissembled.[13]

These same aspects of the dance, and its association with the love matters that are so important to so much drama, only increased its appeal to playwrights. Indeed, dance was so central to theatrical entertainment, and contemporary detractors from the stage condemned it so heartily, that the author of *The Praise of Musicke* excuses himself from dealing with "dauncing and theatricall spectacles" lest he "pull whole swarmes of enimies" upon himself.[14] The children's theater was especially rife with dance, and the beautiful boys who learned other graceful arts clearly excelled at this one. For dance had a place among the liberal arts which such boys were taught routinely:

> And those great Maisters of the liberall arts
> In all their severall Schooles doe daucing teach:
> For humble Grammar first doth set the parts
> Of congruent and well-accorded speach:
> Which Rhoetorick whose state ye clouds doth reach,
> And heav'nly Poetry doe forward lead,
> And divers Measures, diversly doe tread.[15]

The children's versatility in dance is illustrated in so many of their plays, which call for a good cross-section of contemporary social dances and for what are clearly especially choreographed theatrical dances.

Social dance scenes in the children's plays, like masques, serve to gather a group of characters together onto the stage to share in a specific occasion. Such scenes also use music and festivity as a background for displays of emotion, the hatching of plots, and raveling or unraveling tangled webs of intrigue. As in many of the Jacobean masque scenes, the dancers often speak to each other. Since dances are not accompanied by the costumes and allegories of masque, the machinations of the characters in the main world of the drama occupy our full attention; and since the participants wear only their own faces, attention is often drawn to their purposeful interactions and naked emotions. Dance, even more than masque, relies on music for its full effect, for visual symbol and individualized myth have no part in social dance. The participants are not transformed into superhuman figures but remain mortal throughout the dance, completely subject to the petty foibles of any other human being. As in masque, the harmonious element of the dance is often used symbolically, either literally or ironically. And often the dance reshapes the entire world of the play.

Social dances, like masques, fully and properly consist of several parts, these being a group of contrasting dances. Sometimes such a scene in drama is abbreviated by a single dance; but the full, extended scene of a complete social dance permits a great deal of action and dialogue to take place against the musical background, bringing crossed lives and purposes in and out of focus as the dancers glide across the stage in patterned steps. And, though disguises have no central place in social dance, those in drama, as in life, tend to involve so many people that one or two may slip in or out unnoticed, perhaps aided by the slight alteration of normal appearance:

Enter the Queene, Mariana, and waiting women, Philocles and the other lords, the King [of Cyprus] disguised like one of the guard at one end of the stage, and the Duke [of Epyre] so likewise disguised at the other end of the stage.

Queene.	Loud Musicke there, and let the god of Harmonie
	Ravish our senses with delightfull aires.
	Tun'd to the Musicke of the higher spheare,
	And with that mortall signe rarely shew
	The joyes in *Joves* high Court, to feast the gods,
	Making that place abound in happinesse.
	Come noble Philocles I ceaze you first,
	(Mariana there are choice of other Lords)
	In gracing you it is the King I grace.
Mariana.	Come honest Lord, 'tis you must stand to me,
	The Queene in mine doth challenge interest,
	And I must flie for shelter to my friends.

Queene.	Sound musicke, fill the earth with heavens pleasure.
Cyprus.	My Queene is out of time, though she keep measure.
	Here they dance the first straine.
Epyre.	Be luckie villanie,
	Hit now the marke that mine ambition aimes at,
	Me thinkes I see that leane Italian divell, jealousie, dance
	In his eies: possesse him spirit of rage,
	Let passion governe reason, falshood truth,
	Oblivion hide his age, hat kidd his youth.

The first straine ends.

Queene.	This straine contain'd a preticke change.
	Proceed to the next.
	They daunce the second [straine].

Cyprus.	Sinn followes sinne, and change on change doth wait,
	They change doth change my love to cruell hate.

Here in this straine Mariana came [sic] to Philocles.

Philocles.	Madame me thinkes this change is better then the first.
Mariana.	I if the musicke would not alter it.
Queene.	Me thinks tis worse, come we will have another straine.

They dance again.

Philocles.	I pleas'd, let us proceede.
Cyprus.	Rivals in Crownes and beds of Kings must bleed.
	Can that faire house containe so foul a guest
	As lust, a or cloake inordinate and base desires,
	Under so faire a coverture? . . .

(Markham and Machin, *The Dumb Knight,* Act IV, scene i)

The changing partners of the dance permit specific exchanges between individuals that other characters are not meant to hear, and throw jealousies and rivalries into clear view. The dance provides an opportunity for the clandestine observers at either end of the stage, Epyre and Cyprus, to watch the interactions unseen, for the attention of the other characters is firmly focused on the dance. The lack of masks or other disguises permits all of the dancers to be seen as who they are, and the pairing off in what is clearly a series of partner dances permits the observers to know the participants for what they are. The steady musical background of the scene, which changes with each change of the dance, maintains its motion and that of the dancers while reinforcing the emotional changes of dancers and disguised spectators.

Similar devices are used in a number of plays, almost always to emphasize growing love or lust between characters to the musical pulse of the dance. For, as Robert Burton summarizes contemporary attitudes toward the dance in one unusually brief sentence, "Dancing is a pleasant recreation of body and minde, if tempestively used; and a furious motive to burning lust, if abused."[16] Music for the dance could be used to underscore the dominant emotion; in the above scene, a spirited galliard or lavolta would reinforce the Queen's vigorous actions and emotions, while a pavan or almain would support Mariana's constant love. Similarly, a stately measure is called for in Act I, scene i of the anonymous *Blurt, Master-Constable* to whose strains Fontinell and Violetta fall deeply in love, and a "lavolta or a galliard" accompanies Massino's sudden, burning lust for Isabella in Act II, scene i of Marston and Barkstead's *The Insatiate Countess.*

Social dances sometimes come to represent the "pomps, and tryumphs, and soemnities"[17] of courtly settings without directly influencing the plot of the play:

Enter Piero, Antonio, Mellida, Rossaline, Galeatzo, Matzagente, Alberto, and Flavia. As they enter, Feliche & Castilio make a ranke for the Duke to pass through. Forobosco ushers the Duke to his state: then whilst Piero speaketh his first speech, Mellida is taken by Galeatzo and Matzagente, to dance, they supporting her: Rossaline, in like manner by Alberto and Balurdo: Flavia by Feliche & Castilio.

(Marston, *Antonio and Mellida*, Act II, scene i)

Such dances sometimes welcome a dignitary into the court:

The courtiers adresse themselves to dauncing, whilst the Duke enters with Granuffo, and takes his state.

Hercules.   Gallants to dancing, loud musicke, the Dukes upon entrance.

(Marston, The Fawne, Act V, scene i)

Such scenes break the predictable monotony of a simple cornett signal for entrance, and also show that certain courts possess great refinement and artistry. And all social dance scenes show, on one level, that dance has a recreational place in the lives of its noble participants.

Specially choreographed theatrical dances are less common than social dances in children's plays after 1597, when it appears that masques began to take their place as the principal spectacular entertainment in the plays. Furthermore, when the kings, dukes, and even London citizens of real life chose to dance, it was most often in social dances or masques, so that their dramatic equivalents did the same. The fantastic creatures and mythic nymphs and shepherds of the pastoral and related drama still danced special dances after the late 1590s, but fewer children's plays from that time belonged to these outmoded genres. But occasionally a play with an ancient setting made use of spectacular dance to lend credence to the distant time and place of the drama.

Theatrical dance within the drama is less likely than social dance to influence the main plot, since it seems meant mostly to entertain or lend the appropriate atmosphere to a particular scene. A typical example is found in Act I, scene ii of Fletcher's *The Faithful Shepherdess*. Like almost all dance scenes in English Renaissance drama, this one serves to assemble a large group of characters together for a common purpose. But unlike many masques and social dances, it serves not as the background against which major elements of the story can unfold but as the unadorned center of the scene. This dance, performed by shepherds and shepherdesses, is an invocation to Pan, and serves to remind the audience that this scene is laid in mythic Arcadia. For "*Pan* was supposed to be the God of the Shepherds, and . . . was worshipped first in *Arcadia*."[18] The dancers sing a hymn to their deity as they perform a round dance, a simple dance of great antiquity that often had ritual or supernatural associations on the stage:

> Sing his praises that doth keepe,
> > Our Flockes from harme,
> Pan the Father of our sheepe,
> > And arme in arme
> Tread we softly in a round,
> Whilst the hollow neighboring ground,
> Fills the musicke with her sound,
> Pan, O great God, Pan to thee
> > Thus do we sing:
> Thou that keepst us chaste and free,
> > As the young spring,
> Ever be thy honor spoke,
> From that place the morne is broke,
> To that place Day doth unyoke.

Further details of the choreography and music are not given, and no contemporary settings of the song remain extant. But it is clear from the text that the song was accompanied; and, as a hymn to Pan, it is likely that the supernaturally provided music included his instrument, the recorder. For, as well-read Englishmen knew, even in ancient times, *"Pan was figured . . . holding a Pype to his mouth."*[19]

It must be realized that in the theater, the distinction between social dance and spectacular dance was not as sharp as it was in life. As an integral part of a play, any dance on the stage served as part of the larger spectacle, and, like all of the actors' careful movements, had to be completely choreographed ahead of time. Furthermore, the dance named most frequently in children's drama is the measure, which term, as shown above, at least sometimes implied unique choreography. In the courtly masques inserted into plays, social and spectacular dance merged at the revels section as they did in life.

Another special place in the repertoire must be awarded to the Morris dance, a native rustic dance of ancient lineage perforce considered spectacular and not social in life,[20] used in the theater only under the same social circumstances as in contemporary English life. There is only one Morris in the children's repertoire, found at the opening of Marston's *Jacke Drum's Entertainment*, where it sets the stage for Whitsuntide revelry. The Morris itself was associated with festivity, especially Christmas and Whitsunday, and hearkens back with sound and symbol to ancient pagan rites. Toward the end of the Elizabethan era, there was suddenly a great deal of interest in quaint native dances among the nobility,[21] and Marston's Morris is clearly a concession to that interest. But the dance itself, a standard but spectacular sort, occupies a unique place in the children's repertoire.

WEDDINGS

There was no single standard legally binding wedding ceremony in Elizabethan and Jacobean England, though marriage was, especially in propertied families, a very solemn and important rite of passage. Lawrence Stone reminds us that during the period, marriage was an engagement that could be undertaken in a bewildering variety of ways, and that its mere definition is something of a problem.[22] But for persons of property it involved five distinct steps: a written legal contract between the parents concerning financial arrangements, a formal exchange of oral promises, the public proclamation of banns in church to allow the pre-contract claims to be heard, the wedding in church, and the sexual consummation. These necessary steps were often dragged out over a period of time, and their very duration and variety held a great deal of dramatic potential. For example, the exchange of oral promises was as legally binding as the church wedding.[23] In contemporary drama, weddings are usually presented at the fourth step, the church, and a celebration with music, such as a masque or dance, is often held immediately thereafter. But conflict often arises over earlier unseen aspects of the marriage process, and a great deal of dramatic intrigue grows out of the binding nature of a previous contract, as illustrated by the marriage of Bellafront and Scudmore in *A Woman is a Weather-Cocke*. For during the closing years of the sixteenth century and the opening of the seventeenth, arranged marriages were still the norm, but the marriage based on romantic courtship was already a dream of young lovers.

During the late sixteenth and early seventeenth centuries, weddings were considered particularly good excuses for elaborate festivities that included sumptuous music.[24] Numerous masques were written by such men as Ben Jonson and Thomas Campion in honor of marriages between nobles houses, and almost no amount of spectacle was considered too much to celebrate such ultimately public events. Not only did music entertain guests and, in the case of masque, immortalize the bride and groom, but it clearly symbolized the hopes for a harmonious relationship. As Lentulus observes during the climactic wedding celebration in the anonymous *Everie Woman in her Humour*,

> Nay, nay we must have all friendes.
> Jarring discords are no marriage musick,
> Throw not Hymen in a cuckstoole, dimple
> Your furrowed browes, since all but mirth was meant,
> Let us not then conclude in discontent
>
> (*Everie Woman in her Humour*, Act V, scene i)

But, as we have already seen with the masque and the dance, musical harmony was used in the drama to underscore both personal harmony and discord.

Weddings, highly charged emotional events to start with, use music to both ends with unparalleled effect. And, in the case of thwarted love, it is hard to tell for whom the music sounds and whether it is to be interpreted as literal or ironic. Only the outcome of the play will tell which.

Weddings in the children's plays are depicted as great social and religious occasions with as many elaborate trappings as possible. Music normally accompanies the celebration following the church service, but occasionally the ceremony itself includes music. As in life, masques especially are associated with weddings, costly and involved though they may be, "for Comus and Hymen love maskes and all such merriment above measure."[25] And those weddings that are not celebrated on the children's stage with masques almost always include dance, "For dauncing is Loves proper exercise,"[26] and "is the kingdome of Venus and the empire of Cupid."[27]

Like the masques of all sorts and the social dances presented in the children's plays, wedding celebrations allow for the assembly of a large number of characters in a common place for a common purpose. Also like the masques and social dances, those weddings often become dramatic excuses to bring character emotions to the foreground and to further the plot by providing a reason for the confrontation between various individuals. Robert Armin's *The Two Maids of More-Clacke* includes one of the most detailed wedding scenes in the repertoire, and one that is extremely well integrated into the overall plot. The wedding, uniting Sir William Vergir and the widow Mrs. Humil, opens the play and sets up all of its major conflicts. We are brought in on preparations for the wedding, the wedding itself, and the festivities afterward, all of which serve to introduce us to the characters and their assorted conflicts. For contemporary weddings were frequently large public events that brought many people together. In this instance, the guests include James, the still-living husband of the supposed widow, who goes unannounced and unrecognized; the bride's son, who has been promised by his mother that he may wed the groom's eldest daughter, Mary; and Toures, his rival, whom Mary herself loves. Music accompanies the wedding from beginning to end, sounding ironic notes of false harmony against a growing recognition of personal discord.

At the start of the wedding sequence, the Waits of London arrive to play for the ceremony. Even before the solemnization of the marriage they begin to

> Make the gods dance, cause joviall mirth
> Musicke in heaven for this earthes marriage
> Is a triumphant concord in us all

just as the audience begins to understand that there will be little heavenly concord among the guests. The music continues beneath the "solemn shew of the marriage," and continues afterward beneath alternate displays of concord and contention among the characters:

Enter James with the musitions.

James.	Sound proclamation, It is inacted by the bride and bride-groome, And by our selfe chiefe in authoritie That all receive the pleasures From the most high in the assembly To the lowest, all pastimes are made free, Daucing, carding, dicing, revelling. And other dues oftime fit merriments, —Unto the bride and bride-groomes health.
Tabitha.	The daies short and the night's
Filbon.	Stop there.
Tabitha.	I will, to pleasure thee.
James.	There take your places. And in your sweetest key of musique strokes Sound pleasant melody, eccho those sounds Which true-love-hearts, in concords chiefest grounds Have their blest being, use art in times, Which may give welcome to our noblest guests.

Enter [young] Humil.

Toures.	We are betraid, young Humil is at hand, Daunce, and escuse it so.
Filbon.	Sound musique there.
Toures.	Content, a dance, and in againe. Content, no daunce, yet in againe. It is ungently don to snatch her so.
Humil.	I snatch but that which promise saies is mine, Have I offended?
Toures.	I
Humil.	Right what is wrong.
Toures.	Here,
[*Humil.*]	Or where you dare; go seek in Brainford, go.
Toures.	Brainford?
James.	Put up, or I shall be offended unto one, Against the brides sonne, dare ye?
Humil.	I repent not what is done, come you with me.
Toures.	So slaves by violence do hurry hence, The rights of—
James.	Peace, we on you impose a command Yeeld duty in it; a hall, a hall there. Musique sound, and to the bride do consecrate this round.

Enter all the traine to daunce.

Music accompanies the remainder of the scene, playing now beneath personal harmony, now beneath discord, now to reinforce a combination of the two, such as:

> *Humil snatches Mary from Toures and dances.*

> *They daunce a measure.*

Toures. How Goddes-like the elder of the two,
Stations the measure, it is a Joviall sight,
Where beauty guilds the pavement with her light.
How sullen Saturne tooke her by the hand,
With frosty feeling, in whose icy touch,
She shrunke her hold, but with a jealous eie,
She glanst at me, fearfull that standers by
Should be inrich't with't: now she smiles me faire,
Guilding my torture with an after hope.
Thus moroliz'd, I season on my right,
Her love thus challeng'd by inferior might.
> *The Daunce ends.*

The wedding music of Marston's *Sophonisba* is quite different, though no less important to the play. The wedding, which takes place in Act I, scene ii, fatefully unites the title character and the heroic Massinissa just before war wreaks havoc on their lives. The ceremony itself, which is never completed and becomes of central importance to the play for precisely that reason, adds greatly to both the plot and the play's Roman Carthaginian setting. It is presented as a sumptuous pagan ritual that blends ancient authority and contemporary custom in the anachronistic manner typical of the Renaissance. One of Marston's contemporaries reminds us that "The Romanes passed al other nations in pomp, ceremonies, and comlines of marriage,"[28] and the ceremony that we see is as sensual and exquisite as many a theatrical masque. It is the gods of Rome who are invoked in the ritual, yet it is the Renaissance ecclesiastical combination of cornetts, organ, and voices that provides the musical supplication. Furthermore, *The Arte of English Poesie* tells us of the Roman custom of singing at the bedding of the bride,[29] which is precisely what Marston shows us, yet the alternation of hymn and spoken prayer belongs to the church of Marston's time.

In the Prologue, Marston sets the scene for the wedding by telling us that

> . . . now the night
> Yeelds loud resoundings of the nuptiall pompe:
> Apollo strikes his harpe: Hymen his Torch

> Whilst lowring Juno with ill-boding eye
> Sits envious at too forward Venus.

But from this heavenly harmony and splendor we go not to the ceremony itself, but to the discordant plotting of the downfall of the new bride and groom by his rival. Upon this bitter note, we enter the wedding ceremony mid-progress, just as the bride's attendants are preparing her for bed. They lay her "in a faire bed" and draw the curtains about her, just as four boys appear on stage "antiquely attired with bows and quivers dauncing to the cornetts a phantastique measure," and the bridegroom follows with his attendants. When all have entered the stage,

the boyes draw the Curtaines discovering Sophonisba to whom Massinissa speakes.

Massinissa.	You powers of joy: Gods of a happie bed
	Show that you are pleas'd, sister and wife of Jove
	High fronted Juno and thou Carthage Patron
	Smoth chind Apollo, both give modest heat
	And temperat grace.

Mass[inissa] drawes a white ribbon forth of theb ed as from the waste of Sopho[nisba].

Massinissa.	Loe, I unloose thy waste
	She that is just in love is Godlike chaste: Io to Hymen.
	Chorus with cornets, Organ, and voices: Io to Hymen.
Sophonisba.	A modest silence tho'te be thought
	A virgins beautie and hir highest honor
	Though bashfull fainings nicely wrought
	Grace hir that virtue takes not in, but on hir.

> Give no mercy if these bands
> I covet not with unfaigned fervor
> Which zealous vow when ought can force me t'lame
> Loan with that plague Atlas would groane at, shame.
> Io to Hymen.

Chorus. Io to Hymen.

So the ceremony continues with similar spoken vows and hymeneal hymns until, with no warning, Cupid's dainty arrows turn to Mars':

Enter Carthalo his sword drawne, his body wounded, his shield strucke full of darts.

This sudden, unexpected event brings the proceedings to a premature close, as the bridegroom and his attendants are called instantly to arms. The wedding music of cornetts and organ continues as the bride is curtained alone in her bed by her ladies and the men rush heroically off to war, changing the music of love fulfilled to that of dreams destroyed. The exquisite visual detail and the music help implant the incomplete wedding in the minds of the audience. For the nobility and honor of the virgin wife become central to the play, and the theme of love unfulfilled recurs repeatedly in many forms.

BANQUETS

Banquets are most commonly held in children's plays to honor the important guests of the wealthy, and to show the immense hospitality of the host. Banquets were meant to be feasts for all senses, as *The Praise of Musicke* reminds us:

For otherwise why have the feastmakers provided meates for the mouth, sightes for the eye, perfumes for the nose, yea, why have they strowned Violets and Roses for the feet to walke upon, but to allure and detaine their guestes with all manner of delectation? And must the eare sleepe al this while?[30]

The ear certainly did not sleep during stage banquets, for music had a distinct place in contemporary feasts of all sorts:

So kind is Musik at a Feast, dat it is compared to a ric Juel: and is preferred, at dat tim', even befor' wise speaking.[31]

Indeed, even the antimusician Stephen Gosson recognizes positive benefit in the music performed at solemn feasts.[32] Such entertainment was a mark of excellent taste as well as wealth and social status:

Your Princes, Emperors, and persons of any quality, maintaine it in their Courts: no mirth without musicke. So Thomas Moore, in his absolute Utopian commonwealth, allowes musicke as an appendix to every meale, and that throughout, to all sorts. Epictetus calls mensam mutam, praesepe, a table without musicke a manger, for the consent of Musitians at a banquet, is a carbuncle set in gold, and as the signet of an emerald well trimmed with gold, so is the melody of Musicke in a pleasant banket.[33]

The melody of music is featured at banquets of all sorts in children's plays, and, as with music for other occasions, serves to reinforce elements of plot and setting. The type and amount of music varies with the type of banquet, its participants, and its importance to the main plot of the drama, but it nearly always includes a song. Unlike masques, dances, and weddings, there tends to be no central symbolic value to the banquet, and there is little movement to musical accompaniment.

The most common sort of musical feast is that for which the music simply helps to create an atmosphere of festivity and shows the resources and refinement of the host. The music of such feasts ranges from simple supper entertainment that implies music to be a normal part of well-healed dining in the world of the play:

The curtaines are drawn by a page, and Celia and Laverdure, Quadratus and Lyzabetta, Lampatho and Meletza [,] Simplicus and Lucea displayed sitting at dinner. The song is sung, during which a page whispers with Simplicus.

(Marston, *What You Will*, Act V, scene i)

to more spectacular music whose intent is to show diners and the audience that they are not dealing with the ordinary, and should thus be wary of what is to come:

Enter Enchanter, leading Lucilia and Lassingbergh bound by spirits, who being laid down on a green banck, the spirits fetch in a banquet.

THE SONG [by the spirits]

Oh princely face and fayre, that lightens all the ayre,
Would God my eyes kinde fire, might life and soule inspire:
To thy riche beauty shining in my hearts treasure,
The unperfect words refining, for perfect pleasure.

(*The Wisdom of Dr. Dodypoll*, Act III, scene v).

The most musically detailed banquet in the children's repertoire is that in Act II, scene i of Middleton's *A Mad World My Masters*, whose dramatic purpose is principally to show the great wealth of Sir Bounteous Progress and his easy gullibility. Its purpose is to honor a sham "Lord" who, unbeknownst to his host, is actually Sir Bonteous's dishonest grandson, Follywit, in disguise. The episode upholds the contemporary tradition of employing music to honor distinguished guests.[34] The music in this instance is performed by the musicians maintained by Sir Bounteous as part of his impressive household retinue. The first gesture to the visiting "Lord," who secretly plans to carry off some of his host's more portable treasures, is not gastronomic but musical:

Sir Bounteous.   . . . My musick, give my lord a taste of his welcome.

A straine plaid by the consort, Sir Bounteous makes a courtly honor to that l[ord] and seemes to foot the tune.

Sir Bounteous.   So, how like you our aires, my lord?
                  Are they choice?
Follywit.   Theyr seldom match', beleeve it.
Sir Bounteous.   The consort of mine own household.
Follywit.   Yea Sir.
Sir Bounteous.   The musitians are in ordinary, yet no ordinary musitians.
                  Your lordship shall hear my organs now.

Follywit.   O I beseech you, Sir Bounteous.
Sir Bounteous.   My organist.
The organs play and cover'd dishes march over the stage.
[Shortly thereafter, as they partake of the feast, there is *"A song to the Organs."*]

Banquets, like masques, social dances, and weddings, do sometimes provide an excellent cover for underhanded dealings. Of course, with food and drink present and grand visual distraction from overt mischief absent, the obvious deed is the clandestine tampering with the meals of certain guests. In such a scene, especially if the audience is aware of what is going on, music may be used to prolong suspense, as in Act II, scene i of *The Wisdom of Dr. Dodypoll*:

Musick sounds a while; and they sing, Boire a le fountaine.

Cassimere.   How like you him my Lord?
Alberto.   Exceeding well. *Sing Boyre a le fountaine.*
Flores.   Cornelia, do you serve the Prince with wine?
           She puts the powder into the Cup and gives it to the
           Prince [*Alberto*].
Alberto.   I thanke you Lady.
           Earle *Cassimere*, I greete you; and remember
           Your faire Hyanthe.
Cassimere.   I thanke your honour. *Sing boyre a, etc.*
Flores.   Fill my lord Cassimere his right of wine.
Cassimere.   Cornelia, I give you this dead carowse.
Cornelia.   I thanke your Lordship. *Sing boyre a, etc.*
Alberto.   What smoake? smoake and fire?
Cassimere.   What meanes your honour?
Alberto.   Powder, powder, Etna, Sulphure, fier; quench it, quench
           it.
Flores.   I feare the medicine hath distemper'd him, O villaine
           Doctor.
Alberto.   Downe with the battlements, powre water on,
           I burne, I burne; I give me leave to file
           Out of these flames; these flames that compasse me.
                         Exit

On the printed page, this episode moves far faster than it would have in the theater, for the complete song would have been sung each time the incipit is printed. In this manner, suspense over the administration of the potion to the unsuspecting Alberto and its effect on him would have been drawn out over an extended time.

Formal banquets are the province of the wealthy and privileged in these plays, as in life, but many others eat and drink to a musical background on the children's stages. Taverns are almost always musical in English Renaissance drama, as they apparently were in life. Taverns, more so than the banqueting halls of the nobility, were noisy, busy places, as Bishop John Earle reminds us:

Men come here [to a tavern] to make merry, but indeed make a noise, and this musicke above is answered with clanking below.[35]

Such places often attracted a roguish clientele, not the least of whom are the downtrodden fiddlers hired by the guests. But they are frequently joined by the drunken singing of the guests, as in Act III, scene iii of Chapman's *May Day*, in which Quintiliano adds his bawdy song snatches to the playing of the fiddlers. Such music always adds a lively and realistic background to tavern scenes, as in Act II, scene ii of Beaumont and Fletcher's *The Scornful Lady*:

> *Enter Young Lovelesse and his Comrades, with wenches, and two Fydlers.*
>
> **Young Loveless.**   Come my brave man of war, trace out thy darling,
> And you my learned Councell, set and turne boyes:
> Kisse till the Cow come home, kisse close, kisse close knaves.
> My moderne Poet, thou shalt kisse in couplets.
>
> > *Enter with wine*
>
> Strike up merry varlets, and leave your peeping,
> This is no pay for Fidlers.

Tavern music is almost always atmospheric and of little influence on the plot, and is used most frequently in city comedies.

RELIGIOUS RITUAL AND WORSHIP

The pagan dance to Pan from Fletcher's *Faithful Shepherdess* is but one of many examples of musical religious ritual in the children's plays. Formal Christian worship is not depicted on the children's stage, in spite of the chorister background of some of the actors. Pagan worship is, however, vibrant and musical, clearly deriving authority from accounts of the importance of music in the ancient world and in the early Church, and from its use in contemporary English church services.

Nearly every contemporary writer concerned with the use of music stresses its importance as a link between mankind and his creator. Music was literally a harmonious force, capable of appeasing all creation:

Homer makes the Gods to pacify their dissention with musicke: and Achilles with his owne to digest his anger. . . David (who with his harp subdued the evill Spirit which vexed Saule) introduced harmony into the Temple, as suting well with that divine service: Yea even the glorified Spirits are described with harps in their hands, and singing the praises of the Almighty.[36]

The worship of gods on stage was merely a metaphor for the worship of God in church, and it occupied the same social and philosophical position in the lives of stage characters and living Englishmen. Naturally, attitudes such as "Dhe first use of Musick is in devine service and woorship of God,"[37] and "since it [music] is a principall means of glorifying our merciful Creator, it heightens our devotion,"[38] are upheld equally by Elizabethan and Jacobean Englishmen and their stage creatures. While other sorts of musical ceremony and spectacle may include elements of wit, suspense, humor, terror, or pathos, scenes of religious ritual and worship tend to be straightforward and pure, masking no subplots or subtle motivations. They simply serve to glorify the superior beings whom the characters worship.

The majority of religious scenes are rather uninteresting from the perspective of dramatic effect or clever integration of music and drama. They most often consist of a simple entry of the devout, or a rearrangement of the devout on stage, followed by a song in praise of a particular deity. A number of such scenes take place in temples, but others occur in field or forest to show the omnipresence of the deity in the character's world.

However, intense dramatic interest may arise from the integration of such scenes into the larger structure of the drama. The opening act of Beaumont and Fletcher's *Cupid's Revenge* includes an excellent example; it sets the tone of treachery, incompletion, and tragic love for the entire play. In Act I, scene ii, a musical service to the title deity is interrupted in his holy temple:

> *Enter Priest of Cupid, with foure young men and Maydes.*
>
> **Priest.**   Come my children, let your feete
>   In an even Measure meete:
>   And your cheerefull voyces rise,
>   For to present this Sacrifice
>   To great Cupid, in whose name,
>   I his Priest begin the same.
>   Yong men take your Loves and kisse,
>   Thus our Cupid honoured is.
>   Kisse againe, and in your kissing,
>   Let no promises be missing:
>   Nor let any Mayden here,
>   Dare to turne away her eare,
>   Unto the whisper of her Love,
>   But give Bracelet, Ring, or Glove,
>   As a token to her sweeting,

Of an after secret meeting:
Now boy sing, to sticke our hearts
Fuller of great Cupids darts.

SONG

Lovers rejoice, your paines shall be rewarded,
The god of love himselfe grieves at your crying;
No more shall frozen honour be regarded,
Nor the coy faces of a maid denying.
No more shall Virgins sigh, and say we dare not,
For men are false, and what they doe they care not.
All shall be well againe, then doe not greeve,
Men shall be true, and women shall beleeve.

Lovers rejoyce, what you shall say henceforth,
When you have caught your Sweet-hearts in your armes,
It shall be accounted Oracle, and worth:
No more faint-hearted Gyrles shall dreame of harmes,
And cry they are too young: the god hath said,
Fiftene shall make a Mother of a Mayd:
Then wise men, pull your Roses yet unblowne,
Love hates the too ripe fruit that falles alone.

The Measure.

After the Measure enter Nilo and others.

Nilo.   No more of this: here breake your Rights for ever,
The Duke commands it so; Priest doe not stare,
I must deface your temple, though unwilling,
And your god Cupid here must make a Scarcrow
For any thing I know, or at best,
Adorne a Chimney-peece.

This scene, with its sudden defilement of the ceremony and temple, not only sets the mood for the rest of the play, but, like other spectacular scenes, shows a great contrast between the elegant ritual and destructive interruption. The text of the song becomes ironic as the play progresses, for its optimistic promises are thwarted one by one just as the sacred rite was ended suddenly and prematurely.

Only three times are specific sorts of ritual named in children's plays, and all are sacrifices. One is the above example, another is in Lyly's *Love's Metamorphosis* (Act I, scene ii), and the third is Marston's *Sophonisba* (Act III, scene i). *The Praise of Musicke* describes sacrifices as musical, and defines them as "sacred or rather profane churchrites used amon[n]gst the heathe[n] and paga[n]s in reverence to their supposed gods."[39] The sacrifice in *Love's Metamorphosis* is also performed in honor of Cupid, but no details concerning the music are provided. The sacrifice in *Sophonisba* is dedicated to cunning Mercury and chaste Phoebe in the hopes that the two will give the heroine a means to protect her chastity against human or inhuman onslaughts. But the description of the music that accompanies the ritual could well have applied to any Sunday or holy day celebration in Marston's England:

Cornets and organs playing full musick. Enters the solemnity of a sacrifice, which being entered whilst the attendance furnish the altar Sopho[nisba's] songe: which don shee speakes.

(*Sophonisba*, Act III, scene i)

FUNERALS

Death was treated significantly differently in sixteenth- and seventeenth-century England than in succeeding eras.[40] Death was not a time for private grief, but a time for the performance of elaborate public ritual. Funerals themselves were conducted on a grand civic scale which did not allow for private mourning; and among the aristocracy, the funeral was an opulent and expensive ritual.[41] Pomp and pageantry were used to demonstrate the wealth, power, and influence of the family; and, when appropriate, the funeral became an ostentatious symbol of the transfer of authority from the dead man to his successor.[42]

Funerals have certain musical similarities to other rites, both on and off the stage. Like religious rituals of other sorts, music serves as a link during the funeral between this world and the next. Like banquets, the music is but one facet of a display of wealth and propriety. Like weddings, funerals are rites of passage in which music traditionally occupies a prominent place. Like dances, funerals include stylized movement; and, in plays, marches or dead marches are often indicated. Like most musical rituals shown on stage, only part of a complete funeral is generally presented, enough to suggest a real funeral but not enough to alter the careful pacing of the complete play. The specific purposes of music in funerals were considered to be "to solemnize de funerals of honourable Personages: and sweetly to c[h]eer de sad and drooping spirits of de Moorners."[43] Like other musical activities, there was a strong consensus that funerals had been similarly musical in classical antiquity.[44] And, like a number of other musical spectacles of the children's stages, sumptuous funerals are associated overwhelmingly with wealthy and prestigious individuals, no matter what the setting of the play.

The double purpose of funerary music, to honor the dead and cheer the living, could lead to some very striking dramatic effects. These effects depend on the cause of death and the composition of the party of mourners. The stage funeral, like the stage wedding, was often presented in such a manner that varying emotions among the assembled characters came to the foreground in rapid succession, with a musical background to reinforce attitudes toward the dead or lend them a touch of macabre irony. Like the other rituals shown on stage, only a brief part of what was normally a lengthy, elaborate procedure was used by the dramatists.[45] For dramatic purposes, the funeral procession was clearly the favorite and most effective. The children's theaters used quite a number of these funeral processions, whose complete effect could have been greatly increased by the use of appropriate dress, gesture, and music.[46]

The standard funeral on the children's stage consists of an entry of mourners and coffin to music, with perhaps a few lines of dialogue. Most often the entry of the funeral train is presented as a pantomime, and the very absence of the spoken word greatly increases the stark effectiveness of the scene. The typical funeral may be accompanied by instrumental music:

Enter a friar, after him a funerall in white, and bearers in white, after them Borgias, then two dukes, after them a senate, etc.

A solemne march.
(Mason, *Muleasses the Turke*, Act I, scene iii)

Or there may be an additional song of mourning:

Solemnpe [sic] musique to a funerall song the hearse borne over the stage, Duke Lurdo, Polymetes, Angelo, Ivlio, Horatio, and mourners etc. Exeunt.

Manet Horatio.
(Day, *Law Tricks*, Act V)

Some funerals add other details to this basic outline when there is dramatic reason to do so. One such funeral is presented in Act IV, scene iv of Beaumont's *Knight of the Burning Pestle*. This particular episode revolves around the device of the sham funeral. The cheerless entry of the hearse and the time it spends on stage are prolonged for suspense so that the dead man's "reanimation" will come as an even greater surprise. The entry is lengthened by both speech and song, and by a marvelous display of extreme, but ultimately unnecessary, grief. After a man and boy bring her the coffin of her beloved Jasper, Luce dismisses both and launches into a long soliloquy, which concludes:

> And see what I prepare to decke thee with,
> It shall go up, borne on the wings of peace
> And satisfied: first will I sing thy dirge,
> Then kisse thy pale lips, and then die my selfe,
> And fill one Coffin and one grave together.

SONG

Come you whose loves are dead,
And whiles I sing
Weepe and wring
Every hand and every head,
Bind with Cipres and sad Ewe,
Ribands black and candles blew,
For him that was of men most true.
Come with heavy mourning,
And on his grave
Let him have
Sacrifice of sighes and groaning,
Let him have fair flowers enow,
White and purple, green and yellow,
For him that was of men most true.

Thou sable cloth, sad cover of my joyes
I lift thee up, and thus I meete with death.

Jasper.	And thus you meete the living.
Luce.	Save me heaven!
Jasper.	Nay do not flie me faire, I am no spirit, Look better on me do you know me yet?
Luce.	O thou deere shadow of my friend.
Jasper.	Deere substance, I sweare I am no shadow, feele my hand, It is the same it was, I am your Jasper.

The funeral that opens Act II of Marston's *Antonio's Revenge* is prolonged for more sinister reasons. There is no comical outcome here, no happy reunion between lost lovers, but only layer upon layer of corruption. Contrasting attitudes toward the dead are expressed against a background of cornett music, from the tears of the bereaved widow Maria and her son Antonio to the rude talking of the guilty murderer and his accomplice:

The cornets sound a cynet. Enter two mourners with torches, two with streamers: Castilio & Forobosco with torches: a herald bearing Andrugio's helme and sword, the coffin: Maria supported by Lucio and Alberto, Antonio by himselfe Piero and Strotzo talking, Galeatzo and Matzagente, Balurdo and Pandulpho; the coffin set down, helme, sword, and streamers hung up, placed by the herald, whilst Antonio and Maria wet their handkerchers with teares, kisse them, and lay them on the hearse, kneeling. All go out but Piero. Cornets cease and he speakes.

Piero.	Rot there, thou cerecloth that enfolds the flesh Of my loath'd foe; molder to crumbling dust.

The effect of the scene is heightened by the replacement of the spoken word with music as the mimed actions of the participants speak for them against the background of the cornett processional.

ARMED COMBAT

During the Renaissance, war became, like other rituals, a symbol of harmony or of discord. Furthermore, the militarism of bygone days relied on the sounds of loud, piercing instruments to give direction to the soldiers and to sound the changes in the fortunes of both sides of a skirmish. The many battles and other military exercises on the children's stage are accompanied by music, partly for these reasons, and partly because music itself can greatly increase the effectiveness of mimed action on the stage and give the illusion of a far larger space than the tiny stage afforded. There was certainly a high degree of military realism in the music of stage battles, permitting many an author and his players to bring to the theater "A fearefull Battaile rendred you in Musique."[46] The sounds of war emanating from drum and trumpet or cornett helped the audience picture many more soldiers than they saw on the stage, and, in the case of the child actors, imagine that the young men and boys before them were fully grown to manhood—and to war.

The music of war, like that of more peaceful activities brought to the stage, was used for similar reasons on stage and off. "To this end are instruments used in battaile," says Stephen Gosson, "not to tickle the eare, but to teach every soldier when to strike and when to stay, when to flye, and when to followe."[47] A Renaissance military treatise adds:

What the hoste of thyne enemyes is nere, good it is, to com[m]aunde all the fewelers to buylde their fyres, the tro[m]pets blowe up alarum, al the host to make an outcrye, and briefelye to fyll heaven and earth wyth the noise and sounde of tro[m]pettes, and make all on a rore, wherwith thyne enemyes may be afrayed; & thy fre[n]des gladdened.[48]

A battle well fought was a kind of harmony in the Renaissance language of symbol, and the movements of its soldiers a kind a dance. In the theater, where reality and symbol met, the music of battle of course took on both dimensions at once. It governed the choreography of combatants, encouraged the raging fight toward its ordered end, and stood literally or ironically for heroism and order.

No act of physical aggression is without musical accompaniment on the boys' stage, and, if sheer numbers of stage directions are considered, musical indications of warlike matters outnumber those for all peaceful pastimes put together. Most of these directions are extremely simple and indicate the individual signals of battle one by one, such as "cornets sound a charge," "flourish," or "a march." One reason for their comparatively large number, then, is the brevity of each indicated sound; a battle consists of many different brief signals, while a dance or masque that lasts as long needs call for music only once.

The music in scenes of military activity may help to create a cohesive scene when there is a good deal of dialogue and diverse action in rapid succession. It reminds the audience that a fierce battle is raging all the while:

Alarum within: excursions over the stage. The lackies running. Maillard following them.

[dialogue]

Alarum still, and enter Chalon.

[more dialogue]

Showts within. Alarum still. And chambers shot off.
Then enter Aumal.

(Chapman, *The Revenge of Bussy D'Ambois*, Act IV, scene i)

Music can also create the illusion of a larger acting space, and help to imply that what is visible to the audience is merely the periphery of a large battlefield whose main action is far away:

Scena tertia. The cornets afar off sounding a charge, a souldier wounded at one dore, enters at the other Sophonisba, two pages before her with lightes, two women bearing up her traine.

(Marston, *Sophonisba*, Act V, scene iii)

The Cornetts sound a flourish.

[Piero.]	What means this fresh triumphall sound?
Alberto.	The Prince of Milan, and young Florence heir,
	Approach to gratulate your victory.
Piero.	We'll girt them with an ample waist of love
	Conduct them to our presence royally.
	Let volleys of the great artillery
	From off our galleys' bankes play prodigall
	And sound loud welcome from their bellowing mouths.

Exit Piero tantum.

The cornets sound a cynet. Enter above, Mellida, Rossaline and Flavia: enter below, Galeatzo with attendants; Piero meeteth him, embraceth; at which the cornets sound a flourish: Piero and Galeatzo exeunt.

The rest stand still.

Mellida.   What prince was that passed through my father's guard?

(Marston, *Antonio and Mellida*, Act I, scene i)

Music may also add an extra dimension to mimed gestures of fighting and military display:

Here the cornets sound, they fight, and Philocles overcomes the Duke, the queen de[sc]ends.

(Markham and Machin, *The Dumb Knight*, Act I)

Cornets sound a march,. Scipio leads his traine up to the mount.

(Marston, *Sophonisba*, Act V, scene ii)

Scena secunda. Cornets sound marches. Enter Scipio and Lelius with the complements of a Roman generall before them, at the other dore, Massinissa and Juggurth.

(Marston, *Sophonisba*, Act III, scene ii)

SERENADES

The serenade, a common device in contemporary drama, represents a very different social occasion from any so far described. Unlike the others, it is by no means public nor is it held to commemorate some grand occasion, rite of passage, or political event. It involves few people, and centers on only two. But it is a standard sort of social activity with its own social significance. The serenade belongs to the courtship ritual and is but a gentle gesture of love that relies on the great affective power and eloquence of music. Elizabethan and Jacobean thought held that the amorist was naturally driven to music:

Amongst all other good qualities, an amorous fellow is endowed with, he must learne to sing and daunce, play upon some Instrument or other, as without all doubt he will, if hee be truly touched with this Loadstone of Love. For as Erasmus haith it, *Musicam docet amor & poesin,* Love will make them Musitians, and to make ditties, Madrigals, Elegies, and Love Sonnets, and sing them to severall pretty tunes, to get all good qualities may be had.[49]

Women were believed naturally susceptible to such musical pleas:

many things are taken in hande to please women withal, whose tender and soft breastes are soon pierced with melody, and fylled with swetenesse.[50]

In late Renaissance England, serenades must have been both common and effective, for Stephen Gosson advises "the Gentlewomen of London" to stay modestly at home where they belong, and suggests that

if you perceive your selves in any danger at your owne doores, either allured by curtesie in the day, or assaulted with Musick in the night; Close up your eyes, stoppe your eares, tye up your tongues.[51]

However, the serenading amorists of the children's stage cause few moral dangers for the women they love. Almost invariably, they are doltish lovers for whom the ladies have at best pity and at worst contempt. They are so out of tune with the objects of their adoration that they require the artificial aid of music to achieve notice. And the goal of their serenades is to gain the attention of the hard-hearted women who will not return their love. Normally, they request a servant or hired musician to perform the music:

Puff.   Boy cleare thy throate, and mount thy sweetest notes
Upon the bosom of this sleeke cheekt aire:
That it may gently breathe them in the eare
Of my adored Mistresse: Come begin.

THE SONG

Delicious beautie that doth lie
Wrapt in a skin of ivorie,
Lie stil. lie stil upon thy backe,
And fancy let no sweete dreames lacke
To tickle her, to tickle her with pleasing thoughts.
But if thy eyes are open full,
Then daine to view an honest gull,
That stands, that stands, expecting still
When thy Casement open will
And blesse his eyes, & blesse his eyes, with one kind glance.

The casement opens, and Katherine appeares.

Puff.   All happinesse and unconceiv'd delight,
Waite on the love of sweet fac'd Katherine.

Katherine.   Good youth Amen, I do returne your wish
With ample interest of beatitude.

(Marston, *Jacke Drum's Entertainment*, Act II, scene i)

Though the lovelorn man is rarely a competent musician, sometimes he selects or even authors the song he wishes sung. He may suggest how and why the singer perform, and, occasionally dissatisfied, request repeat performances until they yield results:

Jacomo.   Boy could not Orpheus make the stones to dance?

Phylus.   Yes Sir.

Jacomo.   Bir Lady, a sweet touch: did he not bring Euridice out of hell with his lute?

Phylus.   So they say Sir.

Jacomo.   And thou canst bring Celias head out of the window with thy Lute, well hazard thy breath: look see here's a ditty. Tis fowly writ, slight wit cross'd here and there, But where thou findst a blot, there fell a teare.

THE SONG

Fie peace, peace, peace, it hath no passion in't.
O melt thy breath in fluent softer tunes
That evry note may seeme to trickle downe
Like sad distilling teares and make: O God
That I were but a Poet now t'expresse my thoughts
Or a Musitian but to sing my thoughts
Or any thing but what I am, sing't ore once more
My greefes a boundles sea that hath no shore.
Hee sings and is answered, from above a Willow
garland is flung downe and the song ceaseth.

(Marston, *What You Will*, Act I, scene i)

A song is not completely necessary to a serenade; sometimes instrumental music accomplishes the same end, as in Act V of Barry's *Ram Alley*, in which Sir Oliver Small-Shanks hires a troupe of fiddlers to do the job:

Sir Oliver.   Now fresh and youthful as the month of May,
Ile bid my Bride good morrow, musitians on,
Lightly, lightly and by my Knighthood spurres,
This yeere you shall have my protection,
And yet not buy your livery coates your selves.

But, no matter what medium is used, such serenades are rarely successful; poor Sir Oliver is already too late, for his bride is enjoying the fresh morning in the arms of another man.

Lovelorn fools are not the only characters to sing serenades in children's plays. Occasionally, ardent women may sing to men with the hopes of undoing them, but these immodest creatures are clearly unnatural, and wise men shun their siren's ways:

Camelia.   Looke, on my knees I creepe,
Be not impenetrable beautious youth,
But smile on me, and Ile make the aire
Court thy choyce eare with soft delicious sounds.
Bring forth the Violls, each one play his part,
Musick's the quiver of young Cupids dart.

The Song With The Violls

Planet.   Out Syren, peace scritch-owle, hence chattering Pye,
The black beakt Crow, or the howling Dog,
Shall be more gracious then thy squeaking voice:
Go sing to M. John. I shall be blunt

> If thou depart not, hence, go mourne and die,
> I am the scourge of thy light inconstancie.

(Marston, *Jacke Drum's Entertainment*, Act IV)

The music for ceremony, spectacle, and social occasion in the children's plays is at once a mirror of contemporary life and thought and of the dramatist's command of his art.

CHAPTER 7

MUSIC FOR CHARACTERIZATION

Music is not only an art with its own laws and values; it is also a social fact. Composing, performing, listening to music are things which human beings do under certain circumstances just as they fight and make love. Moreover, in the Elizabethan age, music was regarded as an important social fact.

W. H. Auden, "Music in Shakespeare,"
The Dyer's Hand and Other Essays

The use of music for characterization in Elizabethan and Jacobean drama has long fascinated poets, literary critics, and musicologists. In a theater of the spoken word, each musician and each piece of music is conspicuous, literally sounding in a different voice. Numerous scholars have shown that this dramatically exceptional music helped point to an individual's exceptional mental or emotional state, or unusually sympathetic nature.[1] Elizabethan and Jacobean theatrical music for characterization has therefore been considered a simple device through which playwright and audience alike could separate the insane from the rational, the sincere from the deceitful, and the heroic from the villainous. However, this reductive theory, central to previous scholarship, has proven inadequate when applied to the complex dimensions of the English Renaissance theater. Too many irredeemable villains are musical, too few lovers or madmen rely on music to indicate their distracted state, and too many musicians and music lovers lie outside the world of predictable abnormality. Furthermore, when one delves deeply into late Renaissance character and courtesy literature, one begins to realize that gender, social status, and sense of propriety all influenced musical performance in life and on the stage.

Music is much more than a convention for revealing a character's emotional state or trustworthiness. Music, as part of the social fabric of life, joins the other symbols of the stage to illustrate social standing, occupation, and comprehension of propriety. Unlike the classical drama so much admired by Renaissance thinkers, Elizabethan and Jacobean plays bring together characters from many social strata, who must, in the class-conscious world of the time, be separated from each other by any means possible. An individual's music, like his costume, movement, and language, helps to place him in the proper social or professional niche. Music was far from the equal province of all persons in late sixteenth- and early seventeenth-century England. Not everyone had the same amount of time or money to invest in musical training, or the same leisure to enjoy it. Not everyone heard and learned the same sorts of music, and not everyone had equal access to all musical institutions. And not every character on the stage was drawn from life, though each musical individual had a nondramatic antecedent. Each sort of music and each circumstance under which it is performed provides a clue to the character's status in the world of the play. And these things were observed equally in the adults' and children's theaters.

Underlying one vital aspect of musical characterization was the widespread Renaissance concept that all sorts of harmony and discord could be represented in practical terms through audible music. English humanists adopted the Platonic doctrine that showed sympathy between the order of a man's spirit and the ordered harmony of music. William Shakespeare's elegant summary of this principle, from Act V, scene i of *The Merchant of Venice*, speaks for his entire age:

> The man that hath no Musique in himselfe,
> Nor is not moved with concord of sweet sounds,
> Is fit for treasons, stratagems, and spoiles;
> The motions of his spirit are dull as night,
> And his affections darke as Erebus:
> Let no such man be trusted.

Or, in the words of one of the children's playwrights,

> According to my master *Platos* minde
> The soule is musick, and doth therefore joy
> In accents musicall, which he that hates
> With points of discord is togeather tyed
> And barkes at *Reason*, consonant in sense.

(Chapman, *Sir Gyles Goose-cappe*, Act III, scene ii)

The overt connection between internal balance and an outward love of music was quite widespread and completely unambiguous:

I dare not passe so rash a censure as *Pindar* doth, or the *Italian*, having fitted a proverbe to the same effect, *Whom God loves not, that man loves not Musicke*: but I am verily perswaded, they are by nature very ill disposed and of such brutish stupiditie, that scarce any thing else that is good and savoreth of virtue, is to be found in them.[2]

However, only a small percentage of the musical performances on the children's stage provide direct insight into individual souls, and only a few of the most completely honorable characters have an opportunity to reveal their attitudes toward music. Most of the children's characters who savor little of virtue and who are fit for treasons, stratagems, and spoils are far from brutish stupidity. Many know music's power and its place in society, so music becomes as much a part of depravity as of virtue. Marston's malignant Piero of the *Antonio* plays fills his court with as much music as any other Duke, and the same author's Franceschina, *The Dutch Courtesan*, is one of the most musical of all the children's characters. Indeed, nowhere in the repertoire does an individual confess an unqalified dislike of music, for few people are so stupid as to admit themselves churlish and untrustworthy.

The music makers and music lovers depicted on the children's stages between 1597 and 1613 are extremely diverse. Although only a small minority of characters in these potentially very musical plays perform or listen to music, they come from all social classes, genders, and philosophical backgrounds, and even the supernatural world. They represent a good cross-section of the sorts of characters who populate these plays in general, and nearly all use music in accordance with specific nondramatic thought and custom. But each musical individual becomes conspicuous through his or her performance, a technique that helps to develop a fuller, more complex characterization.

The children's musical characters are clearly based on the same body of thought as the adults', but there are a few differences. Intriguingly, there are no singing madmen in children's drama though they are stock figures in the adults' theater. However, the children's plays give us courtiers and courtesans who perform the instrumental accompaniments to their own songs, and numerous groups of professional musicians who provide a fascinating glimpse into their position in society. There are also larger numbers of supernatural beings who participate in elaborate musical numbers than in contemporary adult drama, and there are pert groups of servants whose principal dramatic function seems to be the performance of elaborate polyphonic song. In general, the lower an individual's social status or the farther removed he is from humankind, the more likely he is to sing or play an instrument. But a broader spectrum of individuals may request music, and thus be characterized through the performance of another.

TRADESMEN, ARTISANS, CITIZENS AND ROGUES

More music is assigned to tradesmen, artisans, citizens, rogues, and others who work for their livelihood than to any other group of characters in children's drama. Honest London merchants had little in common with drunken vagabonds in the world outside the theater. But in children's plays, perhaps in response to the higher social standing of the theater audience, both tend to be assigned similar sorts of music. With few exceptions, these characters are assigned pre-existent popular unaccompanied songs or unaccompanied songs written in popular style. These songs range from what may represent genuine "folk song" to broadside ballads to unaccompanied solo versions of some of the more widely circulating lute ayres of such composers as John Dowland and Robert Jones. The two major exceptions to this rule are the servants of classically-inspired comedies who are given a very special musical function, and the rustics of mythological or pastoral comedy who more closely resemble the lofty nymphs and demigods with whom they consort than the low-lives of other sorts of drama. Both of these groups will be given separate consideration.

William R. Bowden has suggested that all tradesmen and other commoners who sing on stage do so because they are joyful.[3] Many such characters do indeed sing for joy or may be described as joyful, but a large body of nondramatic literature from the era explains that laborers of all sorts sang at their work to pass the time and ease the tedium of their tasks. As Robert Burton explains,

[music] cures all irksomeness and heaviness of the soule. Labouring men that sing to their works, can tell as much, and so can Souldiers when they go to fight, whom terror of death cannot so much affright, as Musicke animates.[4]

Therefore, as *The Praise of Musicke* adds,

And hence it is, that manual laborers, and Mechanicall artificers of all sorts, keepe such a chaunting and singing in their shoppes, the Tailor on his bulk, the Shoemaker at his last, the Mason at his wal, the ship-boy at his oare, the Tinker at his pan, & the tylor on the house top. And therfor wel saith Quintilian, that every troublesom & laborious occupation, useth music for a solace & recreatio[n].[5]

Craftsmen and manual workers, then, are not musical because of joyful dispositions, but because music makes their dull, repetitive tasks more bearable.

The laborers of children's drama are frequently shown singing at their work. They often perform or begin long ballads whose detailed stories and multiple stanzas would keep them occupied for quite some time. A typical example is Juniper, the industrious cobbler of Jonson's *His Case is Altered*.

Thomas Deloney reminds us that cobblers are among those men who relieve their tedium with music, for

their minds are never lightly on their business; for it is an old proverb:
They prove Servants kind and good
That sing at their business like birds in a Wood.[6]

In Jonson's play, Juniper "is discovered, sitting at worke in his shoppe and singing." He begins what is clearly meant to be a long ballad, but is discourteously interrupted by the hasty and semihysterical entrance of Onion:

[Juniper.]	*You woefull wights give eare a while,*
	And marke the tenor of my stile
	(Enter Onion in hast)
[Juniper.]	*You woefull wights give eare a while,*
[Juniper.]	*You woefull wights give eare a while,*
	Which shall such trembling hearts unfold
	As seldom hath to fore bene told.
	Such chances rare and doleful newes
Onion.	Fellow *Juniper* peace a Gods name.
[Juniper continues]	*As may attempt your wits to muse*
Onion.	Gods so, heere man. A pox a God on you.
[Juniper,	
ignoring him]	*And cause such trickling teares to passe,*
	Except your hearts be flint or brasse:
Onion.	Juniper, Juniper.
[Juniper continues]	*To heare the newes which I shall tell,*
	That in Castella once befell
[he speaks]	Sbloud, what didst thou learne to corrupt a man
	in the middle of a verse, ha?
	(Act I, scene i)

Juniper's lyric, probably written by Jonson specifically for the play, follows the style of numerous ballads of the era. And a singing cobbler, such as Juniper, did not require formal musical training or literacy, for his songs were part of an oral tradition. All he needed was a keen ear and a good memory, for such songs were strophic, their textual rhythm regular, and their music generally simple. But such a song would not be ill-served should it be sung by a trained choirboy such as the one who probably played the part.

Song was such a central part of a workman's characterization that those who disguised themselves as such had to add music to their tools of the trade. In Robert Armin's *The Two Maids of More-Clacke*, Toures disguises himself as a tinker, and goes to seek appropriate work from any who might require his services—especially the family of his beloved Mary. The tinker was another tradesman who was considered especially musical, for it was believed, "For his art was musick first invented, and therefore is he alwaies furnisht with a song."[7] Toures, being a clever young man, realizes that to be a convincing tinker, he cannot simply be furnisht with pots, pans, tools, and appropriate attire. He also has to have a ready song in his heart and on his lips. In fact, when Madge recognizes him as "the merry tinker of Twitnam," she asks his boy whether he "has his old songs still." And by singing a rollicking ballad in the same scene, he even deceives Mary and her family into believing he is as he appears.

Not all common characters on the children's stage pass their days in tedious labor that needs to be alleviated by the sweet strains of music. Other members of the commonalty, who include apprentices ,, lawyers, merchants, usurers, and men whose occupations are not stated, sing not to help them with their work, but for their own amusement. Some sing for relief from strife or boredom, some for joy, some for love, and some to join their merry companions in tavern revelry. As Robert Burton observes,

Many and sundry are the meanes, which Philosophers and Physitians have prescribed to exhilirate a sorrowful heart, and to divert those fixed and intent cares and meditations, which in this malady so much offended; but in my judgement none so present, none so powerful, none so opposite as a cup of strong drinke, mirth, musicke, and merry company.[8]

The most outstanding common music maker in children's drama is Old Merrythought from Beaumont's *Knight of the Burning Pestle*, for whom the mirth of music can right every wrong and reverse every adversity. He takes a dramatic character convention to the extreme, for he sings at every possible moment. He is "a merry old gentleman," a mirthful soul whose music is the outward manifestation of his extreme joviality, and whose otherwise cavalier insouciance is belied by his common behavior and choice of music. According to Renaissance thought, extremes of anything are pernicious and lead to no good. As Francis Meres reminds us of a surfeit of music,

As too much speaking hurts; too much galling smarts: so too much Musick gluts and distempereth.[9]

Merrythought, with his overzealous love of music, thus becomes a fool. When his favorite son, Jasper, sets off to run away, Merrythought merely sings his blessing (Act I, scene iv); and when the Merchant comes to complain that the same Jasper, who served as his apprentice, has run off with his only daughter, Luce, Merrythought simply sings fragments of popular ballads and ayres in response to each of the Merchant's emotional or accusatory statements (Act II, scene viii). He locks his shrewish wife out of their house and sings at her to go away (Act III, scene v). And when the coffin of his beloved Jasper is brought before him, he bursts neither into tears or an appropriately stoical speech, but into song (Act V, scene iii). His sole obsession in life is to remain merry through music, and he scarcely enters the stage without finding some excuse to sing:

[**Old Merrythought.**] To what end should a man be sad in this world? Give me a man that when he goes to hanging cries, Troll the black bowl to me — and a woman that will sing a catch in her travail! I have seen a man come by my door with a serious face, in a black coat, without a hatband, carrying his head as if he looked for pins in the street; I have looked out of my window half a year after and have spied that man's head upon London Bridge. 'Tis vile. Never trust a tailor that does not sing at his work; his mind is of nothing but filching.

[**Citizen's**] **Wife** [aside to her husband]. Mark this George, 'tis worth noting: Godfrey, my tailor, you know never sings, and he had fourteen yards to make this gown, and I'll be sworn, Mistress Pennystone, the draper's wife, had one made with twelve.

Old Merrythought [sings]   *'Tis mirth that fills the veins with blood,*
More than wine, or sleep, or food.
Let each man keep his heart at ease;
No man dies of that disease.
He that would his body keep
From diseases must not weep;
But whoever laughs and sings
Never he his body brings
Into fevers, gouts, or rheums,
Or ling'ringly his lungs consumes,
Or meets with aches in the bone,
Or catarrhs or griping stone,
But contended lives for aye,
The more he laughs the more he may.

      (Act II, scene viii)

But too much music has clearly distempered him, and he dwells in his own fantastic world whose harmony jars against the rich interplay of concord and discord of normal life.

Not every common character to appear in Elizabethan and Jacobean drama is an industrious laborer, a merry old fool, or even an honest man enjoying music honestly. This body of plays is also populated with assorted and very colorful rascals, representatives of another type of individual thriving in late Renaissance England, and mocked with all the others on the children's stage:

The city rogue lived as a gallant, haunted taverns, ordinaries and theaters, beat the watch, took purses, and outwitted gulls. . . .
    These rogues had more brains and daring than the ordinary vagabonds, and they played for bigger stakes. They formed the gallant company of shifters who lived by

their wits; their business was not begging, but cozening. Elizabethan literature is full of them.[10]

In the children's theater, such characters haunt the city comedies, where they take advantage of wealthy fools, citizen's wives, ambitious schemes, and the considerable vanities of all they meet. They sing often in taverns where they occasionally mistreat the fiddlers they have hired, and their songs tend toward the bawdy and raucous. Indeed, nondramatic writers make it quite clear that the music associated with such scoundrels is of the same low ilk as the rest of their pastimes:

They are carriers of letters between lust and wantonnesse,tellers of old wives tales and singers of wenching Ballads; sweare and forsweare, drinke and gull, laugh and be fat.[11]

One of the most outstanding musical scoundrels of the children's theater is the goldsmith's apprentice, Francis Quicksilver, of Chapman, Jonson, and Marston's *Eastward Ho*.[12] There is scarcely an honest bone in Quicksilver's body, but his great wit and extreme manipulative abilities beg for grudging admiration. Indeed, though Quicksilver is clearly a villainous sort, the dramatists manipulate audience sympathy to lie with him, and he actually becomes the hero of this very satirical play. Robert Burton informs us that "Carmen, Boyes, and Prentises, when a new song is published with us, goe singing that new tune still in the streets,"[13] and, true to form, Quicksilver sings a number of the popular tunes of his day. But instead of repeating the versions he has heard, he fits clever new words to the songs, each of which marks him as quickwitted and resourceful. And his cleverness with words and music, coupled with his great skill at acting and other deceptions, saves his life at the climax of the play.

By Act V, Quicksilver's many misdeeds have been discovered, and he languishes in prison along with his confederates, the bogus knight, Sir Petronel Flash, and the usurer, Security. Death is almost assured, morality seems certain of triumph, and Quicksilver is clearly to go the way of the stereotyped Prodigal of contemporary literature:

fooles are his admirers, and knaves his soothers, whilst hee forgets himself to remember them, and never thinks of shutting the stable-doore till the steed be stolne. . . . He is at last o'retane like a Butterfly in a storm, & left by those that seem'd to love him.[14]

But the harsh realities of imprisonment seem to be leading the dishonest trio toward repentance. By scene ii, the jailer marvels that

I never knew or saw prisoners more penitent or more devout. They will sit you up all night singing of psalms, and edifying the whole prison — only Security sings a note too high sometimes.

In spite of the apparent change of heart, things look pretty grim by scene v, when the goldsmith Touchstone arrives to see his prodigal apprentice and his untrustworthy son-in-law, Sir Petronel, hanged. The righteous goldsmith makes it clear that he shall neither forgive the pair nor extend them a single drop of pity. But the clever Quicksilver is not beaten yet, and decides to add Death to the list of those he has cheated, making a final, desperate play for life and liberty. In the best tradition of repentant criminals, and in a manner patently appropriate for the hero of a mock-prodigal son play, he composes a farewell ballad that traces his fall step by step and warns others not to do as he has done. He models his ballad on a famous old example of the tradition, with which the audience would certainly have been familiar, and to which he refers in his own version.[15] (See Figure 3.) Those who assemble to hear his lamentable swansong are his former confederates; Touchstone and Touchstone's model apprentice, Golding; the jailer, Wolf; and an unnamed "friend":

Quicksilver.	Sir, it [the ballad] is all the testimonie I shall leave behind me to the World, and my Maister, that I have so offended.
Friend.	Good Sir.
Quicksilver.	I writ it when my spirits were opprest.
Petronel.	I, ile be sworn for you *Francis*.
Quicksilver.	It is an imitation of *Manningtons*; he that was hanged at Cambridge, that cut off the Horses head at a blow.
Friend.	So Sir.
Quicksilver.	To the tune of *I waile in wo, I plunge in pain.*
Petronel.	An excellent Dittie it is, and worthy of a new tune.
Quicksilver [singing; see Example 1]	*In Cheapside famous for gold and plate* *Quicksilver I did dwell of late:* *I had a Maister good, and kinde,* *That would have wrought me to his mind.* *He bade me still work upon that,* *But alas I wrought I knew not what,* *He was a Touchstone blacke, but true:* *And told me still what would insue,* *Yet woe is me, I would not learne,* *I saw alas, but could not discerne*
Friend.	Excellent, excellent well.
Goulding.	O let him alone, Hee is taken alreadie.

Quicksilver [singing]   *I cast my Coat and Cap away,*
I went in silkes and sattins gay,
False metal of good manners, I
Did daily coin unlawfully.
I scorned my Maister, being drunke,
I kept my Gelding and my Punke,
And with a knight, sir Flash by name,
Who now is sorie for the same.

Petronel.   I thanke you *Francis.*

[**Quicksilver** continues his song]

I thought by sea to runne away,
But Thames and Tempest did me stay.

Touchstone.   This cannot be fained sure. Heaven pardon my severity. The ragged colt may prove a good horse.

Quicksilver [singing]   *Still Eastward Ho was all my word:*
But Westward I had no regard.
Nor never wrought, what would come after
As did alas his youngest Daughter.
At last the black Oxe trode o' my foote,
And I saw then what longd untoo't
Now cry I, Touchstone, touche me stil,
And make me currant by thy skill.

Touchstone.   And I will do it, *Francis.*

Wolfe.   Stay him Maister Deputie, now is the time, we shall loose the song else.

Friend.   I protest it is the best that ever I heard.

Quicksilver.   How like you it *Gentlemen*?

All.   O admirable Sir!

Quicksilver.   This Stanze now following, alludes to the story of *Mannington*, from whence I tooke project for my invention.

Friend.   Pray you go on sir.

Quicksilver [singing]   *O Mannington thy stories shew,*
Thou cutst a Horse-head off at a blow:
But I confesse, I have not the force
For to cut off the head of a horse,
Yet I desire this grace to winne,
That I may cut off the Horse-head of Sin,
And leave his body in the dust
Of sinnes high way and bogs of Lust,
Whereby I may take Vertues purse,
And live with her for better for worse.

Following further enthusiastic comments from his enthralled listeners, Quicksilver adds a final farewell stanza with an obligatory moral warning to all others who would fall as he fell. By the end of his magnificently insincere performance, the stern Touchstone has been moved to save his former apprentice's life:

Touchstone. I can no longer forebeare to doe your humility right: Arise, and let me honour your Repentance with the hearty and joyfull embraces, of a Father, and Friends love. *Quicksilver*, thou hast eate into my breast, *Quicksilver*, with the dropps of thy sorrow, and kild the desperate opinion I had of thy reclaime . . . . All former passages are forgotten, and here my word shall release you.

Example 1. "In Cheapside Famous for Gold and Plate."

But lest the audience be taken in by the rogue's clever song and crocodile tears, Quicksilver boisterously begins plotting his next audacious and illegal escapade almost immediately after his miraculous pardon.

A forrowfull Sonet, made by M. George
Mannington, at Cambridge Caftle.

To the tnne of Labandala Shot.

I Waſte in wo, I plunge in pain,
   with ſoꝛowing ſobs, I do complain,
   With wallowing waues I wiſh to die,
   I languiſh ſoꝛe whereas I lie,
In feare I faint in hope I holde,
With ruthe I runne, I was too bolde:
As luckleſſe lot aſſigned me,
   in dangerous dale of deſtinie:
Hope bids me ſmile, Feare bids me weep,
   My ſeelie ſoule thus Care doth keep.
¶ Yea too too late I do repent,
   the youthful yeares that I haue ſpent,
The retch leſſe race of careleſſe kinde,
   which hath bewitcht my woful minde.
                    ℂ

Such is the chaunce, ſuch is the ſtate,
Of thoſe that truſt too much to fate.
No bꝛagging boaſt of gentle blood,
What ſo he be, can do thee good:
   No wit, no ſtrength, noꝛ beauties hue,
   No friendly ſute can death eſchue.
¶ The diſmall day hath had his wil,
And iuſtice ſeekes my life to ſpill:
Reuengement craues by rigoꝛous law,
Whereof I little ſtood in awe:
   The dolefull doom to end my life,
   Beded with care and woꝛldlie ſtrife:
And frowning iudge hath giuen his doome.

Figure 3.   The model for Quicksilver's ballad, written in 1576, as it appears in Clement Robinson et al., *A Handefull of Pleasant Delites* (1584). Continued.

O gentle death thou art welcome:
   The losse of life, I do not feare,
   Then welcome death, the end of care.
¶O prisoners poore, in dungeon deep,
Which passe the night in slumbring sleep:
Wel may you rue your youthful race.
And now lament your cursed race.
   Content your selfe with your estate,
   Impute no shame to fickle fate:
With wrong attempts, increase no wealth,
Regard the state of prosperous health:
   And think on me, when I am dead:
   Whom such delights haue lewdly led.
¶My friend and parents, where euer you be
Full little do you thinke on me:
My mother milde, and dame so deer:
Thy louing childe, is fettred heer:

                    Would

   Would God I had, I wish too late,
   Been bred and borne of meaner estate:
Or else, would God my rechlesse eare,
Had been obedient for to heare,
   Your sage aduice and counsel true:
   But in the Lord parents abue.
¶You valiant hearts of youthfull train,
Which heard my heauie heart complain:
A good example take by me,
Which runne the race where euer you be:
   trust not too much to bilbow blade,
   nor yet to fortunes fickle trade.
Hoist not your sailes no more in winde,
Least that some rocke, you chaunce to finde,
   or else be driuen to Lybia land,
   whereas the Barque may sinck in sand.
¶You students all that present be,
To view my fatall destinie,
would God I could requite your pain,
wherein you labour, although in vain,
   if mightie God would think it good,
   to spare my life and vitall blood,

Figure 3. Continued.

For this your profered curtesie,
I would remaine most stedfastly,
    Your seruant true in deed and word,
    But welcome death as please the Lord.
¶Yea welcome death, the end of woe,
And farewell life, my fatall foe:
Yea welcome death, the end of strife,
Aboue the care of mortall life,

                    E ii   For

    For though this life doth fleet away,
    In heauen I hope to liue for ay:
A place of ioy and perfect rest,
Which Christ hath purchasse for the best:
    Til that we meet in heauen most blest:
    Adue, farewell in Jesu Christ.

A sorrowful Sonet, made by M. George Mannington,
at Cambridge Castle.
To the tune of Labandala Shot.

1.   I waile in wo, I plunge in pain,
      with sorrowing sobs, I do complain,
      With wallowing waues I wish to die,
      I languish sore whereas I lie,
          I feare I faint in jope I holde,
          With ruthe I runne, I was too bolde:
      As luckless lot assigned me,
      in dangerous dale of destinie:
          Hope bids me smile, Feare bids me weep
      My seelie soule thus Care doth keep.

Figure 3:   Continued.

2. Yea too too late I do repent,
   the youthful yeares that I haue spent,
   The retch lesse race of carelesse kinde,
   which hath betwitcht my woful mide.
       Such is the chaunce, such is the state,
       Of those that truth too much to fate.
   No bragging boast of gentle blood,
   What so he be, can do thee good:
       No wit, no strength, nor beauties hue,
       No friendly sute can death eschue.

3. The dismall day hath had his wil,
   And iustice seeks my life to spill:
   Reuengement craues by rigorous law,
   Whereof I little stood in awe:
       The dolefull doom to end my lide,
       Bedect with care and worlie strife:
   And frowning iudge hath giuen his doome.
   O gentle death thou art welcome:
       The losse of life, I do not feare
       Then welcome death, the end of care.

4. O prisoners poore, in dungeon deep,
   Which passe the night in slumbering sleep:
   Wel may you rue your youthful race.
   And now lameent your cursed cace.
       Content your self with your estate.
       Impute no shame to fickle fate:
   With wrong attempts, increase no welath,
   Regard the state of prosperous health:
       And think of me, when I am dead:
       Whom such delights hue lewdly led.

5. My friend and parents, where euer you be
   Full little do you thinke of me
   My mother milde, and dame so deer;
   Thy louing childe, is fettred heer;
       Would God I had. I wish too late,
       Been bred and borne of meaner estate:
   Or else, would God my rechlesse eare.
   Had been obedient for to heare,
       Your sage aduice and counsel true;
   But in the Lord parents adue.

Figure 3. Continued.

6.   You valiant hearts of youthfull train,
Which heard my heauie heart complain:
A good example take by me,
Which runne the race where euer you be:
    trust not too much to bilbow blade,
    nor yet to fortunes fickle trade.
Hoist not your sailes no more in winde,
Least that some rocke, you chance to finde,
    or else be driven to *Lybia* land,
    whereas the Barque may sinck in sand

7.   You students all that present be,
To view my fatall destinie,
    would God I could requite your pain,
    wherein you labor, although in vain,
        if mightie God would think it good,
        to spare my life and vitall blood,
For this your profered curtesie,
I would remaine most stedfastly,
        Your seruant true in deed and word,
        But welcome death as please the Lord.

8.   Yea welcome death, the end of woe,
And farewell life, my fatall foe:
Yea welcome death, the end of strife,
Adue the care of mortall life,
        For thought this mortal life doth fleet away,
        In heaven I hope to liue for ay:
A place of joy and perfect rest,
Which Christ hathy purchaste for the best:
        Til that we meet in heauen most hiest:
        Adue, farewell in Iesu Christ.

Figure 3.   Continued.

Quicksilver's song becomes the outward manifestation of his youthful self-confidence, his ready wit, his jubilant insincerity, and his extreme manipulative talent, for he changes its words to suit his needs just as he alters aspects of the world around him for his own ends. His music supplements the most outstanding aspects of his audacious character, and is entirely appropriate for the apprentice of a London goldsmith.

PROFESSIONAL MUSICIANS

One group of lower-class characters whose musical nature in the children's plays merits special attention are the vagabond fiddlers and other professional musicians who add life to numerous scenes. These characters form a musically distinct group, and their position near the bottom of any social hierarchy in which they are depicted helps to unite them further. Professional musicians without regular, steady patronage are especially mocked in children's plays, perhaps because they had less status in the contemporary musical world than those who played them, be those actors privileged choristers, Chapel or Cathedral musicians, or even city waits.

Late Renaissance England took a divided view of its musicians. On one hand were the most excellent practitioners of the art, men such as William Byrd, John Dowland, and Alphonso Ferrabosco, who were praised and held as worthy models for imitation. Such men were considered among the brightest jewels of all England and were commended in the highest terms:

For Motets and Musicke of piety and devotion, as wll for the honour of our Nation, as the merit of the man, I preferre above all other our Phoenix, M. William *Byrd*, whom in that kind, I know not weather any may equall, I am sure none excell, even by the judgement of *France* and *Italy*, who are very sparing in the commendation of strangers, in regard of that conceipt they hold of themselves. His *Cantiones Sacrae*, as also his *Gradualia*, are meere Angelicall and Divine; and being of himselfe naturally disposed to Gravity and Piety, his veine is not so much for light Madrigals or Canzonets, yet his *Virginellae* and some others in his first Set, cannot be mended by the best *Italian* of them all.[16]

But other, lesser sorts of musicians were considered as far from gravity and piety as possible, their music nowhere near angelicall or divine:

I think that all good ministrelles, sober and chast musicions (speking of such drunken sockets and bawdye parasits as ra[n]ge the Cuntryes, ryming and singing of uncleane, corrupt, and filthie songs in Taverns, Alehouses, Innes, and other publique assemblies), may daunce ye wild Moris thorow a needles eye. For how should thei bere chaste minds, seeing that their exercyse is the pathway to all uncleanes. Their is no ship so balanced with massie matter, as their heads are fraught with all kind of bawdie songs, filthie ballads and scurvy rymes for every purpose, and for everie Cumpanie.

Who be more bawdie than they? Who uncleaner than they, who more licentious, and loose minded? Who more incontinent tha[n] they? And briefly, who more inclined to all kind of insolent lewdnes than they?[17]

These common musicians were condemned even by the sort who may have played them in the children's theater. Thomas Ravenscroft's opinion of vulgar musicians, though somewhat less disparaging than the above, undoubtedly speaks for other highly educated practitioners of the musical arts:

As for those common kinde *practitioners*, (truly ycleped *minstrells*, though our city makes *Musitians* of them) who making account forsooth to doe the *art* Honor, now in these daies of the ill opinion [of music], and small credit it beares, have (fairly) brought it downe from a chiefe *liberall science*, to the basest almost of *mechanick functions*.[18]

Nearly all professional musicians portrayed in children's drama are itinerant fiddlers, who were legally defined as vagabonds and beggars during the Elizabethan and Jacobean eras.[19] On the stage, as in life, these men "live by merry begging, mainteyned by almes, and privily encroach uppon everie mans purse."[20] The stage portraits of such rascals are far from flattering. Over half of them are found in the city comedies, where they do indeed haunt taverns, ale-houses, and inns. Such characters have a far rougher life than musicians in the steady employ of gentle households such as Sir Bounteous's in Middleton's *A Mad World My Masters*. Difficult demands and impossible situations are their constant companions:

Monopoly.	Why Chamberlin? Will not these Fidlers be drawn forth? Are they not in tune yet? Or are the Rogues afraid ath Statute, and dare not travell so far without a passe-port?
Whirlpoole.	What chamberlin?
Lynstock.	Where's mine host? What chamberlin.
	Enter Chamberlin.
Chamberlin.	Anon sir, heere sir, at hand sir.
Monopoly.	Wheres this noise? What a lowsie Townes this? Has Brainford no musick int?
Chamberlin.	They are but rozening sir, and theile scrape themselves into your company presently.
Monopoly.	Plague a their cats guts, and their scraping: Dost not see women here, and can we thinkst thou be without a noise then?
Chamberlin.	The troth is sir, one of the poore instruments caught a sore mischance last night: his most base bridge fell downe, and belike they are making a gathering for the reparation of that.

(Dekker and Webster, *Westward Ho*, Act IV)

They belong to the lowest rung of the social ladder, and like similar others often do without great creature comforts:

Musition.	Was ever any marchants band set better I set it: walke Ime a cold, this white sattin is so thin unles it be cut, for then the Sunne enters. . .

(Dekker and Webster, *Northward Ho*, Act V)

Few people appreciate their services though many call for them:

Gozlin. . . . what set of Villains are you, you perpetuall Ragamuffins?
Fidler. The towne Consort Sir.
Gozlin. Consort with a pox? Cannot the shaking of the sheets be danc'd without your Town piping? Nay then let al hel rore.
Fidler. I beseech you sir, put up yours, and wee'le put up ours:
Gozlin. Play you louzie Hungarians.

(Dekker and Webster, *Westward Ho*, Act V, scene i)

And the one certain way to get them to leave others in peace was to pay them:

William Smallshanks. Musitians, minstrils, footrogues,
For Gods love leave your filthy squeaking noyse
And get you gone, the widow and my selfe,
Will scramble out the shaking of the sheets
Without your musicke: we have no neede of fidlers
To our dancing, foote have you no manners?
Cannot a man take his natural rest
For your scraping? I shall wash your gut strings,
If you but stay a while: Yet honest rascalls,
If youle let us have the tother crash
The widow, and ile keepe time, theres for your paines.

(Barry, *Ram Alley*, Act V)

Musicians often serve as the butt of jokes, practical and otherwise:

Maybery. Gods so, see, see whats hee walkes yonder, is he mad.
Fulle-moone. Thats a musition, yet hee's beside himselfe.
Bellamont. A Musition, how fell he mad for Gods sake?
Full-moone. For love of an Italian Dwarfe.

(Dekker and Webster, *Northward Ho*, Act IV)

Of course, musicians demonstrate a great range of musical versatility: they sing, they play a wide variety of musical instruments, and those that inhabit taverns or keep company with equally low sorts of people know the popular repertoire so well that they can play any wenching ballad or dance tune requested of them. Even more than the manual laborers of the stage, musicians perform music to characterize themselves professionally. Their musical instruments become symbols of their occupation as much as the soldier's sword or the tinker's pot. Except for a few dance tunes and ballad fragments, we are given little idea what these characters perform. But it may be assumed that they play music appropriate to each occasion and environment in which they are asked to perform; surely the Waits of London at the wedding in *The Two Maids of More-Clacke*, the household musicians at the banquet in *A Mad*

World My Masters, and the tavern musicians in such plays as *The Scornful Lady* and *May Day* do not play the same repertoire.

SERVANTS

The servants of children's drama and their actual contemporary English equivalents had little in common, though both were believed to be "alway ready furnished with a song."[21] Most of the servant characters in children's drama share more traits with the witty and appealing servants of classical Roman comedy than with their uneducated, underprivileged Elizabethan and Jacobean counterparts. Indeed, servants are introduced into children's plays primarily to act as foils to their masters and to entertain the audience with clever dialogue and skillful song. Most musical servants' roles were clearly designed to give a talented young singer a chance to exercise his skill rather than to contribute significantly to the plot of the play.

Musical servant characters tend to be relegated to subplots or dramatic episodes occurring between scenes of the main drama. Sometimes these episodes take place at the beginnings or conclusions of acts, and may therefore represent inter-act entertainment that has become worked into the fabric of the drama. These individuals, who are frequently provided with humorous names, if named at all, show little development as characters. They are brilliant and ephemeral portraits of lively youth and little more. They tend to appear in groups of two or three and are thus often assigned two and three-part songs, and were probably played by the younger members of the troupes. If the extant music and lyrics are typical, the songs themselves separate these characters from the servants of the time and from most of the other characters of the children's stage. For the songs tend to have self-consciously sophisticated lyrics, complex melodic lines, elaborate instrumental accompaniment, and were probably composed specifically for the plays and singers assigned them. Most of these musical servants belong to Elizabethan comedy.

The three serving boys of *Blurt, Master-Constable* are typical. At the end of Act I, the principal characters have left the stage and the three youths meet apparently by chance as they go about errands for their masters. Pilcher, named for one variety of the dried fish he receives as rations from his parsimonious Spanish master, is teased about his emaciated condition by fellow servants Doyt and Dandiprat, who both have the good fortune to work for less miserly Italians. The boys begin their conversation in speech, but the speech turns into a witty accompanied song:

Dandiprat.	. . . Sirra thin-gut, what's thy name?
Pilcher.	My name? You chops, why I am of the bloud of *Pilchers*.
Dandiprat.	Nay s'foote, if one should kill thee, hee could not be hang'd for't, for hee would shed no bloud, there's none in thee: Pilcher: th'art a most pittiful dryed one.
Doyt.	I wonder thy master does not slice thee, and swallow thee for an *Anchoves*.
Pilcher.	He wants wine Boy to swallow me down, for he wants money to swallow down wine: but farewell I must dog my master.
Dandiprat.	As long as thou dog'st a *Spaniard*, thou'lt nere be fatter: but stay, our hast is as great as thine, yet to endeere our selves into thy leane acquaintance met wee'll meete and be merry, sing:
Pilcher.	Ile make a shift to squeake.
Doyt.	And I.
Dandiprat.	And I, for my profession is to shift as well as you hem:

Sing. Musicke.

Doyt.	What meate eates the *Spaniard*?
Pilcher.	Dry'd *Pilchers* and poore *John*:
Dandiprat.	Alas thou art almost mard.
Pilcher.	My cheekes are falne and gone.
Doyt.	Would'st thou not leape at a piece of meate?
Pilcher.	O how my teeth do water I could eate
	For the heavens; my flesh is almost gone
	With eating of *Pilcher* and poore *John*.

Exeunt

(*Blurt, Master-Constable*, Act I, scene ii)

Both extant contemporary settings of this song, transcribed and discussed in chapter 10, reveal vocal lines that are intended to show off the trained voices of two of the three singers. Both settings are apparently variants of the same original, written for voices and a consort of viols, and the music itself gives the words a sophisticated and clever quality lacking in the lyric alone. The song and the episode to feature it reveal only the most general connection to the rest of the play. Yet, it makes the three servants, who are mostly mute in other scenes in which they appear, come to life on their own and reminds the audience of the double life of the performers as actors and choristers.

Related to such musical servants and also, to a lesser extent, to professional musicians are the nameless "boys" and "pages" who are often introduced for the principal or sole purpose of providing music. Like other servants, they are mostly in the employ of greater men, and like musicians, their expected skills

and duties apparently include music. The dramatic function of these characters is essentially limited to musical performance and mute appearance with
their masters: they are never characterized or developed even to the extent of
Doyt, Pilcher, and Dandiprat. They, too, were probably played by young musicians rather than more seasoned actors, and their parts are the least dramatically demanding in the repertoire. They rarely appear as groups, rarely speak,
and are never assigned scenarios devoted to their antics. They are generally
requested by other characters to sing or play instruments; indeed, their principal purpose is to provide music for those characters who cannot perform
themselves because of lofty social status or lack of skill; or, less likely in the
children's theater, because the character who desires music is played by an
actor who himself cannot sing or play. Most noblemen who wish for music in
more meditative moments call for their "pages" or "boys" to perform for
them; and a few gentlemen do likewise when propriety or supposed lack of
talent demand that they not sing themselves. These dramatically unimportant
though musically vital characters appear in all dramatic genres throughout
the period, and, like classically-inspired servants, are most often assigned accompanied songs. Occasionally they are themselves instrumentalists, and it
is clear that they are highly skilled in music.

GENTRY AND NOBILITY

The privileged elite of Elizabethan and Jacobean England received training
in practical and speculative music. Music was, after all, not only one of the
seven liberal sciences but a godly ornament and an excellent skill for the development of mind and body. Castiglione's *Libro del cortegiano*, whose influence on the English Renaissance can scarcely be overestimated, praises
music's merits repeatedly and makes it one of the necessary accoutrements of
the perfect courtier. As the Count (Ludovico da Canossa) tells us,

For I shall enter into a large sea of the praise of Musicke, and call to rehearsal howe
much it hath alwayes bene renowmed among them of olde time. . . . And remember I
have understood that Plato and Aristotle will have a man that is wel brought up, to be
also a musitien: and declare with infinite reasons the force of musicke to be very great
purpose in us, and for many causes (that should be too long to rehearse) ought
necessarilye to be learned from a mans childhoode, not onely for the superficial
melodie that is heard, but to be sufficient to bring us into a newe habit that is good.[22]

Over half a century after *The Courtyer* was first published in an English
translation and after the influence of humanism had begun to decline in England, Ravenscroft still expresses similar sentiments:

And the *Wise Grecians* therefore educated their children in *it* [music], that by means of *it*, they might *temper* their mindes, and fully settle therin, the *Vertues* of *Modestie* and *Honesty*: and (in a word) *all of worth* ever held it, a very *Direct* and *Necessary* course, for the *Institution of Life*, and *Correction of Ill Manners*.[23]

However, as Ravenscroft, Castiglione, and a host of other writers remind us, music was not suitable for all persons or all occasions. The great dignity and awesome responsibilities of political leadership, for instance, did not harmonize with musical performance, as Agrippa reminds us with an anecdote from the life of Alexander the Great:

When on a time *Alexander* the greate did singe, *Antigonus* his Maister rend his harp a sunder, and cast it awaie, saieing: it is nowe meete for thy age to Rule, and not to Singe.[24]

Thus, the kings and dukes of the children's stage, like the adults', tend to enjoy their music vicariously. Presumably, they have received training in music to know its value and be able to judge many aspects of the art, but it is not appropriate for them to perform before any of their subjects. Instead, they call upon pages to sing to them, they dance with their peers in masques and social dances, and they enjoy all manner of musical spectacle in their courts as we saw in the previous chapter. Requests for music by servant boys are often most revealing about character, for they are most often issued when the great lords are solitary and meditative rather than performing duties of state.

An excellent example is found in Act III, scene iv of Marston's *The Malcontent*, in which the evil Duke, Pietro, seeks music to relieve him of a growing sense of foreboding. Like most villainous usurpers in late Renaissance plays, he has built his position on a foundation of treachery and deceit, but remains insecure and is plagued by nagging feelings of self-doubt and persecution. He and a few loyal companions go hunting in the hopes that the stimulation of the chase will relieve his growing sense of oppression, but suddenly he realizes that in a sense he, too, may be the quarry of a hunt. He hastily dismisses his companions, and is left alone with his young serving boys, with whom he converses kindly. At last, in the time-honored manner of melancholy men, he asks that they sing to him. Between his friendly teasing of the children and his sudden desire for the gentle art of music, the audience is given a hint of the hidden nobility that at last allows the Duke to repent.

Other members of the gentle classes were permitted to perform music under certain circumstances, for excellence in music was a mark of breeding. Henry Peacham admonishes would-be gentlemen to learn and practice music to this extent:

I desire no more in you then to sing your part sure, and at first sight, withall, to play the same upon your Violl, or to the exercise of the Lute, privately and to your selfe.[25]

Lute, viol, and voice were clearly the best-loved instruments of gentlemen on stage and off. Castiglione explains why these fretted instruments are so appropriate and how the voice augments them, though he allows a larger audience than the Puritan Peacham:

Also all instrumentes with freates are ful of harmony, because y[e] tunes of them are perfect, and with ease a manne may do many thinges upon them that fil the minde with the sweetnesse of musike. And the musike of a sette of Violes doth no lesse delite a man, for it is very sweet and artificiall. A mannes breste geveth a great ornament and grace to all these instrumentes, in the whiche I will have it sufficient that our Courtyer have an understandinge. Yet the more counninger he is uppon them, the better it is for him, without medlynge muche with the instrumentes that *Minerva and Alcibiades* refused, because it seemeth they are noisome. Nowe as touchyng the time and season whan these sortes of musike are to be practised: I believe at all times whan a man is in familiar and loving company, having nothing else a doe. But especiallye they are meete to be practised in the presence of women, because those sightes sweeten the minds of the hearers, & make them more apt to be perced with the pleasantnesse of musicke, & also they quicken the spirites of the verye doers.[26]

Most of the gentlemen who play their fretted instruments before loving company, especially women, in the children's plays are portrayed in very unflattering light. Contemporary nondramatic literature was rife with satiric or otherwise derogatory images of self-centered, empty-headed gallants or courtiers, such as

In briefe, his tongue and his heart are most commonly as strangers, as his hands and his actions, or his large promises and lame performances.[27]

and

He puts more confidence in his words than meaning, and more in his pronunciation than his words. *Occasion* is his *Cupid*, and he hath but one receit of making love. He followes nothing but inconstancie, admires nothing but beauty, honors nothing but fortune. Loves nothing.[28]

Of course, similar portraits were brought to the children's stage, often complete with appropriate music.

It is probably no accident that the most effete musical gentlemen of the children's stage, the aptly named courtiers Hedon and Amorphus of Jonson's *Cynthia's Revels*, follow the form of Castiglione's advice about performance on fretted instruments almost to the letter, for the play is a satire on empty court manners and owes other debts to Castiglione's influential book.[29] In Act IV, scene iii of the play, Cynthia's self-loving courtiers wait in their own familar company for the waters of the fountain of self-love to be brought to them. They have nothing else to do but entertain each other, and that entertainment of course includes songs to that excellent fretted instrument, the lyra, by both Hedon and Amorphus. When Amorphus has his turn, he introduces his song by telling us that his deceased mistress bequeathed him a glove, "upon which I composde this *ode*, and set it to my most affected instrument, the *lyra*." The song, like the singer, follows form and convention but lacks the substance to give it true meaning:

> *Thou more than most sweet glove,*
> *Unto my more sweet love,*
> *Suffer me to store with kisses*
> *This emptie lodging, that now misses*
> > *The pure rosie hand, that ware thee,*
> > *Whither then the kid, that bare thee.*
> > > *Thou art sort, but that was softer;*
> > > *CUPIDS selfe hath kist it ofter,*
> > > *Then e're he did his mothers doves,*
> > > *Supposing her the Queene of loves,*
> > > > *That was my Mistresse,*
> > > > *Best of gloves.*

The song is as stilted and artificial as its singer; it is poetically correct but exceptionally trite. Furthermore, it is hardly an appropriate eulogy with which to immortalize one's late beloved. The song and its sentiment ring as hollow as Amorphus himself.

WOMEN

A wide variety of female characters grace the children's plays, and, like their male counterparts, some of them are musicians. Also like their male counterparts, different sorts of music are assigned to different sorts of women, according to their dramatic function and station in life. But the English Renaissance took a divided view about the merits of music for women, and it was generally agreed that the combination of music and feminine beauty was exceedingly powerful for great good or even greater ill. On the one hand, it held that women were extraordinarily musical by nature:

As for Musique, among women it is so familiare, as their very voyce is naturally a hermonie.[30]

and

Great *Caesar* likewise was woont to saye, than mens tunes were learnde from the Birdes chattering on trees: but the voice of women came from the Gods themselves.[31]

On the other hand, it was believed that the sensual nature of music could only ignite the sensual nature of womanhood and lead performer and listener alike from the path of righteousness:

But now adaies it seemeth to some, and that to the moste parte, that it is a godly orname[n]t, and a brave settyng out to a yong Maiden, if emong the rest she can shewe her selfe, to be an excellent fine singer, or a cunnyng plaier uppon Instrumentes, which thyng, although it bee confirmed by some galla[n]t glosyng reasons: I for my part doe not onely discommende, but judge that a thing of no little daunger, which ought by all women to be eschewed. For as Musicke if it be used to a laudable and good intentio[n], hath no evill in it, but deserveth a place emong the other Artes, the which apperteyning properly to menne, be called Liberall: Yet notwithstandyng, under the shadowe of vertue . . . it beareth a sweete baite, to a sowre and sharpe evill. Therefore I wish our Maiden, wholie to refraine from the use of Musicke, and seeing that under the coverture of Vertue, it openeth the dore to many vices, she ought so much the more the be regarded, by how muche the more the daunger is greate, and lesse apparent.[32]

These opposing views are both seen in children's plays, in which women's music is often more affective or more closely related to sexual matters than men's, and in which virtuous gentlewomen are far less likely to sing than virtuous gentlemen.

Female laborers and servants in the drama sing similar music for similar reasons as their male counterparts, and since their music either helps them at their tedious work or serves only to amuse the theater audience, it poses no moral danger to themselves or to other characters. Late Renaissance Englishwomen did not follow such trades as cobbler or tinker, but nonetheless there were more feminine occupations that included wearisome work. And music was believed to cheer and revive industrious women as well as men:

With this [music] the unmannerly countreywoman that aryseth before daye out of her sleepe to spin and carde, defendeth her selfe and maketh her labor pleasant[33]

Audrey, maidservant to the usurer Dampit in Middleton's *A Trick to Catch the Old One*, sings alone at her spinning in Act IV, scene v. Like the wittier male servants of the children's stage, she does not sing a simple ballad such as a realistic servant girl might know, but an accompanied song that demonstrates her cleverness and comprehension of her master's many foibles:

> *[My master is so wise that hee's proceeded wittall,*
> *My mistris is a foole, and yet is the most get all]*
> *Let the usurer cram him, in interest that excell,*
> *There's pits enow to dam him, before he comes to hell.*
> *In Holborne some: in Fleete-street some,*
> *Where ere he come, theres some, theres some.*

This song, though clearly intended as additional entertainment for the audience, nonetheless shows Audrey to be industrious and hardworking as well as witty, for she knows how to make her labor more pleasant. The single extant contemporary setting, for alto voice and a consort of viols, is given in chapter 10.

In spite of admonitions by the more conservative writers of the time that music could only bring women to grief, Elizabethan and Jacobean gentlewomen and noblewomen apparently received the same sort of training in practical music as did their brothers. Like their brothers, they most often learned lute, viols, and keyboard instruments; and also like their brothers, they participated in masques and social dances. A French language tutor for women from the end of the Elizabethan era gives a typical list of the musical instruments and skills taught to the daughters of well-to-do houses:

Lady [to her daughters]. . . . At what hour do your Maisters come?

Charlotte [the eldest]. Our dauncing Maister commeth around nine a clocke: our singing Maister, and he that teacheth us to play on the virginalles, at tenne: he that teacheth us on the Lute and the Violl de Gambo, at foure a clocke in the after noone: and our French Maister commeth commonly betweene seaven and eight a clocke in the morning.[34]

Even more than their brothers, gentlewomen were advised to play their music only in private or in the quiet company of other gentlewomen. As indicated, music was a strong inflamer of the passions and thus carried grave moral danger to the woman who would play before men.[35] Indeed, it was held that

The Phylosophers called Peripateticks, condemned musick in wemen, saying, that betweene it and chastity there could be smal agreement.[36]

Most gentlewomen in the children's plays do remember to exercise their musical skills only to themselves or in each other's company, such as Eynnefred and Annabell who sing at their sewing in Act II, scene i of Chapman's *Sir Giles Goose-Cappe*. But some women, clearly of questionable virtue, sing or dance at the least provocation and in front of any that would see or hear them. One such character is Girtred, the spoiled, bawdy goldsmith's daughter of Chapman, Jonson, and Marston's *Eastward Ho*. Girtred's main goal in life is to be a fine lady, and every aspect of her behavior shows her to be as far from ladylike as possible. She is outspoken, irrepressible, and lascivious. Her extreme love of music supports these other undesirable character traits, for, as Phillip Stubbes tells us,

And right as good edges are not sharpened (but obtused) by being whetted upon soft stones, so good wits by hearing of soft musick are rather dulled then sharpened, and made apt to all wantonnes and sinne: and therefore Writers affirme *Sappho* to have been expert in musick, and therefore whorish.[37]

Girtred sings almost every time she appears on stage, and her very choice of song further portrays her as both wanton and unladylike. Nearly all of her songs were clearly chosen by the authors for their overtly suggestive and sometimes downright crude texts; the only one assigned to her that may be suitable for the fine lady she wishes to emulate is a suggestive quotation from the erotic "Mistress Since You So Much Desire" from Rosseter's 1601 *Book of Ayres*. All of her songs are unaccompanied, many from the ballad repertoire; clearly she never had too much interest in the lute, viol, or virginal of genteel musical training. Even when adversity strikes and she requires song to cheer her flagging spirits, her songs are far from feminine modesty:

> Fond fables tell of old
> How Jove in Danae's Lap
> Fell in a showre of Gold,
> By which shee caught a clappe,
> O had it been my hap
> (How ere the blow doth threaten)
> So well I like the play,
> That I could wish all day
> And night to be so beaten.
>
> (Act V, scene i)

Girtred, like Amorphus of *Cynthia's Revels*, demontrates that she understands proper form but lacks the corresponding substance. She dresses like a lady, marries a supposedly wealthy knight, and imitates ladylike behavior as much as she can. But she lacks the grace and humility that a proper Renaissance lady would have, and her songs serve as a constant humorous reminder of her shortcomings.

Most of the women of the children's stage who would sing outside of their chambers and the company of other gentlewomen are even less innocent than the well-meaning Girtred. Some sing not simply out of exuberant wantonness, but to cunningly entice men into their unclean embraces, as does Cloe of Fletcher's *Faithful Shepherdess*:

> **Cloe**.   Farewell poore swaine, thou art not for my bend,
> I must have some quicker soules, whose words may tend,
> To some free action: give me him dare love
> At first encounter, and as soone dare proove.
>
> THE SONG
> Come Shepheards come,
> Come away without delay,

Whilste the gentle time doth stay,
Greene woods are dumme,
And will never tell to any
Those deere kisses and those many
Sweete imbraces that are given,
Dainty pleasures that would even
Raise in coldest age a fire,
And give virgin blood desire.
    Then if ever,
    Now or never,
    Come and have it,
    Think not I
    Dare deny,
    If you crave it.
(Act I, scene iii)

The most consistently musical of all the sorts of women to appear in children's drama is the whore, not coincidentally the most lascivious. The musical whores of the children's plays are assigned among the most lavish musical numbers, often accompanied by instruments and nearly always including lyrics as highly artificial as the love of a courtesan. Of course, the era's nondramatic literature is full of references to the close relationship between music and whoredom, such as

And if you would have your daughter whoorish, bawdie, and uncleane, and a filthie speaker, and such like, bring her up in musick and dauncing, and my life for yours, you have wunne the goale.[38]

Or, with direct reference to the erotic power of music itself,

To heare a faire young Gentlewoman play upon the Virginalls, Lute, Viall, and sing to it, which as *Gellius* observes *Lib.* I cap. II, are *lascivientium delitiae*, the chiefe delights of lovers, must needs be a great entisement.[39]

So musical was her profession in the eyes of the sixteenth and seventeenth centuries that musical puns even enter the description of a whore's work:

A curtizan is a musitian, Who from her youth being brought up in *pricksong*, hath lost no *time*, but is become a Woman *of note*. She learnt it of the *nightingale*, and in imitation of her sleepes, alwaies against a *Prickle*. She sings sometimes in *parts*, but they are not much respected, because they are grown *common*; yet never was she *put downe* by any but onely in the *closing*, and the reason, as some say, is because she fals ofte[n] too *flat*, she steales away your eares with her voice and in the *mean time* hath many *crotchets* in her head how to *straine* courtesie with your purse. A *large* and a *long* shee is well affected with; but a *briefe* or a *semibriefe*, nothing pleaseth her. Of all *instruments*, shee loves not the *recorder* because it makes her too melancholy. She hath playd at many a Marriage, yet could never affect *the bride-well*, although she hath beene *paid largely* for her *paine*. Imitating the ancient Poets, she sings her poems in *cars,* and the people being much delighted therewith, for the maintainance of her voyce, have bestowed many an *Egge* upon her, which oftentimes have proved as *rotten* as her selfe. Faine would she have beene a *quirister at Pauls,* but she loves not to stand in a *surplisse*: yet many times she repayres thither, especially unto the *lower end* of the *Middle-Ile.* She is never out of the *moode* but when she meetes with a Beadle or a Constable, and then she begins to *quaver,* because she feareth to sing a Counter tenor. If you hagve a desire to heare her, eyther shee is gone to *Lambeth* to take the *ayre*; or else you shall meete her at the next Taverne with her *consorts.*[40]

In the children's theater, where there was no shortage of young, attractive musical actors who could emulate women, song became the trademark of most whores. But the accomplished young courtesan who can sing like a siren and the grotesque old bawd, both of whom earned their livelihood selling flesh, are portrayed very differently in every detail, including and perhaps especially their music. This split may be caused in part by the opposite views of the filthy and corrupt professional whore in the popular writing of the time, and the cultured and esteemed courtesan of the Latin works that inspired so much Elizabethan comic drama. The latter sort, talented, beautiful, and often pure of heart, is represented by Imperia and her two attendants, Trivia and Simperina, in *Blurt, Master-Constable.* Music accompanies Imperia in most of her scenes, and all three characters would have been played by excellent singers. In Act II, scene ii, Simperina and Trivia sing a clever dialogue song about Woman's chief charms to an off-stage accompaniment of "musicke:"

[The Song]

Simperina.   In a faire woman what thing is best?
Trivia.   I think a curral lip.
Simperina.   No no you jest;
She has a better thing.
Trivia.   Then tis a cherry cheeke.
Simperina.   No no you lye.
Were neither lip nor cheekes curral, nor cherry eyes,
Were not her swelling brest stucke with strawberries,
Nor had smooth hand, soft skinne, white necke, pure eye,
Yet she at this alone your love can tye.
It is, O tis the onely joy to men,
The onely praise to women.
Trivia.   What ist then?
Simperina.   This it is, O this it is, and in a womans
Middle it is plaste,
In a most beauteous body, a hart most chaste:
This is the Jewell Kings may buy,
If women sell this Jewell, women lie.

This sweetly playful song stands in marked contrast to that sung unaccompanied by the Bawd of *Northward Ho*, who, in Act IV, sings "scurvily" of a very different feminine virtue. She is in no way subtle about what part of Woman men love best, and in her world in which everything becomes a commodity there is no jewel that women cannot sell forthrightly:

> Methought this other night,
> I saw a pretty sight,
> Which pleas'd me much.
> A comely country mayd,
> Not squeamish or afraid,
> To let gentlemen touch.
> I sold her maiden-head once,
> I sold her maiden-head twice,
> And I sold it last to an Alderman of *Yorke*,
> And then I had sold it thrice.

This song, which perfectly characterizes the grotesque old Bawd as a very fallen woman with her own rules of value and honesty, is a parody of a sweetly suggestive lute ayre by Robert Jones and will be discussed in greater musical detail in chapter 10.

SUPERNATURAL BEINGS

The children's stage is populated by a wide range of supernatural beings, including demigods, enchanters, fairies,ghosts,nymphs, satyrs, spirits, succubi, and a siren. The shepherds and woodsmen of pastoral and forest drama also belong to this category, for they too are *super natura*, as far above the mundane rules of nature as the classical divinities who rule over their eternally verdant landscape. In singing and dancing hand in hand with these others, the rustics of the pastoral and related genres not only share the lives of these higher creatures, but are assigned identical music as well.

Characterizations of this sort are bound by dramatic and nondramatic traditions and by the imagination of the playwrights who add them to their plays. Both tradition and the imagination of the era demand that such superior beings possess qualities by which they may be recognized immediately as belonging to a world beyond humanity. As Frances Yates has noted,

The Elizabethan world was populated not only by tough seamen, hard-headed politicians, serious theologians. It was a world of spirits, good and bad, fairies, demons, witches, ghosts, conjurors. This fact about the Elizabethans, reflected in their poetry, is too well known to need elaboration. . . . And the greatest plays of the greatest poet of the age are suffused with the atmosphere of the occult.[42]

Music was not only a convenient device by which to separate such ethereal beings from more mundane sorts, but the late Renaissance imagination linked music and magic inexorably together. Music was not simply one of the chief delights of the world inhabited by humanity, but one of the controlling forces of all creation, including the invisible world. Music in the theater thus came to stand for the magical or unearthly in all of its guises.[43]

Nondramatic texts from the English Renaissance generally fail to define what sort of music is associated with what sort of supernatural manifestation. In assigning music and even song lyrics to such musicians of the stage as tinkers, common minstrels, or pretentious courtiers, the children's dramatists and directors had actual London examples to draw upon. There were distinct conventions concerning what sort of music was appropriate for whom that could be followed or violated to great dramatic effect. But conventions for supernatural music had to follow different rules and different wisdom. It was quite a bit more difficult to locate an enchanter whose music could be emulated on stage or track down publications of music regularly purchased by spirits. As with the precocious classically-inspired servants who were only slightly less fantastical, the theater had to develop its own musical rules. In fact, the music of the supernatural shares four important characteristics with that of the servants: it is often performed by groups, a large part of its dramatic value lies in the provision of spectacular entertainment outside of the main plot, it is generally accompanied, and the roles could easily be handled by less skilled actors who are trained musicians. Also, like musical servants, there are distinctly more musical supernaturals in children's drama than in adults' from the same years.

Fairies on the English stage are associated with Lylyesque or mythological pastoral drama; they die out with the genre at the turn of the century and do not return with such purer pastorals as Fletcher's *Faithful Shepherdess*. A vast body of English Renaissance literature describes these creatures carefully and sets them apart from other beings. The most immediately recognizable fairy trait, according to contemporary authorities, was a preternatural prediliction for music and dance.[44] Commentaries on occult creatures, written by Englishmen and continental Europeans, often define fairy folk solely by their moonlit dances:

[I]n many places in the North partes, there are certaine monsters or spirits, which taking on them some shape or figure use (cheefly in the night season) to daunce, after the sound of all manner of instrumentes of musicke: whome the inhabitants call companies, or daunces, of Elves, or Fairies.[45]

Although the most sophisticated Elizabethans probably did not believe in such beings,[46] the venerable body of fairy lore allowed a very specific sort of music to be assigned to stage fairies. The fairies of *The Maydes Metamorphosis* are typical. They are a charming and delightful company whose main purpose is to heighten the mood of light-hearted beneficence with their pert dialogue and enchanting song and dance. True to form, they dance at night, illuminated by the moon:

> By the moone we sport and play,
> With the night begins our day:
> As we daunce the deaw doth fall,
> Trip it little urchins all:
> Lightly as the little bee,
> Two by two and three by three:
> And about go we, and about go wee.

> (Act II)

These fairies put in their appearance at the end of the Act, at which point the major characters of the drama have left the stage to a trio of servant boys. The mischevious, unpredictable fairies burst in on the boys with their music. The song and dance not only characterize them as fairies, but the continual movement of the dance illustrates the continual mutability of fairy folk, here one moment, there another, constantly moving, changing, and changing their minds.

Perhaps the most important group of supernatural beings in contemporary drama is that of ghosts. Unlike fairies, they are not especially associated with music; in fact, musical ghosts are exceedingly rare. Ghosts are associated with tragedies of blood and vengeance,[47] and for this reason are less common in children's plays than adults'. The vindictive spirits of Senecan tragedy such as *Antonio's Revenge* would seem to have little use for music nor would music appear to contribute much to their monomaniacal craving for bloody justice. Furthermore, there appears to be no extant English Renaissance literature that associates music with such spirits. However, the laws of harmony that govern all creation must surely apply to ghosts. In the final Act of Chapman's *Revenge of Bussy D'Ambois*, five ghosts revel in their triumph by performing a gleeful dance of death about the body of their murderer. As the hour of their triumph approaches, the ghost of Bussy tells us that they shall celebrate with dance:

> [**Umbra Bussy.**]   The blacke soft-footed houre is now on wing,
> Which for my just wreake, Ghosts shall celebrate,
> With dances dire, and of infernall state.

And, when the body of Monsurry at last lies dead upon the stage and Bussy has been avenged,

Musicke, and the Ghost of Bussy enters, leading the Ghost of the Guise, Monsieur,
Cardinall Guise, and Shatilion, they dance about the dead body, and exeunt.

Ghosts, as the disembodied souls of human beings, still retain some memory
of human behavior, which in this case clearly includes celebratory dance. But
the dance takes on another meaning. For the first time, all five restless spirits
are at peace and in harmony with the cosmos, for they have finally been
avenged. This ultimate harmony is symbolized in the steps of their dance and
in the music that sounds for them. Order has been restored, and the wandering
shades may finally rest in peace.

The shepherds, shepherdesses, nymphs, and demigods of pastoral drama
tend to be quite musical, for Arcadia is the vanished golden world in which all
nature is filled with harmony. Such characters, as part of that world, often
raise their voices in praise of the richness of life around them. At the close of
Fletcher's *Faithful Shepherdess*, order has been restored to the perfect world,
and its shepherds may again deliver harmonious praise to the god who pro-
tects them:

> THE SONG *They all sing.*
> All yee Woodes, and Trees, and Bowers,
> All ye vertues, and yee powers,
> That inhabit in the lakes,
> In the pleasant springs or brakes:
>> Move your feete
>> To our song,
>> Whilst wee greete,
>> All this ground,
> With this honour and his name,
> That defends our flockes from blame.
> Hee is great, and he is just,
> Hee is ever good and must,
> Thus be honnerd: Daffadillyes,
> Roses, Pinckes, and loved Lillyes,
>> Let us fling,
>> Whilst wee sing,
>> Ever holy,
>> Ever holy,
> Ever honerd, ever young,
> Thus great *Pan* is ever sung.

Arcadians are expected to be quite musical, for their music serves as a reminder that the world presented on the stage is a world lost to modern mortals,
a world filled with youthful life and the harmony of a more innocent time.

Thomas Campion gives us the impression that the vogue for spirits and enchanters in English masque and drama came about because these creatures
were then the fashion in the most-admired Italian works:

In ancient times whe[n] any man sought to shadowe or heighten his Invention, he had a store of feyned persons readie for his purpose: as *Satyres, Nymphes,* & their like: such were then in request and beliefe among the vulgar. But in our dayes, although they have not utterly lost their use, yet finde they so little credit, that our moderne writers have rather transferred their fictions to the persons of Enchaunters & Commaunders of Spirits, as that excellent Poet *Torquanto Tasso* hath done, and many others.[48]

But enchanters and their familiar spirits may mingle with other "fained persons" in the same play and to the same background of music:

> *Musicke playing within. Enter a Peasant.*

Pesant. Tis night, and good faith I am out of my way. O harke what brave musick is that under the green hill?

> *Enter fairies bringing in a banquet.*

> O daintie, O rare, a banquet, would to Christ,
> I were one of their guests: Gods ad, a fine little
> Dapper fellow has spyed me: what will he doo?
> He comes to make me drinke. I think you sir,
> Some of your victuals, I pray sir,
> Nay now keepe your meate,
> I have enought I, the cup I faith.
> > *Exit.*

Enter the spirit with banquetting stuffe, & missing the Pesant lookes up & downe for him, the rest wondering at him, to them enters the Enchanter.

> (*The Wisdom of Dr. Dodypoll,* Act III)

True to type, the great power of this Enchanter is demonstrated through his ability to command spirits whose very alien nature is demonstrated by the music that accompanies them. He is not only at home in the musical fairy realm, but, as shown in the previous chapter, commands his own musical spirits. Music is often associated with magic and enchantment in the contemporary theater, and, of course, it is by extension associated with those who practice the occult arts or otherwise perform wonders.

CHAPTER 8

MUSIC TO MOVE THE AFFECTIONS

The symphony & concent of Musick... agreeth with the interior parts & affections of the soule.

The Praise of Musicke (1586)

One of the aims of Elizabethan and Jacobean drama was to move the affections of the audience. In fact, the infamous antitheatrical writer Stephen Gosson strongly objects to plays on the grounds that "*tragedies* and *comedies* stirre up affections, and affections are naturally planted in that part of the mind that is common to us with brute beastes."[1] Long before the revival of the children's companies, English drama had evolved into a highly stylized vehicle for moving the passions, principally because of its close relationship to the affective art of rhetoric:

The Oratour may leade his hearers which way he list, and draw them to what affection he will he may make them to be angry, to be pleased, to laugh, to weepe, and lament to love, to abhorre, and loathe to hope, to feare, to covet, to be satisfyed, to envye, to have pittye and compassion to mervaile, to beleeve, and repent and briefly to be moved with any affection that shall serve best for his purposes.[2]

Music, reserved for special moments in English Renaissance drama, was even more affective than spoken rhetoric, for it literally touched its listeners more immediately and more intensely:

It hath beene anciently held, and observed, that the *Sense of Hearing* and the *Kindes of Musicke,* have most Operation upon manners. . . . The Cause is, for the *Sense of Hearing* striketh the *Spirits* more immediately than the other *Senses* and more corporeally than *Smelling*: for the *Sight, Taste*, and *Feeling*, have their Organs, not of

167

so present and immediate Access to the Spirites, as the hearing hath . . . but Harmony, entering easily and mingling not at all, and Comming with a manifest Motion: doth by custome of often Affecting the Spirits, and Putting them into one kind of Posture, alter not a little the Nature of the *Spirits* even when the Object is removed.[3]

This direct affective power of music was so strong in the theater that the ever-suspicious William Prynne perceived it to be extremely dangerous to the audience because "it workes upon their mindes, to corrupt them, [and] upon their lusts, to provoke them to all voluptuousnesse and uncleanesse what-soever."[4]

English Renaissance drama is full of emotionally intense moments meant to rouse the affections of the audience to all the passions of which human be-ings are capable. The plays often present sensational or even shocking situa-tions, violent clashes between volatile emotional states, and the juxtaposition of opposing action and passion. The supreme affective power of music often comes to represent these passions or emotional states, sometimes literally and at others with a note of irony. Music came to work upon the minds of the audience and provoke them to one passion after another in any way that served the dramatist's purpose. The power of music moved its listeners in all these ways, as Francis Meres reminds us:

The Loadstone draweth iron unto it, but the stone of Aetheopia called *theamedes* driveth it away: so there is a kinde of Musicke that dooth asswage and appease the affections, and a kinde that doth kindle and provoke the passions.[5]

Music, especially in the children's theater where the resources were larger and only dramatic intent was the limit, united with the dramatic text and stage action to reinforce the author's intent and act strongly and directly on the in-nermost part of the human mind and soul.

SPECULATIVE MUSIC AND COSMIC HARMONY

The use of music to move the affections in the drama is intimately related to contemporary thought about the power and universality of the art. "Mu-sicke," wrote Thomas Morley,

is either *speculative* or *practicall. Speculative is that kinde of musicke* which by Mathematical helpes, seeketh out causes, properties, and natures of soundes by themselves, and compared with others proceeding no further, but content with onlie contemplation of the Art. *Practical* is that which teacheth al that may be knowne in songs, eyther for the understanding of other mens or making of ones owne.[6]

Both sorts of music interact in the theater, where practicality and symbolism so often merge. Only practical music sounded from the stage, but all of the children's playwrights, even the "hacks like Day, Sharpham, Barry, and Field,"[7] continually point to the metaphor of music for universal harmony throughout their plays. The English Renaissance had inherited from classical antiquity the belief that music governed the ordered workings of the heavens and the human body and soul, making practical music an easily comprehensible metaphor for order within the human mind, the body politic, the natural world, and the entire universe. As *The Praise of Musicke* tells us,

looke upon the frame & workmanship of the whole worlde, whether there be not above, an harmony betweene the spheares, beneath a simbolisme between the elements. Look upon a man who[m] the Philosophers termed a little world, whether the parts accord not one to the other by consent and unity.[8]

Or, in the stronger words of neo-Platonic numerologist William Ingpen,

Musicall harmony bringeth not a little faculty of discoursing, seeing her power and vertues are so great, that shee is called The Imitatrix of the starres, of the soule and body of man. And when she followeth celestiall bodies so exquisitely, it is incredible to think, how she provoketh those heavenly influxes, how she tempereth the affections of her hearers, their intentions, gestures, motions; changeth their actions and manners, allureth them to her properties, either to mirth or sadnes, boldnes or tranquility; and so forth.[9]

There has been a great deal of debate over just how familiar this concept was to contemporary Englishmen.[10] Far too many Elizabethan and Jacobean writers on far too many topics casually mention music as a governing force in the universe for there to be any doubt whatsoever that literate individuals such as those who patronized the children's theater were familiar with the concept of speculative music. Such widely circulating and influential works as Castiglione's *The Courtyer* and Burton's *The Anatomy of Melancholy* repeatedly refer to nonpractical music, and a great many books, including Byrd, Bull, and Gibbons's landmark *Parthenia or the Maydenhead*, Dowland's *Second Booke of Songs or Ayres*, and Ravenscroft's highly derivative and very fashionable *Briefe Discourse*, mention it offhandedly in their introductory material as if anyone who purchased these books would surely have seen the idea before. Furthermore, the frequent references in the dramatic texts to aspects of speculative music and music as a symbol of order prompt the audience to listen to music with their ears and their intellects. As Stephen Gosson reminds us even as he condemns music in the theater,

Pythagoras bequeathes them a Clookbagge, and condemnes them for fooles, that judge Musicke by sound and eare. If you will be good Schollers, and profite well in the Art of Musicke, shutte your Fidels in their cases, and looke up to heaven the order of the *Spheares*, the unfaillible motion of the Planets, the juste course of the yeere, and varietie of seasons, the concorde of the Elementes and their qualyties, Fyre,

Water, Ayre, Earth, Heate, Colde, Moysture and Droughte concurring togeather to the constitution and sustenance of every creature.[11]

According to the vast and influential body of Renaissance neo-Platonism, the music of humanity was analogous to that of the heavens and could be represented and affected by the earthly sound of practical music:

it hath bene the opinion of most wise Philosophers that the world is made of Musicke, and the heavens in their moving make a melody, and our soule is framed after the very same sort, and therefore lifteth up it selfe and (as it were) reviveth the vertues and force of it with musick.[12]

The Renaissance regarded this human soul as a substantive entity, physically affected by man's five senses. Corporeal perception most often reached the soul through the spirit, which relayed those sensory impulses that entered the body. Robert Burton best explains this phenomenon:

Spirit is a most subtile vapour, which is expressed from the *Blood*, & the instrument of the soule, to performe all his actions: a common tye or *Medium*, betwixt the body and soule. . . . *Melancthon* holds the fountaine of these spirits to be the *Heart*, begotten there, and afterward convaied to the *Braine*.[13]

But music touched the very soul as it reached the body and intermediary spirits, drawing it through the ear to become one with universal harmony. This direct seduction of the soul by music resulted from a substantive similarity between the two, for both were perceived as vivified air.[14] Again, Burton summarizes the physical effects of music as the later English Renaissance knew them:

In a word it [music] is so powerful a thing, that it ravisheth the soule, *regina sensuum*, the Queene of the senses, by sweet pleasure (which is an happy cure) and corporeall tunes pacifie our incorporeall soule, *sine ore loquens, dominatum in animam exercet*, and carries it beyond it selfe, helpes, elevates, extends it. *Scaliger exercit*. 302. gives a reason of these effects, *because the spirits about the heart, take in that trembling and dancing aire into the body, are moved together, and stirred up with it*, or else the mind as some suppose, harmonically composed, is roused up at the tunes of musicke. And 'tis not only men are so affected, but almost all other creatures.[15]

The early seventeenth-century English classicist George Sandys adds that

Yet musicke in it selfe most strangly works upon our humane affections. Not in that the Soule (according to the opinion of the *Platonists*) consisting of harmony, & rapt with the sphearicall musick before it descended from heaven to inhabit the body, affects it with like desire. . . but beacuse the Spirits which agitate in the heart, receave a warbling and dancing aire into the bosome, and are made one with the same where they have an affinity; whose motions lead to the rest of the Spirits dispersed through the body, raising or suppressing the instrumental parts according to the measures of the Musick; sometimes inflaming and againe composing the affections the sence of hearing stricking the Spirits more immediately, then the rest of the sences.[16]

The author of another of the fashionable treatises on melancholy explains just how music moves the diverse affections of its hearers:

For as the heart is most delicat and sensitive, so it perceaveth the least motions and impressions that may be and it seemeth that musicke in those celles playeth with the vital and animate spirits, the onely instruments and spurres of passions. . . . In musicke, divers consorts stirre up in the heart, divers sorts of joyes, and divers sorts of sadnesse or paine the which as men are affected, may be diversly applied let a good and Godly man heare musicke, and hee will lift up his heart to heaven let a bad man heare the same, and hee will convert it to lust let a souldiour heare a trumpet or a drum, and his blood will boile and bend to battell; let a clowne heare the same, and he will fall a dauncing; let the common people heare the like, and they will fall a gazing, or laughing and many never regard them, especially if they bee accustomed to heare them. So that in this, mens affections and dispositions, by meanes of musicke, may stirre up divers passions, as in seeing we daily proove the like. True it is, that one kind of musicke may be more apt to one passion than another, as also one object of sight is more proportionat to stirre up love, hatred, or pleasure, or sadnesse, than another. Wherefore the naturall disposition of a man, his custome or exercise, his vertue or vice, for most part as these sounds diversificate passions for I cannot imagine, that if a man never had heard a trumpet or a drum in his life, that he would at first hearing be mooved to warres.[17]

In the theater, then, musical characterization had a strong and direct influence on musical affect, for different characters use and perceive music differently. Dialogue further reinforces precisely what affect the music should have not only on the characters in the drama but on the passions of the audience. The use of musical affect in the contemporary theater, then, is based on philosophical views of the nature of music but is essentially dependent on each specific dramatic instance and the way in which author and director use language and gesture as well as music.

THE MUSICAL COSMOS IN THE CHILDREN'S THEATER

The children's playwrights and audience were by and large educated and fashionably intellectual, and the children's companies had the musical resources to play almost anything for any reason. It is, therefore, no surprise that the ideas of cosmic harmony and the affinity between the soul and music appear again and again in this diverse body of plays. Musical affect is used in an almost infinite variety of ways and for many reasons in these works, but always to the same end: to temper or illustrate the mood of individuals and to affect or explain their behavior. These rules of course extend to the world in which the characters live, for, as we have seen, the music of the human condition is analogous to the music of the external world. As Francis Meres tells us, the individual had to be in tune with himself and his environment in order to receive the higher form of harmony:

Even as he that would play upo[n] an harp, or anye other instrument of Musick, ought before all things to have his strings well tuned, that they may fitly and melodiously agree with one another: so it is necessary also that our heart (seeing it is the chiefe instrument of that heavenly Musicke) be first well tuned and prepared, for there can bee no harmonious consort in a jarring and untuned instrument.[18]

In the concluding dialogue of Middleton's *The Phoenix*, we see the restoration of harmony to the world of the play through the restoration of well-tuned music to an individual:

> Tanglemad.   Haile sacred patience, I begin to feele
> I have a conscience now, truth in my words,
> Compassion in my hart, & above all, in my blood
> Peaces musick,
> Use me how you can,
> You shall find me an honest-quiet man.
> O pardon that I dare behold that face!
> Now I've at lest law I hope I have most grace.
>
> Phoenix.   We both admire the work-man and his peece:
> Thus when all hearts are tunde to honors strings,
> There is no musicke to the quire of kings.

The effectiveness of these words is greatly increased when we recall that music traditionally closed the children's plays, for in this case such practical music is elevated to the status of metaphorical harmony.

A contrasting episode opens Marston's *The Malcontent*, and in that case there is absolutely no doubt left that music added to the affect of the dialogue. As noted earlier, the play opens with literal and figurative discord to set the stage for the corruption of the Genoese court and to show the inner restlessness and eccentricity of the title character:

> *The vilest out of tune musicke being heard, enter* Bilioso *and* Prepasso.
>
> Bilioso.   Why how now! Are ye mad, or drunk, or both, or what?
> Prepasso.   Are ye building Babylon there?
> Bilioso.   Here's a noise in court! You think you are in a tavern, do you not?
> Prepasso.   You think you are in a brothel-house, do you not?—This room is ill-scented.
>   *Enter One with a perfume.*
> So perfume, perfume; some upon me, I pray thee—
> The duke is upon instant entrance; so make place there!
> *Enter Pietro, Ferrando, Equato; Celso and Guerrino before.*

Pietro.	Where breathes that musicke?
Bilioso.	The discord rather than musicke is heard from the malcontent Malevole's chamber.

A different use of music to represent both the human condition and the external environment is found in Act I, scene ii of Chapman's *Conspiracy of Charles Duke of Byron*. The title character has just been named Duke, and accepts his new status in harmonious wonder. As the standard ceremonial entry music sounds, he fancies that he hears within it the harmony of the heavens, for the entire frame of being seems in tune with him:

Lowde musique, and enter Byron.

Byron.	What place is this? What ayre? What region?
	In which a man may heere the harmony
	Of all things mooving? *Hymen* marries here,
	Their endes and uses and makes me his temple.

Musique again

Heere too? They follow my steps with musique
As if my feete were numerous, and trod sounds
Out of the centre with Apollos vertue,
That out of every thing his each part touchd
Strook musicall accents: wherefoe're I goe,
They hide the earth from me with coverings rich,
To make me thinke I am heere in heaven.

In this manner, the audience may see how Byron perceives his place in the cosmos and accepts his new responsibilities as Duke.

Most often, music does not simply symbolize harmony or discord within the individual or his world, but is requested by one or more characters to heal a distressed spirit. The music itself not only acts upon an introspective, grief stricken, or even mad character, but audibly represents the healing process as he is made whole again. In Act V of Marston's *Jacke Drum's Entertainment*, Pasquil has lost his wits by thinking he has lost his Katherine forever. His friends are clearly aware of the common wisdom that "musicke restoreth mad-men to their wits,"[19] and arrange for his sanity to be restored through music. They also explain precisely why it is music that must accomplish the task:

Sir Edward.	I am quite sunck with griefe, what shall we do
	To get recovery of his wits againe?
Brabant.	Let sweet musicke sound, for I have often heard
	It hath such sweet agreement with our soules,

> **Planet.** That it corrects vaine humours, and recalls
> His struggling fancies to faire union.
>
> **Planet.** Why the soule of man is nought but symphonies,
> A sound of disagreeing parts, yet fair unitie
> By heavens hand, divine by reasons light.
>
> **Sir Edward.** Sound musicke, then pray God it takes effect.
>
> (The musicke sounds and *Pasquils* eye is fixt upon *Catherine*.)
>
> **Brabant.** Mark with what passion he sucks up the sweets
> Of the same delicately harmonious breath.
>
> **Planet.** Observe him well, me thinkes his eye is fixt
> Upon some object that seemes to attract
> His verie soule forth with astonishment.
> Marke with what vehemence his thoughts do speake
> Even in his eies, some creature stands farre off,
> That has intranc'te him with a pleasing sight.
>
> **Pasquil.** Amazement, wonder, stiffe astonishment,
> Stare and stand gazing on this miracle,
> Perfection, of what e're a humane thought
> Can reach with his discoursive faculties,
> Thou whose sweet presence purifies my sence,
> And doest create a second soule in me,
> Deare *Katherine*, the life of *Pasquils* hopes.

Of course, the music has taken effect, for the power of music is omnipotent.

Music is similarly used under radically different circumstances in Act III, scene i of the same author's *Antonio and Mellida*. At this point in the drama, Andrugio, the defeated Duke of Genoa, wanders through a gloomy Venetian marsh where he has been cast ashore and muses over a notice that offers twenty thousand double pistolets for the delivery of his head to his conquering enemy, Piero. He seems to have lost everything, even his dear son Antonio. In the company of only his faithful friend Lucio and a pageboy, he requests a song to ease the heaviness of his soul:

> **Andrugio.** No sun will shine where poore *Andrugio breathes*
> My soule growes heavy: boy, let's have a song:
> Weele sing yet, even despite of fate.
>
> CANTANT
>
> **Andrugio.** Tis a good boy, and by my troth well sung.
> O, and thou felt'st my griefe, I warrant thee,
> Thou would'st have strook division to the height,
> And made the life of musicke breath[e].

Although the song scarcely expresses Andrugio's infinite woe to his liking, it eases his distraught spirits and rouses him to action. Instead of continuing to sigh, at last he tells us that "ere yon sunne set, Ile shew myselfe myselfe,/

Worthy my blood." The song banishes his distraction and allows him to proceed as the noble Duke he truly is.

Music to heal the downtrodden or discordant spirits does not always accompany such dire situations as Pasquil's or Andrugio's. But no matter why music is requested, it always has a profound affect on both the dramatic atmosphere and the characters involved. In Act III of Day's *Law Tricks*, the Countess and her ladies sit "sowing by an howre-glass," the age-old symbol of the mercilessly steady passage of time and human mortality. Their discussion turns rapidly to such moribund subjects as aging and mortality, creating an aura of repressive gloom about their cozy task and intimate setting. One wise gentlewoman suggests the standard cure for oppressed spirits to banish their cares:

> **2 Gentlewoman.** Be not so sad, good madam, do but smile
> Weele have a song sad sorrow to beguile.
> *Cantant*

The song immediately begins to reverse the solemn atmosphere of the sewing circle and restores the ladies to better humor.

In Act IV, scene i of Mason's *Tragedy of Muleasses the Turk*, the song Amada sings to comfort Julia in her despair becomes a vehicle for extreme dramatic irony and a jarring juxtaposition of ordered action:

> **Julia.** Sad thoughts opresse me: may I have no musique?
>
> **Amada.** Yes Madam
>
> **Julia.** Some say that when the Thracian entered hell,
> The tortur'd soules enchanted with his tunes,
> Felt not their torments: *Syciphus* sate downe,
> Ixions wheele stood still: the thirsty sonne of *Jove*,
> Forgat to drinke, and all the rest did stand
> Catching the aire from his delicious hand:
> I would I might pertake their happines.
>
> **Amada.** Madam you shall: give your eares a while,
> And you shall heare such musicke as would make
> The greedy wolf forsake the tender lamb,
> And listen to it: such as the sonne of *Neptune*
> Playd to the Dolphins: when they in a ring
> Danct their crookt measures but to heare him sing.
>
> A SONG
>
> Madam how fare you now?
>
> **Julia.** Even as the laboring dayman after sleepe.
> *Enter Timoclea like a Ghost*
> Refresht and cherisht. . . .

Orpheus-like herself, Amada has driven all torment from her companion's soul. However, Timoclea, the singer's mother, arrives instantly after the song clad in the costume of a vengeful ghost from hell to kill her daughter in a jealous rage that has been mounting for some time. The audience knows that Timoclea is bent on murder, and she arrives too late to feel the healing power of Amada's song. But the order imposed by the music on Julia's troubled mind stands in clashing contrast to the chaotic act of murder that it precedes, having lulled audience and victim alike. The peaceful atmosphere summoned forth by the healing power of the song is shattered through the sudden act of bloody horror.

Music to move the affections did not always reverse despair, for the limitless power of music was capable of provoking many passions. Indeed, it was held by many Elizabethan and Jacobean thinkers that music simply amplified the affect it found. As Burton tells us, music can make "him that was merry much merrier than before, a lover more inamoured, a religious man more devout."[20] And Francis Bacon in all his wisdom reminds us that

Tunes and *Aires*, even in their own Nature, have in them some affinitie with the Affections. . . considering that Tunes have a predisposition to the Motion of the Spirits in themselves. But yet it hath beene noted, that though this variety of Tunes doth dispose the *Spirits* to variety of Passions, conform to them; yet generally, *Musicke* feedeth that disposition of the *Spirit* which it findeth.[21]

In Act IV, scene i of Marston's *Antonio and Mellida*, Antonio languishes in the cold Venetian marsh where he, his father, and their faithful men have been variously cast ashore. Although he has been reunited with his father, Andrugio, in that dismal place, he fears that he has lost his beloved Mellida forever. Alone with his page, he requests that the boy express his despair in the passionate language of music:

> **Antonio.**   . . . Boy, prethee stay a little.
>   Thou hast had a good voice, if this cold Marsh,
>   Wherein we lurke, have not corrupted it.
> *Enter Mellida, standing out of sight, in her pages sute.*
>   I prethee sing, but sirra (marke you me)
>   Let each note breathe the heart of passion,
>   The sad extractature of extreamest griefe.
>   Make me a straine speake groaning like a Bell
>   That towles departing soules.
>   Breathe me a poynt that may inforce me weepe,
>   To wring my hands, to breake my cursed breast,
>   Rave and exclaime, lie groveling on the earth,
>   Straight start up frantick, crying, *Mellida*
>   Sing but, *Antonio hath lost Mellida*,
>   And thou shalt see me (like a man possest)

> Howle out such passion, that even this brinish Marsh
> Will squease out teares from out his spungie cheekes,
> The rockes even groane, and
> Pree thee, pree thee sing,
> Or I shall nere ha done; When I am in
> Tis harder for me end, then to begin.
> *The* boy *runnes a note*: Antonio breakes *it*.
> For looke thee, boy, my griefe that hath no end
> I may begin to plaine, but—Pree thee sing.

CANTANT

This grief-enforcing song is integrated into an especially effective piece of theater. For as soon as it ends Antonio is reunited with Mellida, who has escaped from her father's watchful eye in the guise of a page. His sad despair, expressed musically by his page, only contrasts all the more with the lovers' joyous reunion.

A contrasting example of song to augment despair involves the same characters but a much less joyous ending. In Act II, scene ii of *Antonio's Revenge*, the title character has come to speak with his wrongfully convicted beloved through the grate of her prison door. The deviously evil Piero and his creature Strotzo enter just in time to see the young man weep in despair, and Piero calls for a song to augment his young adversary's depressed spirits:

> **Piero.** He grieves; laugh, Strotzo, laugh, he weepes. Hath he
> teares?
> O pleasure! hath he teares?
> Now doe I scourge *Andrugio* with steele whips
> Of knotty vengeance. *Strotzo*, cause me straight
> Some plaining ditty to augment despair:
> Triumph, *Piero*; harke, he groanes; O rare!
> **Antonio.** Behold a prostrate wretch layd on his tombe.
> His epitaph thus: *Ne plus ultra*. Ho,
> Let none out-woe me, mine's *Herculean woe*.

CANTANT

The power of music and the obscene villainy of Piero unite to oppress Antonio even further, and to increase audience sympathy for the desperately wronged young lovers.

LOVE

No passion is expressed more frequently and more variously with music in the children's plays than love. The examples of music used to enhance the emotion of love in these works, ranging from expressions of dejection to overt sexual metaphor, could easily fill volumes. After all, love itself is a multifarious affect that must be expressed in a variety of ways in drama:

And because love is of all other humane affections the most puissant and passionate, the most generall to all sortes and ages of men and women, so as whether it be of the yong or old or wise or holy, or high estate or low, none could ever truly bragge any exemptio[n] in that case: it requireth a form of Poesie variable, inconstant, affected, curious and most witty of any others, whereof the joyes were to be uttered in one sorte, the sorrowes in an other, and by many formes of Poesie the many moodes and pangs of lovers, thoroughly to be discovered: the poore soules sometimes praying, beseeching, sometime honouring, avancing, praising: an otherwhile railing, reviling, and cursing: then sorrowing, weeping, lamenting: in the ende laughing, rejoysing, & solacing the beloved againe, with a thousand delicate devises, odes, songs, elegies, ballads, sonets and other ditties, mooving one way and another to great compassion.[22]

The relationship between music and love was commented on as frequently by Englishmen of the late sixteenth and early seventeenth centuries as that between music and the soul. Music could content the lovelorn:

we see the *Soveraignty* of *Musicke* in this *Affection* [love], by *Cure* and *Remedy* it affoords the *Dispassionate* and *Infortunate Sonnes of Love*, thereby to asswage the *turmoyles* and quiet the *tempests* that were raised in them.[23]

Men and women could even become better musicians by using music in love:

Tis their chiefest study to sing, dance, and without question, so many Gentlemen and Gentlewomen would not be so well qualified in this kinde, if love did not incite them.[24]

The music of love could be instrumental or vocal. In its instrumental manifestation, it was particularly associated with bowed or plucked strings:

> And when your Ivory fingers touch the strings
> Of any silver-sounding instrument,
> Love makes the[m] daunce to those sweet murmurings
> With busie skill, and cunning excellent.[25]

A special category of instrumental love music was the dance, for the combination of music and ordered motion was an especially apt metaphor for love. The dance itself was, like love, associated with universal harmony, as Antinous reminds Penelope in Sir John Davies's terpsichorean poem, *Orchestra*:

> Daemon (bright Lady) then began to be,
> When first the seeds whereof the world did spring,
> Then Fire, Ayres, Earth, and Water—did agree,

> By Loves perswasion,—Natures mighty King,—
> To leave their first disordered combating;
> And in a dance such measures to observe,
> As all the world their motion shall preserve.[26]

The music of the dance also served to ignite the burning passion of love in the dancers, or, as the Puritans would have it, fanned the flames of lust.[27] When love's sweet music was vocal, it most often served to enhance amorous lyrics, which made it even more affective than instrumental music under certain circumstances:

enamoring [is] a passion as (more or lesse) possessing and affecting all, so truely exprest by none, but musick, that is Song or Poetry: the former whereof, gives herein both as a relish, and a beauty to the latter, inasmuch as Passionate Tunes make Amorous Poems both willinglier heard and better remembred.[28]

However, ultimately the combination of "A swet voice and musick are powerful enticers" to love.[29]

Renaissance thought, especially that influenced by the ideas of neo-Platonism, related love to music, for both are universal and both depend on a concord of independent but sympathetic elements. The same soul that could leave the body and ascend the heavenly heights by music could do the same through love and the contemplation of earthly beauty. The analogy between love and music because of their similar inspirational affect on the airy human soul was stressed repeatedly by contemporary writers. One of the more elegant examples is from a neo-Platonic poem by children's playwright George Chapman:

> Never was any sence so sette on fire
> With an immortal ardor as myne eares;
> Her fingers to the strings doth speech inspire
> And numbred laughter; that the deskant beares
> To hir sweete voice; whose species through my sence
> My spirits to their highest function reares;
> To which imprest with ceasles confluence
> It useth them, as proper to her powre
> Marries my soul, and makes it selfe her dowre.[30]

And as Thomas Morley cites the revered Plato on the topic, "*Musicke*, saith he, *is a science of love matters occupied in harmonie and rhythmos.*"[31]

Again and again, we see this idea in the children's plays, where music comes frequently to represent love matters through its harmony and rhythm. But this association between the moving experience of love and moving ability of music was broadly based and included many diverse elements and actions, as Ravenscroft reminds us:

I have heard it said, that Love teaches a man *musicke*, who ne're before knew what perteyned thereto: and the Philosophers three *Principall Causes of Musick*, 1. *Dolour*, 2. *Joy*, 3. *Enthusiasme* or *Ravishing of the Spirit*, are all found by him within *Loves* Territories.[32]

The reverse of the chaste love that could ravish the spirit was the baser lust that could ravish the body and corrupt both soul and mortal flesh. The music of the theater was applied to both extremes and all that lay between.[33] Again, children's plays tend to use love music in the same dramatic way as adults' plays; if the music of love appears more frequently and takes more diverse forms in the children's theater, it is only because the Children of the Chapel and the Children of Paul's had a larger number of available musicians.

All sorts and phases of love, from the first amorous glances to the final consummation, were accompanied by and represented in music on the children's stage. The beginning of a new love relied especially on harmonic symbolism and on the metaphorical relationship among the music of the individual, the cosmos, and the sound of practical music. Falling in love, often an extremely lengthy process in life, could be symbolically compressed into a very brief period of time through the use of music.

One of the most interesting and detailed instances of falling in love quickly against a musical background takes place during the wedding masque of Act II, scene i of Marston and Barkstead's *The Insatiate Countess*. The masque belongs to the celebration of the marriage between the title character, Isabella, and the Count, Robert. The masque is structured in the manner of most masques in Jacobean plays, with the taking-out dance occupying a position of dramatic prominence. The music of the entire masque becomes symbolic love music as Isabella beholds the young and handsome Massino, appropriately costumed as a torchbearer. A stage direction following the second of three "changes" of the taking-out dance calls for her to fall in love with him. An impassioned speech assigned to her reinforces the direction. And lest the symbolism of the music and dance be lost to the audience, Massino, equally taken with the new Countess, remarks at the close, "The spheres ne're danced to a better tune." Following the end of the revels section of the masque, Massino "dances a Levalto or a galliard, and in the midst of it falleth into the Brides lap, but straight leaps up and danceth out." The sexual symbolism of this action is as obvious as the metaphor of the dance for his new passion, and the musical symbolism is again reinforced when Isabella asks her maid to discover his name with "Speake Musicke, what's his name?". The very choice of the galliard or lavolta for Massino's display of musical virility is quite appropriate, for both dances were considered especially fit for displaying the attributes of masculinity. Either was regarded as

> A gallant daunce, that lively doth bewray
> A spirit and a vertue Masculine,
> Impatient that her house on earth should stay
> Since she her selfe is fierie and divine:
> Oft doth she make her body upward flune,
> > With loftie turnes and capriols in the ayre
> > Which with the lustie tunes accordeth fayre.[34]

The mounting passion between Isabella and Massino that could not be expressed through simple dialogue is instead shown very effectively through music and gesture. But the irony that this sudden surge of amorous desire is accompanied by music to celebrate the wedding of Isabella and another man is as obvious as the emotion itself. And dialogue makes it quite clear that Isabella's desire for the handsome masked man is far from chaste or spiritual. The music that sounds for it, then, is heavenly only to the two of them, and their love is obviously headed for a destructive end since it springs from earthly desire.

The most diverse stage of love, generally following the first stirrings of the passion, is courtship, which makes as much use of music as do the first pangs of love on the children's stage. But music in courtship often becomes an artificial tool to help the suitor and thus comes to the foreground of the scene in which it is used. An elegant example is found in Act III, scene i of Lyly's *Love's Metamorphosis*, which combines neo-Platonic love metaphor, practical courtship music, and fashionable love melancholy. This brief scenario also includes the almost obligatory musical puns that so many contemporary discussions of love embrace. At this point in the play, the melancholy Silvestris comes upon the object of his unrequited love, the sweetly wanton nymph, Niobe. The poor youth has been all but driven mad with love for her. But he, being a fine lutenist, knows well the power of music in love matters and asks her to sing with him to ease the yearning in his soul. She, inconstant but honest, warns him that their music will only make him sigh and burn all the more. Nonetheless, she yields to his simple request, and for a brief instant his troubled soul is soothed:

Silvestris.	A woman hath but one hart.
Niobe.	But a thousand thoughts.
Silvestris.	My Lute, though it have many strings, maketh a sweet consent, and a ladies heart, though it harbour many fancies, should embrace but one love.
Niobe.	The strings of my heart are tuned to a contrastie keye to your Lute, and make as sweet harmonie in discords, as yours in concord.
Silvestris.	Why, what strings are in Ladies hearts? Not the base.
Niobe.	There is no base in a womans heart.

Silvestris.	The meane?
Niobe.	There was never meane in womans heart.
Silvestris.	The treble?
Niobe.	Yea, the treble double and treble, and so are all my heart strings. Farewell.
Silvestris.	Sweet *Niobe*, let us sing, that I may die with the Swanne.
Niobe.	It will make you sigh the more and live with the Sala-mich.
Silvestris.	Are thy tunes fire?
Niobe.	Are yours death?
Silvestris.	No but when I have heard thy voice, I am content to die.
Niobe.	I will sing to content thee.

Cantant

Silvestris.	Inconstant Niobe! Unhappie Silvestris! Yet I had rather shee should rather love all then none: for nowe though I have no certaintie, yet doe I find a kinde of sweetnesse.

Late Renaissance thought held that the music of love would only increase despondency in those who, like Silvestris, had become melancholy through unfulfilled love:

Provided alwaies, his disease proceed not originally from it [love], and that he be not some light *inamorato*, some idle phantasticke, who capers in conceit all day long, and thinkes of nothing else, but how to make Gigges, Sonnets, Madrigals, in commendation of his Mistresse. In such cases Musicke is most pernitious, as a spurre to a free horse, will make him run himselfe blinde, or break his winde, it will make such mealncholy persons mad. . . . *Plato* for this reason forbids, Musicke and wine to all young men, because they are most part amorous, *ne ignis addatur igni*, least one fire encrease another.[35]

Such a case is shown in Act IV, scene v of Jonson's *His Case is Altered*, in which amorous young Onion asks Juniper to stop singing when he has been stricken melancholy with love:

Enter Juniper in his shop singing; to him Onion.

Onion.	Fellow Juniper, no more of thy songs and sonets, sweet Juniper, no more of thy hymnes and madrigals, thou singst but I sigh.
Juniper.	Whats the matter Peter ha? What an Academy still, still in sable, and costly black array? Ha?
Onion.	Prithee rise mount, mount sweet Juniper, for I goe downe the wind, and yet I puffe: for I am vext.
Juniper.	Ha bully? What intoxicate? . . .
Onion.	I confesse Cupids carouse, he plaies super *negulum with my liquor of life*.

The serenade, considered at length in chapter 6, of course belongs to the courtship ritual, and, as we have seen, was particularly associated with the unsuccessful, doltish lover who attempted to win his lady with the sweet melody to which she was believed so susceptible. The children's plays, always quick to parody conventions of the stage or life and thought, of course include parodic serenades and parodic musical courtship. One of the most outstanding examples in the repertoire occurs in Act III, scene ii of Marston's *Antonio's Revenge* in which the delicate harmony of music is perverted into a grotesque parody of an amorous serenade that becomes part of an obscene travesty of true love. Everything about this scene is a violation of convention and propriety, right down to the absence of the love and the use of lyrics hardly meant to make an amorous tune more willingly heard. Furthermore, the scene is placed between two jarringly discordant actions, helping to illustrate the corruption and perversion of every normal ritual of life that pervades this masterful play. The scene hardly arouses the affect of love in either audience or characters, but succeeds only to shock and sicken with a deft and purposeful dramatic hand. We are given by the playwright a world in which beauty has no place and love is only a matter of convenience.

At the start of the third Act, Antonio visits the tomb of his murdered father at the stroke of midnight. True to form, the ghost of his father, Andrugio, rises to speak. His grim message is twofold: Antonio must avenge his unnatural death; and his widow, Maria, must be prevented from marrying his murderer, Piero. The scene closes with the first and most hideously wanton act of vengeance as Antonio murders Piero's trusting young son and sprinkles the stage with the child's blood. Immediately, the scene shifts to Maria's bedchamber. The hapless widow is to be married against her will the next day to Piero, and her bridegroom-to-be has sent the eccentric Sir Jeffrey Balurdo to woo her by proxy with tasteless love songs:

> [Balurdo.]   The Duke [Piero] hath sent you the most musical Sir
>   Jeffrey. With his not base but most enobled viol, to
>   rock your baby thoughts in the cradle of sleep.

Piero does not accompany Balurdo as would have been traditional, nor does the musician stop outside Maria's chamber door, but instead serenades her in the intimate setting of her bedroom. Balurdo's amorous music is as ill-timed in Maria's life as it is in the play, and his songs are ill-conceived. The first of the three sets the tone of grotesque and unseemly sensuality that pervades the scene. The song represents not only the absurd character who performs it, but also the unfeeling Piero, who has only the basest reasons for wishing to marry the reluctant widow. It is the music of love where no love can exist, jolting the audience as much as the gruesome scene of horror that it follows. No matter how exquisite the musical accompaniment that Balurdo may have played, it could hardly have given relish and beauty to the lyric, as the music of love songs was supposed to do:

[THE SONG]
My mistresse eye doth oyle my joynts,
And make my fingers nimble:
O love come on, untrusse your poynts,
My fiddlestick wants a rozzen.
My ladies dugges are all so smooth
That no flesh must them handle:
Her eyes do shine, for to say sooth,
Like a new-snuffed candle.

After Balurdo leaves and Maria dismisses her attendants, she discovers the spectre of her late murdered husband sitting on the bed, hurling accusations of faithlessness and wantonness at her. His grim presence is shocking after the ludicrously inappropriate scene with the bufoonish Balurdo, and his harsh accusations of her unfaithfulness are as grossly inappropriate as the crude serenade. Furthermore, the song that Maria has just heard could hardly inspire wantonness any less. Marston has carefully placed the musical courtship scenario between two shocking moments of high drama to lull the audience temporarily with something approaching comedy while the horror mounts, and to express the extreme impropriety of the loveless match between Maria and Piero.

Another sort of musical courtship found often in the children's plays is that between a courtesan and her customer. Because of the unearthly power of music in love matters, the music of the whore serves both to entice her customers and to represent her trade. As shown in the previous chapter, she is often as skilled in the arts of music as in the artifical allurements of love. And because music is so extremely potent an aid to love, those men who hear the siren song of the courtesan are rendered completely helpless before her. As the author of a treatise in praise of women reminds us, "the Astronomers do holde, that *Venus* is the patronesse of Musique, and that the influence of her Planet, brings most speciall felicitie to such as deal in that facultie."[36]

One of the most musical courtesans of children's drama is Imperia of *Blurt, Master-Constable,* who sings almost every time she comes on stage. In Act V, scene ii, she has lured Fontinell into the privacy of her bordello where she entertains him with all the arts of her trade. Fontinell himself has seemingly abandoned the pure Violetta, for whom he realized his true love to the strains of a dance in the first Act of the play. The contrast between Fontinell's two loves is as obvious as that between Imperia's siren song of erotic delight and Violetta's heavenly pure dance.

The scene between Imperia and Fontinell is one of the most overtly sexual in the repertoire, full of passionate embraces and the obligatory double entendres of speech and gesture. Imperia sings twice, the first time unaccompanied, and the second time to an instrumental accompaniment. The first song is only a simple "la la" burden, a spontaneous response to Fontinell's "moiste and moving" lip. The second song, which she sings as he lies in her lap, represents a relaxing calm after ardent embraces and increasingly passionate speech. The song also represents the climax of their brief relationship, and comes to stand for the passionate sexuality that could only be represented symbolically in a theater in which all the actors were boys. In fact, the sly reference to Jove and Ganymede slipped into the song text serves as an overt reminder that the audience was actually witnessing a fervent love scene played between two beautiful young men. The song itself is prepared by dialogue and by an instrumental introduction that becomes its accompaniment. It upholds the feeling of leisurely and understated ardor that pervades the entire scene:

> Love for such a cherrie lip,
> Would be glad to pawne his arrows:
> Venus heere to take a Sip
> Would sell her Doves and teeme of Sparrows.
> But they shall not so,
> Hey nony nony no:
> None but I this lip must owe,
> Hey nony nony no.
> Did *Jove* but see this wanton eye,
> Ganimede must waite no longer;
> Phoebe heere one night to lye,[37]
> Would change her face and looke much younger,
> But they shall not so,
> Hey nony nony no:
> None but I this lip must owe,
> Hey nony nony no.

Sexual union between other characters and under other circumstances is also given musical treatment in children's plays. When music is used in a scene of sexual fulfillment, it not only enhances the amorous affect but also becomes a symbol of physical and spiritual concord. Music, the philosophical emblem of harmonious union in the literature of the English Renaissance and seventeenth century, becomes especially important in representing erotic fulfillment in a theater in which mature male and female lovers were really young boys. The affect created by the music thus becomes indispensable in making adult heterosexuality believable under such circumstances.

The most outstanding example of music as strict sexual metaphor in the children's repertoire is found in Act III, scene iv of Marston and Barkstead's *The Insatiate Countess*. In that scene, the authors themselves indicate that the specific choice of music is not as important as the fact that it is included. They further remind the audience of the philosophical association between music and love in the speeches of the lovers:

> **Isabella.** Cease admiration, sit to Cupid's feast,
> The preparation of Paphian dalliance;
> Harmonious musick, breathe thy silver airs
> To stir up appetite to Venus' banquet,
> That breath of pleasure that entrances sould
> Making that instant happiness a heaven,
> In the true taste of love's deliciousness.
>
> **Gniaca.** Thy words are able to stir cold desire
> Into his flesh that lies entombed in ice,
> Having lost the feeling use of warmth in blood;
> Then how much more in me, whose youthful veins,
> Like a proud river, overflow their bounds?
> Pleasures ambrosia, or love's nourisher,
> I long for privacy; come, let us in;
> Tis custom, and not reason, makes love sin.
>
> **Isabella.** I'll lead the way to Venus paradise,
> Where thou shalt taste that fruit that made men wise.
>
> *Exit Isabella*
>
> **Gniaca.** Sing notes of pleasure to elate our blood:
> Why should heaven frowne on joyes that do us good?
> I come Isabella keeper of loves treasure,
> To force thy blood to lust and ravish pleasure.
>
> *Exit.*
>
> *After some short song enter Isabella and Gniaca againe,*
> *she hanging about his neck lasciviously.*

It is easy to imagine the erotic off-stage scenario so cleverly represented by a short musical number, making this a highly effective piece of theater. The emphasis in the dialogue and action is on lust and not the higher, spiritually uplifting form of love. The audience would know at this point of the action, if not before, that these two adulterous lovers are destined for trouble, for it was held that "Musique is delectable to the mynde, but carnally liked, is hurt to the soule."[38] And it is hardly for the delectation of the mind that Gniaca calls for music.

A very different use of the standard musical metaphor for sexual union occurs in Act V, scene iii of Marston's *Sophonisba*, in which the prelude to love fulfilled ironically becomes the music of martyrdom. At this point in the play, the cornetts of war have finally ceased, and Massinissa comes home to enjoy a delayed wedding night with the faithful Sophonisba. The only direction for "soft music" in a completely human context in the entire play occurs in this scene, a stirring contrast to the bellicose cornetts that play so many times. This music, the sound of peace and a prelude to the ultimate union between these two heroic lovers, accompanies their passionate reunion:

Sophonisba.	We cannot now be wretched.
Massinissa.	Stay the sword.
	Let slaughter cease: Sounds soft as Leda's breast
	Soft musique
	Slide through all eares, this night be loves high feast.
Sophonisba.	Oerwhelm me not with sweets; let me not drink
	Till my breast burst, O jove thy nectar, thinke—
	She sinkes into Massinissas armes
Massinissa.	She is orecome with joy.
Sophonisba.	Helpe, helpe to beare
	Some happinesse yee powers, I have joy to spare,
	Inough to make a God, O Massinissa.

But the atmosphere of peace, joy, and love fulfilled is shattered suddenly as Laeius bursts in and demands the delivery of Sophonisba to the Romans as a hostage. The nectar that she finally drinks is not that of heavenly love or ultimate bliss, but the poison that she takes to resolve her beloved husband's conflict of loyalty. The theme of thwarted love, which runs throughout the play to the accompaniment of music which makes that love believable and possible, has reached its ultimate tragic conclusion. Marston, master of the unexpected use of music, has taken the convention of music for love fulfilled to a bitter and ironic end.

MELANCHOLY

Another important affect that often becomes musical in children's drama is melancholy, which, as we have seen, is sometimes closely connected to love. Toward the end of the Elizabethan era, there sprang up a cult around melancholy that lasted well into the seventeenth century. Though most modern writers associate the melancholy vision of life with the Jacobean era, by the 1580s it was already a highly fashionable affliction with a vital influence on literature.[39] Interest in this disease of the spirit arose in part from the educated elite's fascination with the literature and learning of the ancient world,[40] and some of the best-selling books of the period, including Timothy Bright's *Treatise of Melancholy* and Robert Burton's *Anatomy of Melancholy*, were devoted to the subject. By the end of the sixteenth century, numerous English writers described the disease in fanciful and technical terms, and all of the arts felt the influence of the vogue for melancholy.

The term "melancholy" had originally been used to denote one of the basic personality types, the gloomy temperament that resulted from the predominance of the melancholy humor, or black bile, in the human body. However, the Elizabethan and Jacobean preoccupation was not with the melancholy temperament but with a mental or spiritual illness that resembled the humorous temperament; indeed, by the seventeenth century, the term had become an all-embracing label for disease, particularly that of spiritual origin.[41] Melancholy was characterized by a morbid depression, gloominess, and generalized sorrow that could lead to madness or death if left untreated.[42] It was a disease associated with the wealthy in both literature and life; more members of the upper classes suffered from melancholy than from other mental maladies, and most patients treated for the ailment were of gentle birth.[43]

Music was very closely associated with the disease, particularly as a cure, but also occasionally as an inducement. William Barley, for instance, used as a selling point for his *New Booke of Tabliture* of 1596 the fact that it could "benefit such, as desire to have a tast of so ravishing a sweet Science as Musique is, being the soveraigne salve of a melancholy and troubled minde."[44] And Robert Burton tells us in no uncertain terms that

Musica est mentis medicina maestra, a roaring-meg against Melancholy, to ereare and revive the languishing Soule, y affecting not only the eares, but the very arteries, the vitall and animall spirits, it erects the minde, and makes it nimble . . . his it will effect in the most dull, severe, and sorowfull Soules, expell griefe with mirth, and if there bee any cloudes or dust, or dregges of cares yet lurking in our thoughts, most powerfully it wipes them all away.[45]

He adds that not only does music aggravate the symptoms of love melancholy, as we have already seen, but that

Many men are melancholy by hearing Musicke, but it is a pleasing melancholy that it causeth, and therefore to such as are discontent, in woe, feare, sorrow, or dejected, it is a most present remedy, it expells cares[,] alters their grieved mindes, and easeth in an instant.[46]

So closely, then, were music and melancholy intertwined for all purposes that Batren Holyday, in his Oxford comedy *Technogamia: or the Marriages of the Arts*, has Melancholico, a servant to Poeta, fall in love with Musica, a servant to Astronimia in Act I; and has them marry in Act V.[47] Thomas Nabbes, in his masque *Microcosmus*, personifies Melancholy as "A Musician. His complexion[,] haire and clothes black: A Lute in his hand."[48]

Numerous descriptions of the symptoms and cures of melancholy show that nearly all diseases of the spirit on the children's stage, especially those provided with musical cure or reinforcement, fall under the general rubric of "melancholy." However, after the late 1590s, when children's drama turned heavily to satire and to the mockery of convention, and when the fashionable cult of melancholy was wide open to burlesque interpretation, characters displaying the more overt symptoms of the condition tended to represent parodies of the disease. By the Jacobean era, a burlesque of melancholy in the distinct guise of a socially or philosophically alienated young man, black-clad and sullen, had become a convention of the stage.[49]

As in so much else, the children's playwrights led the way, beginning almost instantly after the revival of the two principal companies; and nowhere else is the parodic convention more prevalent than in the children's plays, which were aimed at the very same class of people among whom melancholy was a fashionable affectation. Of course, melancholy was taken seriously in some children's plays; Pasquil, Andrugio, the Countess, Julia, and even Silvestris are all clearly victims of the damaging disease. But each of them seeks a cure and does not emphasize his condition for its own sake. Onion, on the other hand, is a perfect example of the burlesque of the ailment. Instead of quietly seeking a cure, he broadcasts his state in every manner possible and according to every convention. The word is not applied to the condition in any of the above instances, but when the label "melancholy" is used in children's plays, it seems to signal a playful parody of the more serious literary treatments, more like Onion's exaggerated affectation than the debilitating ailment of the others. And, of course, the standard parodic treatment normally included a burlesque of the more serious uses of music as a cure for spiritual ills, for music was a constant companion of the melancholy man, and the children's companies had the resources to express any affect through any sort of music.

One of the most outstanding examples of melancholy that is so labeled occurs in Act II of *The Maydes Metamorphosis*, complete with music. The incident is a typically witty servant's scene, related little to the remainder of the play. Mopso, Frisco, and Joculo each enter the stage singing a popular song. The first is a shepherd's boy, the second a ranger's boy, and they sing the simple ditties of bucolic life that convention assigned to such rustics as they. Joculo, on the other hand, is a courtier's page, and seems to take on the fashionable affects that belong to the stereotyped courtier of literature and the stage, most notably the overstated accoutrements of melancholy. His song is the desperate, dirgelike "Fortune my Foe." Joculo not only breaks with tradition by providing his own melancholy song, but also appears to seek and maintain the company of two strangers, in spite of a feeble protest to the contrary, when melancholia normally demands solitude or the presence of only a close confidant or two. It is easy to see this scenario, especially acted by imp-

ish young rascals in a parodic style, as a parody of the courtly preoccupation
with melancholy:

> *Enter at one doore. Mopso singing*

Mopso.   Terliterlo, terliterlo, terliterlee, terlo,
           So merrily this shepheards Boy
           His horne that he can blow,
           Early in a morning, late, late in an evening,
           And ever sat this little Boy,
           So merrily piping.

> *Enter at the other Doore, Frisco singing.*

Frisco.   Can you blow the little horne?
           Weel, weel, and very weel.
           And can you blow the little horne,
           Amongst the leaves greene?

> *Enter Joculo in the midst singing.*

Joculo.   Fortune my foe, why doest thou frown on mee?
           And will my fortune never better bee:
           Wilt thou I say, for ever breed my paine?
           And wilt thou not restore my Joyes againe?

Frisco.   Cannot a man be merry in his owne walke,
           But must be thus encombred?

Joculo.   I am disposed to be melancholy,
           And I cannot be private for one villaine or another.

The merry songs of Mopso and Frisco do not cure Joculo's affected melancholy as they should, but instead Joculo's song causes the merriment of Mopso and Frisco to cease. This is a complete reversal of the standard convention
by which melancholy is cured by mirth; and neither does the song appear to
cause Joculo a particularly carefree or pleasing melancholy. Instead, he and
his song, affected as they both are, simply serve to annoy the merry boy rustics, for melancholy courtiers have no place in the midst of pastoral revelry.
Undoubtedly, Joculo's costume and appropriately mimed action added to the
merry hilarity of this scenario in the original production.

DEATH

The dramatic tradition of funerary music, as discussed in chapter 5, is simply
one manifestation of the association between death and music on the children's stage. Not only was music used in funeral processions as it would have
been in the world outside the theater, but it became emblematic of death under
other circumstances and was occasionally used to increase the pathos of a
death foreshadowed. The symbolic association between music and death is
ancient and widespread,[50] and, like the equally venerable association be-

tween music and the human soul, could be used for a variety of affects in the drama.

Perhaps the simplest and most direct use of music in conjunction with death in the children's plays is the sounding of a bell to toll departed souls, most often used for the off-stage death of one of the characters. In Act IV, scene ii of Middleton's *Michaelmas Term* such a bell announces Quomodo's death to all within hearing distance, causing a momentary break in the action with its sudden solemn sound. But such a sound and such a brief moment, based on Renaissance custom rather than affect alone, scarcely demonstrate the great power of music in the drama of death, for it is hardly more than an official announcement of the passage of a human soul from this world to the next. Song and instrumental music are used in a wide variety of ways to remind the audience and the other characters of death. The most common and most varied use of music in conjunction with death is the lament after the fact. The lament is especially associated with the children's plays of the 1570s and 80s, when it often took the musical form of a consort song.[51] But after the later 1590s it was still as viable and affective a device as ever before, with increased stylistic and dramatic versatility.

In Act II, scene i of Chapman's *Revenge of Bussy D'Ambois*, a private, personal lament serves to remind the audience of the treacherous murder of the title character at the end of the previous play, *Bussy D'Ambois*. Tamyra, the adulterous mistress of the deceased, grieves for him alone. Her despondent mood, which could not be fully expressed through rational speech, is instead reinforced by a heartfelt lament that also serves to signify her own spiritual imbalance since her lover's death. Her pitiful song is harshly interrupted by her unfeeling husband, the guilty murderer. But the atmosphere of despair and sorrow has already been reinforced by the song and by the verbal reminder of the close relationship between music and the human spirit:

> [Tamyra.]   . . . Here, O here where still
> Earth (mov'd with pittie) yelded and embrac'd
> My Loves faire figure, drawne in his deare bloud,
> And mark'd the place, to show thee where was done
> The cruell'st murther that ere fled the Sunne.
> O Earth! why keep'st thou not as well his spirit,
> To give his forme life? No, that was not earthly:
> That (rarefying the thinne and yeelding ayre)
> Flew sparkling up in Sphaere of fire,
> Whence endlesse flames it sheds in my desire:
> Here by my daily pallet, here all nights
> That can be wrested from thy rivals armes;
> (O my deare Bussy) I will lye, and kisse
> Spirit into thy bloud, or breathe out mine

In sighes, and kisses, and sad tunes to thine. *She sings.*

Enter Montsur[ry]

Montsurry.   Still on this hant? Still shall adulterous bloud
                   Affect thy spirits?

In this way, the audience is reminded of the tragic outcome of the previous play and of where their sympathies should lie in a dramatic world full of moral ambiguity.

The opposite dramatic use of lament is found in Act I, scene ii of Jonson's *Cynthia's Revels*, in which the song becomes an emblem of the play to come. The lament, sung by Eccho over Narcissus, expresses the theme of warning to self-lovers that recurs throughout the play. At this point in the action, Jove has sent his heavenly messenger, Mercury, to restore "vocall and articulate power" to Eccho, who has remained dumbly beside the fountain where her beloved Narcissus pined and died of self-love three thousand years before. At long last, she is briefly given power to lament the death of

> that too beauteous boy,
> That trophaee of selfe-love, and spoile of nature,
> Who (now transform'd into a drouping flowre)
> Hangs the repentant head, back from the streame,
> As if it wish'd, would I had never look'd
> In such a flattering mirror.

She sings out her ancient misery to the accompaniment of "musicque from the spheares" that shows the accord of all nature with her sorrowful sentiment that "natures pride is, now, a whither'd daffodil."

A very different and far less formal sort of vocal lamentation that borders on the farcical is found in Act V, scene iii of Beaumont's burlesque *Knight of the Burning Pestle*. Old Merrythought, forever singing to purge himself of all vexing thoughts, sings over the coffin of his favorite son in spite of a spoken warning that song may be inappropriate at such a time. Though the unaccompanied snatch of song he selects is not inappropriate, his lament is not delivered to immortalize the dead or express a sorrow too deep for normal speech. For Merrythought, snatches of song are the language of daily speech, and he prides himself on never feeling sorrow because he always sings. Thus, his lament is not really set apart from normal behavior. The lament, one of the most affective expressions of deep personal grief in English Renaissance drama, here loses all meaning and becomes instead a routine part of life. But, fortunately, the lamented son is actually alive and well, welcomed back to the world of the living by his overly musical father in the same way that his "demise" was mourned:

Enter a boy *with a coffin.*

Boy.	God save you, sir.
Old Merrythought.	Its a brave boy. Canst thou sing?
Boy.	Yes, sir, I can sing: but 'tis not so necessary at this time.
Old Merrythought [singing].	*Sing wee and chant it* *Whilst love doth grant it.*
Boy.	Sir, sir, if you knew what I have brought you, you would have little list to sing.
Old Merrythought [singing].	*O the Mimon round,* *Full long, long I have thee sought,* *And now I have thee found,* *And what hast thou here brought?*
Boy.	A coffin, sir, and your dead son Jasper in it.
Old Merrythought [singing].	Dead? Why farewell he. Thou wast a bonny boy And I did love thee.

Enter Jasper.

Jasper.	Then, I pray you sir, do so still.
Old Merrythought.	Jasper's ghost! [He sings] *Thou art welcome from Stygian lake* *so soon;* *Declare to me what wondrous things* *in Plutos court are done.*
Jasper.	By my troth, sir, I ne're came to that; tis too hot for me, sir.
Old Merrythought.	A merry ghost, a very merry ghost!

Musical expressions of grief and tragic loss are not always sung; sometimes an instrumental reinforcement of spoken text can be just as effective. In Act I, scene ii of Marston's *Antonio's Revenge*, Antonio, Alberto, and Pandulpho lament the murder of young Feliche. They are members of the nobility for whom public song would be inappropriate, and none have been sufficiently distempered by the murder and its aftermath to lose their sense of propriety and break into song. Therefore, a stage direction calls for music to sound beneath the spoken eulogy, and this expresses the sorrowful sentiment more intensely than words alone:

[Pandulpho].	Come sit, kind nephew; thou and I Will talk as chorus to this tragedy. Entreat the musick strain their instruments With a slight touch whilst we—say on fair coz.

Alberto.   He was the very hope of Italy,
                 Musicke sounds softly
                 The blooming honor of your drooping age.

In spite of dramatic convention, sometimes musical lamentation following violent death would be too harmonious and is therefore purposefully omitted. In Act IV, scene v of the same play, the trio of mourners and their assisting servants have finally found the opportunity to bury Feliche. Antonio requests a dirge from his page, for the moment is right to memorialize the dead with music, but Pandulpho tells him that musical harmony at such a time would not accord with circumstance:

Antonio.   Wilt sing a Dirge boy?
Pandulpho.   No, no song: twill be vile out of tune.
Alberto.   Indeede hes hoarce: the poor boys voice is crackt.
Pandulpho.   Why cuz? Why should it not be hoarce & crackt,
                 When all the strings of natures symphony
                 Are crakt, & jar? Why should his voice keepe tune,
                 When ther's no musicke in the breast of man?

In this instance, the sounding metaphor of practical music for cosmic and human harmony is avoided for the very reason that it is so powerfully affective: the world in *Antonio's Revenge* is too darkly discordant for the sweet strains of sounding music to restore harmony. Feliche's death is too unnatural for any analogue of harmonious nature to ease him into the next world, or wipe out the discord of his violent end.

The technique of foreshadowing death with music, used so beautifully by Shakespeare in *Richard II* and *Othello*, is by no means absent from the children's stage. The trial of Mellida in Act IV, scene ii of *Antonio's Revenge* includes an excellent and subtle example. It begins with a formal sennet played on cornetts as all but Mellida enter. But "the still flutes sound softly" for her entrance, their muted tones as soft and weak in comparison to the robust cornetts as Mellida's case and true justice are in comparison to Piero and his biased witness. As we have seen, the flute was an instrument associated with death and funeral processions. This association further reinforces the final outcome of the sham trial—the death of an innocent young woman who has entered the courtroom as if to the music of her own funeral.

A playfully ironic use of the musical foreshadowing of death may be found in Act I, scene ii of Field's *A Woman is a Weather-Cocke*. At the double wedding of Bellafront and Count Frederick and Katherine and Strange, Sir Abram Ninny has been spurned by his love, Lucida. He launches straight into a speech of despair, full of the standard imagery of death and thwarted love, and at last says that he shall pine and die:

Abram.	Well since I am disdain'd; off Garters blew;
	Which signifies Sir *Abrams* love was true
	Off Cypresse blacke, for thou befits not me;
	Thou art not Cypresse, of the Cypresse Tree,
	Befitting Lovers. . .
	Now to thy Fathers Countrey house at *Babram,*
	Ride post; There pine and dle, poore, poore sir *Abram.*
Omnes.	Oh dolefull dumpe.

Musicke plays.

But the music that plays is hardly a doleful dump, suitable for Abram's predicament or his tale of woe, nor is it even a funeral march to speed the young fop on his way. It is instead the music that signals the start of the wedding, as we are told by the next line of dialogue. The music that plays is not the knell of death, but the bright sound of new beginnings.

An actual thwarting of expected death, prepared by music, occurs in the first Act of *The Maydes Metamorphosis*. Eurymine, grieving for the love of Ascanio, has found a willing executioner to end her misery forever. Distracted beyond the ability to express herself in rational words, she sings a swan song before the final blow is struck. At the end of the song, "Orestes offers to strike her with his rapier, and is stayed by Phylander." Phylander's gallantry and Eurymine's acceptance of his life-saving action recall the principle that "musical harmony recalleth furious and frantick persons from sudden and desperate attempts,"[52] for Eurymine's song arouses the pity that saves her life even after the audience has been prepared for her premature death.

MAGIC AND THE FANTASTIC

Children's plays are not only populated with a wide variety of fantastic beings whose music helps create their distant, normally invisible place in the cosmos, but are pervaded with the iridescent aura of magic. And these occult things, musical in all English Renaissance drama, are especially musical in the children's plays. The same neo-Platonic doctrine that postulated the effect of music on the rest of the universe also allowed for such beings to occupy a place among the same spheres,[53] so it is hardly surprising to discover that the music of the marvelous includes the same affective ability as the music of humanity. The Elizabethan cosmos held many things in it that have been lost to the modern world, including good and evil spirits and several sorts of magic. The last was especially associated with music, because both were numerical arts. The kind of white magic known as natural magic, actually a Renaissance form of natural science that relied both on the obvious and occult properties of objects, was considered to be a "naturall wisdome . . .

the exact and absolute knowledge of all naturall things,"[54] and was especially musical, for

There is nothing of greater efficacy then the hymnes of *Orpheus*, in naturall Magick, if the fitting musick, intention of the minde, and other circumstances which are knowne to the wise, bee considered and applyed. And againe—*that they are of no lesse power in naturall magick*, or to the understanding thereof, then the *Psalmes of David are to the Caball* or to understand the *Cabalistick Science* by.[55]

Previous writers on music in Elizabethan and Jacobean drama have been unable to ignore the extreme wealth of magical and fantastic music, but have generally attributed it to authorial creativity in transcending the limits of the natural world or the contemporary stage.[56] Indeed, such music, as omnipresent as the aura of magic and the marvelous, belongs in part to authorial creativity (for it sounded on common, mundane instruments in the theater) and undoubtedly helped to overcome the limits of stage machinery and lack of scenery, but it also belongs to the now-vanished tradition of the Renaissance occult sciences. Music itself at once combined the literal with the symbolic, the mortal with the divine, the mundane with the celestial, and as such could express any of these. "For there is a twofold harmony of musick," says a seventeenth-century classicist, "the one of divine providence, and the other of humane reason. To humane judgement (which is as it were to mortall eares) the administration of the World, of the creature, and more secret degrees of the highest, sound harsh and disconsonant."[57] Occult scientist and mathematician John Dee adds that "as *Astronomie* hath a more divine Contemplation and co[m]modity, then the mortall eye can perceive: So is *Musicke* to be considered, that the Minde may be preferred before the eare.[58] As we have seen, the theater audience was encouraged to listen to dramatic music with both the ear and the mind; and though only one sort of music could sound to mortal ears in the theater, dialogue and action made it clear when the music played belonged to the secret world beyond humanity.

Often in scenes of superhuman wonder, music is meant to represent a component of magic, or contribute to the atmosphere of mystery and superhuman power. In Act III of the anonymous *Wisdom of Dr. Dodypoll*, the Enchanter commands musical spirits to do his bidding, and their music shows both his unearthly power and the magical world in which mere mortals are helpless. His entrances are all preceded by fantastic music, produced by fairies, spirits, or unspecified forces that are all at his command. While the Enchanter has been demonstrating his power to the Peasant who stumbled upon his charmed domain, Lucilla has been pursuing her reluctant lover, Lassenburgh, over the magical green hills. The Enchanter is himself charmed

by the girl, and decides to seduce her through magical means. His erotic
magic uses music as an agent at each step:

*Enter Enchanter, leading Luc. and Lass. bound by spirits, who being laid down on a
green banck, the spirits fetch in a ba[n]quet.*

THE SONG

> *O princely face and fayre, that lightens all the ayre,*
> *Would God my eyes kindle fire, my life and soule inspire;*
> *To thy riche beauty shining in my hearts treasure,*
> *The unperfect words refining, for perfect pleasure.*

Enchanter.	Lie there and lose the memory of her,
	Who likewise forgot the thought of thee
	By my inchantments: come sit downe faire Nimphe
	And taste the sweetnesse of these neavenly cates,
	Whilst from the hollow craines of this rocke,
	Musick shall sound to recreate my love.
Lucilla.	I had a lover I thinke, but who it was,
	Or where, or how long since, ayre me, I know not:
	Yet beat my timorous thoughts on such a thing,
	I feele a passionate heate, but find no flame:
	Thinke what I know not, nor what I thinke.
Enchanter.	Hast thou forgot me then? I am thy love,
	Whom sweetly thou wert wont to entertaine,
	With lookes, with vowes of love, with amorous kisses,
	Looskt thou so strange, doost thou not know me yet?
Lucilla.	Sure I should know you.
Enchanter.	Why, love, doubt you that?
	Twas I that led you through the painted meades
	Where the light Fairies daunst upon the flowers,
	Hanging on every leafe an orient pearle,
	Which strooke together with the silken winde,
	Of their loose mantels made a silver shime.
	Twas I that winding my shrill bugle horne,
	Made a guilt pallace breake out of the hill,
	Filled suddenly with troopes of knights and dames,
	Who daunst and reveld whilst we sweetly slept,
	Upon a bed of Roses wrapt in goulde.

It is clear that the sound of music throughout the episode, and even in the Enchanter's seductive story, is the sound of his powerful magic at work, not
meant for mortal ears to hear but represented in the theater with the available
musical media.

Sometimes supernatural beings sing as they work selfless miracles, as does
the God of the River in Act III, scene i of Fletcher's *Faithful Shepherdess*;

again, it is the sound of music beyond mere humanity, music of greater power. Amoret, wounded by her lover Perigot, has been flung into a well by the Sullen Shepherd and left to die. However, the God of the River "Riseth with Amoret in his armes" shortly thereafter and restores her to health. Unlike the Enchanter above, he makes all of his own music because his power is entirely within himself. And he needs but a single song to accomplish his deed and make his point to the audience. But even his speech is songlike in its poetry, for poetry, too, was considered harmonious.[59] When he beholds the wounded maiden, he speaks in metrical verse:

[God of the River.]   See she pants and from her flesh
                        The warme blood gusheth out a fresh
                        She is an unpoluted mayde:
                        I must have this bleeding stayde.
                        From my banckes, I pluch this flower,
                        With holy hand whose vertuous power,
                        Is at once to heale and draw.

After he has brought her "back out of the Armes of death," the deity introduces himself and completes the healing process, which must include striking the wounded soul more harshly than the flesh. Then the God turns from poetry to song:

THE SONG
Doe not feare to put thy feete,
Naked in the River sweete,
Think not leach, or Neute, or Toad,
Will byte thy foote when thou hast trod,
Nor let the water rising hye,
As thou wadest in make thee cry
And sobb but ever live with mee,
And not a wave shall trouble thee.

The God of the River is concerned and healing, and the Enchanter's power is rendered comically impotent when he misuses it for lustful gain. However, the spells worked by such beings and their music are not always benign or innocuous to human beings. Music has power over the human soul in the realm of the marvelous in contemporary drama, and this power makes men easy victims of malevolent magic that uses a musical component. There are a number of practitioners of harmful musical magic in children's drama. All of them work their spells to the accompaniment of music, which serves both to illustrate the working of the magic and to provide additional power over their mortal victims.

All practitioners of musical black magic in children's drama are women, such as the powerful Erictho of *Sophonisba*. The identification of musical malevolence with the feminine gender is undoubtedly not accidental in these plays. Rudolf Felber points out how very pervasive in Western thought is the union of "the evil aspect of music, its demonic, sense-exciting effect in certain situations as personified by woman, and . . . the infatuating diablerie of feminine nature expressed in the artful seduction of music."[60] Indeed, the harmful sense-exciting aspect of music was often likened by English Renaissance thinkers to a siren, their quintessential personification of female musical magic:

to some it [music] seemes offensive, bycause it carrieth away the eare, with the sweetnesse of the melodie, and bewitcheth the mind with a *syrens* sound, pulling it from the delite, wherein of duetie it ought to dwell, unto harmonicall fantasies, and withdrawing it, from the best meditations, and most vertuous thoughtes to forreigne conceits and wandring devises.[61]

And in children's drama, perhaps the best example of the evil aspect of womanly musical magic is the Siren of Lyly's *Love's Metamorphosis*. She is truly feminine deviltry personified, and her enchanting voice and fair face are but the unavoidable call to certain destruction. Indeed

the *Sirens* are now taken for inticing pleasures, as formerly for the Muses: and their musick for that eloquence which perswades to destruction. They are called *Sirens*, of attracting . . . which signifie no other then the motives of the minde to amorous delights, by beauty, youth, and bewitching eloquence.[62]

In Act IV, scene i of Lyly's mythological comedy, the Siren attempts to lure the pure Petulius to a watery grave with her overwhelming charms. In her hand she holds the customary symbols of the mermaid, the comb and glass, and she has about her all the traditionally irresistible enticements of her kind:

> Syren.   Here commeth a brave yuth. Now, *Syren*, leave out nothing that may allure—thy golden lockes, thy entising lookes, thy tuned voice, thy subtile speeche, thy faire promises which never missed the heart of any but *Ulisses*.
>
> *Sings, with a glasse in her hand and a combe.*
>
> Petulius.   What divine godess is this? What sweete harmonie! My heart is ravished with such tickling thoughts and mine eyes stayed with such a bewitching beautie, that I can neither find the meanes to remove my affection, nor turne aside my lookes. *Sing againe Syren.* I yeeld to death, but with such delight, I would not wish to live, unlesse it were to heare thy sweete layes.

The fair fiend promises her immortal love to the enchanted Petulius, and he seems caught in her harmonious snare. But his mortal love, Protea, enlists the aid of the divine Neptune to save the youth from the Siren's wet and fatal embrace. Not only would the literate audience have known the legend of the sirens and their great danger, but they, too, would undoubtedly have been captivated by the voice of the singer playing the ravishing creature.

One of the most amusing scenes of musical marvel in the children's repertoire is found in Act IV, scene ii of *Blurt, Master-Constable.* Lazarillo de Tormes, the unlucky Spaniard who serves as the butt of most of the jokes in the play, is made to believe that he is in a haunted chamber. Music, the standard vehicle for the supernatural, convinces him of the occult presences in the area, and adds to the well-calculated, all-too-human "unearthly" atmosphere, also for the benefit of the audience:

Musicke sodainly plaies, and birds sing: Enter Lazarillo bare headed in his shirt: a pair of pantaples on, a rapier in his hand and a tobacco pipe: he seems amazed, and walkes so up and downe. A song presently within.

Lazarillo speaks at length to the unseen presences (presumably Frisco, Imperia, and their comrades masquerading as spirits), and receives an occasional laugh "from within." Another "song within" follows the mostly one-sided dialogue, and its text contributes to the merrily eerie feeling of this scenario:

A SONG WITHIN

Midnights bell goes ting, ting, ting, ting,
Then dogs do howle, and not a bird does sing:
But the Nightingale, and she cries twit, twit, twit, twit.
Owles then on everie bowe do sit
Ravens Croake on Chimnes toppes.
The Cricket in the Chamber hoppes:
And the Cats crie mew, mew, mew,
The nibling Mouse is not a sleepe
But he goes peepe, peepe, peepe, peepe,
And the Cats cryes mew, mew, mew,
And the Cats cryes mew, mew, mew.

Lazarillo. I shall be mowz'd by pusse-cattes: but I had rather dye a dogs death; they have nine lives (apeece like a woman) and they will make it up ten lives, if they and I fall a scratching: Bright *Helena* of this house, wod thy *Troy* were a fire, for I am a colde. . .

The Spanish Pavin

The Spanish Pavin: I thought the devill could not understand Spanish: but since thou art my countriman, o thou tawnie Satin, I will daunce after thy pipe.

He daunces the Spanish Pavin

The thoroughly ridiculous portrait of Lazarillo as a superstitious, gullible fool places him completely within the unflattering Spanish stereotype that sprang up in literature shortly after the defeat of the Spanish Armada, adding to the amusement value of the scene. This nonthreatening scenario, a perfect parody of musical magic, stands in marked contrast to the sinister one that bridges Acts IV and V of Marston's *Sophonisba*, although both use music similarly to represent unearthly happenings. Only human imagination limited what sort of music could be called to sound for the marvelous in English Renaissance drama.

CHAPTER 9

THE SOURCES OF THE MUSIC

What time and diligence I have bestowed in the search of Musicke, what travel in forren countries, what successe and estimation even among strangers I have found, I leave to the report of others.

John Dowland, *The First Booke of Songes or Ayres* (1597)

Although previous scholars have identified and transcribed a number of seventeenth-century musical settings of children's dramatic lyrics, it has remained to present scholars to do a comprehensive search and complete study of the musical sources for the plays. Like the children's plays themselves, these sources are extremely varied; and like the archival documents connected to the children's companies, they are extremely rare. Central London, where the brief history of children's drama unfolded, has been exceptionally vulnerable to the ravages of time; and therefore, many precious manuscript documents from the sixteenth and early seventeenth centuries have been lost. Among these are all of the theatrical promptbooks for the children's plays and, apparently, any manuscripts of musical settings for theatrical use maintained by the children's companies or their associated musical establishments. Furthermore, during the early seventeenth century, there was apparently none of the later interest in publishing anthologies of music from the theater; nor did such theatrical musicians as Robert Jones and Philip Rosseter include dramatic settings in those collections they published. However, because such a high percentage of children's dramatic music after the late 1590s is pre-existent, and because a number of eclectic musical manuscripts and publications include one or two original theatrical pieces, settings of a representative sample of lyrics from the children's theaters have been preserved.

A look at the extant sources of children's dramatic music after 1597 resembles a brief overview of English secular music from the Elizabethan and Jacobean eras with a few later examplars thrown in. These sources include a goodly cross-section of the published collections of lute song, madrigals, and lessons for musical instruments that became so popular during these years; the earliest surviving British attempts to commit music from the vast oral tradition to writing; major manuscript collections of lute songs and viol music; a theoretical treatise with appended musical examples; mid-seventeenth century autograph manuscripts; and some very eclectic musical miscellanies. In spite of these differences a common feature unites these works: they all remain only peripherally related to the children's stage, for none are principally collections of Elizabethan or Jacobean theatrical music.

These sources can be divided into several categories, both temporally and in terms of content or presentation. From the Elizabethan and Jacobean eras come published collections devoted to homogeneous works by single composers, and diverse published anthologies. The relevant pieces in both categories of books tend to predate the plays that use them by several years and to appear in those plays only as fragments or quotations that attest to previous popularity. Also from the Elizabethan and Jacobean periods come the Ravenscroft anthologies that must be given separate consideration because they include pieces written specifically for the theater and settings of popular songs that were independently appropriated for dramatic use. From the Caroline era and later seventeenth century come publications which include long-lived popular tunes that were finally committed to print, publications that present settings of children's lyrics by composers too young to have been responsible for music in the original productions, and manuscripts with settings of children's lyrics by the same younger generation of composers. Finally, there are a number of miscellaneous popular songs from widely scattered sources such as printed broadsidesand parts of the oral repertoire that were only committed to writing in much later eras.

ELIZABETHAN AND JACOBEAN PUBLICATIONS
BY SINGLE COMPOSERS

There are an even dozen publications of homogeneous works by single composers from the Elizabethan and Jacobean eras that include a total of fifteen musical settings of lyrics from the children's stage. (These publications include Philip Rosseter's 1601 *Booke of Ayres* whose contents are divided between Rosseter and Thomas Campion.) All but two of the relevant pieces were incorporated into the plays after the printed collections had appeared, and the remaining two may be completely independent settings or later arrangements of songs from children's plays. Eleven of the fifteen pieces in question are sung by London citizen characters in plays with city comedy elements, eleven are represented in the plays by quotations of less than a single stanza, and two are given as satiric parodies. This information would imply that most of these pieces were well-known among the privileged audiences who attended the children's theaters and were perhaps associated with urban citizenry.

John Dowland's *First Booke of Songes or Ayres* is perhaps the most famous and most widely circulating publication to enjoy such a relationship to the children's stage. Furthermore, the pieces borrowed from this book are given typical treatment in the plays. This landmark publication, which first appeared in 1597, set the quarter-century long English vogue for printed collections of lute songs.[1] It is also noteworthy for its commercial success, which was greater than any previous English publication of secular music.[2] Dowland's *First Booke* went through five editions between 1597 and 1613, corresponding precisely to the final phase of children's drama, and a number of later manuscripts attest to the lasting popularity of some of its songs. Three of these songs are used in children's plays, each quoted unaccompanied by a solo singer who is assigned a large number of other contemporary popular songs.

Number six in Dowland's book, "Now O Now I Needs Must Part," is quoted in Act I, scene i of the anonymous *Everie Woman in her Humour* and misquoted in Act III, scene ii of Chapman, Jonson, and Marston's *Eastward Ho*. It is possible that the tune is older than Dowland's setting; certainly, it later became quite common and even served as the basis for broadside ballads.[3] And a number of Jacobean manuscripts include the song, further testimony to its great popularity: British Library MS Add. 36526A (fol. 7ᵛ); King's College Cambridge MS Rowe 2, "The Turpyn Book of Lute Songs" (fol. 2ᵛ); and Christ Church Oxford MS Mus 439 (p. 45).

Number thirteen in the collection, nearly as popular in Jacobean England, is "Sleep Wayward Thoughts," which is sung in Act I, scene i of *Everie Woman in her Humour* and quoted in Act I, scene i of *Eastward Ho*. Again, there are a number of Jacobean manuscript collections that pay homage to its extreme popularity: British Library MS Add. 15117 (fol. 7); British Library MS Add. 15118 (fol. 4ᵛ); British Library MS Add. 24665, "Giles Earle his Booke" (fol. 29ᵛ); and Christ Church Oxford MS Mus 439 (p. 46). Finally, number fifteen in the collection, "Wilt Thou Unkind Thus Reave Me," is quoted in Act I, scene iv of Beaumont's *The Knight of the Burning Pestle*.

Only a single later manuscript concordance attests to its lasting popularity, British Library MS Add. 15118 (fol. 5ᵛ).

It is quite clear that these songs transcended the narrow limits of Dowland's book to become the common property of music-lovers everywhere in Elizabethan and Jacobean England. There is no evidence that the printed book served as the direct source or inspiration for the inclusion of any of these three songs in the plays. Severed from their polyphonic accompaniments, their narrow vocal ranges and clear syllabic textual underlays are little different from many broadside and ballad tunes. It is, in fact, quite telling that in all three plays, Dowland's once-elegant ayres receive dramatic treatment similar to a wide range of unaccompanied popular songs sung by the same characters, including rounds, catches, ballads, and other similarly treated lute songs and madrigals.

Only two pieces from Jacobean musical publications by single composers have a significantly different relationship to children's drama than the above Dowland songs. One is "What Thing is Love?" from John Bartlet's 1606 *Booke of Ayres*, and the other is "Slow, Slow Fresh Fount" from Henry Youll's 1608 *Canzonets to Three Voyces*. Both were published after the relevant plays were produced, both are provided with complete texts in the plays, and one was definitely sung to an accompaniment on stage. There is no evidence that either one is the setting originally used in the play.

"What Thing is Love?," sung in Act I, scene i of the anonymous *The Wisdom of Dr. Dodypoll*, is a particularly interesting case, for there are two sources to which Bartlet may have turned for the text. The lyric first appeared in George Peele's 1591 "The Hunting of Cupid," probably a pastoral poem that survives only in fragmentary form.[4] The *Dr. Dodypoll* version, which uses only part of a longer passage from Peele's poem, is the earliest to call for a musical setting for the text. And Bartlet's collection was published at least a half-dozen years after the play was first presented between 1597 and 1600. All three texts exhibit variants that make it difficult to tell whether Bartlet's was drawn from the play or the pastoral poem; furthermore, Bartlet's lyric varies more from extant versions of the Peele and the *Dr. Dodypoll* than they do from each other:

Peele version A (William Drummond's 1609 transcription):[5]

> what thing is love for (wel I wot) love is a thing
> it is a pricke; it is a sting
> it is a prettie, prettie thing
> it is a fire it is a cole
> whose flame creepes in at evrie hole.
> and as my wit doth best devise
> loves dwelling is in ladies eies:

from whence do glaunce loves pearcing darts
that mack such holes into our harts
and all the world herin accord
love is a great and mightie lord
and when he list to mount so hie
with Venus he in heven doth lie
and ever more hath been a God
since Mars and sche plaid even and od.

Peele version B (Bodleian MS Rawlinson Poet. 85, fol. 13):[6]

What thing is love? fore sure love is a thinge
Love is a pricke, love is a stynge, love is a pretye,
    pretye thing,
Love is a fyre love is a colle,
Whose flame creeps in at everye hoole,
And as my selfe can beste devyse
His dwelling is in ladyes eyes
From whence he shootes his dayntye dartes
In to the lusty gallunts hartes.
    And ever since was callde a god
    That Mars with Venus playde even and odd,
                Finis   Mr. G: Peelle.

Dr. Dodypoll Version

What Thing is love? For sure I am it is a thing,
it is a prick, it is a thing,
it is a prettie prettie thing,
it is a fire, it is a coale,
whose flame creeps in at every hoale.
And as my wits do best devise,
Loves dwelling is in ladies eies.

Bartlet Version

What thing is love, what thing is love I pray thee tel,
it is a prickle it is a sting,
it is a prety prety thing,
it is a fire it is a coale
whose flame creeps in at every hole,
and as my wits do best devise,
Loves darling lies in Ladies eyes.

All that is completely clear is that Bartlet set only that portion of the text used in the play, and that his source of the lyric is no longer extant. There is no evidence that Bartlet's song was written for the theater nor that he was connected in any way to the Children of Paul's, for whom the play was written. However, it is worth noting that Bartlet's song is set for solo singer with lute accompaniment, that stage directions in the play call for a solo singer, and that the Children of Paul's maintained competent lutenists.

In Henry Youll's case, the only textual source of "Slow, Slow Fresh Fount" is Act I, scene ii of Ben Jonson's *Cynthia's Revels*, acted by the Children of the Chapel in 1600, eight years before Youll's *Canzonets to Three Voyces* were published. Youll's canzonet is set for two treble voices and a tenor, and the song as given in the play calls for a vocal soloist with the accompaniment of "musicque from the spheares." Scholars have argued about whether his setting may have been written for the original production of the play. Mary Chan argues that Youll's setting was probably written for the original production, and that the text was probably added to the two original instrumental lines prior to publication.[7] David Fuller counters that because Youll was not connected to the theater in any known capacity and did not set any other identifiable dramatic lyrics, this song must have been written independently of the theater.[8] Fuller's argument is not entirely conclusive, but further evidence strengthens his position. There are no extant settings of children's lyrics in the three-part madrigalian style that marks the piece, and Youll's setting of "Slow, Slow Fresh Fount" is not stylistically distinct from the other pieces in the collection, none of which has even the slightest connection to the drama. Furthermore, as we shall see, Jonson's usually elegant lyrics, which stand quite well on their own, attracted the attention of later composers for their own sake.

THE COLLECTIONS AND THEIR CHILDREN'S SETTINGS

1. John Bartlet, *A Booke of Ayres* (1606). STC number 1539.
   "What Thing is Love," sung in the anonymous *The Wisdom of Dr. Dodypoll* (Act I, scene i).
2. Thomas Bateson, *The First Set of English Madrigals* (1604). STC number 1586.
   "Sister Awake, Close Not Your Eyes," sung as an unaccompanied solo in the anonymous *Everie Woman in her Humour* (Act II, scene ii).
3. John Dowland, *The First Booke of Songes or Ayres* (1597, 1600, 1603, 1606, 1608, and 1613). STC numbers 7091-7094.
   "Now O Now I Needs Must Part," misquoted in Chapman, Jonson, and Marston's *Eastward Ho* (Act III, scene ii) and quoted in the anonymous *Everie Woman in her Humour* (Act I, scene i).
   "Sleep Wayward Thought," quoted in Chapman, Jonson, and Marston's *Eastward Ho* (Act I, scene i) and the anonymous *Everie Woman in her Humour* (Act I, scene i).
   "Wilt Thou Unkind Thus Reave Me?" quoted in Beaumont's *The Knight of the Burning Pestle* (Act I, scene iv).

4. John Dowland, *The Second Booke of Songs or Ayres* (1600). STC number 7095.
   "Sorrow Stay," quoted in Beaumont's *The Knight of the Burning Pestle* (Act II, scene viii).
5. John Dowland, *The Third and Last Booke of Songs or Aires* (1603). STC number 7096.
   "Say Love if ever Thou Didst Find," quoted parodically in Chapman's *The Widdowes Teares* (Act V, scene i).
6. John Dowland, *Lachrimae or Seaven Teares* (c. 1604). STC number 7097.
   "Lachrimae," called for in Beaumont's *The Knight of the Burning Pestle* (between Acts II and III).
7. Robert Jones, *The First Booke of Songs or Ayres* (1600). STC number 14732.
   "Farewell Dear Love," quoted in Beaumont's *The Knight of the Burning Pestle* (Act II, scene viii).
   "My Mistris Sings No Other Song," quoted in the anonymous *Everie Woman in her Humour* (Act II, scene ii and Act V, scene i), and parodied in Marston's *The Dutch Courtesan* (Act II, scene i).
8. Robert Jones, *The Second Booke of Songs and Ayres* (1601). STC number 14733.
   "My Thought This Other Night," parodied in Dekker and Webster's *Northward Ho* (Act IV).
9. Thomas Morley, *The First Booke of Balletts to Five Voyces* (1595 and 1600). STC numbers 18116 and 18117.
   "Sing Wee and Chaunt It," quoted as an unaccompanied solo in Beaumont's *The Knight of the Burning Pestle* (Act V, scene iii).
10. Thomas Morley, *The First Booke of Ayres* (1600). STC number 18115.5
    "Mistris Mine," quoted in the anonymous *Everie Woman in her Humour* (Act II, scene i).
11. Philip Rosseter, *A Booke of Ayres* (1601). STC number 21332.
    "Mistris Since You So Much Desire," by Thomas Campion, quoted in Chapman, Jonson, and Marston's *Eastward Ho* (Act III, scene ii).
12. Henry Youll, *Canzonets to Three Voyces* (1608). STC number 26105.
    "Slow, Slow Fresh Fount," performed in Jonson's *Cynthia's Revels* (Act I, scene ii).

ELIZABETHAN AND JACOBEAN ANTHOLOGIES INCLUSIVE OF INSTRUCTIONS FOR PLAYING

Four anthology collections that open with instructions for playing instruments preserve tunes used in children's plays. All four were published during the final phase of children's drama, and all four were carefully marketed as music tutors. Like the music from homogeneous collections by single composers, most of the music from these anthologies apparently found its way to the stage because it was popular at the time, and was probably performed on stage in alternate arrangements. Most of the titles included in the collections are also found in different settings in contemporary manuscripts, and many serve as common ballad tunes.[9] Again, the music from these collections that is associated with children's drama tends to be used in plays that feature common characters and familiar urban settings. And it is obvious that it was the great popularity of these pieces that inspired their inclusion in stage plays.

Anthony Holborne's *Cittharn Schoole* of 1597 is the earliest of these anthologies and is typical of the group. It opens with simple rudimentary instructions for playing the cittern. However, most of the book is devoted to music arranged for the instrument and presented in cittern tablature, which includes exercises, dance tunes, fantasies, and a good selection of popular and ballad tunes. Holborne carefully chose familiar music for this anthology, and explains why he selected and presented the pieces as he did:

For in the fronte of the booke (as in the first step or keye to open a way to thy beginnings) I have prefixed some fewe tastes, which by another name I call *praeludia*: things short and not hard: delivered unto thee of purpose to guide thy hand to some proper use of plaie. . . . Next unto them as in ordinary consequence I have conjoyned the most usuall and familiar grounds of these our times. . . together with some such other light fantasies and vulgar tunes for variety as I could best call to memory. . . . To these as they increase of performance riseth, I have annexed some of the same groundes in variable division: done after a more quicke maner of plaie: thereby to teach thee the neerest course to shift thy hand from string to string. Lastly, (as a complet summary of this little worke) I conclude with thinges grave and more judicious then the rest with their Bases in pricksong notes, which I have set downe on every Page opposite to the same lesson.[10]

The Cittharn Schoole, then, like the elementary musical instruction books of any age, includes familiar tunes that will be easily recognizable to the beginner. And because it is an instrumental tutor, those vulgar tunes with which text is associated are presented without words. Some of these tunes are also heard in the children's theaters, performed by familiar and vulgar characters in scenes or plays featuring the familiar and vulgar. Many of the melodies undoubtedly belonged to the tradition of orally-transmitted music and were only set in writing in this case for didactic purposes. The tunes included in Holborne's collection that were also heard in the children's theater are "Go From My Window," quoted with text in Act III, scene v of Beaumont's *The Knight of the Burning Pestle*; "As I Went to Walsingham," misquoted with text in Act II, scene viii of the same play; and "The Spanish Pavin," played in Act IV, scene ii of the anonymous *Blurt, Master-Constable* and which provides the tune for the parodic ballad "When Sampson was a Tall Young Man" in Act II, scene iii of Chapman, Jonson, and Marston's *Eastward Ho*. Further theatrical interest in the collection lies in "Bonny Sweet Robin," quoted as one of Ophelia's mad fragments in Act IV, scene v of Shakespeare's *Hamlet*.

It is quite possible that other tunes in the book were also used in contemporary drama in some of those instances where music is called for but no piece is named.

Thomas Morley's *First Booke of Consort Lessons, made by Divers Exquisite Authors* of 1599 is probably the most famous Elizabethan printed anthology to share tunes with the children's plays. Unlike the Holborne collection, which was written for a single instrument, this one is intended for the mixed consort that was associated with the contemporary theater, and originally included partbooks for treble lute, pandora, cittern, bass viol, flute, and treble viol. In fact, a number of the pieces in the collection demonstrate a broad association with plays performed in the public and private theaters of the era.[11] The *Lessons* also includes instrumental arrangements of madrigals, a canzonet, two masques, and numerous dances. Morley, like Holborne, advances a reason for the variety of his collection. But his reason is slightly different from Holborne's:

The songs are not many, least too great plenty should breede a scarcenes of liking: They be not all of one kinde, because mens fansies seeke after variety; They bee not curious, for that men may be diligence make use of them—and the exquisite Musitian may adde in the handling of them to his greater commendation.[12]

Thus, he recognizes not only the need for familiarity and student progress, but with a shrewd sense of business he openly appeals to the widest possible market by including something to please all musical tastes.[13]

As with Holborne's collection, the pieces that these *Lessons* share with the children's stage are those of the common Londoner, arranged for performance by instruments alone. Number seven, the "lachrimae pavin," is called for simply as "lachrimae" between Acts II and III of Beaumont's *The Knight of the Burning Pestle*; number ten, the "Frogge Galliard," is an instrumental version of the tune used for Dowland's "Now O Now I Needs Must Part," which is misquoted in Act II, scene ii of Chapman, Jonson, and Marston's *Eastward Ho*; number twelve, "Goe from my Window," is quoted with text in Act III, scene v of Beaumont's *The Knight of the Burning Pestle*; and, finally, number eighteen, "Balowe," is called for between Acts II and III of the same play. Two of these tunes are made famous by John Dowland, two are arrangements of popular songs, and all four tunes appear repeatedly in different arrangements in numerous musical works of the era. It is significant that the Dedication to Morley's collection stresses the suitability of the contents for the London waits, for the inter-act dialogue in *The Knight of the Burning Pestle* that includes requests for "lachrimae" and "baloo" informs us that waits are supposed to be providing the entertainment. It is quite plausible, then, that Morley's arrangements are those intended by the Citizen when he asks the musicians to play them.

THE COLLECTIONS AND THEIR CHILDREN'S SETTINGS

1. Anthony Holborne, *The Cittharn Schoole* (1597). STC number 13562.
   "As I Went to Walsingham," misquoted in Beaumont's *The Knight of the Burning Pestle* (Act II, scene viii).
   "Go From My Window," quoted in Beaumont's *The Knight of the Burning Pestle* (Act III, scene v).
   "The Spanish Pavin," played in the anonymous *Blurt, Master-Constable* (Act IV, scene ii); is also the tune for the ballad "When Sampson Was A Tall Young Man," parodied in Chapman, Jonson, and Marston's *Eastward Ho* (Act II, scene iii).
2. Thomas Morley, *The First Booke of Consort Lessons, made by Divers Exquisite Authors* (1599 and 1611). STC numbers 18131 and 18132.
   "Balowe," requested in Beaumont's *The Knight of the Burning Pestle* (between Acts II and III).
   "Frogge Galliard," whose tune is also that of Dowland's "Now O Now I Needs Must Part," misquoted in Chapman, Jonson, and Marston's *Eastward Ho* (Act III, scene ii).
   "Goe from my Windowe," quoted with text in Beaumont's *The Knight of the Burning Pestle* (Act III, scene v).
   "Lachrimae Pavin," requested as "lachrimae" in Beaumont's *The Knight of the Burning Pestle* (between Acts II and III).
3. Thomas Robinson, *New Citharen Lessons* (1609). STC number 21127.
   "O Hone," quoted with text in Chapman, Jonson, and Marston's *Eastward Ho* (Act V, scene i).
4. Thomas Robinson, *The Schoole of Musicke* (1603). STC number 21128.
   "The Spanish Pavin," played in the anonymous *Blurt, Master-Constable* (Act IV, scene ii); the tune is the musical basis for the ballad beginning "When Sampson Was a Tall Young Man," parodied in Chapman, Jonson, and Marston's *Eastward Ho* (Act II, scene iii).[14]

THE RAVENSCROFT SOURCES AND THEIR CONCORDANCES

Thomas Ravenscroft, music theorist, composer, collector, editor, and one-time chorister of St. Paul's Cathedral, is the single most important figure in the preservation of the meagre repertoire of children's dramatic songs that have survived to the present day. Ravenscroft published four very eclectic collections of secular music between 1609 and 1614, each of which includes musical settings of contemporary dramatic lyrics. But it has recently been shown that the only plays for which he preserves unique settings of indisputably dramatic origin were acted by the Children of Paul's between c. 1597 and c. 1604, the approximate years for which Ravenscroft was a member of the St. Paul's Cathedral choir.[15] Since the musical manuscripts actually used by the children's companies have apparently vanished into the mists of time, Ravenscroft's collections are extremely important. They not only add significantly to the extant body of late English Renaissance theatrical songs, but preserve a unique musical record, sparse though it may be, of a once-celebrated London dramatic company.

Each of the four collections has its own unique musical flavor, and each relates differently to the drama. *Pammelia* and *Deuteromelia*, both published in 1609, are marked by simple, popular songs. *Pammelia* consists entirely of rounds, catches, and canons, selected for variety and simplicity, for Ravenscroft, like Morley before him, was a shrewd businessman who wished the widest possible market for his work:

Good Art in all, for the most musicall, good mirth and melodie for the most joviall, sweet harmonie, mixed with varietie, and both with great facilitie. Harmonie to please, varietie to delight, facilitie to invite thee. Some toyes yet musicall, without absurdity, some very musicall, yet pleasing without difficulty, light, but not without musickes delight, musickes pleasantnes, but not without easines, what seems old, at least renewed, Art having reformed what pleasing tunes injurious time and ignorance have deformed. The onely intent is to give generall content, composed by Art to make these disposed to mirth.[16]

Pammelia is the earliest English publication devoted to popular rounds and catches, and its editor explains why he chose to collect these items and commit them to print:

Amongst other liberall Arts, Musicke for her part, hath alwayes beene as liberall, in bestowing her melodious gifts, as any one whatsoever, and that in such rare manner, for diversitie: and ample measure, for multiplicitye as more cannot be expected, except were more then it is respected: yet in this kind onely, it may seem some what niggardly and unkind, in never (as yet) publikely communicating, but alwayes privately retaining: and as it were, envying to all, this more familiar mirth and jocund melodie. But it may be Musicke hath hitherto beene defective in this vaine, because this vaine indeed, hath hitherto beene defective in Musicke: and therefore, that fault now being mended, this kind of Musicke also is now commended to all mens acceptation.[17]

This collection, then, made a certain kind of popular music available to those who could not learn it orally or who simply preferred a written copy, and those who wished to have a quantity of such music available in print. None of the music claims to be original, and none of the four songs preserved here and used in children's plays is originally dramatic. Ravenscroft was hardly the first or only Renaissance collector of popular English song, and his

Pammelia should never be considered without a look at the two extant concordant manuscripts. The first of these, King's College Cambridge MS KC 1, is a parchment roll which measures sixteen feet in length, and whose fifty-seven rounds, catches, and canons were collected by Thomas Lant in 1580.[18] The second, Library of Congress MS M1490.M53A5, is a small quarto-sized manuscript of 152 pages, collected by Scotsman David Melvill, and dated 1612. Its title page bears the designation "Ane Buik off Roundels," which describes its contents perfectly except for a few appended partsongs.[19] Both of these manuscripts overlap significantly in content with each other, with *Pammelia*, and with its immediate successor *Deuteromelia*. The Lant collection demonstrates the antiquity of some of the songs set down by Ravenscroft over a quarter-century later; and Melvill, whose texts are all written in a Scottish dialect, attests to the wide circulation of many of these songs.

"Jolly Shepherd," number three in *Pammelia*, is typical of the songs preserved in Ravenscroft's first collection and used in the theater. It clearly predates the play in which it appears, the anonymous *The Maydes Metamorphosis*, for it is also given in the Lant manuscript. The same tune is given in the Ravenscroft, Lant, and Melvill collections, and all three indicate that it is a round for three voices. But there are textual variations between all three musical sources, and the play introduces yet a fourth variant. "Jolly Shepherd" is unusual only in that the entire text is given in the play, for, as we have seen, it was far more standard to print only the title or incipit of a well-known song. The Ravenscroft and Lant versions are quite close; indeed, only the spellings and textual underlay differ. The Melvill version is closely related, but a few words have been changed to conform to Scottish dialect. The version sung in *The Maydes Metamorphosis*, indicated as a solo in the play, differs strikingly from all three musical sources but can clearly use the same tune. The song was therefore probably collected independently in all four instances:

The Maydes Metamorphosis (Act II)

Terliterlo, terliterlo, terliterlee, terlo,
So merrily this shepheards boy
His horne that he can blow,
Early in the morning, late, late in an evening,
And ever sat this little boy,
So merrily piping.

Ravenscroft

Jolly shepheard and upon a hill as he sate,
So lowd he blew his little horne,
And kept right well his gate:
Earely in a morning, late, late in an Evening,

And ever blew this little boy,
So merrily piping:
Tere liter lo, terli ter lo, terli ter literlo.

Lant (number 22)
As above; only the spellings differ.

Melvill
("The Secund Roundells to Thrie Voices," p. 2)

Jolly scheiphird and upone a hill as he sat
So lowde he blew his little horne,
And keip't richt veil his gait.
Airlie in a morning lait in an evening
And ewer blew this little boy
So mirrilie piping.
Terliter lo, ij.
Terliter lo terli, terliter lo, terliter lo, terliter lo, terli.

Deuteromelia was published the same year as Pammelia, and was clearly meant as a sequel. For, in spite of differences in the subtitles (Pammelia's is actually "Musicks Miscellanie"), Deuteromelia pronounces itself on the title page to be "The Second Part of Musicks Melodie, or Melodius Musicke." Like Pammelia, it includes rounds and catches, but half of its contents are "freemens' songs" of three and four voices, several of which exhibit greater musical sophistication. Again, there is significant overlap between the Ravenscroft, the Lant, and the Melvill collections, especially the rounds and catches. Two songs given in Deuteromelia are used in children's plays, one which appears to have been borrowed for the drama, the other probably collected by Ravenscroft from the drama. "Of All the Birds," the simplest freeman's song for three voices included in Deuteromelia, is also given as the fourth "Song for thrie voices" in Melvill's *Buik*, and is quoted as a solo in Act I, scene i of Beaumont's *The Knight of the Burning Pestle*. On the other hand, the four-voice "Give Us Once a Drink," whose setting is apparently unique to Ravenscroft, may well have dramatic origin. The song is stylistically similar to other four-voice pieces in *Deuteromelia*, but its full twelve stanzas are given in Act V of the first (1601) quarto of Marston's *Jacke Drum's Entertainment*, where they take up over a page. The text in both cases is identical. In *Deuteromelia*, this rather simple drinking song is arranged for a soloist to sing in alternation with a four-voice choir. In *Jacke Drum's Entertainment*, Ellis alone is asked to sing the "high Dutch song" for which he is admired, but he has a large audience of good friends and there is every indication that the song is well known to them. Therefore, there is no reason to assume that Ellis was not joined on the refrains by a chorus of his friends. The song may well have been written especially for this drinking scene in the play, and in it both John Marston and the anonymous composer have captured the style of the common urban drinking songs of the day.

The Dedication to Ravenscroft's next collection, *Melismata* of 1611, indicates that the editor and compiler wished to follow his earlier successes in publication with yet more variety:

To the noblest of the court, liberallest of the countrey, and freest of the cittie.

You may well perceive by the much variety herein composed, that my desire is to give contentment in this kinde of Musicke to the skilfull, and most judicious of all sortes. And being little or much beholding to some of each rancke, I studie and strive to please you in your owne element.[20]

In keeping with his promise and with the subtitle of the work "Musicall Phansies Fitting the Court, Citie, and Countrey Humours," *Melismata* is a mixture of catches, ballad tunes, consort songs and madrigalian pieces on subjects befitting the court, city, and country. Among these varied pieces is one song from a children's play entitled "The Scriveners Servants Song of Holborne," which begins "My Master is so Wise." The same text is found, in a corrupt form without its first two lines, in Act IV, scene v of Middleton's *A Trick to Catch the Old-One*. In spite of the textual difference, there is every reason to believe that Ravenscroft's setting is the one used in the play, and that the complete text may be restored to the play from *Melismata*. The song is set for mezzo-soprano and the consort of viols so beloved by the Children of Paul's. In the play, it is sung by a soloist, and its text is set apart from surrounding dialogue with the indication "song," a directive most often used to indicate an accompanied song. It is assigned to a London usurer's servant, and, like most similar servant's songs, relates only peripherally to the main action of the play. However, its text suits the drama and characters quite well and includes a pun on the name of the Master at whom it is aimed, Harry Dampit.

Andrew Sabol has suggested that *Melismata* may include several other stage songs whose texts were omitted from the printed versions of the plays, and further suggests several specific songs for specific points in Paul's boys' plays.[21] Certainly a number of songs in the collection are extremely dramatic in and of themselves, and many are quite suitable for the high, clear voices of boy singers. The texts vary as widely as those that remain attached to other children's plays. And there are a large number of songs indicated in Paul's plays from the years of Ravenscroft's tenure in the choir (not to mention the earlier and later history of the company to whose songs Ravenscroft may also have access) without the benefit of text. Some of the songs in *Melismata* are so very dramatic that they may even represent inter-act entertainment. Such pieces as "A Song of Pages, Cashiered from their Masters" or "Servants out of Service, are going to the Citie to looke for new" would lend themselves well to limited action and thus provide the sort of self-contained entertainment associated with inter-acts.

There are three songs among the "harmonicall examples" of Ravenscroft's 1614 *Briefe Discourse of the True (but neglected) Use of Charact'ring the Degrees* that clearly belong to plays acted by the Children of Paul's. All three settings perfectly fit the musical clues given in stage directions, and all vocal lines lie easily in the soprano and alto ranges. The *Briefe Discourse* itself includes some of the most sophisticated musical settings published by Ravenscroft, and the composers include the editor himself, his former master Edward Pearce, and madrigalist John Bennet. Ostensibly, all of the settings included in this conservative theoretical treatise serve to exemplify the correct methods of notation and composition. But the settings may also have been intended to help Ravenscroft fight his battle against detractors from native English music by providing exemplary native compositions:

The *Forraigne Artist* saith, that an *Englishman* is an excellent *Imitator*, but a very bad *inventor*; and indeed it should so appeare; for we observing such *Inventions* which they ensample to us, as *Madrigalls, Pastorals, Neapolitaines, Ballads*, and divers other light *Harmonies*, doe bend our courses onely to surpasse the *tuning* of such *strings*; Among whome if divers excellent *Composers* have exceeded their *Ensamples*, why should not we (seeing our *Art* is as copious and ample, our *Clymate* not exceeding moist, and our *Artists* (as they confesse) farre surpasse them in the accuratenes thereof, which is upon the *Plaine Song*, and *Multiplicitie of Parts*, wherein they do admire us) finde some *Invention* to set them on work? . . .

Wherefore let us for the honour of our *Art*, of our *Selves* and *Countrye* . . . endeavour to bring *Her* unto that *Life, Reputation, Estimation* and honour, which she formerly did sustaine.[22]

In the collection, foreign inventions mix with more native musical genres to produce a very eclectic miscellany, organized around the activities associated with music in life and on the stage: hunting, hawking, dancing, drinking, and enamoring.

Numbers eight and nine in the *Briefe Discourse*, the unattributed "Urchin's Dance" and "The Elves Dance" by John Bennet, are the paired dance songs from the end of Act II of the anonymous *The Maydes Metamorphosis*. Both are four-part madrigalian compositions for two sopranos and two altos, and are sung in the play by a troupe of fairies. Both texts were probably written for the play, for they discuss common fairy activity that is reiterated in the brief dialogue between them in the drama, and the fairies mostly speak in the same poetic meter as the first song. Furthermore, phrases from the song text appear in their spoken dialogue to unite the sung and spoken portions of the scenario.

Number fifteen in the collection, "The Mistris of her Servant," is attributed to "Edw. Piers [Pearce]," the Master of the Children of Paul's. It is Imperia's professional love song to Fontinell from Act V, scene ii of the anonymous

Blurt, Master-Constable. The song is set for mezzo-soprano and a consort of three unspecified instruments whose ranges and melodic idioms suggest the consort of viols that was the vogue at Paul's playhouse. In the play, Imperia is accompanied by "Musicke" which begins shortly before her song text. The setting opens with an instrumental introduction from which the singer could take his pitch and tempo, corresponding perfectly to the "strain" of music that Imperia must catch to enter on time and in tune.

As with *Melismata*, there are a number of songs in the *Briefe Discourse* that present self-contained dramatic situations and whose vocal lines lie easily within the soprano and alto ranges. And a number of songs include at least one simple line that could easily be handled by an individual not yet sure of his ability in part-singing. All of the stage songs presented in the Ravenscroft volumes and nowhere else belong to the repertoire of the Children of Paul's from the period during which the editor-compiler was associated with the Cathedral choir, and there may also be lost songs from the same repertoire preserved in these collections, especially in *Melismata* and *A Briefe Discourse*. It is not improbable that Ravenscroft's editorial and collector instincts led him, when he sought material to supplement the rounds, catches, and part-songs gathered for anthologies meant to satisfy diverse musical taste, back to the secular repertoire that he had learned as a young chorister.

THE COLLECTIONS AND THEIR CHILDREN'S SETTINGS

1. Thomas Ravenscroft, *Pammelia: Musicks Miscellanie* (1609). STC number 20759.

    "Hey Ho Nobody at Home," sung in Beaumont's *The Knight of the Burning Pestle* (Act IV, scene iv). Concordance: King's College Cambridge MS KC 1, no. 12. Concordance: Library of Congress MS M1490.M535A5, p. 46.

    "Jolly Shepheard," sung in the anonymous *The Maydes Metamorphosis* (Act II). Concordance: Library of Congress MS M1490.M535A5, p. 2.

    "Now God Bee with Old Simeon," quoted in Beaumont's *The Knight of the Burning Pestle* (Act II, scene viii). Concordance: King's College Cambridge MS KC 1, no. 29. Concordance: Library of Congress MS M1490.M535A5, p. 6.

    "Sing We Now Merrily," quoted in Beaumont's *The Knight of the Burning Pestle* (Act IV, scene iv). Concordance: King's College Cambridge MS KC 1, no. 7. Concordance: Library of Congress MS M1490.M535A5, p. 80.

2. Thomas Ravenscroft, *Deuteromelia: or the Second Part of Musicks Melodie, or Melodius Musicke* (1609). STC number 20757.

   "Give us Once a Drink," sung in Marston's *Jacke Drum's Entertainment* (Act V).

   "Of All the Birds," quoted in Beaumont's *The Knight of the Burning Pestle* (Act I, scene i). Concordance: Library of Congress MS M1490.M535A5, p. 130.

3. Thomas Ravenscroft, *Melismata. Musicall Phansies Fitting the Court, Citie and Countrey Humours* (1611). STC number 20758.

   "The Scriveners Servants Song of Holborne," performed in Middleton's *A Trick to Catch the Old-One* (Act IV, scene v).

4. Thomas Ravenscroft, *A Briefe Discourse of the True (but neglected) use of Charact'ring the Degrees* (1614). STC number 20756.

   "The Elves Dance" by John Bennet, performed in the anonymous *The Maydes Metamorphosis* (Act II).

   "The Mistris of her Servant," by Edward Pearce, performed in the anonymous *Blurt, Master-Constable* (Act V, scene ii).

   "The Urchin's Dance," performed in the anonymous *The Maydes Metamorphosis* (Act II).

JACOBEAN MANUSCRIPTS

A number of manuscripts from the Jacobean era include settings of songs from children's plays. Though each of these manuscripts is unique, several features unite them. First, apparently none served as a repository for the musicians from any of the children's theaters or as a teaching manuscript for the boy actors. Second, the contents tend to be quite eclectic; most include accompanied songs and purely instrumental selections that range from previously published lute songs to original theater pieces, from dances to arrangements of popular tunes. Third, none can be dated precisely. Finally, like the eclectic printed anthologies considered above, they tell as much about contemporary musical taste as they do about any of the music itself. Several of these manuscripts have attracted a great deal of previous scholarly attention, including work done on the identification of sources for music from the children's plays. But it must be stressed again that, in spite of previous suggestions to the contrary, not one of these manuscripts includes enough music from the children's plays to substantiate any claim of connection to, or particular interest in, any of the companies.[23] It simply seems that theatrical tunes occasionally caught the fancy of contemporary collectors, along with popular arrangements and well-loved songs by the most famous composers of the day.

One of the most famous and most typical of these manuscripts is Christ Church Oxford MS Mus 439, an eclectic mixture of lute songs and dance tunes, the former principally from previously printed collections by such composers as William Byrd, John Dowland, and Robert Jones. The songs are set in two-octave score without tablature, and the vocal line is frequently ornamented with divisions. There is no evidence to support the claim that some of the settings were specifically intended for the lyra viol.[24] The dance pieces are notated in lute tablature or for unfigured bass alone. Most of the songs are by Alfonso Ferrabosco (including settings from Jonsonian masques) and Robert Jones. Ian Spink has dated the manuscript c. 1620 - 1630.[25]

The contents included four Dowland pieces that were used by the children's companies, and one unique song that clearly originated in a children's play. The Dowland pieces, whose dramatic contexts have already been considered, are "Pavan Lachrimae" with its complete text of "Flow My Tears" on pp. 6-7; "Now O Now I Needs Must Part," on p. 45 and there attributed to "Dowland in First Book of Ayres"; "Sleep Wayward Thoughts" on p. 46 and there attributed to "Dowland's First Book"; and "Sorrow Stay" on p. 70. This manuscript is one of two extant sources for the song "Heares Non but Onelie I," twice quoted in the anonymous *Everie Woman in her Humour* as if pre-existent (Act I, scene i and Act IV, scene i), given in the manuscript on p. 39.

However, the principal interest of the manuscript to the study of children's drama lies in its unique setting of "O the Joyes so soone should waste," on pp. 38-39, from Act IV, scene iii of Jonson's *Cynthia's Revels*. The song, first put into its dramatic context by Andrew Sabol,[26] presents a corrupt version of the text from Jonson's play. But it is generally agreed that the melodic line given in the manuscript is that of the original production, for there is a reference in the play to an aspect of the music that is preserved in the given setting.[27] In the play, Hedon proudly performs the song which he has written, and then asks Amorphus his opinion of the work. The latter replies

A prettie ayre! In generall, I like it well: but in particular, your long *die*-note did arride me most, but it was somewhat too long.

The setting given in MS Mus 439 preserves this feature in the form of an extremely long note beneath which is the word "die." The accompaniment given in the manuscript suits the text and melody beautifully, and there is no reason to believe that it, too, did not belong to the play presented by the Children of the Chapel in 1600.

An especially interesting manuscript is British Library MS Add. 24665, "Giles Earle His Booke," for it is the only contemporary manuscript to include settings for more than one original song from the children's repertoire. The manuscript bears the date 1615 on the flyleaf, and has been dated as c. 1615–1626.[28] It includes the typical mixture of songs found in contemporary secular or predominantly secular manuscripts: mostly songs from assorted earlier publications by William Byrd, Thomas Campion, John Dowland, Robert Jones, Thomas Morley, and so on, with a few popular tunes and miscellaneous songs in addition. But this manuscript presents only vocal songs, all arranged for voice and unfigured bass. There are none of the purely instrumental selections that mark so many similar manuscript miscellanies. Dowland's "Flow my Teares," using his famous Lachrimae melody, is given on p. 12, and "Sorrow Stay" is given on p. 32. As we have seen, both were used in children's plays.

But far more interesting are two other songs, which appear to be originally dramatic, both from the repertoire of the Children of the Chapel. "The Darke is my Delight," Franceschina's siren song from Act I, scene ii of Marston's *The Dutch Courtesan*, is given on pp. 59 and 61. In the play, it is sung to the lute. The given test is identical in the play imprint and the manuscript. This is one of two extant settings of the song, the other being included in the roughly contemporary British Library MS Edgerton 2971 where it is arranged for voice and unfigured bass with two additional parts given on the facing page to make a consort song. The tunes in both manuscripts are identical, but the bass parts are different; indeed, that in MS Add. 24665 was copied quite carelessly and includes two corrections made in the original hand. And it is still "in need of extensive emendation"[29] before it makes melodic or harmonic sense.

The following piece in the manuscript, on p. 60, is "Yf I Freely May Discover," from Act II, scene ii of Jonson's *The Poetaster*, which was acted by the Children of the Chapel about two years after *The Dutch Courtesan*. The text is identical in the play and the manuscript, and the manuscript includes the only extant contemporary setting of the lyric. In Jonson's play, the solo song is accompanied by an unspecified instrument or instruments; and in the manuscript it is arranged, like all the contents, for voice and bass. Like "The Darke is my Delight," the bass part is full of harmonic errors. Also like "The Darke is my Delight," both words and music are unattributed. The fact that two songs from plays acted by the same company about two years apart appear together in the same manuscript may indicate that the compiler collected both from a single source. Therefore, at least the melodies of both are likely to belong to the original productions.

Another interesting, though quite different, case is provided by British Library MSS Add. 17786–91, a set of six instrumental partbooks from the early seventeenth century. They include music principally for viols alone, dominated by fantasies and dances, but are also a major source of the Elizabethan consort song and may be of Oxford origin.[30] Identifiable composers include William Byrd and John Dowland, and there are several intricate arrangements of popular tunes from both the ballad and printed repertoires. Among these latter are a setting of "Mr. Dowland's Lachrimae" and William Wigthorpe's arrangement of "Sorrow Stay." But more important and central to the children's repertoire is an anonymous setting of the delightful dialogue song "What Meate Eates the Spaniard?" from Act I, scene ii of the anonymous *Blurt, Master-Constable.*[31] From the text of the play, it may be surmised that the three singers had an instrumental accompaniment, for both "song" and "musicke" are requested at once in the extant imprint. The part-books, of course, assign the accompaniment to a consort of viols, but only one (MS Add. 17791) includes text beyond the incipit "What meate eates the Spaniard." For one part-book of the original set has been lost, and with it the text for two of the three singers, who share a part in the song. However, because instruments are intended to double the vocal lines, the piece is musically complete, and the missing text can be restored from the play. This setting clearly emphasizes instrumental writing over vocal expression: the texture is constantly thick. There are intricate instrumental interludes between the texted portions in each part, which sometimes turn into lively counterpoint against the other vocal line. The elegant polyphony therefore rarely requires fewer than all of the parts to sound at once. The anonymous arranger was clearly fond of intricate consort writing, for the instrumental parts rarely act as mere support for the singers but continually play elaborate figuration around the vocal lines. This is not an arrangement in which text remains the mistress of the music as in most contemporary theater songs. The alternative extant version, preserved in a rather haphazard state in Royal College of Music MS 2049, is probably closer to the theatrical original because its instrumental writing is far simpler,[32] though the vocal parts and bass line are similar enough in both versions to suggest a common source.

THE COLLECTIONS AND THEIR CHILDREN'S SETTINGS

1. British Library MS Edgerton 2971.[33]
    "Here's None But Only I," on fol. 15, quoted in the anonymous *Everie Woman in her Humour* (Act I, scene i and Act IV, scene i).
    "The Darke is my Delight," arranged for voice and viols on fol. 8[v]-9, performed in Marston's *The Dutch Courtesan* (Act I, scene ii).
2. British Library MS Add. 15117.[34]
    "Sleep Wayward Thoughts," by John Dowland on fol. 4[v], quoted in Chapman, Jonson, and Marston's *Eastward Ho* (Act I, scene i) and the anonymous *Everie Woman in her Humour* (Act I, scene i).
3. British Library MS Add. 15118.[35]
    "The Spanish Pavin," on fol. 30[v], played in the anonymous *Blurt, Master-Constable* (Act IV, scene ii); also provides the tune for the ballad "When Sampson was a Tall Young Man," parodied in Chapman, Jonson, and Marston's *Eastward Ho* (Act II, scene iii).

"Walsingham," given in an instrumental version on fol. 32^v, quoted with text in Beaumont's *The Knight of The Burning Pestle* (Act II, scene viii).

"Wilt Thou Unkind Thus Reave Me," by John Dowland on fol. 5^v, quoted in Beaumont's *The Knight of the Burning Pestle* (Act I, scene iv).

4. British Library MSS Add. 17786–91.

"Mr. Dowland's Lachrimae," arranged for consort of viols as no. 29, requested as "lachrimae" in Beaumont's *The Knight of the Burning Pestle* (between Acts II and III).

"What Meate Eates the Spaniard," arranged for voice(s) and consort of viols as no. 28, performed in the anonymous *Blurt, Master-Constable* (Act I, scene ii).

"Sorrow Stay" [by John Dowland], arranged for consort of viols by William Wigthorpe, quoted as a song fragment in Beaumont's *The Knight of the Burning Pestle* (Act II, scene viii).

5. British Library MS Add. 24665, "Giles Earle His Booke."

"The Darke is my Delight," arranged for voice and unfigured bass on pp. 59 and 61, performed in Marston's *The Dutch Courtesan* (Act I, scene ii).

"Sorrow Stay," by John Dowland on p. 32, quoted in Beaumont's *The Knight of the Burning Pestle* (Act II, scene viii).

"Yf I Freely May Discover," arranged for voice and unfigured bass on p. 60, performed in Jonson's *The Poetaster* (Act II, scene ii).

6. British Library MS Add. 29481.[36]

"Sleep Waiward Thoughts" by John Dowland on fol. 2, quoted in Chapman, Jonson, and Marston's *Eastward Ho* (Act I, scene i) and the anonymous *Everie Woman in her Humour* (Act I, scene i).

7. Royal College of Music MS 2049.

"What Meate Eats the Spaniard?" arranged for voices and viols in four parts, performed in the anonymous *Blurt, Master-Constable* (Act I, scene ii).

8. Christ Church Oxford MS Mus. 439.

"Hears Non But Onelie I," on p. 39, quoted in the anonymous *Everie Woman In her Humour* (Act I, scene i and Act IV, scene i).

"Now O Now I Needs Must Part," by John Dowland on p. 45, misquoted in Chapman, Jonson, and Marston's *Eastward Ho* (Act III, scene ii) and quoted in the anonymous *Everie Woman in her Humour* (Act I, scene i).

"O the Joyes so soone whould waste," arranged for voice and unfigured bass on pp. 38–39, performed in Jonson's *Cynthia's Revels* (Act IV, scene iii).

"Pavan Lachrimae" by John Dowland on pp. 6-7, requested as "lachrimae" in Beaumont's *The Knight of the Burning Pestle* (between Acts II and III).

"Sorrow Stay" by John Dowland on p. 70, quoted in Beaumont's *The Knight of the Burning Pestle* (Act II, scene viii).

9.   New York Public Library MS Drexel 4175, "Ann Twice's Book."[37]

"Sorrow: Sorrow Stay," by John Dowland is no. 31, quoted in Beaumont's *The Knight of the Burning Pestle* (Act II, scene viii).

"Tell Mee Dearest" [by Robert Johnson] is no. 42, arranged for two voices and unfigured bass, performed in Beaumont's *The Knight of the Burning Pestle* (Act III, scene i), but included here with the textual variants from Beaumont and Fletcher's later adult play, *The Captain* (Act II, scene ii).[38]

CAROLINE AND LATER PUBLISHED ANTHOLOGIES

Numerous lyrics used in children's plays continued to attract musical interest through most of the seventeenth century. But the extant sources dating from after the Jacobean era preserve virtually no musical settings that could possibly originate in the first productions of children's plays. As with the earlier period, there are older popular songs that were finally committed to print, and there are sophisticated art songs newly composed in the latest style. Works from the latter category that set children's lyrics from the mid-seventeenth century and later almost always name the composer, and he is almost always too young to have written music for turn-of-the-century productions; the brothers Lawes and John Wilson are the most obvious examples.

By the reign of Charles I, several Elizabethan and Jacobean plays had achieved the status of classics, their authors venerated as they have been ever since. Some of these plays were revived, and it is quite likely that some of the musical settings of their songs by mid-century composers were intended for specific productions. The favorite children's authors during the final three-quarters of the seventeenth century, at least as well beloved as William Shakespeare, were Francis Beaumont, John Fletcher, and Ben Jonson. Fletcher's *The Faithful Shepherdess*, a dismal failure when first presented by the Children of the Chapel in 1608, met with wide acclaim when revived in 1633. And some of the music probably written for this production continued to appear in print for some time thereafter.

As with Elizabethan and Jacobean publications that preserve songs used in children's plays, a number of later publications are devoted to popular music. A great deal of the popular music used in children's plays, particularly ballad tunes, clearly enjoyed a long period of familiarity, because many of these songs were still being sung and printed in one form or another throughout the seventeenth century. There was certainly increasing interest in committing common tunes to print as the century went on, for more and more collections preserve more and more popular music throughout the century.

No discussion of published sources of popular music from seventeenth-century England can possibly ignore John Playford's landmark *Dancing Master*, which is undoubtedly the most famous English musical publication of the entire century. It is a massive collection of popular tunes from the sixteenth and seventeenth centuries. The work was originally published in 1651 as *The English Dancing Master*, and it went through an unprecedented eighteen editions between then and c. 1728, each including more dances than the last.[39] *The English Dancing Master* was Playford's first venture into music publishing and was so successful that from then on he published nothing but music.[40] Many of the dance tunes in the collection were old by the time Playford gathered them "with the assistance of a knowing friend,"[41] or, more likely, friends,[42] and a large number of these had served as Elizabethan and Jacobean ballad tunes. Given the tremendous scope of the collection, it is not surprising to discover that some of the tunes used in children's plays are included in various incarnations of *The Dancing Master*; it is only surprising that there are so few children's tunes in the collection. "The New Exchange," whose tune is also known as "Go From My Window," on p. 8; and "The Maid peept out at the Window, or the Frier in the Well" on p. 42 are the only tunes presented in the first edition that had also been used in children's plays. The former is quoted as a ballad fragment in Beaumont's *The Knight of the Burning Pestle* (Act III, scene v), and the latter as a ballad fragment in the anonymous *Everie Woman in her Humour* (Act II, scene iv). By the fifth edition of 1675, "The Shepherd's Daughter" had been added, on p. 83. This tune is quoted as a ballad fragment in Act II, scene viii of Beaumont's *The Knight of the Burning Pestle*. It is not coincidental that it is the two children's plays that rely most heavily on popular balladry that share tunes with *The Dancing Master*.

Mid-to-late seventeenth century collections of original English art song enjoy a very different relationship with the children's plays than do such popular anthologies as Playford's *Dancing Master*. No books of solo song were published in England between John Attey's *First Booke of Ayres* in 1622 and the *Selected Musicall Ayres and Dialogues* published by John Playford in 1652. However, various editors and publishers, especially Playford, include songs from the intervening years in later publications. Two such collections include settings of children's lyrics which can be linked to specific revivals of the plays: John Playford's publication, *The Treasury of Musick: Containing Ayres and Dialogues to Sing to the Theorbo-Lute or Basse-Viol*, Composed by Mr. Henry Lawes . . . and other excellent masters, of 1669; and John Wilson's *Cheerful Ayres and Ballads* of 1660. The more famous and more inclusive of the two is Playford's, which includes two settings of lyrics from Jacobean children's plays, both of which were probably composed for specific later performances. The collection itself is typical of Playford's song miscellanies. It is a folio-sized volume divided into three "books" or sections; one contains songs for voice and *basso continuo*, another of which consists of dialogues for two voices and *basso continuo*, and the final section is composed of three-part vocal pieces arranged in parts on the page so that singers could read from the same book while seated around a table. Many of Playford's songs come from plays from the reign of James I onward, and many of the three-part songs appear elsewhere in slightly different solo versions.[43] This collection is no exception.

The first of the two settings of children's lyrics in the collection is found on p. 98 of Book I, and is a three-voice arrangement of "Do Not Fear to put Thy Feet," the song of the River God from Act III, scene i of Fletcher's *The Faithful Shepherdess*. The setting is attributed to John Wilson and is probably a three-part arrangement of an accompanied solo which he wrote for the play.[44] *The Faithful Shepherdess* was revived for a Court performance at Somerset House on Twelfth Night, 1633,[45] and Wilson probably composed his song for this performance. The play and its new music must have enjoyed a renewed popularity after the revival, for a new quarto of the drama was issued the following year, and several songs from the play, written by composers active at Court and in the theater during the early 1630s, remain extant in a variety of sources.

"Still to be Neat," arranged for solo voice and unfigured bass, is found at the bottom of p. 51 of the second part of *The Treasury of Musick*. The song comes from Act I, scene iii of Jonson's *Epicoene*, where it is performed by a solo singer. The setting is unattributed in the Playford collection, but is assigned to William Lawes in New York Public Library MS Drexel 4041. It was probably written by Lawes for a documented 1635 revival of the play.[46]

THE COLLECTIONS AND THEIR CHILDREN'S SETTINGS

1. *The English Dancing Master*, published by John Playford (1651–c.1728). STC numbers P2477-P2486.
    "The Maid peept out at the Window, or the Frier in the Well," quoted as a ballad fragment in the anonymous *Everie Woman in her Humour* (Act II, scene iv).
    "The New Exchange," quoted with its text of "Go From My Window" in Beaumont's *The Knight of the Burning Pestle* (Act III, scene v).
    "The Shepherd's Daughter," quoted as a ballad fragment in Beaumont's *The Knight of the Burning Pestle* (Act II, scene viii).

2. *Musicks Hand-Maide*, published by John Playford (1663). STC number P2492.

> "Bow Bells," given in a keyboard arrangement, sung unaccompanied in Chapman, Jonson, and Marston's *Eastward Ho* (Act I, scene i).

3. *The Treasury of Musick: Containing Ayres and Dialogues to Sing to the Theorbo-Lute or Basse Viol, Composed by Mr. Henry Lawes. . . and other excellent Masters*, published by John Playford (1669). STC numbers L645 and P2504.

> "Do Not Fear to put Thy Feet," by John Wilson, arranged for three voices, performed as an unaccompanied solo in Fletcher's *The Faithful Shepherdess* (Act III, scene i), probably written for a 1633 Court performance.
>
> "Still to be Neat," [by William Lawes], performed in Jonson's *Epicoene* (Act I, scene iii), probably written for a 1635 performance.

4. John Wilson, *Cheerful Ayres or Ballads* (1660). STC number W2908.

> "Doe not feare to put thy feete," arranged for three voices, performed as an accompanied solo in Fletcher's *The Faithful Shepherdess* (Act III, scene i), probably written for a 1633 Court performance.

5. *Wit and Mirth: or Pills to Purge Melancholy: Being a Collection of the Best mery Ballads and Songs, Old and New*, published by Henry Playford (1699 and 1700; reissued in 1719). No STC listing.

> "Begone, Begone, my Juggy, my Puggy," sung in Beaumont's *The Knight of the Burning Pestle* (Act III, scene v).
>
> "Fading," presented with the text of "A Ballad of the Courtier and the Country Clown," requested in Beaumont's *The Knight of the Burning Pestle* (between Acts III and IV).

CAROLINE AND LATER MANUSCRIPTS

The mid-century manuscripts that include settings of lyrics from children's drama tend, like their predecessors, to be quite eclectic; and several are quite famous. But by the middle of the seventeenth century, music manuscripts with secular vocal content tend to be somewhat more homogeneous than those from the previous era. They are generally easier to categorize and tend to give attributions more regularly. Those later manuscripts that include songs from children's drama are not only rather limited to contemporary secular art song but tend to include a variety of theatrical settings or be the work of a single composer. An excellent example of the former sort is New York Public Library MS Drexel 4041, which is considered "a treasure-house of early seventeenth-century song and dramatic lyric worthy of the attention of any student of seventeenth-century literature and drama."[46] Ian Spink has dated it c. 1650, but John P. Cutts shows that it has to have been compiled before 1649 and probably before 1644.[47] The manuscript appears to have belonged to a theatrical musician or to an individual with access to those manuscripts circulating among court and theater musicians.[48] The composers represented are those of court and theater at mid-century, such as Robert Johnson, Nicholas Lanier, and Henry and William Lawes.

There are three settings of lyrics from children's plays included in this monumental manuscript. The first, number 19 in the collection, is "Com Shepherds Com Com Away," from Act I, scene iii of Fletcher's *Faithful Shepherdess*, here attributed to William Lawes. It is arranged as the accompanied solo indicated in the play, and was undoubtedly written for the 1633 revival of Fletcher's pastoral tragicomedy. The same setting of "Still to be Neate" from Jonson's *Epicoene* that is included in Playford's *Treasury of Musick* is here attributed to William Lawes as number 64. Finally, an arrangement of "Tell Mee Dearest," the song found in both Act III, scene i of Beaumont's *The Knight of the Burning Pestle* and Beaumont and Fletcher's later adult play *The Captain* and which we have already seen in the earlier MS Drexel 4175, is given as number 124. The song is here attributed to Robert Johnson, differs little from the version in Drexel 4175, and follows the textual variants from *The Captain*.

A different sort of manuscript from the same era to include children's settings is Henry Lawes's autograph manuscript, British Library MS Add. 53723. This folio-sized manuscript contains 325 songs, and was compiled over a number of years in roughly chronological order, from before 1634 until the composer's death in 1662.[49] The two children's songs in this collection are the only ones to have survived in both contemporary settings and these later arrangements. Both are from Jonson plays that did not enjoy documented revivals during Lawes's lifetime, and both Willa McClung Evans and David Fuller feel that the composer was simply attracted to these lyrics independently of any dramatic performance.[50] Both lyrics, "O y^t Joye so soone should waste" on fol. 5, from Act IV, scene iii of *Cynthia's Revels* and "If I freely may discover" on fol. 7, from Act II, scene ii of *The Poetaster* are up to Jonson's usual exquisite standards and stand quite well on their own. Pamela J. Willets has noted that a few settings of Elizabethan poems are found near the beginning of the manuscript but that Lawes mostly set the words of his contemporaries.[51] It would, then, appear that these Jonson settings belong to an early experimental phase of Lawes's career, in which he briefly tried his hand at setting the lyrics of an older generation of poets and composers.

THE COLLECTIONS AND THEIR CHILDREN'S SETTINGS

1. British Library MS Add. 31432, William Lawes's autograph.[52]
    "Lovers Rejoice" on fol. 36, performed in Beaumont and Fletcher's *Cupid's Revenge* (Act I, scene ii), probably written for a 1637 Court performance.
2. British Library MS Add. 53723, Henry Lawes's autograph.
    "If I freely may discover," on fol. 7, performed in Jonson's *The Poetaster* (Act II, scene ii).
    "O y^t Joye so soone should waste," on fol. 5, performed in Jonson's *Cynthia's Revels* (Act IV, scene iii).
3. Edinburgh University Library MS Dc.1.69.[53]
    "Do not feare to put thy feete," by John Wilson, arranged as the accompanied solo performed in Fletcher's *The Faithful Shepherdess* (Act III, scene i) on fol. 155, probably written for a 1633 Court performance.
    "Singe his Praises" by Will[iam] Lawes on fols. 24^v-25, performed in Fletcher's *The Faithful Shepherdess* (Act I, scene ii), probably written for the 1633 Court performance.
4. New York Public Library MS Drexel 4041.
    "Com Shepherds Com Com Away" by William Lawes is number 19, performed in Fletcher's *The Faithful Shepherdess* (Act I, scene iii), probably written for the same 1633 Court performance.
    "Still to be Neate" by William Lawes is number 64, performed in Jonson's *Epicoene* (Act I, scene iii), probably written for a 1635 production.
    "Tell mee Dearest" by Robert Johnson is number 124, performed in Beaumont's *The Knight of the Burning Pestle* (Act III, scene i), but this arrangement sets the textual variants given in Beaumont and Fletcher's later adult play, *The Captain* (Act II, scene ii).
5. New York Public Library MS Drexel 4257, "John Gambles Commonplace Book."[54]
    "If I freely may discover" by Henry Lawes is number 25, performed in Jonson's *The Poetaster* (Act II, scene ii).
    "Still to be neat" by William Lawes is number 179, performed in Jonson's *Epicoene* (Act I, scene iii), probably written for a 1635 performance.
    "Tell me Dearest" by Robert Johnson is number 35, performed in Beaumont's *The Knight of the Burning Pestle* (Act III, scene i), but this arrangement sets the textual variants given in Beaumont and Fletcher's later adult play, *The Captain* (Act II, scene ii).

MISCELLANEOUS SOURCES OF POPULAR BALLADRY

No discussion of the sources of English theatrical music from the sixteenth and seventeenth centuries would be complete without some consideration of the multitude of sources of popular ballads and their tunes. Some settings of popular ballad tunes were included in the printed and manuscript volumes considered in the previous pages. However, in addition there are a staggering number of printed books and manuscripts from the mid-sixteenth century to the nineteenth century that include the texts and/or tunes of some popular ballads that were sung in the theater. To consider all of them would exceed the scope of this study. Nevertheless, they must be mentioned, if only to reiterate the point that music for the children's plays was drawn from a wide variety of traditions; not all of it was composed especially for the plays or drawn from the repertoire of art songs.

Balladry deserves separate consideration from the equally popular rounds, catches, and street cries, which belong to completely different traditions. There were ballads that circulated orally, and those more literary examples that were published as broadsides. The line of distinction between the two sometimes becomes blurred because some traditional ballads found their way into print even as some broadsides circulated orally; and the traditional oral ballads of earlier ages were meticulously collected and committed to print by such later individuals as Francis James Child, Thomas Percy, and Joseph Ritson. However, the contrasting genres of orally circulating traditional ballad and the broadside ballad ultimately remain distinct.[55] Dozens of examples of both categories found in hundreds of sources appear in Elizabethan and Jacobean drama, which, of course, includes children's plays.

Traditional, or oral, ballads have been carefully collected since the eighteenth century, and numerous quotations from works in this category are given in children's plays. Like other pre-existent musical material, they are mostly found in plays with realistic English Renaissance settings. More than any other kind of music that predates the play that includes it, these ballads are sung by tradesmen with not even the slightest pretension to personal sophistication, the "merry worker" type of character or the country bumpkin. The original function of this sort of ballad was to provide entertainment and perhaps edification to an illiterate populace. Most of these ballads are quite long, and often include ten or a dozen stanzas. They are never presented in full in the children's plays, and most of the quotations show a tale already in progress. Numerous eighteenth- and nineteenth-century ballad collections, particularly the famous ones of Child, both Percys, and Ritson, include material used in the children's plays, and provide valuable information on the genre itself.[56]

A great deal has been written about the broadside ballad in the past century,[57] and each subsequent work has added significantly to our knowledge of the genre and its musical sources. The present study does not even pretend a comprehensive investigation of the sources of the broadside tunes used on the children's stage, but I have identified over twenty lyrics with extant broad-side tunes, all of which are listed in Appendix A; the comprehensive sources of these are listed by title in Claude Simpson's landmark *The British Broad-side Ballad and its Music*, supplemented by John Ward's "Apropos *The Brit-ish Broadside Ballad and its Music.*"[58]

The word "broadside" means a single sheet, usually of folio size, printed on one side. Broadsides thus include proclamations, heroic epistles, news let-ters, poetic odes, and theatrical prologues or epilogues as well as ballads.[59] The broadside ballad was usually written by a hack versifier to a common tune, printed without music but with the name of the tune to which the words were to be sung, becoming part of "de infinite multitude of Balads (set to sundry pleasant and delightful tunes, by cunning and witti Composers.)"[60] Such ballads were sold in bookstalls or fair booths, or they were hawked about cities and towns by street singers. Subjects tend toward the sensational, such as the birth of monsters or the final farewell and execution of notorious criminals, although standard lover's complaints are also well represented. Many broadside ballads have a distinctly moralizing tone, using the fate of some poor soul as a sensational example of what will happen to others who live as he or she did, as Elizabethan satirist Edward Guilpin reminds us in an epigram addressed to the most famous broadside-ballad writer of the era:

> Like to the fatall ominous Raven which tolls,
> The sicke mans dirge within his hollow beake,
> So every paper-clothed post in Poules,
> To thee (*Deloney*) mournfully doth speake,
> And tells thee of thy hempen tragedie;
> The racks of hungry Tyburn naught to thine.
> Such massacre's made of thy balladry,
> And thou in griefe, for woe thereof must pine.[61]

More literate poets and critics almost universally condemned balladeers and their works:

So as nowe a dayes our Philosophers are all our Poets, or what our Poets should bee; and our Poesies growne to bee little better than fardles of such small ware as those Marchats the French call pedlers, carry up and downe to sell; whistles, painted rattles, and such like *Bartholomew*-babyes. For what other are our common uninstructing fabulous rimes, those amusements for fools and children? But our Rimes (say they) are full of Morall doctrine. Be it so. But why not delivered then in plaine prose, and as openly to every mans understanding, as it deserves to be taught, and commonly knowne by every one. The Auncients (say they) were Authors of Fables, which they sung in measured numbers, as we in imitation of them. True: but sure enough their meanings were of more high nature, and more difficult to be found out.[62]

The broadside ballad was essentially an urban variety of subliterary expression, and London was its undisputed headquarters.[63] In the children's plays, some of the same characters are assigned broadside and traditional ballads in almost indistinguishable combinations. But the former tend to be sung by denizens of London, social-climbing rogues who can conceal neither their lowly origins nor their lofty designs. These same characters may sing their broadsides mixed with traditional ballads and previously published lute songs and madrigals, but the broadsides distinctly belong to them.

An excellent explanation of the popularity and influence of the broadside ballad is that it was written to music that was already familiar, for the ballad maker had to have a specific tune in mind as he began to frame his stanzaic pattern.[64] These tunes were indeed popular; one reason why so many indicated on the broadsheets have survived is that they were used over and over in collections of instrumental music, printed and manuscript, for lute, keyboard, viols, cittern, and mixed consort. Aside from the lesson books, manuscripts like British Library MS Add. 15118, and Playford publications like *The Dancing Master* or *Wit and Mirth*, sources for the broadside ballad tunes used in children's plays include British Library MS RM.24.d.3 (*The Forster Virginal Book*), British Library MS Add. 10337 (*Elizabeth Rogers hir virginall booke*), Cambridge University MS Music 32.G.29 (*The Fitzwilliam Virginal Book*), Cambridge University Library MS Dd.5.78.3, Trinity College Dublin MS D.3.30 (*The Thomas Dallis Lute Book*), and Folger Shakespeare Library MS 1610.1. In addition, several of these tunes, such as the Spanish Pavan (the Pavan D'Espagne in Arbeau's *Orchesographie* of 1588), can be traced to continental European sources.[65] Many other collections, dating from the sixteenth to the twentieth centuries, present the texts of broadside ballads in convenient volumes and, of, course provide the names of the appropriate tunes.

Chapter 10

THE MUSICAL STYLES

Benigne Reader, heere is offered unto thy courteous acceptation, Musicke of sundry sorts, and to content divers humors.

William Byrd, *Psalmes, Sonets & Songs of Sadnes and Pietie* (1588)

All that remains of the music in Elizabethan and Jacobean dramatic imprints are song lyrics and often-cryptic stage directions or fragments of dialogue. Information about musical dramaturgy, and to a certain extent about the sound of the music, can be gleaned from these scattered verbal impressions. But it is only through recovery of the music itself that we can glimpse the full dramatic meaning of the songs and instrumental pieces that once gave life to the plays. For, as Sir Philip Sidney reminds us, it was not poetic text but music that was considered "the most divine striker of the senses."[1]

Nearly all of the extant music from the final phase of children's drama is texted song, since original musical settings may only be restored through text, title, or incipit. In addition, song is given a more prominent place in the plays than purely instrumental music, for it expresses specific ideas through its text. In Elizabethan and Jacobean drama, music was frequently used to express specific ideas for which speech and action were not sufficient. Song depends as much on music as on text, for only through the balanced union of text and music can the complete meaning of a song be revealed. In a song setting, music may emphasize certain words or phrases more than others by assigning them longer note values or simpler accompaniment. Musical settings may require verbal repetition that is absent from the printed lyric, or may alter spoken rhythms to draw attention to certain words or concepts. Musical settings may obscure parts of a text with thick polyphony and rapid tempi, and emphasize others with clear, deliberate homophonic writing. In the theater, as part of the temporal art of drama, the full impact of a song must be complete in a single hearing. Therefore, it must be written so that everything of importance is apparent at once, for there is no chance to listen a second time for subtlety or hidden meaning.

Between 1597 and 1613, there were a wide variety of musical styles for dramatists, directors, and theatrical composers to choose among. As we have seen, pre-existent compositions, no matter how they were originally conceived, were sung unaccompanied on the children's stages. But there is a great deal of variety among original theatrical compositions. The years between 1597 and 1613 proved exciting ones for English secular music. During the early part of this period, the celebrated English madrigal reached full fruition. Throughout the period, the English ayre, born even as children's drama was revived, blossomed into brilliant color. The consort song, whose very history is intimately connected to the first phase of children's drama,[2] was still as vital as ever, especially at the start of the period.

As we have seen, the audience who patronized the children's theaters was especially partial to novelty, and the playwrights supplied it amply with avant-garde experiment and innovation in the text and conception of the plays. The music, too, followed this pattern. As the solo song or ayre, devised for a single singer and one instrument alone, soared to popularity outside of the theater, it also did so in children's drama. It is difficult to draw conclusions about songs for which musical settings have yet to be recovered, but numbers of singers are almost always indicated in the dramatic text, and accompanying instruments are often named. It appears that solo song to the lute or viol came quickly to dominate the children's plays after 1600 as the same genre rose to prominence outside the theater. By the accession of James I, choral song, and therefore anything even possibly madrigalian in style, had all but faded from the plays; and the consort song, too, seems to have become less common.

It is also vital to recall that text is most clearly audible in a solo song, especially one with a simple homophonic accompaniment. As far back as Castiglione's time, the greater expression of text permitted by a single singer and solo instrument had been preferred above the full texture of partsong:

to sing to the lute is much better [than partsong], because al the sweetnesse consisteth in one alone, and a manne is much more heedfull and understandeth better the feate maner and aer or veyne of it, when the eares are not busyed in hearing any moe then one voyce.[3]

Music was, of course, considered "a sister to Poetry,"[4] and even those great masters of expressive English polyphony, William Byrd and Thomas Morley, recognized the great importance of text to the affect of a song.[5] Therefore, in the theater where text and music united to affect the audience in a single hearing, the least polyphonic setting often proved most desirable.

MADRIGALIAN COMPOSITIONS

Since madrigal texts tend to be obscured by their settings, it is not surprising that the genre seems to be underrepresented in the children's repertoire. Only two madrigalian compositions stand among extant settings associated with the original performance of children's plays, both preserved by Ravenscroft, and both from the anonymous *Maydes Metamorphosis*. They are the charming fairy dances from the end of Act II, and everything about them sings of Italy and Italian influence. It is probably no accident that this mythological pastoral comedy of 1597-1600, whose literary antecedents include Italian imports, includes at least two songs whose musical inspiration comes from the same country. Even the fairies who perform were considered to be the native equivalents of the fantastic populace of the Italian pastoral:

The Robbin-good-fellowes, Elfes, Faires, and Hobgoblins of our latter age, which idolatrous former daies and the fantasticall world of *Greece* ycleped *Fawnes, Satyrs, Dryades*, and *Hamadryades*, did most of their merry prankes in the *Night*.[6]

The nymphs of Diana who play such a part in true pastoral were therefore interchangeable with English fairies:

The fourth kinde of spirits, which by the gentiles was called *Diana*, and her wandring court, and amongst us called the *phairie* (as I told you) to our good neighbors, was one of the sorts of illusions that was rifest in the time of Papistry.[7]

In fact, the earliest Italian-English dictionary to include the terms "nymph" and "fairy" equates the two by broadly translating *"Nimfa"* as "any kinde of Nymph, Elfe, or Fairie."[8] The songs assigned to the fairies in the play are light and cheerful, typical of those English madrigals of the 1590s that were stylistically closest to the lighter Italian forms,[9] and whose affinity lay with "the time and mood of Shakespeare's comedies."[10]

Reaching a simple, accurate definition of the term "madrigal" to cover all existing species at the close of the sixteenth century is not easy. Only the most general, such as "a secular composition for unaccompanied voices (two to eight), each singing a separate part. . . [whose] music was sometimes contrapuntal, sometimes harmonic,"[11] or "an omnibus term [to] include all the vocal music published in madrigal collections,"[12] will suffice. By the later sixteenth century, stylistic characteristics of the madrigal and related lighter genres had merged sufficiently that the lines of distinction became blurred even in Italy; and Joseph Kerman stresses that in England distinctions between the ballett, canzonet, and madrigal were not sharply made.[13]

These two exceptional little pieces from Ravenscroft's *Briefe Discourse* certainly fail to fit strict modern definitions of specific madrigalian subgenres. But Thomas Morley's simple definition of *balletti* describes them perfectly and elevates them to a position of unique importance in the history of the English madrigal:

> There is also another kind [of secular music] more light than [the villanelle] which they tearme *ballette* or daunces, and are songs which being sung to a dittie may likewise be daunced.[14]

Both of these songs are danced in *The Maydes Metamorphosis* by the same company of fairies who sings them, and the importance of seeing the settings in their proper dramatic context cannot be overestimated. It has long been assumed that the ballett was not danced in England and that Morley simply referred to an Italian practice learned from the title page of Giovanni Giacomo Gastoldi's *Balletti a cinque voci* of 1591.[15] These two fairy dance-songs, however, overlooked by previous commentators on the English ballett, provide the only evidence as yet discovered to suggest that Morley's statement applied to England. And they represent a further link between the English ballett and the Italian *balletto*.[16]

In *The Maydes Metamorphosis*, as shown earlier, a company of fairies surprises a merry gathering of a shepherd's boy, a ranger's boy, and a courtier's page and proceeds to dance by moonlight and make mischief at the boys' expense. They enter with song and dance, and the introductory ballett they perform is the anonymous "Urchin's Dance," Number 8 in Ravenscroft's *Briefe Discourse*. The text, practically identical in the play and the musical anthology, is a six-line poem with an added refrain. The rhyme scheme is AABBCC(C), and each of the first six lines consists of seven syllables in homage to Italian poetry. The seventh line appears to fulfill the function of the nonsense refrain that is appended to so many balletts, although it makes perfect sense and rhymes with the fifth and sixth lines:

> By the moone we sport and play,
> With the night begins our day;
> As we daunce[17] the dew doth fall;
> Trip it little urchins all,
> Lightly as the little Bee,
> Two by two and three by three:
> And about go wee, and about go wee.

The setting (Example 2) is truly a miniature gem of English madrigalian writing, and it reflects the fairies' playful and capricious nature in its changing textures, dainty rhythms, and shifting meter. The text is set for four high voices in a bright G-major tonality, lightened further by a cadence in A-major. Each line of poetry receives surprisingly different musical treatment, perhaps to illustrate the whimsical character of the fairies as well as to work in simple madrigalisms at the words "lighly," "little," "two by two," and "three by three." Declamation is excellent, and the proper accentuation of the words "begins" and "about" shifts the rhythm of the entire piece as each is sung. The vocal ranges are limited and therefore eminently suitable for the display of young voices. The piece is full of dancelike rhythms, and the shifts from duple to triple meter may relate to the choreography of the dance, for, as Francis Bacon tells us,

the *Tripla's* and *Changing of Times*, have an Agreement with the *Changes of Motions*; as when *Galliard Time* and *Measure Time* are in the *Medley* of one *Dance*.[18]

This entertaining, aesthetically pleasing piece is thus both functional and impressive, suitable for the talents of its youthful performers and creatures they impersonate, . It is a perfect example of how a dramaturgically appropriate piece of music could become extra-spectacular entertainment for the audience.

The other fairy dance from the same scene, preserved as number 9, "The Elves Dance," in the *Briefe Discourse* and there attributed to John Bennet, is separated from the first by witty banter between the fairies and the boys. As it ends, the young mortals are forced into joining a dance in the traditional fairy ring by the threat of a severe pinching. This dance closes the second act of the play on a note of graceful merriment; its musical setting has been described as "perfect in its daintiness and delicacy."[19] Ravenscroft has only the highest praise for its composer, in whose works he claims that

the very *life* of that *Passion* which the ditty sounded, is so truly exprest, as if he had measured it alone by his owne *Soule*, and invented no other *Harmony*, then his own sensible feeling in that *Affection* did afford him.[20]

In this brief ballett, Bennet captures all the grace and whimsy of fairy magic. In the play, the poem consists of three stanzas, the first two of which are identical. Each stanza is four lines long, and each is extended to an Italiante eleven-syllable length and given a faminine ending by means of the artificial syllable "a." The rhyme scheme is AABB in each stanza:

Example 2.   From "The Urchins Dance." (Continued on p. 239.)

Example 2.   (Continued from p. 238.)

Round about,round about, in a fine ring a,
Thus we daunce, thus we daunce, and thus we sing a:
Trip and go, to and fro, over this Greene a,
All about, in and out, for our brave Queene a.

Round about, round about, in a fine ring a,
Thus we daunce, thus we daunce, and thus we sing a:
Trip and go, to and fro, over this Greene a,
All about, in and out, for our brave Queene a.

We have daunc't round about in a fine Ring a,
We have daunc't lustily and thus we sing a:
All about, in and out, over this Greene a,
Too and fro, trip and go, to our brave Queene a.

Bennet's musical setting (Example 3) preserves only the first stanza of the poem, varied so that the phrase "for our brave Queene a" is replaced by a repetition of "over this Greene a." Again, each of the four lines of text receives different musical treatment, and only the final one is repeated. The composer was clearly aware of the dictum on madrigalian writing that is expressed so beautifully by Thomas Morley:

You must in your musicke be wavering like the wind, sometimes wanton, sometime drooping, sometime grave and staide, otherwhile effeminat, you may maintaine points and revert them, use triplaes and shew the verie uttermost of your varietie, and the more varietie you shew the better shal you please.[21]

Example 3.   From John Bennet, "The Elves Dance." (Continued on p. 241.)

Example 3. (Continued from p. 240.)

Of course, this dance song is set for the same combination of voices in the same comfortable range as its companion piece; its third vocal part, labelled "tenor," is especially simple to sing. Some variety from the other fairy ballett is provided by its solid C-major tonality. And although the song shifts between two meters, its "changing of times" is never as pronounced or as rapid as any of those in the first fairy piece, and it is less insistent on simple word painting. Instead, it achieves a very different sort of interest through the alternate use of homophony and counterpoint in the opening section, a technique later praised by Charles Butler, who observed that

bothe in Madrigalz and Canzonets, Counterpoint with Discant, and Discant with Counterpoint, are soomtime enterchangeably and artificially mixt."[22]

Bennet's exquisite setting brings the utterly simplistic lyric to life as part of an enchanting piece of music. It is unfortunate that these two charming dance songs are the only extant madrigalian pieces from the children's repertoire, and it is impossible to judge how typical they may be. But a number of song lyrics in the children's plays, especially those from the waning years of the Elizabethan era, retain the lure of Italy in their poetry and are sung by small groups. Perhaps these, too, had been given madrigalian settings.

THE CONSORT SONG

There are three extant examples of consort songs from the final phase of children's drama. As with the madrigalian pieces, all three belong to the early years of the revival and all three come from the repertoire of the Children of Paul's. Two of the three were preserved by Thomas Ravenscroft, and the third apparently achieved a certain degree of popularity outside of the theater. Again, it is impossible to judge just how typical these pieces may be because so few examples have survived. But it is clear from stage directions and dialogue that the consort song belongs principally to the earlier phase of children's drama.

The consort song, "made for Instruments to expresse the harmonie, and one voyce to pronounce the ditie,"[23] is a specifically English form that has been considered the most characteristic late Renaissance expression of the native musical idiom.[24] The term itself is of modern origin, but it is a perfect description of song for solo voice accompanied by a consort of viols. The stylistic development of the genre during the 1560s and 70s apparently owed a great deal to the children's drama of the time, and the form became fully mature as the children's fame reached its first zenith in the 1580s.[25] The consort song permits the composer all the intricacies of part-writing without obscuring the text with multiple vocal lines, and permits competent instrumentalists to display a great deal of skill. In the drama, this means an opportunity to articulate the lyric clearly while impressing the audience with learned contrapuntal writing and pleasing performances from an entire ensemble of musicians.

Both principal children's companies began the revival at the close of the sixteenth century with plays similar to their earlier successes, and with these plays clearly came some of their older musical styles. But the 1590s, the missing decade in the history of the children's companies, had seen as many changes in musical style and taste as in dramatic. And so it is quite probable that as the "musty fopperies of antiquity" and newly-clothed spectres of older plays were abandoned before they scared away an audience partial to novelty, older musical styles also gave way to the new. The venerable consort song, so long a part of children's drama, appears to have quickly become less common. Both principal companies undoubtedly used consort songs after 1597, especially during the waning years of the Elizabethan era, but the Children of the Chapel produced no Thomas Ravenscroft to commit their songs to print.

Two of the three extant consort songs from the revival period come from the anonymous *Blurt, Master-Constable*. The first of these, "What Meate Eats the Spaniard?" from Act I, scene ii, is the sole extant setting of the sort of accompanied dialogue song that appears in so many children's plays. This type of piece is of great dramatic importance, for it is often relegated to the end of an act and may thus represent inter-act entertainment. It is also an especially distinctive musical feature of children's drama, especially Elizabethan comedies. It is usually performed by a trio of servants, and it normally becomes the centerpiece of a brief scenario that includes comical dialogue. Indeed, Andrew Sabol has described such pieces as resembling "self-contained five-minute operettas."[26] "What Meate Eats the Spaniard?" is dramatically quite typical, but, of course, as sole musical exemplar, it is impossible to judge its music in relation to similar pieces.

Settings of this song are extant in British Library MSS Add, 17786-91 and Royal College of Music MS 2049. Both settings are clearly based on the same original, for the vocal lines and bass part are almost identical; and these very different treatments of the piece would seem to indicate that it enjoyed a certain popularity outside of its dramatic context. The setting in British Library MSS Add. 17786-91 (Example 4) is more elaborate than the other extant consort songs built on children's dramatic lyrics, and its thicker texture does not permit the words to come across as clearly as the other setting. Both vocal lines are doubled by viols that play lively interludes between sung phrases, and the entire setting clearly favors elaborate instrumental writing over vocal expression. The alternate setting (Example 5), though copied quite careless-

Example 4. From "What Meat Eats the Spaniard?" version 1. (British Library Manuscripts Additional 17786–91.) (Continued on p. 245.)

Example 4. (Continued from p. 244.)

Example 5.   "What Meat Eats the Spaniard?" version 2. (Royal College of Music Manuscript 2049.) (Continued on p. 247)

Example 5. (Continued from p. 246.)

Example 5.   (Continued from p. 247.)

ly into the manuscript, is probably much closer to the dramatic original. But what is outstanding about the piece itself is its playfully ironic treatment of the text. In fact, it becomes a sly parody of the famed laments from the earlier phase of children's drama, at least some of which were set as consort songs.

As indicated earlier, "What Meate Eats the Spaniard?" is the high point of a chance meeting between three pert serving boys, one of whom, Pilcher, is grossly underfed by his miserly Spanish master. Doyt and Dandiprat, the healthier servants, tease him about his emaciated state and finally ask him to sing with them. Separated from its theatrical context, the lyric of "What Meate Eats the Spaniard?" appears inconsequential at best. When seen within the context of the play, the lyric becomes a sorrowful lamentation of the pathetic mistreatment of an overworked servant, recalling the type of lament so common in the children's plays of earlier times.[27] But when the words and the setting are regarded together in proper dramatic context, the song becomes a witty parody of the famed laments of former times. The cheerful setting, with its bright G-major tonality and graceful, rapid motion serves as an unexpectedly comical foil for the sorrowful lyric. Doyt and Dandiprat, the healthy servants, sing in the soprano range in contrast to the deeper tones used by the starving Pilcher, an alto. But the setting shows Pilcher's desperate state of starvation to be amusingly exaggerated, for he sings rapidly of his monotonous and insubstantial diet (Example 5, bars 6-9), and becomes even more excited about how poorly he is fed after better fare is suggested (bars 24-38). His song is completely contrary to what English Renaissance theoriests prescribe for musical depictions of woe. Thomas Morley, for example, tells us that

if the subject be light you must cause your musicke to go in motions, which carrie with them a celeritie or quicknesse of time. . . ; if it be lamentable the note[s] must goe in slow and heavie motions.[28]

And Charles Butler adds that

Plain and slow Musik is fit for grave and sad matter: qik Notes or Triple time, for Mirth and rejoicing. A manly, hard, angry or cruel matter is to be exprest by hard and harsh short tones.[29]

Pilcher's short tones are never hard or harsh, nor are those of his comrades; the only dissonance in the piece is the occasional passing note that is such a vital part of contemporary viol consort writing. Only when Pilcher describes his fallen cheeks does his part move in slow and heavy motions to its lowest point (bars 14-18). Pilcher's sympathetic friends are shown by their music to be scarcely more worried than he about his emaciated and deprived state. Doyt constantly sings in merrily moving notes, and even leaps upward with

Example 6.   From Edward Pierce, "Of Enamouring. The Mistris of Her Servant." (Continued pn p. 251.)

Example 6.   (Continued from p. 250.)

appropriate madrigalisms when consoling poor Pilcher with thoughts of a real piece of meat (bars 20-24). Only Dandiprat behaves with anything resembling musical appropriateness, offering his repeated, stereotypically breathy "alas" motive in overly gallant consolation (bars 10-12). Pilcher's final three notes, spare and static as his diet, come far too late to undo the musical sense of mirth expressed by the rest of the piece. The text and music in this piece stand in humorous contrast to each other. It is a carefully conceived satire of a serious lament and a fine example of musical irony. The song is also clearly intended to show off beautifully trained voices, for Doyt and Pilcher are assigned unusually wide vocal ranges for a consort song: Doyt's treble part spans a twelfth and Pilcher's alto an eleventh. In contrast, the vocal parts of most extant consort songs are limited to an octave or a ninth.

The other consort song from Act V, scene ii of the same play is Imperia's serenade to Fontinel, "Love for Such a Cherrie Lip," preserved as number 15 in Ravenscroft's *Briefe Discourse*. It is there entitled "Of Enamoring. The Mistris of her Servant" and attributed to "Edw: Piers" [Edward Pearce], Master of the Children of Paul's at the time the play was presented. This song is quite different from the other, though it includes its own ironic touch. It is a far more typical consort song with its single singer and limited vocal range, and belongs to the central action of the play instead of to a servant interlude. And, as we have seen, the song functions as a sexual metaphor.

The atmosphere of playful sensuality that pervades the entire scene is greatly enhanced by the musical setting of the song (Example 6). The viols provide a rich background for Imperia's mezzo-soprano voice, making the setting as elaborate and blatantly artificial as the love of a courtesan. The pacing of the setting is stately without being solemn, much like the langorous love scene whose climax it represents. The continuous, graceful motion of the instrumental lines and the short vocal phrases separated by liberal rests are as indicative of leisurely passion as the playfully understated text. The instrumental parts exhibit some of the independent polyphony of the other consort song from the same play, but they tend more toward homophonic support and anticipation of vocal motives (bars 1-4 and 14-15). There are passing note dissonances and cadential suspensions, which, though common, simple musical devices, are particularly appropriate to a love song performed by a courtesan. Francis Bacon notes the effect of this sort of musical device on the human affections:

Againe, the Falling from a Discord to a Concord, which maketh a great Sweetnesse in musik, hath an Agreement withe the Affections, which are reintegrated to the better, after some dislikes; it agreeth also with the Taste, which is soone glutted with that which is sweet alone.[30]

Therefore, Imperia can only increase Fontinel's desire through her varied, teasing performance. The delayed artificeof the fall from discord to concord is especially suitable for the cunning love of the courtesan, which has drawn Fontinel away from the simple sweetness of his beloved Violetta.

The choice of a consort song for this moment in the drama provides added humor and not a little musical irony. For, true to the Italian setting of the play, Imperia introduces her song to the French Fontinel (and to the audience) as "a poor Italian song." The text, like many Italian Renaissance and early Baroque lyrics, pays tribute to erotic incidents from classical mythology. But the setting is the most English of genres, the consort song; and the nonsense refrain is the very English "hey nony nony no" instead of the more Italiante "fa la la" of so many other songs. The play was performed in 1601 or 1602, at the height of the English madrigal craze and long enough after the first English publications of Italian and strictly Italianate madrigals for a musically literate audience to recognize an "Italian song." Imperia's is truly a poor Italian song--but a very fine English one. And the limited vocal range and constant instrumental interest makes this a model consort song.

The final extant consort song from the later children's repertoire belongs to Act IV, scene v of Middleton's *A Trick to Catch the Old-One* and is printed as number 12, "The Scriveners Servants Song of Holborne," in Ravenscroft's *Melismata* (Example 7). It exhibits few important stylistic features not shared with the previous examples. The solo voice here occupies the alto line, and the setting involves more imitative and motivic interaction between vocal and instrumental parts than the other two surviving consort songs from the same period, but is otherwise musically unremarkable. Its main interest is dramatic and historical, for it represents a slightly anachronistic blend of the old and the new.

My mas - ter is so wise, so wise, that hee's pro - cee - ded whit - tal, My

mis - tris is a foole, a foole, and yet tis the most get - all.

Let the u - sur - er cram him in inter - est that ex - cell,

Example 7. From "The Scriveners Servants Song of Holborne."

A Trick to Catch the Old-One, first presented around the time of James I's accession to the English throne, is one of the first citycomedies devised, and therefore predates many conventions later associated with the genre. Middleton's play stands at the temporal crossroad where the wise and witty servant characters of Latin-inspired comedy step aside for the crude and cunning London servants of the city comedy. As we have seen, characters in the city comedies are normally assigned appropriate urban music, principally pre-existent unaccompanied songs of the sort that their real-life equivalents might sing under similar circumstances. Audrey, the singer, is a contemporary London maidservant who serves a contemporary London usurer, but her song is closer to the sort of vehicle for vocal display and gratuitous entertainment given to the less realistic servants of romantic comedy, such as "What Meate Eats the Spaniard?". Her ditty, unlike most earlier servant's songs, relates to the main action of the play, for it characterizes her hypocritical master perfectly and prepares for the "discovery" of him lying drunkenly on his bed. The setting is dominated by a learning and delicacy that is somehow incongruous with Middleton's presentation of the seamy side of early Jacobean London.

THE AYRE

Most extant settings of songs that are provided with complete text in the imprints of the children's plays after 1597, those songs that were probably written specifically for the plays in which they were included, must be considered ayres. Technically, an ayre is an accompanied solo song in which there is a distinct polarity between the melody and the instrumental support. In children's drama, ayres are accompanied by solo stringed instruments, especially lute or bass viol. The ayre itself was born at the time of the revival of the children's companies, but its antecedents stretch back to the early sixteenth century. Like so many English art forms, it is a hybrid whose ancestry is highly diversified and whose form is unique. Numerous musical genres influenced its development, including the simple partsongs of early Tudor times, the consort song with its clear functional division between vocal and instrumental parts, the native ballad and dance, the Italian madrigal, the French chanson, the *voix de ville* and *chanson à danser*.[31] Diana Poulton suggests that the practice of performing partsong as a solo with lute accompaniment may be as old in England as on the continent, which would push it back into the fifteenth century.[32] However, the influence of Italian monody, born in Italy even as the ayre was born in England, did not reach England until after the demise of children's drama.[33]

The native ayre proved a more suitable vehicle than the madrigal for native English poetry at the turn of the century,[34] and shortly after 1600 began to increase in popularity until the number of published collections of ayres surpassed that of madrigals.[35] It is not surprising that the children's plays, written by the most innovative poets for the most fashionable audience, clearly favor the ayre over both madrigal and consort song. Many late English Renaissance intellectuals explain why the solo ayre was the choice of contemporary poets. The Address to the Reader of Rosseter's *Book of Ayres* of 1601, perhaps written by coauthor and poet-composer Thomas Campion, attacks salient features of both the madrigal and consort song while asserting the superiority of the ayre in expressing the text:

> What Epigrams are in Poetrie, the same are Ayres in musicke, then in their chiefe perfection when they are short and well seasoned. But to clogg a light song with a long Praeludium, is to corrupt the nature of it. Manie rests in Musicke were invented either for necessity of the fuge, or granted as a harmonicall license in songs of many parts: but in Ayres I find no use they have unlesse it be to make vulgar, or triviall modulation seeme to the ignorant strange, and to the judiciall tedious. . . . The Lyricke Poets among the Greekes and Latines were the first inventors of Ayres, tying themselves strictly to the number, and values of their sillables. . . But there are some, who to appeare the more deepe, and singular in their judgement, will admit no Musicke but that which is long, intricate, bated with fuge, chaind with sincopation, and where the nature of evrie word is precisely exprest in the Note, like the old exploided action in Comedies. . . . But such childish observing of words is altogether ridiculous, as we ought to maintaine as well in Notes, as in action a manly carriage, gracing no word, but that which is eminent and emphaticall.[36]

Charles Butler emphasizes the importance of verbal clarity to the setting, especially if the words themselves are well written:

> In Ditti-mixt-Musik is alwasy to bee observed, dat de Instruments dooe eider sound Submisely, or by Turns; dat de Ditti bee not obscured. For dowgh de Singers can soometime content demselvs wit de Musik of de Note; yet de Hearers ar not so well satisfyed witout de Ditti, if it bee good.[37]

These rules are especially applicable to the theater, where, if the text is at all important it must be clearly heard. Under some circumstances, such as the musical fairies of *The Maydes Metamorphosis*, the text is less important than the fact of the music. In these rare cases, the music alone may dazzle the audience. But after the revival, music became increasingly better integrated into the main action of the play, so that its every aspect came to have direct bearing on the outcome of the action. As we have seen, song was limited to particularly appropriate moments in this predominantly spoken drama, and was often meant to affect the audience in a particular way. Butler tells us that it is only when melody is added to poetry that the listener's affections can be moved:

> Dis numerous Ditti, or Rhyme applying to de Note, de Pilosper equalizest to de *Melodi* itself, for Resembling and Mooving manners and affections. . . . And afterward hee makest it a Parte of Musik: shewing dat Musik is made as well by *Poesi* as by *Melodi*.[38]

It is most significant that the writer specifies melody only, and omits reference to accompaniment or harmony from the passage. The music must help the poetry to be heard and understood, not obscured. For this, the ayre was unsurpassed.

If one can judge from extant examples, the ayres from the children's plays are as tunefully melodic as most of those published between 1597 and 1613. They tend to have vocal ranges of an octave, not atypical of other ayres of the time; and the accompaniments are more melodic than true thoroughbass, often anticipating or imitating motives from the vocal line. The text itself seems to have as great an influence on the settings of children's dramatic ayres as on the finest nondramatic settings of the same era. Declamation also apparently motivates the settings from the children's plays, for the musical rhythms flow freely with all the pleasing irregularities of the English tongue. Literal repetition of melodic material is less frequent in the ayres from the children's plays than in many published collections, whose contents often make use of repeated strains that set new lines of text. Children's dramatic ayres generally accord each new line of text new musical treatment.

One of the most outstanding ayres from the children's repertoire is "O that Joy So Soone Should Waste," from Act IV, scene iii of Jonson's *Cynthia's Revels*. It is preserved in Christ Church Oxford MS Mus 439, pp. 38-39, and is the only extant setting about which characters make stylistic comments in the play. It is also one of two songs to survive in both a contemporary version and a later one; the lyric is given very different treatment by Henry Lawes in his autograph manuscript, British Library MS Add. 53723, fol. 5. This song serves as an outstanding example of how musical style can augment a dramatic scene, and how dramatic context can make a great difference in setting a text.

In this scene, Jonson mocks effete court gallantry through the affected behavior of the aptly named Hedon and Amorphus. The two offer rival performances of songs which they have written to entertain a group of their equally empty-headed colleagues as they await delivery of a draught from the fountain of self-love. "O That Joy So Soone Should Waste" is Hedon's offering, prepared by descriptive dialogue in typically overblown prose:

Philautia.	Phantaste, Argurion! what? you are sodainely strooke me thinkes! for loves sake let's have some musicke, till they come. *Ambition*, reach the *lyra*, I pray you.
Hedon.	Any thing to which my Honour shall direct mee.
Philautia.	Come, *Amorphus*, cheare up *Phantaste*.
Amorphus.	It shall bee my pride, faire ladie, to attempt all that is in my power. But here is an instrument that (alone) is able to infuse soule into the most melancholique and dull disposde creature upon earth. O! let me kisse thy faire knees. Beauteous eares attend it.

Hedon.   Will you have the Kisse, *Honour*?
Philautia.   I, good *Ambition*.

SONG

O, that joy so soone should waste?
or so sweet a blisse
As a kisse,
Might not for ever last!
So sugred, so melting, so soft, so delicious,
The dew that lyes on roses,
When the morne her selfe discloses,
Is not so precious.
Or rather then I would it smother,
Were I to taste such another;
It should be my wishing
That I might dye, kissing.

Hedon.   I made this dittie, and the note to it, upon a kisse that my
Honour gave me, how like you it, sir?
Amorphus.   A prettie ayre! in general, I like it well: but in particular
your long *die*-note did arride me most, but it was some-
what too long. I can shew one almost of the same nature,
but much before it, and not so long, in a composition of
mine own.

Even without the music, the song and its performance characterize the shallow, narcissistic young gallant quite effectively. Both language and structure are affected, elegant, eloquent, and ridiculously trivial. In magnificent but essentially empty hyperbole, Hedon sings of the raptures of an idealized union with his beloved, effectively reducing it to a mere trifling passion. Hedon therefore adheres to the formal ideas of the neo-Platonic love poem, but gives it neither direction nor substance. The kiss, earthly prelude to spiritual bliss in the Platonic tradition, is here an end in itself. For Hedon, the first small step on the ladder of love is its pinnacle.

The anonymous setting from Christ Church Oxford MS Mus 439 (Example 8) is as affected as the poem and the scenario, a perfect complement to both. It is longer than most extant song settings from the children's repertoire, and the long "*die*-note" (bars 50-53) is certainly not the only aspect of the piece that is "somewhat too long." Almost every aspect of the text is repeated, and every musical device is used to the point of banality, perhaps expressing the singer/poet/composer's overfondness of his own cleverness. Butler tells us that

de most pouerful Musicians (suc as were *Orpheus* and *Arion*: yea, suc as was dat Divine *Psalmist* were also Poets. And suc shoolde our Musicians bee, if dey will be

Example 8.   From "O the Joyes that Soone Should Wast." (Continued on p. 259.)

complete: for hee dat knowest bode, can best fit his Poesi to his own Musik, and his Musik to his own Poesi.[39]

Hedon is presented as poet and musician, each certainly well fitted to the other and each exemplifying his shallow, self-loving manner. The song is everything that the Address to the Reader of Rosseter's *Booke of Ayres*

Example 8.   (Continued from p. 258.)

condemns: it becomes genuinely tedious in its use of imitation (bars 37–41), syncopation (bars 22-24), many rests, and the "childish observing of words" throughout. None of these devices serves any useful purpose, but simply shows that the composer knew how to use them. The sequentially repeated motivic devices for "as a kisse," "was not so pretious," "were I to taste," and especially "such another" are nothing short of ridiculous. The short rests that punctuate the choice repeated phrases not only emphasize the words, but they exaggerate the artificially breathless passion of the singer/composer.

The style of composition is as full of form and devoid of substance as everything else about this song. As if to keep pace with the latest fashion in musical style, Hedon uses a rather free, declamatory melodic line to complement the varying line-lengths and specific syllabification of the poem. In the almost flawless declamation that dominates the melody, the anonymous composer perfectly follows the stylistic injunction that Thomas Campion articulated so beautifully:

In joining of words to harmony there is nothing more offensive to the ear than to place a short syllable with a long note, though in the last the vowel often bears it out. The world is made by symmetry and proportion, and is in that respect compared to music, and music to poetry.[40]

The unique rhythmic and melodic disposition of the text provides a novel contrast to the regular, repeated, symmetrical phrases and less sensitive declamation of most ayres published before 1600, the year in which *Cynthia's Revels* was performed. In this respect, the setting at first appears quite remarkable and ahead of its time. However, the accompaniment to this sophisticated melody follows the most elementary rules of sixteenth-century counterpoint with its short but impeccable points of imitation and its almost perfect contrary motion. It provides a surprisingly conservative foundation for an avant-garde overlay, again illustrative of Hedon's characteristic mistaking of outward appearance for true substance. For all of its flashy syncopation, dotted rhythms, and sustained notes at the top of the range, the vocal part is limited to an octave, an easy octave in the most comfortable part of the soprano range. Hedon's vocal ability is thus also reduced to the same level of trivial brilliance. This setting cleverly fits the complete context and therefore enhances the drama.

By contrast, Henry Lawes's later setting (Example 9), which cannot be connected to any known production of *Cynthia's Revels*, suits the text and mood of the poem alone far better than the earlier anonymous version. But it fails to characterize Hedon or contribute to the scene from which it was severed. It is a perfect expression of the detached poem's mannerism, and provides musical support for its breathless ardor and momentous insignificance without the extreme overstatement necessitated by the dramatic context. It becomes quite clear that this is a setting of the poem for its sake alone, not as part of the broader dramatic context. The brief setting is a vehicle for virtuosic vocal display, and its lack of useless musical devices and senseless repetition allows the simple affect of the text to come through unhindered. The earlier anonymous setting, clearly intended for the play, does not express the lyric as clearly but enhances the dramatic context tremendously. A comparison between these two settings, which do indeed possess a few striking similarities, shows just how important a musical setting can be to its dramatic context.

A very different sort of ayre and of a more common type is "The Dark is My Delight" from Act I, scene ii of Marston's *The Dutch Courtesan*. This com-

Example 9. From Henry Lawes, "O yt Joye Soe Soone Should Wast."

plete song, too, is eminently suitable to its dramatic context and adds a great
deal to the meaning of the scene in which it is performed. It is preserved in
British Library MS Add. 24665, where it is set for voice and unfigured bass
on pp. 59 and 61; and British Library MS Edgerton 2971, fol. 8ᵛ-9, where it
includes a pair of apparently optional instrumental parts to make it into a consort song. In the play, it is sung as a solo with lute accompaniment.

As with "O that Joy so Soone Should Waste, "The Dark is my Delight" is
sung and accompanied by the same performer, helps to characterize the per-

former, and is performed purposefully before an audience of other characters from the play. In both cases, the performer is a central figure in the drama. Both songs deal with physical aspects of love, both have identical vocal ranges and the same basic tonality, and both arouse a reaction from other characters. Yet, both are quite different, representing the extremes of the ayre on the children's stages in spite of their outward similarities.

In the play, Freevil has brought his unhappy friend, Malheureux, to meet his mistress, Franceschina, the Dutch courtesan, to convince him that woman's beauty alone is virtue. The puritanical Malheureux regards prostitutes with disgust, and states, "The most odious spectacle the earth can present is an immodest vulgar woman." His opinion continues upon meeting Franceschina:

Enter Franceschina

Freevil.	See, sir, this is she.
Malheureux.	This?
Freevil.	This.
Malheureux.	A courtezan? Now, cold blood defend me! What a proportion afflicts me!
Franceschina.	O mine aderliver love, vat sall me do to requit dis your mush affection?
Malheureux.	Marry, salute my friend, clip his neck, and kiss him welcome.
Franceschina.	A mine art, sir, you bin very velcome.
Freevil.	Kiss her, man, with a more familiar affection, so. Come, what entertainment? Go to your lute.

❖ ❖ ❖ ❖ ❖ ❖ ❖

Malheureux.	Ha! She is a whore is she not?
Freevil.	Whore! Fie, whore! You may call her a courtezan, a cockatrice, or (as that worthy spirit of eternal happiness said) a suppository. But whore! Fie, 'tis not in fashion to call things by their right names. . . .

Enter Franceschina, with her lute.

Come siren, your voice.

Franceschina.	Vill not you stay in my bosom to-night, love?
Freevil.	By no means, sweet breast; this gentleman has vowed to see me chastely laid.
Franceschina.	He shall have a bed too, if dat please him.
Freevil.	Peace, you tender him offence; he is one of a professed abstinence. Siren, your voice and away.

She sings to her lute

THE SONG

> The darke is my delight,
> Soe tis the nightingale's
> My musick's in the nighte,
> Soe is the nightingales.
> My bodie is but little,
> Soe is the nightingales,
> I love to sleep 'gainst prickle,
> Soe doth the nightingale.

Like the siren to which Freevil likens her, Franceschina completely enchants Malheureux, who falls instantly in love with her:

Malheureux.	Is she unchaste—can such a one be damn'd?
	O love and beauty! ye two eldest seeds
	Of the vast chaos what strong right you have
	Even in things divine—our very souls!
Freevil.	What ho, ha! come bird, come. Stand, peace.
Malheureux.	Are strumpets then such things so delicate?
	Can custom spoil what nature made so good?
	Or is their custom bad? . . .
Freevil.	By the Lord! he's caught! Laughter eternal!
Malheureux.	Soul, I must love her! Destiny is weak
	To my affection. . . .

Franceschina's song of enchantment, presented without the outrageous Dutch accent that dominates her spoken lines and at least one other song, is strikingly unaffected. In eight lines of regularly metrical poetry she compares herself to the nightingale: their common evening activity, famed music, and daintiness of body—and even draws a clever erotic parallel between her own professional posture and the Classical image of the sleeping nightingale pierced by a thorn. The prepossessing simplicity of the text has an honest, almost innocent, appeal, at odds with the artifice of the singer's profession. Instead, it characterizes Franceschina's earnest amorality, driven by passion rather than cunning.

Both settings (Examples 10 and 11) use essentially the same melody and basic harmonic support. The piece moves rapidly in a bright G-major tonality,[41] and the setting transforms a rather dull poem into a charming song. The lute part of the original production has not survived, but the bass line of both manuscripts provides simple harmonic support, and the additional instrumental parts of the Egerton manuscript provide polyphonic interest and occasional points of imitation although they are idiomatic of viol consort writing.

Example 10. From "The Darke is My Delight" version 1. (British Library Manuscript Additional 24665.)

The piece is divided into two sections, typical of many contemporary ayres, and the second section is repeated. It exhibits the tunefulness and limited vocal range of many ayres from the first years of the seventeenth century. It also includes an example of simple word painting in its use of eighth-note motion and short rests on the repeated motive for "little" (bars 10-11). This spirited song does not demand a great deal of vocal virtuosity from its singer, but, unlike Hedon's song, this does not reflect negatively on the singing character.

Example 11. From "The Dakre is My Delight" version 2. (British Library Manuscript Egerton 2971.)

Franceschina, a simple woman of action and passion rather than of rational thought, is characterized perfectly by the complete song. And like Hedon's song, it may be performed effectively by an excellent actor with a pleasing voice and some training on a stringed instrument.

A consideration of the ayre on the children's stage must not overlook the curious category of the parodied pre-existing ayre. Such songs are sung unaccompanied in the manner of popular song, but this is an acceptable practice:

... one of de upper Partes is necessarily to have a special Melodi aboov de rest: whic is called de *Cantus* or tune: suc as may delight a Musical ear, dowgh it bee sung alone by it self.[42]

By removing the accompaniment, which frequently includes imitation or anticipation of various vocal motives and provides melodic interludes during short rests, part of the character of the original composition becomes lost. And a change of text most often brings a once-elegant art song closer to the common ballad, which gives new words to a pre-existing tune.

An excellent example is "Methought This Other Night" from Act IV of Dekker and Webster's *Northward Ho*, a parody of the ayre of the same title in Robert Jones's *Second Book of Songs and Ayres* (1601). Jones's original song is the simple, elegant setting of an anonymous text concerning a typically courteous dream of sincere love and innocent pleasure. A simple alteration of the text renders it as irreverently obscene as the grotesque old Bawd who sings the parody, for the intense emotion and frustrated passion of the original are transformed into a hilariously unsentimental image of the basest sort of physical love (Example 12). Only the first stanza is used, but in it the coy virginity of the five-stanza original is reduced to a marketable commodity, and gallant masculine love descends to a mixture of unabashed lust and easy gullibility. Minimal changes in textual rhythm, such as the substitution of the word "gentlemen" for the monosyllabic "me" of the original in bar 9, add a rough, folk like quality to the polished metrical regularity of the original poem; and the omission of the lively, supportive instrumental accompaniment furthers the song's fall from its original grace. But these changes still permit the song to remain an obvious parody of a specific original, probably known to the original audience. To further the song's descent from its original beauty and delicacy, a stage direction calls for the Bawd to sing it "scurvily."

MISCELLANEOUS POPULAR SONG

The boundary between popular and art song on the children's stages becomes quite nebulous at the point of such parodies, of newly composed songs in popular style, or of brief unaccompanied quotations from widely circulating pre-existent ayres or madrigals. But several sorts of distinctly popular song appear in children's plays and are important to a discussion of musical style, because popular songs account for a goodly number of the extant lyrics with extant settings, and contribute as much to dramatic context as any other sort of song.

It is clear that there were many kinds of popular music in late Renaissance England, but the modern scholar must characterize and categorize them. Most Renaissance literary and musical theorists, if they even considered pop-

Example 12. "Me Thought This Other Night." (After Robert Jones.)

ular music at all, lumped all sorts together disdainfully, or discussed only one form, such as the ballad. But the texts of these songs tend to be quite distinctive, whether gathered outside of the theater or written in imitation of genuinely popular originals. Their language is simple and often colloquial, they refer to common trivial pursuits, their appeal is extremely broad, and they are conspicuously lacking in pretension or sophisticated literary devices of any sort.

One form of popular music that was recognized as a discrete category by contemporary writers is the drinking song, classified more by subject and purpose than by musical style. Thomas Morley considers drinking songs a compendium of musical vulgarity:

The slightest kind of musick (if they deserve the name of musicke) are the *vinate* or drincking songes, for, as I have said before, there is no kind of vanitie whereunto they have not applied some musicke or other, as they have framde this to be sung in their drinking.[43]

The children's plays exhibit as wide a variety of drinking songs as may be found in musical sources. Some are monophonic, others rounds or catches, and, according to stage directions, some were accompanied by "fiddlers." And a few are simple part songs.

   One of the most interesting drinking songs with extant music from the children's plays is "Give Us Once a Drinke," sung in Act V of Marston's *Jacke Drum's Entertainment.* It is presented as number 17 in Ravenscroft's *Deuteromelia*, a "Freeman's Song of Four Voices," where it is given the full twelve stanzas presented in the play. It is a simplistic song that alternates between soloist and chorus (Example 13), and, though the lowest part as given in the Ravenscroft collection is too low for a boy singer, the fact that its complete text is given in the play implies that it was originally written for the play. The combined styles of the music and the lyric have a truly popular appeal. The vocal ranges are extremely limited, rhythms are simple, and the text requires free addition of the names of successively larger drinking containers ad infinitem. The song was probably performed with appropriate gestures (there is a butler on hand who continues to serve the drinkers), and would seem to owe its origin to the sort of drinking game-song still practiced today, in which participants alternate the solo section and each person who misses a prescribed word or note of the successively longer solo is required to pay for the next round of drinks or down his own before wishing better luck to the next soloist.

   Rounds, catches, and canons formed another category of popular song recognized during the age of children's drama. All three types were defined as simple canonic songs with trivial texts and extremely limited vocal ranges, and even half a century later there was no formal distinction made among the three terms: round, catch, canon.[44] Topics range from sacred to profane and include just about anything their anonymous writers could imagine. Those used in children's drama all appear to be on secular subjects.

   In children's plays, rounds, catches, or canons are sometimes sung as solo songs. One extant example is "Jolly Shepherd," used in Act II of *The Maydes Metamorphosis*, and preserved as a three-voice round in King's College Cambridge MS KC 1 (number 22), Thomas Ravenscroft's *Pammelia* (number 3), and Library of Congress MS M1490.M535A5 (the Secund Roundels to Thrie Voices, p. 2). Any joyful piece suitable for a shepherd's boy would

Example 13. From "Give Us Once a Drink."

Example 14. From "Jolly Shepheard."

have sufficed in the dramatic context, which simply shows a shepherd boy singing for his own amusement. Though the song may be sung as a round, it has a charming simplicity as a solo (Example 14; text and underlay as given in the Ravenscroft collection). It is far more tunefully melodic than many similarly canonic pieces, and its vocal range is unusually wide for the genre.

Those canonic pieces sung in parts in the children's plays are generally introduced as catches in stage directions or dialogue. An excellent example comes from Act IV, scene iv of Beaumont's *The Knight of the Burning Pestle*, in which Old Merrythought introduces a song with "Let's have a catch. Boy, follow me; come." Their song, "Ho, ho nobody at home" is presented in King's College Cambridge MS KC 1 (number 12), Thomas Ravenscroft's *Pammelia* (number 85), and Library of Congress MS M1490.M535A5 (the XLI Roundell for four voices, p. 46) as "Hey ho, nobody at home" (Example 15; text and underlay as given in the Ravenscroft collection). This catch is but one of several songs in the scene, each one belonging to a popular genre, each one unaccompanied. Like the others, it serves as trivial a dramatic function as its text: it enhances a mood of simple, mundane joviality. Any well-known catch, canon, or round would have sufficed in this situation.

Many writers of the era refer to ballads, most often in derogatory terms. Ballads in the children's plays are easy to distinguish by their texts, for they

Example 15. "Hey Ho Nobody at Home."

tell a story, or present part of a story, in simple language and simple meter. As William Webbe explains, ballad text is simplistic and formulaic, ballad music borrowed from among a wide range of popular tunes, and they belong to rogues and common people:

> If I let passe the uncountable rabble of ryming ballett makers, and compylers of senceless sonets who be most busy, to stuffe every stall full of gross devises and unlearned Pamphlets: I trust I shall with the best sort be held excused. For though many such can frame an Alehouse song of five or six score verses, hobbling uppon some tune of a Northern Jygge, or Robyn Hoode, or La Lubber, etc. And perhaps observe the just nu[m]ber of sillables, eyght in one line, sixe in an other, and there withall an A to make a jerke at the end.[45]

And, as we have seen, more literate poets and musicians disdained ballads, ballad makers, and ballad singers. But ballads, especially of the urban printed variety, were extremely common; and balladeers were perceived as artists in certain lowly circles, condemned for pretense in others:

> In these later times every Ballad-maker will be a Poet, as if every Pedler would seeme a Merchant, and every Pettifogger a lawyer.[46]

"When Sampson was a Tall Young Man," from Act II, scene iii of Chapman, Jonson, and Marston's *Eastward Ho*, is an excellent example of a ballad from the children's repertoire. Sung by that master rogue and balladeer, Francis Quicksilver, it is a parody of a popular ballad made to a foreign dance-tune, the oft-used Spanish Pavan (Example 16). The ballad genre itself is, of course, broadly parodic, for tunes must be selected to which new words can be framed with ease. The earliest reference to the ballad which Quicksilver parodies is to a song entitled "A Most Excellent and Famous Ditty of Samson Judge of Israel," to be sung to the tune of the Spanish Pavan, registered in

Example 16. "When Sampson was a Tall Young Man."

1586.[47] The ballad, which spawned other imitations and whose earliest text is now lost, had thus been circulating for nineteen years before the first production of *Eastward Ho* in 1605. As Webbe's astute observation tells us of the style of ballad texts, both the earliest extant version of the song and Quicksilver's own clever rendition have eight syllables in lines 1-3 and 5-7, and six in lines 4 and 8. The ballad presents Quicksilver's situation at the point of singing, shortly after he leaves his master, the goldsmith Touchstone. It shows him to be a man of quick wit and able imitative ability, traits that he uses again and again throughout the play as he cheats and gulls his way to the very abyss of misfortune and back on his prodigal progress. As a city comedy, *Eastward Ho* presents realistic music for each of its singing characters, and a young apprentice certainly would have known popular ballad tunes.

APPENDIX A

EXTANT PLAYS PRESENTED BY CHILDREN'S COMPANIES, c. 1597–1613

The following list, arranged alphabetically by dramatist, is based on information from Michael Shapiro's company-by-company list of all plays known or believed to have been acted by English children's companies from the reign of Henry VIII onward; on A. R. Braunmuller and Michael Hattaway's chronological table of English plays between 1485 and 1642; and on the most recent revision of Alfred Harbage's compendium of plays acted in England before 1700.[1] This list is necessarily uncertain, since English Renaissance drama companies did not maintain repertoire lists, and play imprints rarely include complete information about their original performing companies. Furthermore, though all plays were written for specific troupes to present at specific times, occasionally plays were stolen, revived, or revised for new actors or a new season. It is even sometimes difficult to establish an author, for collaboration was common, many plays were printed without authors' names, and still others were misattributed. There are also a number of plays known to have been acted by the children's companies that are now lost. These are given by both Harbage and Shapiro in the above works, but because they could not be consulted for musical content they have been omitted here.

Anonymous

    Blurt, Master-Constable or the Spaniard's Night Walk. Presented by the Children of Paul's in 1601–02. (Often attributed to Thomas Middleton or Thomas Dekker.)

The Contention Between Liberality and Prodigality. Presented by the Children of the Chapel in 1600–01; possibly a revival of a play first presented by the Children of Paul's in 1567–68.

Every Woman in Her Humor. Presented by the Children of the King's Revels (?) in 1607.

Hieronimo. Presented by the Children of the Chapel between 1600 and 1604; possibly a revival of Thomas Kyd's *The Spanish Tragedy* which had first been presented between 1582 and 1592 by the Lord Strange's Men and previously resurrected by the Lord Admiral's Men in 1597; or of the anonymous *The Spanish Comedy* which had been presented between c. 1584 and 1592 by the Lord Strange's Men and the Lord Admiral's Men; or the Children's original burlesque *The First Part of Hieronimo.*

The Maydes Metamorphosis. Presented by the Children of Paul's between 1597 and 1600.

The Puritan. Presented by the Children of Paul's (?) in 1606.

Wily Beguiled. Presented by the Children of Paul's (?) between 1596 and 1606.

The Wisdom of Dr. Dodypoll. Presented by the Children of Paul's between 1597 and 1600.

Robert Armin.

The Two Maids of More-Clacke. Presented by the Children of the King's Revels (?) in 1607–08.

William Barkstead. (See under John Marston.)

Lording Barry.

Ram Alley. Presented by the Children of the King's Revels in 1607–08.

Francis Beaumont.

The Knight of the Burning Pestle. Presented by the Children of the Chapel in 1607.

Francis Beaumont and John Fletcher.

The Coxcomb. Presented by the Children of the Chapel in 1609.

Cupid's Revenge. Presented by the Children of the Chapel in 1607–08.

The Scornful Lady. Presented by the Children of the Chapel (?) c. 1610.

The Woman Hater. Presented by the Children of Paul's between 1605 and 1607.

George Chapman.

All Fools. Presented by the Children of the Chapel in 1604.

Bussy D'Ambois. Presented by the Children of Paul's in 1604.

The Conspiracy and Tragedy of Charles Duke of Byron.
(Also known as *The Contention and Tragedy of Byron.*)
Presented by the Children of the Chapel in 1608.

The Gentleman Usher. Presented by the Children of the Chapel (?) in 1602–03.

May Day. Presented by the Children of the Chapel in 1601–02.

Monsieur D'Olive. Presented by the Children of the Chapel in 1604–05.

The Revenge of Bussy D'Ambois. Presented by the Children of the Chapel in 1610.

Sir Gyles Goose-Cappe. Presented by the Children of the Chapel between 1601 and 1603.

The Widow's Tears. Presented by the Children of the Chapel c. 1605.

George Chapman, Ben Jonson, and John Marston.

Eastward Ho. Presented by the Children of the Chapel in 1605.

Samuel Daniel.

Philotas. Presented by the Children of the Chapel in 1604.

John Day.

Humor Out of Breath. Presented by the Children of the King's Revels in 1608.

The Isle of Gulls. Presented by the Children of the Chapel in 1606.

Law Tricks. Presented by the Children of the Chapel (?) between 1604 and 1607 (?) and by the Children of the King's Revels (?) in 1607.

Thomas Dekker. (See also under Anonymous and Thomas Middleton.)

Thomas Dekker (and John Marston?).

Satiro-Mastix. Presented by the Children of Paul's in 1601.

Thomas Dekker and John Webster.

Northward Ho. Presented by the Children of Paul's in 1605.

Westward Ho. Presented by the Children of Paul's in 1604.

Nathan Field.

Amends for Ladies. Presented by the Children of the Chapel in 1610–11.

A Woman is a Weather-Cock. Presented by the Children of the Chapel in 1609–10.

John Fletcher. (See also under Francis Beaumont.)

The Faithful Shepherdess. Presented by the Children of the Chapel in 1608.

Ben Jonson.

His Case is Altered (also known as *The Case is Altered*). Presented by the Children of the Chapel between 1600 and 1608; originally written for an unknown adult company in 1597–98, but revised for the Children.

Cynthia's Revels. Presented by the Children of the Chapel in 1600.

Epicoene or the Silent Woman. Presented by the Children of the Chapel in 1609–10.

The Poetaster. Presented by the Children of the Chapel in 1601.

Thomas Kyd. (See under Anonymous.)

John Lyly.

Love's Metamorphosis. Presented by the Children of Paul's in 1597 (?) and by the Children of the chapel in 1600.

Lewis Machin. (See under Gervase Markham.)

Gervase Markham (?) and Lewis Machin (?).

The Dumb Knight. Presented by the Children of the King's Revels in 1607–08.

John Marston. (See also under Thomas Dekker and George Chapman.)

Antonio and Mellida. Presented by the Children of Pauls in 1599–1600.

Antonio's Revenge. Presented by the Children of Paul's in 1599–1600.

The Dutch Courtesan. Presented by the Children of the Chapel between 1603 and 1605.

Histrio-Mastix. Presented by the Children of Paul's (?) in 1599 (?).

*Jack Drum's Entertainment.*Presented by the Children of Paul's in 1600.

The Malcontent. Presented by the Children of the Chapel c. 1603.

Parasitaster or the Fawn. Presented by the Children of Paul's c. 1604 and by the Children of the Chapel c. 1604.

What You Will. Presented by the Children of Paul's c. 1601.

The Wonder of Women or the Tragedy of Sophonisba. Presented by the Children of the Chapel in 1605–06.

John Marston and William Barkstead.

The Insatiate Countess. Presented by the Children of the Chapel between 1609 and 1611.

John Mason.

Mulleasses the Turk (also known as *The Turk*). Presented by the Children of the King's Revels in 1607.

Thomas Middleton. (See also under Anonymous.)

A Trick to Catch the Old-One. Presented by the Children of Paul's in 1604 and the Children of the Chapel between 1604 and 1607.

Thomas Middleton (and Thomas Dekker?).

The Family of Love. Presented by the Children of Paul's (?) between 1602 and 1603 and by the Children of the King's Revels in 1607.

A Mad World My Masters. Presented by the Children of Paul's between 1604 and 1606.

Michaelmas Term. Presented by the Children of Paul's between 1604 and 1606.

The Phoenix. Presented by the Children of Paul's in 1603–04.

Your Five Gallants. Presented by the Children of the Chapel between 1604 and 1607.

Edward Sharpham.

Cupid's Whirligig. Presented by the Children of the King's Revels in 1607.

The Fleer. Presented by the Children of the Chapel in 1606.

John Webster. (See under Thomas Dekker.)

*A LIST OF LYRICS AND MUSICAL SOURCES TO 1700**

The following list supplements the discussion of musical sources given in Chapter 9, and is a more convenient way to locate the music for the lyrics given in the dramatic imprints by title, incipit, or opening line. I have included all song texts from all children's plays in the hopes that future scholars can identify additional musical sources. I have listed all known extant sources of the original theatrical songs. But, as shown in Chapter 9, much of the popular music that was incorporated into plays circulated in enough arrangements to require a source-study in itself. In fact, there have been several such studies done, and a number of modern collections have published popular and ballad tunes in convenient volumes. For this reason, and for the convenience of the producer who is more concerned about reuniting words with music than with the process that makes the union possible or with variant settings of the same tune, I have listed a few representative sixteenth- and seventeenth-century sources for settings of the most widely circulating popular music. I have also listed modern works that provide the complete lyrics in cases in which only an incipit is given in the drama. For the interested reader, abundant details regarding popular song and balladry from the Elizabethan and Jacobean eras are given in such classic works as William Chappell, *Popular Music of the Olden Time*; Joseph Ritson, *A Select Collection of English Songs*; and Claude

---

*Organized by title and first given line.

Simpson, *The British Broadside Ballad and its Music.* These book-length studies are supplemented by such detailed articles as Diana Poulton, "The Black-Letter Broadside and its Music"; and John Ward, "Apropos *The British Broadside Ballad and its Music.*"

ABBREVIATIONS

The following more modern collections of ballads and popular tunes are referred to repeatedly in this Appendix with the following abbreviations:

Chappell.   William Chappell, *The Ballad Literature and Popular Music of the Olden Times*, 2 vols. (London: 1855–59; reprint ed., New York: Dover Books, 1965). This is a source for tunes and a few texts.

Child.   Francis James Child, ed., *The English and Scottish Popular Ballads*, 5 vols. (London, 1882–94; reprint ed., New York: Dover Books, 1965). This is a source for text only.

Percy.   Thomas Percy, *Reliques of Ancient English Poetry*, 3 vols. (London, 1886; reprint ed., New York: Dover Books, 1966). This is a source for text only.

Ritson.   Joseph Ritson, *A Select Collection of English Songs*, 3 vols. (London: Printed for J. Johnson, 1783). This is a source for text and some tunes.

Simpson.   Claude Simpson, *The British Broadside Ballad and its Music* (New Brunswick: Rutgers University Press, 1966). This is a source for tunes, lists of contemporary sources, and broadside ballad titles which made use of the given tunes.

All other such works are given more complete citations in this Appendix, and may be located easily in the Bibliography that follows.

"A Ladies Daughter of Paris"
Beaumont, *The Knight of the Burning Pestle*, Act V, scene iii.
Presented by the Children of the Chapel in 1607.
    This ballad, whose opening line is "It was a ladies daughter of Paris properly," was printed as a broadside under the title of "A Rare Example of a Vertuous Maid in Paris." It is sung in full in the play, but only the opening words are given, followed by an "etc." The complete text is given in William Chappell, ed., *The Roxburghe Ballads*, vol. 1 (London: Printed for the Ballad Soci-

ety by Taylor and Co., 1871), p. 34. The ballad is to be sung to the tune of "O Man of Desperation," which is given in Simpson, p. 533.

"A Maiden Sitting All Alone"
Armin, *The Two Maids of More-Clacke*, no act divisions.
Presented by the Children of the King's Revels in 1607–08.

"A Merry Heart Lives Long-A"
Beaumont, *The Knight of the Burning Pestle*, Act I, scene i.
Presented by the Children of the Chapel in 1607.

"All Haile Faire Phoebus in thy Purple Throne"
The Maydes Metamorphosis, Act V.
Presented by the Children of Paul's between 1597 and 1600.

"All Ye Woods and Trees and Bowers"
Fletcher, *The Faithful Shepherdess*, Act V, scene v.
Presented by the Children of the Chapel in 1608.

"Amidst the Mountaine Ida Groves"
The Maydes Metamorphosis, Act III.
Presented by the Children of Paul's between 1597 and 1600.

"And Ever and Anon She Doubled in her Song"
Chapman, Jonson, and Marston, *Eastward Ho*, Act I, scene i.
Presented by the Children of the Chapel in 1605.

"And Ever She Cride Shout Home"
Chapman, Jonson, and Marston, *Eastward Ho*, Act I, scene i.
Presented by the Children of the Chapel in 1605.

"And If She Will Not Go To Bed"
Chapman, Jonson, and Marston, *Eastward Ho*, Act I, scene i.
Presented by the Children of the Chapel in 1605.

"And If Thou Wilt My True Lover Be"
Marston, *Antonio and Mellida*, Act V, scene i.
Presented by the Children of Paul's in 1599–1600.

"And Some They Whistled, And Some They Sang"
Beaumont, *The Knight of the Burning Pestle*, Act V, scene iii.
Presented by the Children of the Chapel in 1607.
    The opening line of the fourteenth stanza of a ballad entitled "Little Musgrave and Lady Barnard," which is given in full in Chappell, vol. 1, p. 170; Child, vol. 2, p. 243; Percy, vol. 3, p. 58; and Ritson, vol. 2, p. 215.

"And Then to Apollo, Hollo Trees, Hollo"
Every Woman in her Humor, Act IV, scene i.
Presented by the Children of the King's Revels in 1607.

"And Was Not Good King Salomon"
Marston, *Antonio and Mellida*, Act III, scene i.
Presented by the Children of Paul's in 1599–1600.

This ballad, whose opening line is as given in the play, was printed as a broadside under the title of "The Panges of Love and Lovers Fittes" in 1559, directed to be sung to the tune of "Lady, Lady." It is reprinted in Herbert L. Collman, ed., *Ballads and Broadsides Chiefly of the Elizabethan Period* (Oxford: Oxford University Press, 1912), p. 111. The tune is given under the title of "King Solomon" in Simpson, p. 412. John Ward claims that this tune was originally the almain "Guerre, Guerre Gay," "Music for a *Handefull of Pleasant Delites*," *JAMS* 10 (1957): 175.

"And Where Is Your True Love?"
Beaumont, *The Knight of the Burning Pestle*, Act V, scene iii.
Presented by the Children of the Chapel in 1607.

"Arise, Arise"
Beaumont, *The Knight of the Burning Pestle*, Act V, scene v.
Presented by the Children of the Chapel in 1607.

The title/opening of a song whose third stanza, beginning "Begone, begone, my juggy, my puggy," is used in the play. The song is given in Henry Playford, *Wit and Mirth, or Pills to Purge Melancholy*, The Second Part (London: William Pearson for Henry Playford, 1700), p. 44.

"A Little Lambes Lift Up Their Snowie Sides"
The Maydes Metamorphosis, Act IV.
Presented by the Children of Paul's between 1597 and 1600.

"As You Came From Walsingham"
Beaumont, *The Knight of the Burning Pestle*, Act II, scene viii.
Presented by the Children of the Chapel in 1607.

This is the opening line of the well-known and well-beloved ballad of "Walsingham," arrangements of which are included in William Barley, *A New Book of Tabliture* (London: William Barley, 1596); Anthony Holborne, *The Cittharn Schoole* (Peter Short, 1597); British Library MS Add. 15118, fol. 32^v; British Library MS RM.24.d.3, The Forster Virginal Book, fol. 39^v; and numerous other sources listed in Chappell, vol. 1, p. 121; Poulton, "The Black-Letter Broadside and its Music," p. 434; Simpson, p. 741; and Ward, "Apropos *The British Broadside Ballad and its Music*," pp. 79–82. The tune is given in all of the above except the latter. The complete text is given in

Thomas Deloney, *A Garland of Good Will* (London: Robert Bird, 1631); British Library MS Ass. 27829, "Bishop Percy's Folio Manuscript," fol. 251; and Percy, vol. 2, p. 101.

"Baloo"
Beaumont, *The Knight of the Burning Pestle*, between Acts II and III.
Presented by the Children of the Chapel in 1607.

The title is more commonly spelled "ballow" or "ballowe," and arrangements are included in Thomas Morley, *The First Booke of Consort Lessons* (London: William Barley, 1599 and 1611); British Library MS Add. 10337, Elizabeth Roger's Virginal Book, p. 6; New York Public Library MS Drexel 4257, John Gamble's Commonplace Book, p. 46; and other sources listed in Simpson, p. 31; and Ward, "Apropros *The British Broadside Ballad and its Music*," p. 29. The text is given in British Library MS Add. 27879, Bishop Percy's Folio Manuscript, fol. 257^v; and Percy, vol. 2, p. 209.

"Begone, Begone, My Juggy, My Puggy"
Beaumont, *The Knight of the Burning Pestle*, Act III, scene v.
Presented by the Children of the Chapel in 1607.

This is the opening of the third stanza of "Arise, Arise," which see above.

"Better Musicke Nere Was Known"
Beaumont, *The Knight of the Burning Pestle*, Act V, scene iii.
Presented by the Children of the Chapel in 1607.

"Blush, Folly, Blush"
Jonson, *The Poetaster*, Act V, scene iii.
Presented by the Children of the Chapel in 1601.

"Boe-Bell"
Chapman, Jonson, and Marston, *Eastward Ho*, Act I, scene i.
Presented by the Children of the Chapel in 1605.

The title of this piece is more commonly spelled "bow bells," and sources include Playford, *Musicks Hand-Maide* (London: John Playford, 1663), no. 30; and Playford, *A Musicall Banquet* (London: John Benson and John Playford, 1663) no. 12. A modern transcription and more complete list of sources of the tune are given in Simpson, p. 64. Additional information is provided in Ward, "Apropros *The British Broadside Ballad and its Music*," p. 31.

"Boire a le fountaine"
Anon., *The Wisdom of Dr. Dodypoll*, Act II.
Presented by the Children of Paul's between 1597 and 1600.

"Brave Lads Come Forth and Chant It"
Marston, *Histriomastix*, Act II.
Presented by the Children of Paul's (?) in 1599 (?).

"Bugs Song"
Chapman, *The Gentleman Usher*, Act II.
Presented by the Children of the Chapel in 1602–03.

"But A Little Higher, But A Little Higher"
Chapman, Jonson, and Marston, *Eastward Ho*, Act III, scene ii.
Presented by the Children of the Chapel in 1605.
    Refrain of Thomas Campion's "Mistress Since You So Much Desire,"
Campion's no. 16 in Philip Rosseter's *A Booke of Ayres* (London: Peter Short
for Thomas Morley, 1601).

"But Yet, Or Ere You Part"
Beaumont, *The Knight of the Burning Pestle*, Act I, scene iv.
Presented by the Children of the Chapel in 1607.
    A quotation from "Wilt Thou Unkind," no. 15 in Dowland's *First Booke of
Songs or Ayres* (1597, 1600, 1603, 1608, and 1613), given parodically in the
play.

"By Gorden Me Must Needs Now Sing"
Marston, *Jack Drum's Entertainment*, Act IV.
Presented by the Children of Paul's in 1600.

"By the Moone We Sport and Play"
The Maydes Metamorphosis, Act II.
Presented by the Children of Paul's between 1597 and 1600.
    Text of "The Urchin's Dance," no. 8 in Thomas Ravenscroft's *A Briefe
Discourse of the True (but neglected) Use of Charact'ring the Degrees* (Lon-
don: Edward Allde for Thomas Adams, 1614), given and performed in full in
the play.

"Can You Blow the Little Horne?"
The Maydes Metamorphosis, Act II.
Presented by the Children of Paul's between 1597 and 1600.

"Chaunt Birds on Everie Bush"
Everie Woman in Her Humour, Act V, scene i.
Presented by the Children of the King's Revels in 1607.

"Chunck, Chunck, Chunck, His Bagges Do Ring"
Marston. *Jacke Drum's Entertainment*, Act II.
Presented by the Children of Paul's in 1600.

"Coll Her And Clip Her"
Everie Woman in Her Humour, Act II, scene i.
Presented by the Children of the King's Revels in 1607.
    Refrain from "Mistress Mine," no. 8 in Thomas Morley's *First Booke of Ayres* (London: William Barley for Thomas Morley, 1600).

"Come Follow Me My Wagges"
Jonson, *Cynthia's Revels*, Act II, scene v.
Presented by the Children of the Chapel in 1600.

"Come No More There Boyes"
Beaumont, *The Knight of the Burning Pestle*, Act V, scene iii.
Presented by the Children of the Chapel in 1607.

"Come Shepherds Come"
Fletcher, *The Faithful Shepherdess*, Act I, scene iii.
Presented by the Children of the Chapel in 1608.
    New York Public Library MS Drexel 4041, no. 19, attributed there to William Lawes.

"Come Sleepe, And With Thy Sweet Deceiving"
Beaumont and Fletcher, *The Woman Hater*, Act III, scene i.
Presented by the Children of Paul's between 1605 and 1607.

"Come You Whose Loves Are Dead"
Beaumont, *The Knight of the Burning Pestle*, Act IV, scene ii.
Presented by the Children of the Chapel in 1607.

"The Darke Is My Delight"
Marston, *The Dutch Courtesan*, Act I, scene ii.
Presented by the Children of the Chapel between 1603 and 1605.
    British Library MS Egerton 2971, fol. 8^v (listed as fol. 14^v in the table of contents); and British Library MS Add. 24665, Giles Earle His Booke, pp. 59 and 61.

"Dead? Why Fare-Well He"
Beaumont, *The Knight of the Burning Pestle*, Act V, scene iii.
Presented by the Children of the Chapel in 1607.
    A variant of the Twentieth Stanza of "The Friar of Orders Gray," presented in Percy, vol. 2, p. 245. This ballad was also used in Shakespeare's *Hamlet*, where Ophelia quotes two stanzas in her mad scene in Act IV, scene v. No extant tune is definitely identified with the ballad, but John Long suggests the use of "Walsingham," *Shakespeare's Use of Music*, vol. 3, pp. 123–24.

"Delicious Beauty That Doth Lie"
Marston, *Jack Drum's Entertainment*, Act II.
Presented by the Children of Paul's in 1600.

"Doe Not Feare To Put Thy Feet"
Fletcher, *The Faithful Shepherdess*, Act III, scene i.
Presented by the Children of the Chapel in 1608.

   John Playford, *The Treasury of Musick* (1669), p. 98; John Wilson, *Cheerful Ayres and Ballads* (London: William Godbid for John Playford, 1660), pp. 24–25; and Edinburgh University Library MS Dc.1.69, no. 96. The piece is attributed in all instances to John Wilson.

"Downe, Downe, Downe:/Let the Chimney Sweeper In"
Chapman, *May Day*, Act III.
Presented by the Children of the Chapel in 1601–02.

"Downe, Downe, Downe:/They Fall Downe"
Beaumont, *The Knight of the Burning Pestle*, Act II, scene viii.
Presented by the Children of the Chapel in 1607.

   Misquotation from "Sorrow Stay," number 3 in John Dowland, *The Second Booke of Songs or Ayres* (London: Thomas Easte for Thomas Morley, 1600); also included in British Library MS Add. 24665, Giles Earle His Booke, p. 32; Christ Church Oxford MS Mus 439, p. 70; and New York Public Library MS Drexel 4175, Ann Twice's Book, no. 31.

"The Dutchman For A Drunkard"
Marston, *The Malcontent*, Act V, scene i.
Presented by the Children of the Chapel c. 1603.

"The Elves Dance"
The Maydes Metamorphosis, Act II.
Presented by the Children of Paul's between 1597 and 1600.

   Title given to the lyric beginning "Round about, round about, in a fine ring-a" in Thomas Ravenscroft's *A Briefe Discourse*, no. 9, there attributed to John Bennet.

"Fading"
Beaumont, *The Knight of the Burning Pestle*, between Acts III and IV.
Presented by the Children of the Chapel in 1607.

   The tune is used in Henry Playford's *Wit and Mirth*, the Second Part (1700), p. 99, for "A Ballad of the Courtier and the Country Clown." Other sources and further information about the tune are given in Chappell, vol. 1, p. 234; and Simpson, p. 792.

"Fair Forester And Lovely Shepherd Swaine"
The Maydes Metamorphosis, Act IV.
Presented by the Children of Paul's between 1597 and 1600.

"Fair Margaret and Sweet William"
Beaumont, *The Knight of the Burning Pestle*, Act II scene viii and Act III, scene v.
Presented by the Children of the Chapel in 1607.

This ballad provides quotations beginning "When it was growne to darke midnight" and "You are no love for me, Margaret." The complete text is provided in Child, vol. 2, p. 199; Percy, vol. 3, p. 124; and Ritson, vol. 2, p. 190. The tune and further information are given in Chappell, vol. 1, p. 382; and Simpson, p. 785.

"Farewell, Adieu: Saith Thy Love True"
Marston, *Antonio's Revenge*, Act III, scene iv.
Presented by the Children of Paul's in 1599–1600.

"Farewell Dear Love"
Beaumont, *The Knight of the Burning Pestle*, Act II, scene viii.
Presented by the Children of the Chapel in 1607.

This song, number 12 in Robert Jones's *The First Booke of Songes or Ayres* (London: Peter Short for Thomas Morley, 1600), is quoted beginning with "Why an if she be, what care I?"

"Fond Fables Tell Of Old"
Chapman, Jonson, and Marston, *Eastward Ho*, Act V, scene i.
Presented by the Children of the Chapel in 1605.

This text begins the song entitled "Song O the Golden Shower" in the play.

"For I Did But Kiss Her"
Everie Woman in Her Humour, Act II, scene ii.
Presented by the Children of the King's Revels in 1607.

A quotation from "My Mistress Sings No Other Song," no. 19 in Robert Jones's *The First Booke of Songes or Ayres* (1600).

"For Jillian Of Berry She Dwells On A Hill"
Beaumont, *The Knight of the Burning Pestle*, Act IV, scene iv.
Presented by the Children of the Chapel in 1607.

"Fortune My Foe"
1. *Everie Woman in Her Humour*, Act IV, scene i.
    Presented by the Children of the King's Revels in 1607.
2. Beaumont, *The Knight of the Burning Pestle*, Act V, scene iii.
    Presented by the Children of the Chapel in 1607.

3. *The Maydes Metamorphosis*, Act II.
    Presented by the Children of Paul's between 1597 and 1600.
    This is one of the favorite and most widespread ballad tunes of the late six-
teenth and early seventeenth centuries. It has its own set of words, which are
used in all of these plays, and served as the basis for many other ballads. A
great deal of information is given in Chappell, vol. 1, p. 162; Diana Poulton,
"The Black-Letter Broadside and its Music," p. 429; and Simpson, p. 225.

"The Friar In The Well"
Everie Woman in Her Humour, Act II, scene iv.
Presented by the Children of the King's Revels in 1607.
    Quoted, beginning "The fryer was in the sol, sol." The tune is given in
Playford's *The English Dancing Master* (London: Thomas Harper for John
Playford, 1651; with numerous subsequent reprints) under the title of "The
Maid peept out at the window, or the Frier in the well," no. 42, p. 36 in the first
(1651) edition. Further information and lists of sources are given in Chappell,
vol. 1, p. 274; and Simpson, p. 240.

"The Friar of Orders Gray"
Beaumont, *The Knight of the Burning Pestle*, Act V, scene iii.
Presented by the Children of the Chapel in 1607.
    A variant of the twentieth stanza of this ballad is quoted, beginning
"Dead? Why fare-well he," which see above for further information.

"The Fryer Was In The Sol, Sol"
Everie Woman in Her Humour, Act II, scene iv.
Presented by the Children of the King's Revels in 1607.
    A quotation from "The Friar in the Well," which see above.

"The Gentleman Ushers Voluntarie"
Day, *Humor Out of Breath*, Act IV.
Presented by the Children of the King's Revels in 1608.

"Give Him Flowers I'now Palmer"
Beaumont, *The Knight of the Burning Pestle*, Act II, scene viii.
Presented by the Children of the Chapel in 1607.

"Give Us Once A Drinke"
Marston, *Jack Drum's Entertainment*, Act V.
Presented by the Children of Paul's in 1607.
    No. 17 in Thomas Ravenscroft's *Deuteromelia* (London: Thomas Adams,
1609), headed as a "Freemans Song of Four Voices."

"Give Your Scholler Degrees & Your Lawyer His Fees"
Marston, *Histrio-Mastix*, Act II.
Presented by the Children of Paul's (?) in 1599 (?).

"Go From My Window"
Beaumont, *The Knight of the Burning Pestle*, Act III, scene iv.
Presented by the Children of the Chapel in 1607.

  The tune for this ballad is included in Anthony Holborne, *The Cittharn Schoole* (1597); John Playford, *The English Dancing Master* under the title of "The New Exchange," no. 8, p. 11 of the first (1651) edition; and British Library MS RM.24.d.3, *The Forster Virginal Book*, fol. 163^v (marked p. 324), arrangement attributed to "Bird" (i.e. William Byrd). The tune is also given, along with further information and lists of sources, in Chappell, vol. 1, p. 141; and Simpson, p. 257.

"Grand Sot Mamon"
Marston, *Jack Drum's Entertainment*, Act II.
Presented by the Children of Paul's in 1600.

"Guy of Warwick"
Beaumont, *The Knight of the Burning Pestle*, Act II, scene viii.
Presented by the Children of the Chapel in 1607.

  A parody quotation of the beginning of this ballad, opening with "Was never man for ladies sake," is used in the play. The complete text of the original is given in Percy, vol. 3, p. 170; and Ritson, vol. 2, p. 296. The tune and sources are given in Chappell, vol. 1, p. 171; and Simpson, p. 283.

"He Set Her On A Milk-White Steed"
Beaumont, *The Knight of the Burning Pestle*, Act II, scene viii.
Presented by the Children of the Chapel in 1607.

  A quotation from the ballad of "The Knight and the Shepherd's Daughter," which see below.

"He Tooke Her By The Lilly-White Hand"
Chapman, *May Day*, Act IV, scene i.
Presented by the Children of the Chapel in 1601–02.

"Here's None But Only I"
Everie Woman in Her Humour, Act I, scene i and Act IV, scene i.
Presented by the Children of the King's Revels in 1607.

  The complete song, which is quoted but indicated to be sung in full in the play, is preserved in British Library MS Add. 2971, fol. 15; and Christ Church Oxford MS Mus 439, p. 39.

"Hey Ho, Farewell Nan"
Beaumont, *The Knight of the Burning Pestle*, Act I, scene i.
Presented by the Children of the Chapel in 1607.

"His Head As White As Milk"
Chapman, Jonson, and Marston, *Eastward Ho*, Act III, scene ii.
Presented by the Children of the Chapel in 1605.

A parody of the song sung by the mad Ophelia in Shakespeare's *Hamlet*,
Act IV, scene v, whose second stanza begins with "His beard was as white as
snow," and which opens with "And will 'a not come again?" William Chap-
pell fits Ophelia's song to the tune of "The Merry, Merry Milkmaids," Chap-
pell, vol. 1, p. 237. "The Merry, Merry Milkmaids" can be found in John
Playford, *The English Dancing Master*, p. 29 of the first (1651) edition; and
Simpson provides information about the tune and its other sources, p. 490.
John Long fits Ophelia's song to the tune of "Who List to Lead a Soldier's
Life," *Shakespeare's Use of Music*, Vol. 3, p. 127. That Tune is given, along
with a list of sources and further information, in Simpson, p. 773.

"His Mans Red Hose Were The Colour of Nose"
Sharpham, *The Fleer*, Act II, scene i.
Presented by the Children of the Chapel in 1606.

"Ho, Ho, Nobody At Home"
Beaumont, *The Knight of the Burning Pestle*, Act IV, scene iv.
Presented by the Children of the Chapel in 1607.

Variant of "Hey Ho Nobody at Home," found in Thomas Ravenscroft's
Pammleia (1609), no. 85; King's College Cambridge MS KC1, no. 12; and
Library of Congress MS M1490.M535A5, p. 46, "The XLi Roundell for four
voices."

"Holyday, O Blessed Morne"
Marston, *Histriomastix*, Act I.
Presented by the Children of Paul's (?) in 1599 (?).

"I Am Three Merry Men, & Three Merry Men"
Beaumont, *The Knight of the Burning Pestle*, Act II, scene viii.
Presented by the Children of the Chapel in 1607.

Quotation from "Three Merry Men Be We," which see below.

"I Come Not Hither For Thee To Teach"
Beaumont, *The Knight of the Burning Pestle*, Act III, scene v.
Presented by the Children of the Chapel in 1607.

"I Waile In Woe, I Plunge In Pain"
Chapman, Jonson, and Marston, *Eastward Ho*, Act V, scene v.
Presented by the Children of the Chapel in 1605.

The song of this name furnishes the tune and inspiration for the ballad "In Cheapside Famous for Gold and Plate," as the authors tell us through the mouth of the singing character. "I Waile in Woe, I Plunge in Pain" is the opening line of "A Sorrowful Sonet, Made by M. George Mannington," in Clement Robinson et al., *A Handefull of Pleasant Delites* (London: Richard Jhones, 1584), whose tune is indicated in the collection as being "Labandala Shot." The tune, information, and a list of sources are given in Simpson, p. 419.

"I Would Not Be A Serving-Man"
Beaumont, *The Knight of the Burning Pestle*, Act IV, scene v.
Presented by the Children of the Chapel in 1607.

"If I Freely May Discover"
Jonson, *The Poetaster*, Act II, scene ii.
Presented by the Children of the Chapel in 1601.

British Library MS Add. 24665, Giles Earle His Booke, fol. 59^v. A later setting of this lyric by Henry Lawes is given in British Library MS 53723, Henry Lawes's Autograph Manuscript, no. 11, fol. 7; and New York Public Library MS Drexel 4257, John Gamble's Commonplace Book, no. 25.

"If Pleasure Be The Only Thing"
The Contention Between Liberality and Prodigality, Act V, scene iii.
Presented by the Children of the Chapel in 1600–01 (a revival of the same play first acted by the Children of Paul's in 1567–68).

"If Such Danger Be In Playing"
Beaumont, *The Knight of the Burning Pestle*, Act IV, scene iii.
Presented by the Children of the chapel in 1607.

"In A Faire Woman What Thing Is Best"
Blurt, Master-Constable, Act II, scene ii.
Presented by the Children of Paul's in 1601–02.

"In Cheapside Famous for Gold and Plate"
Chapman, Jonson, and Marston, *Eastward Ho*, Act V, scene v.
Presented by the Children of the Chapel in 1605.

Ballad based on the extant example, "I Waile in Woe, I Plunge in Paine," which see above.

"In Crete When Daedalus"
Beaumont, *The Knight of the Burning Pestle*, Act I, scene iv.
Presented by the Children of the Chapel in 1607.

The tune, information, and a list of sources for the music to this ballad are given in Simpson, p. 364. Further information about the ballad is provided in Poulton, "The Black-Letter Broadside Ballad and its Music," p. 432.

"Io To Hymen"
Marston, *Sophonisba*, Act I, scene ii.
Presented by the Children of the Chapel in 1605–06.

"It Was A Ladies Daughter"
Beaumont, *The Knight of the Burning Pestle*, Act V, scene iii.
Presented by the Children of the Chapel in 1607.

This is the opening of the ballad "A Ladies Daughter of Paris," which see above.

"Jolly Shepherd"
The Maydes Metamorphosis, Act II.
Presented by the Children of Paul's between 1597 and 1600.

This song is found in slightly varied form in Thomas Ravenscroft's *Pammelia* (1609), no. 3; King's College Cambridge MS KC 1, no. 22; and Library of Congress MS M1490.M535A5, "The Secund Roundells to Thrie Voices," p. 2.

"The Knight and the Shepherd's Daughter"
Beaumont, *The Knight of the Burning Pestle,* Act II, scene viii.
Presented by the Children of the Chapel in 1607.

This ballad is quoted in the play, beginning with the line "He set her on a milk-white steed." The complete text is given in Child, vol. 2, p. 475; and Percy, vol. 3, p. 76. The tune is given in John Playford, *The Dancing Master*, beginning with the fifth (1675) edition, under the title of "The Shepherd's Daughter," p. 83. The tune, further information, and a list of sources are given in Simpson, p. 658.

"Lachrimae"
Beaumont, *The Knight of the Burning Pestle*, between Acts II and III.
Presented by the Children of the Chapel in 1607.

This is one of the most widespread and well-loved tunes of the era, sometimes, as in the play, used as an instrumental piece, and sometimes with its text of "Flow My Teares" from John Dowland's *Second Booke of Songs or Ayres* (1600), no. 2. The lachrimae tune is found in instrumental versions in John Dowland's *Lachrimae or Seaven Teares* (London: John Windet, [c. 1604]); Thomas Morley, *The First Booke of Consort Lessons* (1599 and

1611), "lachrimae pavin," number 7; British Library MS RM.24.d.3, The Forster Virginal Book, "Lachrimy," arranged by "Bird" (i.e. William Byrd), fol. 167 (marked as p. 331); and Christ Church Oxford MS Mus 439, texted but indicated as "Pavan Lachrimae," pp. 6–7.

"Let The Usurer Cram Him"
Middleton, *A Trick to Catch the Old-One*, Act IV, scene v.
Presented by the Children of Paul's c. 1604.

From a song entitled "The Scrivener's Servant's Song of Holborne," beginning "My Master is so Wise," in Thomas Ravenscroft's *Melismata* (London: William Stansby for Thomas Adams, 1611), no. 12. The musical setting apparently gives the opening lines of the song that were omitted from the dramatic imprint.

"Little Musgrave and Lady Barnard"
Beaumont, *The Knight of the Burning Pestle,* Act V, scene iii.
Presented by the Children of the Chapel in 1607.

Quoted, beginning with the fourteenth stanza "And some they whistled/ And some they sang," which see above.

"Love For Such A Cherry Lip"
Blurt, Master-Constable, Act V, scene iii.
Presented by the Children of Paul's in 1601–02.

This song is given as "Of Enamoring: The Mistris of Her Servant" in Ravenscroft's *A Briefe Discourse* (1614), there attributed to "Edw. Piers" (i.e. Edward Pearce).

"Love Is Blinde, And A Wanton"
Jonson, *The Poetaster*, Act IV, scene iii.
Presented by the Children of the Chapel in 1601.

"Love Is Like A Lambe, And Love Is Like A Lyon"
Blurt, Master Constable, Act II, scene iii.
Presented by the Children of Paul's in 1601–02.

"Lovers Rejoice, Your Paines Shall Be Rewarded"
Beaumont and Fletcher, *Cupid's Revenge*, Act I, scene i.
Presented by the Children of the Chapel in 1607–08.

British Library MS Add. 31432, William Lawes's autograph manuscript, fol. 36.

"Mary Ambree"
1. Armin, *The Two Maids of More-Clacke* (no act divisions given).
    Presented by the Children of the King's Revels in 1607–08.

2.   Sharpham, *Cupid's Whirligig*, Act IV.
        Presented by the Children of the King's Revels in 1607.
        This ballad is quoted, beginning "Mortall downe, thistle soft" in Armin's play; and "They marched out manly by three and by three" in Sharpham's. The complete text of the ballad is given in British Library MS Add. 27879, Bishop Percy's Folio Manuscript, fol. 93; and in Percy, vol. 2, p. 231. The ballad is indicated to be sung to the tune of "The Blind Beggar," also known as "The Blind Beggar's Daughter of Bethnal Green." Two different versions of the tune are given in Chappell, vol. 1, pp. 159–60.

"Me Thought This Other Night"
Dekker and Webster, *Northward Ho*, Act IV.
Presented by the Children of Paul's in 1605.
        A parody of "My Thought This Other Night," no. 5 in Robert Jones's *Second Booke of Songs and Ayres* (London: P. S. for Matthew Selman by the assent of Thomas Morley, 1601).

"Mine Mettre Sing No Oder Song"
Marston, *The Dutch Courtesan*, Act II, scene i.
Presented by the Children of the Chapel between 1603 and 1605.
        A dialect versions of "My Mistress Sings No Other Song," which see below.

"Midnights Bell Goes Ting, Ting, Ting, Ting, Ting"
Anon., *Blurt, Master-Constable*, Act IV, scene ii.
Presented by the Children of Paul's in 1601–02.

"Mistress Since You So Much Desire"
Chapman, Jonson, and Marston, *Eastward Ho*, Act III, scene ii.
Presented by the Children of the Chapel in 1605.
        This song is Thomas Campion's no. 16 in Philip Rosseter's *A Booke of Ayres* (1601). The refrain, which begins with "But a little higher," is given in the play.

"Mistress Mine"
Everie Woman in Her Humour, Act II, scene i.
Presented by the Children of the King's Revels in 1607.
        This song is no. 8 in Thomas Morley's *The First Booke of Ayres* (1600). Its refrain, beginning "Coll her and clip her," is given in the play.

"Mortall Downe, Thistle Soft"
Armin, *The Maids of More-Clacke* (no act divisions given).
Presented by the Children of the King's Revels in 1607–08.
        This is a quotation from the ballad of "Mary Ambree," which see above.

"Musicke, Tobacco, Sack and Sleepe"
Marston, *What You Will*, Act II, scene i.
Presented by the Children of Paul's c. 1601.

"My Love Can Sing No Other Song"
Everie Woman in Her Humour, Act V, scene i.
Presented by the Children of the King's Revels in 1607.
   Misquotation from "My Mistress Sings No Other Song," which see below.

"My Master Is So Wise"
Middleton, *A Trick to Catch the Old-One*, Act IV, scene v.
Presented by the Children of Paul's c. 1604.

   This is the opening of a song entitled "The Scriveners Servants Song of Holborne," no. 12 in Thomas Ravenscroft's *Melismata* (1611). The song is given in the play beginning with its third line, "Let the usurer cram him." The entire song is undoubtedly meant to be sung in the play, but the first quarto and subsequent editions give only the incomplete version.

"My Mistress Sings No Other Song"
1.   Marston, *The Dutch Courtesan*, Act II, scene i.
     Presented by the Children of the Chapel between 1603 and 1605.
2.   *Everie Woman in Her Humour*, Acts II, scene ii and V, scene i.
     Presented by the Children of the King's Revels in 1607.
   This is no. 19 in Robert Jones's *The First Booke of Songes or Ayres* (1600). It is quoted, beginning with the line "For I did but kisse her," in *Everie Woman in Her Humour*, Act II, scene ii; misquoted, beginning "My love can sing no other song," in Act V, scene i of the same play; and given in a dialect version in Marston, *The Dutch Courtesan*, Act ii, scene i.

"My Mistresse Eye Doth Oyle My Joynts"
Marston, *Antonio's Revenge*, Act III, scene iv.
Presented by the Children of Paul's in 1599–1600.

"Nose, Nose, Jolly Red Nose"
Beaumont, *The Knight of the Burning Pestle*, Act I, scene i.
Presented by the Children of the Chapel in 1607.
   A quotation from "Of All the Birds," which see below.

"Now Dally Sport and Play"
Marston, *Jack Drum's Entertainment*, Act III.
Presented by the Children of Paul's in 1600.

"Now Each One Dry His Weeping Eyes"
Jonson, *Cynthia's Revels*, Act V, scene v.
Presented by the Children of the Chapel in 1600.

"Now God Be With Old Simeon"
Beaumont, *The Knight of the Burning Pestle,* Act II, scene viii.
Presented by the Children of the Chapel in 1607.

This song is quoted, beginning with "Troll the bowl to me," in the play. It is given as no. 7 in Thomas Ravenscroft's *Pammelia* (1609); no. 29 in King's College Cambridge MS KC 1; and as "The VI Roundel," p. 6, in Library of Congress MS M1490.M535A5.

"Now If I List Will I Love No More"
Middleton, *The Family of Love,* Act I, scene ii.
Presented by the Children of Paul's in 1602–03; and by the Children of the King's Revels in 1607.

"Now O Now I must Depart"
Chapman, Jonson, and Marston, *Eastward Ho,* Act III, scene ii.
Presented by the Children of the Chapel in 1605.

This is a parody of "Now O Now I Needs Must Part," which see below.

"Now O Now I Needs Must Part"
1. Chapman, Jonson, and Marston, *Eastward Ho*, Act III, scene ii.
    Presented by the Children of the Chapel in 1605.
2. *Everie Woman in Her Humour*, Act I, scene i.
    Presented by the Children of the King's Revels in 1607.

This song is no. 6 in John Dowland's *The First Booke of Songes or Ayres* (1597, 1600, 1603, 1606, and 1613), and which appears in a number of other contemporary sources. It is parodied in *Eastward Ho*, beginning as "Now o now I must depart;" and quoted in *Everie Woman in Her Humour*, beginning with the line "Sad despair doth drive me hence." Other sources that give this song include Christ Church Oxford MS Mus 439, p. 45; and King's College Cambridge MS Rowe 2, *The Turpyn Book of Lute Songs*, fol. 2^v. The tune itself, better known as "The Frog Galliard," appears in many sources, which are listed in Chappell, vol. 1, p. 127; and Simpson, p. 242.

"The Nut-Brown Ale"
Marston, *Histriomastix*, Act I.
Presented by the Children of Paul's (?) in 1599 (?).

"O For A Bowle Of Fat Canary"
Middleton, *A Mad World, My Masters*, Act V, conclusion (1640 edition only).
Presented by the Children of Paul's between 1604 and 1606.

This song, for which no musical source has yet been discovered, may or may not have belonged to the original production. It is first associated with the play in the 1640 quarto as the "Catch for the Fifth Act, Sung by Sir Bounteous Progresse to his Guests," right before the indication of "finis," sig. K4.

This quarto was printed following a Caroline revival of the play. However, the first dramatic use of the song is in a variant form in John Lyly's *Campaspe*, Act I, scene ii, first presented by the Children of Paul's between 1580 and 1584. Again, it is a later (1632) edition of the play in which the song first appears, Lyly's *Six Court Comedies* (London: Edward Blount, 1632), sig. G11ᵛ. The song may have been originally dramatic, may have belonged to the repertoire of the Children of Paul's, may have been borrowed from Lyly by Middleton, or may have been added to the later revival of *A Mad World, My Masters* by a later producer as an attractive old theater song.

"O Hone, Hone, O No Nera"
Chapman, Jonson, and Marston, *Eastward Ho*, Act V, scene i.
Presented by the Children of the Chapel in 1605.

The refrain "O Hone, O Hone" is common to a great many contemporary broadside ballads; and it is also the given name of a contemporary tune. The tune is included in Thomas Robinson, *New Citharen Lessons* (London: William Barley, 1609), no. 33. Further information and an inclusive list of sources are included along with the tune in Simpson, p. 232.

"O Love How Strangely Sweet"
Marston, *The Dutch Courtesan*, Act V, scene i.
Presented by the Children of the Chapel between 1603 and 1605.

"O Master Touchstone"
Chapman, Jonson, and Marston, *Eastward Ho*, Act V, scene v.
Presented by the Children of the Chapel in 1605.

Dramatic circumstances make it amply clear that this ballad is a parody, but the playwrights give no hint as to what served as the model, nor does it particularly resemble any ballad that has yet come to light. The closest is "Cuckhold's Haven," given in Chappell, *The Roxburghe Ballads*, vol. 1, p. 47, whose tune is "The Spanish Gipsie." "The Spanish Gypsy" tune fits this ballad quite well. It is given as "The Spanish Jeepsie" in John Playford's *The English Dancing Master*, no. 23, p. 21 of the first (1651) edition. Further information on the tune and its source may be found in Simpson, p. 675; and perhaps a ballad that clearly served as the model for "O Master Touchstone" will yet come to light.

"O Noble Hercules"
Chapman, *May Day*, Act IV, scene i.
Presented by the Children of the Chapel in 1601–02.

"O Princely Face And Fayre"
The Wisdom of Dr. Dodypoll, Act III.
Presented by the Children of Paul's between 1597 and 1600.

"O That Joy So Soone Should Wast"
Jonson, *Cynthia's Revels*, Act IV, scene iii.
Presented by the Children of the Chapel in 1600.

   Two very different settings of this lyric remain extant. The first, Christ Church Oxford MS Mus 439, pp. 38–39, is probably that of the original production. The second is found in Henry Lawes's autograph manuscript, British Library MS Add. 53723, fol. 5, written much too late to belong to the original production.

"O The Mimon Round"
Beaumont, *The Knight of the Burning Pestle*, Act V, scene iii.
Presented by the Children of the Chapel in 1607.

"Oares, Oares, Oares, Oares"
Dekker and Webster, *Westward Ho*, Act V, conclusion.
Presented by the Children of Paul's in 1604.

"Of All the Birds That Ever I See"
Beaumont, *The Knight of the Burning Pestle*, Act I, scene i.
Presented by the Children of the Chapel in 1607.

   This song is given as no. 7 in Ravenscroft's *Deuteromelia* (1609); and as the fourth "Song for thrie voices," p. 130, in Library of Congress MS M1490.M535A5. In the play, it is quoted from the line "Nose, nose, jolly red nose."

"The Olde Downe A Downe"
Everie Woman in Her Humour, Act II, scene iv.
Presented by the Children of the King's Revels in 1607.

"Olde Tithon Must Forsake His Deare"
Wily Beguiled (no act division given).
Presented by the Children of Paul's (?) between 1596 and 1606.

"Peace, Peace, Peace, Make No Noyse"
Day, *Humor Out of Breath*, Act IV.
Presented by the Children of the King's Revels in 1608.

"Pitty, Pitty, Pitty"
The Contention Between Liberality and Prodigality, Act II, scene iv.
Presented by the Children of the Chapel in 1600–01; a revival of the same play first presented by the Children of Paul's in 1567–68.

"Queene And Huntresse, Chaste And Fayre"
Jonson, *Cynthia's Revels*, Act V, scene i.
Presented by the Children of the Chapel in 1600.

"Religion, Arts, & Merchandise"
Marston, *Histrio-Mastix*, Act VI, conclusion.
Presented by the Children of Paul's (?) in 1599 (?).

"Reverence, Due Reverence"
The Contention Between Liberality and Prodigality, Act I, scene vi.
Presented by the Children of the Chapel in 1600–01; a revival of the same
play first presented by the Children of Paul's in 1567–68.

"Rise Lady Mistresse Rise"
Field, *Amends for Ladies*, Act IV.
Presented by the Children of the Chapel in 1610–11.

"Round About, Round About, In A Fine Ring A"
The Maydes Metamorphosis, Act II.
Presented by the Children of Paul's between 1597 and 1600.
      The opening text of "The Elves Dance," which see above.

"Sad Despair Doth Drive Me Hence"
Everie Woman in Her Humour, Act I, scene i.
Presented by the Children of the King's Revels in 1607.
      A quotation from "Now O Now I Needs Must Part," which see above.

"Satyres Sing, Let Sorrow Reep Hir Cell"
Wily Beguiled (no act divisions given).
Presented by the Children of Paul's (?) between 1596 and 1606.

"Say Love If Ever Thou Didst Find"
Chapman, *The Widow's Tears*, Act V, scene i.
Presented by the Children of the Chapel c. 1605.
      No. 7 in Dowland's *The Third and Last Book of Songs or Aires* (London: P.
S. for Thomas Adams, 1603), whose refrain is parodied in the play, beginning
with "She, she, she, and none but she."

"The Scriverner's Servant's Song of Holborne"
Middleton, *A Trick to Catch the Old-One*, Act IV, scene v.
Presented by the Children of Paul's c. 1604.
      This song begins in the extant play imprints with the line "Let the Usurer
Cram Him," which see above.

"She Cares Not For Her Daddy"
Beaumont, *The Knight of the Burning Pestle*, Act II, scene viii.
Presented by the Children of the Chapel in 1607.

"She, She, She, And None But She"
Chapman, *The Widow's Tears*, Act V, scene i.
Presented by the Children of the Chapel c. 1605.

   This is a parody of the refrain from "Say Love If Ever Thou Didst Find,"
which see above.

"Since Hope of Helpe My Froward Starres Denie"
The Maydes Metamorphosis, Act IV.
Presented by the Children of Paul's between 1597 and 1600.

"Since Painfull Sorrowes Date Hath End"
The Maydes Metamorphosis, Act V, conclusion.
Presented by the Children of Paul's between 1597 and 1600.

"Sing Boyre a le Fountaine"
The Wisdom of Dr. Dodypoll, Act II.
Presented by the Children of Paul's between 1597 and 1600.

   The song is sung several times in the same scene, also introduced simply
as "Boire a le Fountaine" and "Sing Boire a etc." No musical source has yet
come to light.

"Sing His Prayses That Doth Keepe"
Fletcher, *The Faithful Shepherdess*, Act I, scene ii.
Presented by the Children of the Chapel in 1608.

   Edinburgh University Library MS Dc.1.69, no. 15, fol. 24^v–25; and number 126, fol. 106^v–107. The setting is here attributed to William Lawes and
probably belongs to a Carolingian revival of the play.

"Sing Wee And Chaunt It"
Beaumont, *The Knight of the Burning Pestle*, Act V, scene iii.
Presented by the Children of the Chapel in 1607.

   This is a quotation from the opening of no. 4 in Thomas Morley's *The First
Book of Balletts* (London: Thomas Este, 1595 and 1600), which title is the
same.

"Sing We Now Merrily"
Beaumont, *The Knight of the Burning Pestle*, Act IV, scene iv.
Presented by the Children of the Chapel in 1607.

   No. 100 in Ravenscroft's *Pammelia* (1609); no. 7 in King's College
Cambridge MS KC1; and the "LXIX Roundell," p. 80, in Library of Congress
MS M1490.M535A5, quoted in the play beginning with the line "Who can
sing a merrier noate?".

"Sir Guy of Warwick"
Beaumont, *The Knight of the Burning Pestle*, Act II, scene viii.
Presented by the Children of the Chapel in 1607.

Parody quotation of the beginning of this ballad, opening "Was never man for ladies sake," given in the play and noted below. For complete reference, see "Guy of Warwick" above.

"Sister Awake, Close Not etc."
Everie Woman in Her Humour, Act II, scene ii.
Presented by the Children of the King's Revels in 1607.

No. 21 from Thomas Bateson's *First Set of English Madrigals* (London: Thomas Este, 1604), whose full title is "Sister, Awake, Close Not Your Eyes."

"Skip It, & Trip It, Nimbly, Nimbly"
Marston, *Jack Drum's Entertainment*, Act I.
Presented by the Children of Paul's in 1600.

"Sleep Wayward Thoughts"
1.   Chapman, Jonson, and Marston, *Eastward Ho*, Act I, scene i.
     Presented by the Children of the Chapel in 1605.
2.   *Everie Woman in Her Humour*, Act I, scene i.
     Presented by the Children of the King's Revels in 1607.

No. 13 in John Dowland's *The First Booke of Songes and Ayres*, sung from the beginning in *Everie Woman in Her Humour*; and quoted from the line "Thus whilst [sic] she sleepes" in *Eastward Ho*. The song was evidently quite popular at the time and is preserved in a number of contemporary manuscripts: British Library MS Add. 15117, fol. 7; British Library MS Add. 15118, fol. 28^v; British Library MS Add. 29481, fol. 2; and Christ Church Oxford MS Mus 439, p. 46.

"Slow, Slow Fresh Fount"
Jonson, *Cynthia's Revels*, Act I, scene ii.
Presented by the Children of the Chapel in 1600.

No. 8 in Henry Youll, *Canzonets to Three Voices* (1608).

"Some Up & Some Down, Thers Players In the Towne"
Marston, *Histriomastix*, Act II.
Presented by the Children of Paul's (?) in 1599 (?).

"Song O' The Golden Showre"
Chapman, Jonson, and Marston, *Eastward Ho*, Act V, scene i.
Presented by the Children of the chapel in 1605.

The text begins "Fond fables tell of old," and is introduced as the "Song O the Golden Showre."

"Sorrow Stay"
Beaumont, *The Knight of the Burning Pestle*, Act II, scene viii.
Presented by the Children of the Chapel in 1607.

No. 3 in John Dowland's *The Second Book of Songs or Ayres*: misquoted in the play beginning with "Down, downe, downe:/They fall downe," which see above.

"Sound Lute, Bandora, Gitterne"
Middleton, *Your Five Gallants*, Act V.
Presented by the Children of the Chapel between 1604 and 1607.

"The Spanish Ladies Love"
Sharpham, *Cupid's Whirligig*, Act IV.
Presented by the Children of the King's Revels in 1607.

This ballad is given in Thomas Deloney's *A Garland of Good Will* (1631). Its opening, which begins "Will you heare of a Spanish lady," is quoted in the play. More recent sources of the complete text are Percy, vol. 2, p. 247; and Ritson, vol. 2, p. 205. The tune, further information, and a list of sources are given in Chappell, vol. 1, p. 186; and Simpson, p. 677.

"The Spanish Pavin"
Blurt, Master-Constable, Act IV, scene ii.
Presented by the Children of Paul's in 1601–02.

This very popular dance tune is included in Anthony Holborne's *The Cittharn School* (1597); and British Library MS Add. 15118, fol. 30ᵛ. Further information on this piece and its numerous other sources may be obtained from Chappell, vol. 1, p. 240; Poulton, "Notes on The Spanish Pavin," pp. 5–16; Simpson, p. 678; and Ward, "Apropros *The British Broadside Ballad and its Music*," p. 75.

"Still To Be Neat, Still To Be Drest"
Jonson, *Epicoene,* Act I, scene iii.
Presented by the Children of the Chapel in 1609–10.

John Playford's *The Treasury of Musik*, p. 51; New York Public Library MS Drexel 4041, no. 64; and New York Public Library MS 4257, John Gamble's Commonplace Book, no. 179. The piece is attributed in all instances to William Lawes.

"Sweet Mony The Minion That Sayles With All Winds"
The Contention Between Liberality and Prodigality, Acts II, scene iv and III, scene ii.
Presented by the Children of the Chapel in 1600–01; a revival of the same play first presented by the Children of Paul's in 1567–68.

"Tell Me (Deerest) What Is Love?"
Beaumont, *The Knight of the Burning Pestle*, Act III, scene i.
Presented by the Children of the Chapel in 1607.

This song is also used, in variant form, in Beaumont and Fletcher's later adult play, *The Captain*, and was possibly written for that play, which was presented before the first quarto of *The Knight of the Burning Pestle* was published. A setting by Robert Johnson, whose text is closer to the version in *The Captain* in all instances, is found in New York Public Library MS Drexel 4041, no. 124; New York Public Library MS Drexel 4175, no. 42 (the table of contents also lists it as no. 44); and New York Public Library MS Drexel 4257, John Gamble's Commonplace Book, no. 35.

"Terliterlo, Terliterlo, Terliterlee, Terlo"
The Maydes Metamorphosis, Act II.
Presented by the Children of Paul's between 1597 and 1600.

The first given line of "Jolly Shepherd" as presented in the play imprint, which see above.

"Th'art Over Long At Thy Pott, Tom, Tom"
Beaumont and Fletcher, *The Coxcomb*, Act I, scene vi.
Presented by the Children of the Chapel in 1609.

Also quoted in the same scene as "Thou art over long at the pot, Tom, Tom." No musical source has yet been discovered.

"Then In A Free And Lofty Straine"
Jonson, *The Poetaster*, Act IV, scene v.
Presented by the Children of the Chapel in 1601.

"Then Set Your Foot To My Foot & Up Tails All"
Beaumont and Fletcher, *The Coxcomb*, Act I, scene vi.
Presented by the Children of the Chapel in 1609.

From the ballad, "Up Tails All," whose tune is included in John Playford's *The English Dancing Master*, no. 97, p. 82 in the first (1651) edition. For further information, a modern transcription of the tune, and a more complete list of sources, see Simpson, p. 727.

"They Marched Out Manly By 3 & by 3"
Sharpham, *Cupid's Whirligig*, Act IV.
Presented by the Children of the King's Revels in 1607.

Quotation from the ballad of "Mary Ambree," which see above.

"They That For Worldly Wealth Do Wed"
Field, *A Woman is a Weather-Cock*, Act II.
Presented by the Children of the Chapel in 1609–10.

"Thou Art Over Long At The Pot, Tom, Tom"
Beaumont and Fletcher, *The Coxcomb*, Act I, scene vi.
Presented by the Children of the Chapel in 1609.
    Also quoted in the same scene as "Th'art over long at thy pott, Tom, Tom."
No musical source has yet come to light.

"Thou Art Welcome From Stygian Lake So Soon"
Beaumont, *The Knight of the Burning Pestle*, Act V, scene viii.
Presented by the Children of the Chapel in 1607.

"Thou More Than Most Sweet Glove"
Jonson, *Cynthia's Revels*, Act IV, scene iii.
Presented by the Children of the Chapel in 1600.

"Thou That Dost Guide The World By Thy Direction'
The Contention Between Liberality and Prodigality, Act II, scene iv.
Presented by the Children of the Chapel in 1600–01; a revival of the same
play first presented by the Children of Paul's in 1567–68.

"Three Merry Men, And Three Merry Men"
1.   Barry, *Ram Alley* (no act division given).
    Presented by the Children of the King's Revels in 1607–08.
2.   Beaumont, *The Knight of the Burning Pestle*, Act II, scene viii.
    Presented by the Children of the Chapel in 1607.
    Sung from the beginning in *Ram Alley*, and from the line "I am three merry
men" in *The Knight of the Burning Pestle*. The tune for the song, information,
and sources are given in Chappell, vol. 1, p. 216. The song is not, as Vincent
Duckles claims in "The Music for the Lyrics in Early Seventeenth-Century
English Drama," in *Music in English Renaissance Drama*, ed. John H. Long
(Lexington: University of Kentucky Press, 1968), p. 124, part of the famous
catch "Hold Thy Peace" given in Ravenscroft's *Deuteromelia* (1609).

"Troll The Bowl To Me"
Beaumont, *The Knight of the Burning Pestle*, Act II, scene viii.
Presented by the Children of the Chapel in 1607.
    This is a quotation from "Now God Bee With Old Simeon," which see
above. This song is not to be confused with the one that begins "Troll the
black bowl to me" found in Ravenscroft's *Pammelia* (1609) and concordant
sources.

"Thus Whilst She Sleeps"
Chapman, Jonson, and Marston, *Eastward Ho*, Act I, scene i.
Presented by the Children of the Chapel in 1605.

This is a misquotation from "Sleep Wayward Thoughts," which see above.

"Up Tails All"
Beaumont and Fletcher, *The Coxcomb*, Act I, scene vi.
Presented by the Children of the Chapel in 1609.
 Quoted in the play from the line "Then set your foot to my foot," which see above.

"The Urchin's Dance"
The Maydes Metamorphosis, Act II.
Presented by the Children of Paul's between 1597 and 1600.
 No. 8, in Ravenscroft's *A Briefe Discourse*, whose opening line is "By the moone we sport and play," which see above.

"Wake, Our Mirth Begins To Die"
Jonson, *The Poetaster*, Act IV, scene v.
Presented by the Children of the Chapel in 1601.

"Walsingham"
Beaumont, *The Knight of the Burning Pestle*, Act II, scene viii.
Presented by the Children of the Chapel in 1607.
 The opening lines of the ballad are quoted in the play, beginning with "As You Came From Walsingham." The tune was a great favorite at the time, and arrangements are included in William Barley, *A New Book of Tabliture* (1596); Anthony Holborne, *The Cittharn Schoole* (1597); British Library MS Add. 15118, fol. 32^v; and British Library MS RM.24.d.3, The Forster Virginal Book, fol. 39^v. Numerous other musical sources are given in Chappell, vol. 1, p. 121; Poulton, "The Black-Letter Broadside Ballad and its Music," p. 434; Simpson, p. 741; and Ward, "Apropros *The British Broadside Ballad and its Music*," pp. 79–82. The complete text is given in Deloney's *A Garland of Good Will* (1632); British Library MS Add. 27879, Bishop Percy's Folio Manuscript, fol. 251; and Percy, vol. 2, p. 101.

"Was Never Man For Ladies Sake"
Beaumont, *The Knight of the Burning Pestle*, Act II, scene viii.
Presented by the Children of the Chapel in 1607.
 A parody quotation from the beginning of the ballad "Sir Guy of Warwick," also known as "Guy of Warwick," which see above.

"What Meate Eates the Spaniard?"
Blurt, Master-Constable, Act I, scene ii.
Presented by the Children of Paul's in 1601–02.

British Library MSS Add. 17786-91, no. 28; and Royal College of Music MS 2049, fol. 7^v (treble partbook), fol. 9 (medius partbook), fol. 8 (tenor partbook); and fol. 6^v–7 (bass partbook).

"What Thing Is Love?"
The Wisdom of Dr. Dodypoll, Act I.
Presented by the Children of Paul's between 1597 and 1600.

This song, whose lyric first appears in George Peele's earlier pastoral poem *The Hunting of Cupid,* is set with a slightly varied text as number 13 in John Bartlet's *A Booke of Ayres* (London: John Windet for John Browne, 1606).

"What Voice Is That That Calleth At Our Door?"
Beaumont, *The Knight of the Burning Pestle,* Act V, scene iii.
Presented by the Children of the Chapel in 1607.

"When Earth And Seas From Me Are Reft"
Beaumont, *The Knight of the Burning Pestle,* Act I, scene iv.
Presented by the Children of the Chapel in 1607.

"When It Was Grown To Darke Midnight"
Beaumont, *The Knight of the Burning Pestle,* Act II, scene viii.
Presented by the Children of the Chapel in 1607.

This is a quotation from the ballad "Fair Margaret and Sweet William," which see above.

"When Sampson Was A Tall Young Man"
Chapman, Jonson, and Marston, *Eastward Ho,* Act II, scene iii.
Presented by the Children of the Chapel in 1605.

This is a parody of a ballad entitled "A Most Excellent and Famous Ditty of Sampson Judge of Israel," whose complete text is given in Chappell, *The Roxburghe Ballads,* vol. 2, p. 460. The ballad is indicated to be sung to the tune of "The Spanish Pavin," which see above.

"Whilst Thou Dost Spent With Friend & Foe"
The Contention Between Liberality and Prodigality, Act II, scene iv.
Presented by the Children of the Chapel in 1600–01; a revival of the same play first presented by the Children of Paul's in 1567–68.

"Who Can Sing A Merrier Noate?"
Beaumont, *The Knight of the Burning Pestle,* Act IV, scene iv.
Presented by the Children of the Chapel in 1607.

A quotation from "Sing We Now Merrily," which see above.

"Why An If She Be, What Care I?"
Beaumont, *The Knight of the Burning Pestle,* Act II, scene viii.
Presented by the Children of the Chapel in 1607.
   A quotation from "Farewell Dear Love," which see above.

"Will You Heare Of A Spanish Lady?"
Sharpham, *Cupid's Whirligig*, Act IV>
Presented by the Children of the King's Revels in 1607.
   The opening of the ballad, "The Spanish Ladies Love," which see above.

"Willowe, Willowe, Willowe/Our Captaine Goes Down"
Chapman, *Sir Gyles Goose-Cappe*, Act V, conclusion.
Presented by the Children of the Chapel between 1601 and 1603.

"Wilt Thou Unkind Thus Reave Me?"
Beaumont, *The Knight of the Burning Pestle*, Act I, scene iv.
Presented by the Children of the Chapel in 1607.
   No. 15 in Dowland's *The First Booke of Songs or Ayres* (1597, 1600, 1603, 1606, 1608, and 1613), quoted in the play beginning with "But yet, or ere you part (O cruel)."

"With Hey Trixie Terlery Whiskin"
Beaumont, *The Knight of the Burning Pestle*, Act V, scene iii.
Presented by the Children of the Chapel in 1607.

"With That Came Out His Paramoure"
Beaumont, *The Knight of the Burning Pestle,* Act V, scene viii.
Presented by the Children of the Chapel in 1607.

"Ye Sacred Fyres, & Powers Above"
The Maydes Metamorphosis, Act I.
Presented by the Children of Paul's between 1597 and 1600.

"You Are No Love For Me Margaret"
Beaumont, *The Knight of the Burning Pestle*, Act III, scene v.
Presented by the Children of the Chapel in 1607.
   A quotation from the ballad "Fair Margaret and Sweet William," which see above.

"You Woeful Wights Give Eare A While"
Jonson, *His Case Is Altered*, Act I, scene i.
Presented by the Children of the Chapel between 1600 and 1608; originally written for an unknown adult company.

NOTES*

CHAPTER 1. THE CHILDREN'S DRAMATIC COMPANIES

1. The most inclusive studies of children's drama are E. K. Chambers, *The Elizabethan Stage*, vol. 2 (Oxford: Clarendon Press, 1923), pp. 1–76; Reavley Gair, *The Children of Paul's: The Story of a Theatre Company, 1553–1608* (Cambridge: Cambridge University Press, 1982); Harold Newcomb Hillebrand, *The Child Actors* (Urbana: University of Illinois Studies in Language and Literature, vol. 11, nos. 1 and 2, 1926); Michael Shapiro, *Children of the Revels: The Boy Companies of Shakespeare's Time and Their Plays* (New York: Columbia University Press, 1977); and Charles William Wallace, "The Children of the Chapel at Blackfriars, 1957–1603," *University Studies* 8 (April–July 1908), republished as *The Children of the Chapel at Blackfriars* (New York: AMS Press, 1970), each of which presents different evidence and arrives at slightly different conclusions.
2. Richard Flecknoe, *A Short Treatise of the English Stage* (London: Printed by R. Wood for the author, 1664), sigs. G4ᵛ–G5. Although Flecknoe confuses several facts, his very succinct summary of changing attitudes toward children's drama and its increasingly bold content is quite accurate.
3. The Children of the Chapel and the Children of Paul's were the principal and longest-lived English children's troupes, but a number of others presented plays, particularly during this early period; see Chambers, *Elizabethan Stage*, vol. 2, pp. 61–76; and Shapiro, *Children of the Revels*, pp. 2–7 and 266–68.
4. These Children's participation in courtly entertainment under the first four Tudor monarchs is described in Trevor Lennam, *Sebastian Westcott, The Children of Paul's, and "The Marriage of Wit and Science"* (Toronto: University of Toronto Press, 1975), p. 34; Shapiro, *Children of the Revels*, pp. 5–6; and John E. Stevens, *Music and Poetry in the Early Tudor Court* (London: Methuen and Co., 1961), pp. 247–51.

---

*Abbreviations are the standard ones used in the *MLA International Bibliography* and the *New Grove Dictionary of Music and Musicians*.

5. London, Public Records Office, Patent Rolls, 4 Elizabeth, pt. 6, C66/981, m. 14ᵛ. This document is transcribed in full in Chambers, *Elizabethan Stage*, vol. 2, pp. 33–34.
6. Claude Desainliens [Claudius Hollybande], *The French Schoolemaister* (London: Imprinted by William Howe for Abraham Veale, 1573), pp. 132–34.
7. The Children of Paul's may have presented plays as early as 1378, but documentary evidence is weak; see Chambers, *Elizabethan Stage*, vol. 2, p. 11; and Gair, *Children of Paul's*, p. 2.
8. Trevor Lennam feels that Westcott's association with the choristers of St. Paul's Cathedral may have begun in 1537, and that he may have belonged to a St. Paul's literary and musical circle at the time that also included his predecessor John Redford and playwright John Heywood; see *Sebastian Westcott*, pp. 33–34.
9. A number of possible locations for the theater have been proposed, but none has been completely convincing to historians of the English theater; see Gair, *Children of Paul's*, pp. 52–56; Lennam, *Sebastian Westcott*, pp. 43–48; and Michael Shapiro, "The Children of Paul's and their Playhouse," *Theatre Notebook* 36 (1982): 3–13.
10. See Lennam, *Sebastian Westcott*, p. 43; and Shapiro, *Children of the Revels*, p. 13.
11. Desainliens, *The French Schoolemaister*, p. 74.
12. Chambers, *Elizabethan Stage*, vol. 2, pp. 16–17; and Shapiro, *Children of the Revels*, p. 16.
13. London, British Library MS Sloane 2035b, fol. 1ᵛ–2. This document is transcribed in Chambers, *Elizabethan Stage*, vol. 2, pp. 17–18 n. 2.
14. See Shapiro, *Children of the Revels*, pp. 18–19.
15. Edward F. Rimbault, ed., *The Old Cheque-Book of the Chapel Royal* (Westminster: J. B. Nichols and Sons, 1872), pp. 5–6.
16. Thomas Ravenscroft, *A Briefe Discourse of the True (but neglected) use of Charact'ring the Degrees by their Perfection. Imperfection & Diminution in Measurable Musicke, against the Common Practise and Custome of these Times* (London: Printed by Edw[ard] Allde for Tho[mas] Adams, 1614), sigs. A2ᵛ–A3.
17. Gair, *Children of Paul's*, p. 185.
18. John Marston, *Jacke Drums Entertainment: or The Comedy of Pasquil & Katherine* (London: Richard Olive, 1601), Act II [scene ii].
19. London, Guildhall Library MS 9537/9, *The Visitation Report of Bishop Richard Bancroft for the London Diocese 1598*, fol. 56ᵛ. Gair quotes from the same account at greater length, *Children of Paul's*, pp. 40–41.
20. *The Maydes Metamorphosis* (London: Printed by Thomas Creede for Richard Olive, 1600), Act III.
21. Thomas Dekker [T. Deckar], *The Guls Horne-Booke* (London: Imprinted for R. S., 1609), p. 20.
22. John Marston, *What You Will* (London: Imprinted by G. Eld for Thomas Thorppe, 1607), Act II, scene i.
23. For information about the grammar school students as actors, see *A Brief Account of Cathedral and Collegiate Schools* (London: J. B. Nicholls, 1827), Appendix; Chambers, *Elizabethan State*, vol. 2, pp. 9–11; Gair, *Children of Paul's, p. 2; Hillebrand*, Child Actors, pp. 105–7; and Shapiro, *Children of the Revels*, p. 267. For further information about the shared education of the choristers and grammar students, see Michael F. McDonnel, *A History of St. Paul's School* (London: Chapman and Hall, 1909), pp. 20, 29–31.
24. Mulcaster had been headmaster of the Merchant Taylor's School when its students had acted plays between 1573 and 1583; see Shapiro, *Children of the Revels*, pp. 19–20.
25. London, Public Record Office, Star Chamber Proceedings, Elizabeth I, STAC 5C.46/39. This document is often cited or quoted in accounts of the Elizabethan theater. The most complete transcription is found in James Greenstreet, "Blackfriars Theatre in the Time of Shakespeare," *The Athenaeum* no. 3224 (August 10, 1889): 203–4.
26. Chambers, *Elizabethan Stage*, vol. 2, pp. 44–45.
27. [Thomas Middleton,] *Father Hubburds Tales: or the Ant, and the Nightingale* (London: Printed by T. C. for William Cotton, 1604), sig. C5.

28. London, Public Record Office, Patent Rolls 1 James I, pt. 8, C66/1614, memb. 13. This document is transcribed in Chambers, *Elizabethan Stage*, vol. 2, p. 49. To avoid confusion, I refer to this company as the Children of the Chapel throughout this work.

29. London, Public Record Office, Patent Rolls 4 James I, pt. 18, C66/1708, memb. 6ᵛ–7ᵛ. A complete transcription of this account is found in Malone Society, *Collections*, vol. 1, pts. 4–5 (Oxford: Oxford University Press, 1911), pp. 362–63. Excerpts are printed in Chambers, *Elizabethan Stage*, vol. 2, p. 52; and Shapiro, *Children of the Revels*, p. 27.

30. From a letter written by Sir Thomas Lake, Clerk of the Signet, to Robert, Lord Salidbury, on 11 March 1607 [1608], as transcribed in Malone Society, *Collections*, vol. 2, pt. 2 (Oxford: Oxford University Press, 1923), pp. 148–49.

31. London, Public Record Office, Patent Rolls 7 James I, pt. 13, C66/1801, no. 15. A transcription of this document is included in Malone Society, *Collections*, vol. 1, pt. 3 (Oxford: Oxford University Press, 1910), pp. 271–72.

32. Hillebrand, *Child Actors*, p. 220. Knowledge about the company comes principally from the legal suit of George Andrews v. Martin Slater, 1609, described in Hillebrand, pp. 221–31.

33. Ibid., p. 271. Similar views are expressed in Anthony Caputi, *John Marston, Satirist* (Ithaca: Cornell University Press, 1961), p. 101; and Brian Gibbons, *Jacobean City Comedy*, 2nd ed., (London: Methuen and Co., 1980), p. 14.

34. See Maurice Charney, "The Children's Plays in Performance," *Research Opportunities in Renaissance Drama* 18 (1975): 19–23; and R. A. Foakes, "Tragedy at the Children's Theatres after 1600: A Challenge to the Adult Stage," *The Elizabethan Theatre* 2 (1970): 40.

35. See Charney, "Children's Plays in Performance," p. 23; and Shapiro, *Children of the Revels*, p. 104.

36. Ibid., pp. 113–38.

37. Henry Peacham [the younger], *The Compleat Gentleman* (London: Francis Constable, 1622), p. 103. See also Henry Peacham, Minister, *The Garden of Eloquence, conteyning the figures of grammar and rhetorick* (London: Imprinted by H. Jackson, 1577), sigs. A2ᵛ–A3.

38. See Linda Phyllis Austern, "Musical Parody in the Jacobean City Comedy," *Music and Letters* 66 (1985): 363–65.

39. William Shakespeare, *Comedies, Histories, & Tragedies* (London: Printed by Issac Jaggard and Ed[ward] Blount, 1623), *As You Like It*, Act III, scene ii.

40. George Chapman, *The Gentleman Usher* (London: Printed by V. S. for Thomas Thorppe, 1606), Act II, scene i.

41. Gordon Lell, "'Ganymede' on the Elizabethan Stage: Homosexual Implications of the Use of Boy-Actors," *Aegis* 1 (Spring 1973): 5–15.

42. Stephan Gosson, *Playes confuted in Five Actions* (London: Imprinted for Thomas Gosson [1582]), sig. E5. For further information about boy actresses on the English Renaissance stage, see Stephen Orgel, "Nobody's Perfect: Or Why Did the English Stage Take Boys for Women?" *The South Atlantic Quarterly* 88 (1989): 7–30.

43. As quoted in Chambers, *Elizabethan Stage*, vol. 2, pp. 46–47. Translation: *From there we went to a children's play. Now this is the situation with these children's plays: The Queen has a number of young boys, who are required to devote themselves earnestly to the art of singing and learn to play all sorts if instruments, while they continue their [other] studies. These boys have excellent instructors in all subjects, especially outstanding music teachers.*
     . . . For an entire hour before [a play] one hears an exquisite instrumental concert of organs, lutes, pandoras, mandoras, bowed strings, and woodwinds, such as this time when a boy sang so beautifully in a warbling voice to a bass viol, that unless the nuns in Milan may have outdone him, we did not hear the like on our travels.

44. Ben Jonson, *Cynthias Revels or the Fountayne of Selfe-Love* (London: Printed by William Stansby, 1616), Induction.

45. Anthony, Munday, *A Second and Third Blast of Retrait from Plaies and Theaters* (London: Allowed by Authoritie, 1586), pp. 110–11.

46. John Northbrooke, *A Treatise Wherein Dicing, Dauncing Vaine Playes or Enterluds are Reproved* (London: Printed by H. Bynneman for G. Byshop [1577]), p. 76.
47. Shakespeare, *Comedies, Histories, & Tragedies*, Hamlet, Act II, scene ii.

CHAPTER 2. THE PERFORMERS AND THEIR THEATERS

1. Thomas Gainesford, *The Rich Cabinet* (London: Printed by J. B. for Roger Jackson, 1616), p. 118.
2. See Gerald Eades Bentley, *The Profession of Player in Shakespeare's Time* (Princeton: Princeton University Press, 1984), pp. 5–11 and 234–35; and Andrew Gurr, *The Shakespearean Stage, 1574–1642*, (Cambridge: Cambridge University Press, 1970), pp. 60–69.
3. Gosson, *Playes Confuted*, sig. G6^v. See also Thomas Dekker, *The Seven Deadlie Sinns of London* (London: Printed by E. A. for Nathaniell Butter, 1606), pp. 39, 41.
4. Stephen Gosson, *The Schoole of Abuse* (London: Printed for Thomas Woodocke, 1579), sig. B3. See also Henry Cornelius Agrippa [von Nettesheim], *Of the Vanitie and Uncertaintie of Artes and Sciences*, Englished by Ja. San[ford] (London: Henry Wykes, 1569), fol. 29; Gosson, *Playes Confuted*, sig. E6; William Prynne, *Histrio-Mastix: The Players Scourge. or, Actors Tragedie* (London: Printed by E. A. and W. I. for Michael Sparke, 1633), pp. 237–90; and Phillip Stubbes, *The Anatomy of Abuses* (London: Richard Jones, 1583), sigs. L7 and L8–L8^v.
5. [Ben Jonson,] *The Workes of Benjamin Jonson* (London: Printed for William Stansby, 1616), p. 270.
6. Ibid., p. 354.
7. Ibid., p. 600.
8. See Henry Cart De Lafontaine, *The King's Musick* (London: Novello and Co., 1909), p. 44; and Alan Smith, "The Gentlemen and Children of the Chapel Royal of Elizabeth I: An Annotated Register," *RMARC* 5 (1965): 15.
9. Opposing views are expressed in John H. Long, *Shapespeare's Use of Music*, 3 vols. (Gainesville: University of Florida Press, 1955–71), vol. 1 (1955): *A Study of the Music and its Performance in the Original Production of Seven Comedies*, pp. 32–33, which considers all of the Children of the Chapel to have been choristers; and Wallace, *The Children of the Chapel at Blackfriars*, pp. 73–76, which states that the actors and choristers were two entirely separate groups.
10. From "A Collection of Papers relating to Shares and Sharers in the Globe and Blackfriars Theatres, 1635, from contemporary transcripts formerly preserved amongst the official manuscripts of the Lord Chamberlain of the Household at St. James Palace," as transcribed in James Orchard Halliwell-Phillipps, *Outlines of the Life of Shakespeare*, 6th ed. (London: Longmans, Green, and Co., 1886), vol. 1, p. 291.
11. Shakespeare, *Comedies, Histories, & Tragedies*, sig. A8.
12. William Barkstead, *Hiren: Or The Faire Greeke* (London: Printed for Roger Barnes, 1611); and idem., *Mirrha, the Mother of Adonis: Or, Lustes Prodegies* (London: Printed by E. A. for John Bache, 1607). Barkstead's name replaces that of John Marston in some copies of the third quarto of *The Insatiate Countesse* (London: Printed by J. N. for Hugh Perrie, 1631).
13. James A. Riddell, "Some Actors in Ben Jonson's Plays," *Shakespeare Studies* 5 (1969): 285, 287.
14. John Field, Minister, *A Godly Exhortation, By Occasion of the Late Judgement of God, Shewed at Parris-Garden* (London: Printed by Robert Waldgrave for Henry Carre, 1583). John Field was dead and buried before his son was a year old.
15. Foakes, "Tragedy at the Children's Theatres After 1600," p. 58.
16. See Chambers, *Elizabethan Stage*, vol. 2, p. 317; Gurr, *Shakespearean Stage*, p. 68; and William Perry, *The Plays of Nathan Field* (Austin: University of Texas Press, 1950), p. 23.
17. Ben Jonson, *Bartholomew Fayre* (London: J. B[eale] for R. Allott, 1631), Act V, scene iii.
18. Flecknoe, *Treatise of the English Stage*, sig. G6^v.

19. Nathan Field, *Amends for Ladies* (London: Printed by J. Okes for Math[ew] Walbanke, 1639); and idem., *A Woman is a Weather-Cocke* (London: John Budge, 1612).

20. P[hilip] M[assinger] and N[athan] F[ield], *The Fatall Dowry* (London: J. Norton for Francis Constable, 1632).

21. See C. J. Bulliet, *Venus Castina: Famous Female Impersonators Celestial and Human* (New York: Bonanza Books, 1956), pp. 154–57; and Vern L.Bullough, *The Subordinate Sex: A History of Attitudes Toward Women* (Urbana: University of Illinois Press, 1973), p. 228.

22. John Davies of Hereford, *The Scourge of Folly* (London: Printed by E. A. for Richard Redmer, 1610).

23. *The Workes of Benjamin Jonson*, pp. 808–9.

24. From the Visitation Report of Bishop Richard Bancroft, London, Guildhall Library, MS 9537/9, fol. 5ᵛ. This list is also given in Gair, *Children of Paul's*, p. 184; and Hillebrand, *Child Actors*, p. 111.

25. From the Visitation Book of Bishop Thomas Ravis, as printed in Hillebrand, *Child Actors*, p. 112. This list is also given in Gair, *Children of Paul's*, p. 184.

26. John Marston , *The History of Antonio and Mellida, the first part* (London: Printed for Mathewe Lownes and Thomas Fisher, 1602), Act IV, scene i.

27. Ravenscroft, *Briefe Discourse*, sig. A2; and idem., "A Treatise of Musick," London, British Library MS Add. 19758, fol. 19.

28. See Linda Phyllis Austern, "Thomas Ravenscroft: Musical Chronicler of an Elizabethan Theater Company," *JAMS* 38 (1985): 238–63; and Andrew J. Sabol, "Ravenscroft's *Melismata* and the Children of Paul's," *Renaissance News 12 (1959): 3–9.*

29. The only contemporary reference to Ravenscroft's age or date of birth is a commendatory poem in his *Briefe Discourse* that puts him at 22 when the book was published in 1614 (Ravenscroft, *Briefe Discourse*, sig. qqq2). The accuracy of this statement and its implied birthdate of 1592 are highly questionable; see *The New Grove Dictionary of Music and Musicians*, 1980 ed., s.v. "Ravenscroft, Thomas," by David Mateer.

30. Nan Cook Carpenter, *Music in the Medieval and Renaissance Universities* (Norman: University of Oklahoma Press, 1958), p. 206. The traditional 1607 date of the degree has been questioned by Mateer, who proposes an earlier date, *New Grove Dictionary*, s.v. "Ravenscroft," p. 623.

31. Thomas Ravenscroft, *Pammelia, Musics Miscellanie* (London: Printed by William Barley, 1609); and idem., *Deuteromelia: Or the Second Part of Musicks Melodie, or Melodius Musicke* (London: Thomas Adams, 1609).

32. Ravenscroft, *Briefe Discourse*, sigs. qq3–qqq.

33. Thomas Ravenscroft, *The Whole Booke of Psalmes: With the Hymnes Evangelicall, and Songs Spiritual* (London: n. p., 1621).

34. Carpenter, *Music in the Medieval and Renaissance Universities, p. 206.*

35. Henry and William Lawes, *Choice Psalmes put into Musick, for Three Voyces* (London: Printed by James Young, for Humphrey Moseley and Richard Wodenothe, 1648), bass partbook, sig. IIII4ᵛ.

36. David Bevington, *Action is Eloquence: Shakespeare's Language of Gesture* (Cambridge, MA: Harvard University Press, 1984), pp. 67–69; and Jackson I. Cope, *Dramaturgy of the Daemonic* (Baltimore: Johns Hopkins University Press, 1984), pp. 62–63. See also W. Robertson Davies, *Shakespeare's Boy Actors* (London: J. M. Dent and Sons, ltd., 1939), pp. 34–35; and Gurr, *Shakespearean Stage*, p. 70.

37. Abraham Fraunce, *The Arcadian Rhetoric* (London: Printed by Thomas Orwin, [1588], sigs. H6ᵛ–K4ᵛ.

38. Agrippa, *Vanitie and Uncertaintie*, fol. 18ᵛ.

39. Fraunce, *Arcadian Rhetoric*, sig. I7ᵛ.

40. Agrippa, *Vanitie and Uncertaintie*, fol. 32.

41. Ibid., fol. 19.

42. Richard Mulcaster, *Positions Wherein Those Primitive Circumstances Be Examined, Which are Necessarie for the Training Up of Children* (London: Printed by Thomas Vautrollier for Thomas Chare, 1581), p. 38.

43. Francis Meres, *Palladis Tamia* (London: Printed by P. Short for Cuthbert Burbie, 1598), p. 288.

44. William Byrd, *Psalmes, Sonets & Songs of Sadnes and Pietie* (London: Printed by Thomas East, the asigne of W. Byrd, 1588), sig. A3ᵛ.

45. Peacham, *Compleat Gentleman*, p. 98.

46. Mulcaster, *Positions*, p. 36.

47. Richard Rastall, "Female Roles in All-Male Casts," *Medieval English Theatre* 7 (1985): 28–34.

48. See Sydney Beck, ed., *The First Book of Consort Lessons, Collected by Thomas Morley 1599 and 1611* (New York: Published for the New York Public Library by C. F. Peters Corp., 1959), p. 3; Mary Chan, *Music in the Theatre of Ben Jonson* (Oxford: Clarendon Press, 1980), p. 32; R. W. Ingram, "Operatic Tendencies in Stuart Drama," *MQ* 44 (1958): 491; and Walter L. Woodfill, *Musicians in English Society from Elizabeth to Charles I* (Princeton: Princeton University Press, 1953), pp. 30, 40–41.

49. Bevington, *Action is Eloquence*, pp. 14–15.

50. R. B. Graves, "Daylight in the Elizabethan Private Theatres," *Shakespeare Quarterly* 33 (1982): 81–82.

51. R. A. Foakes, "Playhouses and Players," in *The Cambridge Companion to English Renaissance Drama*, ed. A. R. Braunmiller and Michael Hattaway (Cambridge: Cambridge University Press, 1990), pp. 27–28.

52. Richard Hosley, "The Playhouses and the Stage," in *A New Companion to Shakespeare Studies*, ed. Kenneth Muir and S. Schoenbaum (Cambridge: Cambridge University Press, 1971), p. 32.

53. Ibid.; and D. F. Rowan, "The English Playhouse: 1595–1630," *RenD*, n. s., vol. 4 (1971): 46.

54. Hosely, "The Playhouses and the Stage," p. 33; and Glynne Wickham, *Early English Stages, 1300 to 1600* (London: Routledge and Kegan Paul, 1972), vol. 2: *1576 to 1660*, pt. 2, pp. 206–7.

55. See Bevington, *Action is Eloquence*, pp. 11–12.

56. See Gair, *Children of Paul's*, p. 55; and Shapiro, "The Children of Paul's and their Playhouse," p. 4.

57. Gair, *Children of Paul's*, p. 67. See also Joseph Quincy Adams, *Shakespearean Playhouses* (Boston: Houghton Mifflin and Co., 1917), p. 112; and Chambers, *Elizabethan Stage*, vol. 2, p. 554. Gair has estimated the area of the main stage as 170 square feet and the area for spectators as 300 square feet, but these figures are based on questionable assumptions about the identity and location of the theater building; see *Children of Paul's*, p. 66; and Shapiro, "The Children of Paul's and their Playhouse," pp. 3–5.

58. Thomas Middleton, *A Mad World My Masters* (London: Printed by H. B. for Walter Burre, 1608), Act II, scene i.

59. John Marston, *Antonios Revenge, The Second Part of the History of Antonio & Mellida* (London: Printed for Thomas Fisher, 1603), Act V, scene v.

60. See, for example, *The Maydes Metamorphosis*, Act IV.

61. Chambers, *Elizabethan Stage*, vol. 2, p. 512; R. A. Foakes, *Illustrations of the English Stage, 1580–1642* (London: Scolar Press, 1985), pp. 39–40; and Richard Hosley, "A Reconstruction of the Second Blackfriars," *The Elizabethan Theatre* 1 (1969): 74.

62. For detailed reconstructions of the theater and the stage, see Adams, *Shakespearean Playhouses*, pp. 183–98; Hosley, "Reconstruction of the Second Blackfriars," pp. 74–88; Irwin Smith, *Shakespeare's Blackfriars Playhouse* (New York: New York University Press, 1964), pp. 290–425; and Wickham, *Early English Stages*, vol. 2, pt. 2, pp. 129–36.

63. Hosley, "Playhouses and the Stage," pp. 28–29; and idem., "Reconstruction of the Second Blackfriars," pp. 76–77, 79.

64. John Marston, *The Wonder of Women or the Tragedy of Sophonisba* (London: Printed by John Windet, 1606), Act III, scene ii and Act IV, scene i.
65. See, for example, Chapman, *The Gentleman Usher*, Act II, scene i.
66. Chambers, *Elizabethan Stage*, vol. 2, p. 516.
67. Wickham, *Early English Stages*, vol. 2, pt. 2, p. 123.
68. Adams, *Shakespearean Playhouses*, pp. 312–313.

CHAPTER 3. THE PLAYS AND PLAYWRIGHTS

1. Ejner J. Jensen, "The Boy Actors: Plays and Playing," *RORD* 28 (1975): 11.
2. See, for example, Chan, *Music in the Theatre of Ben Jonson*, pp. 14–15; Edward J. Dent, *The Foundations of English Opera* (Cambridge: Cambridge University Press, 1928), p. 6; Long, *Shakespeare's Use of Music*, vol. 1, p. 5; and Frederick W. Sternfeld, *Music in Shakespearean Tragedy* (London: Routledge and Kegan Paul, 1963), p. 15.
3. Shapiro, *Children of the Revels*, pp. 235–36.
4. William Webbe, *A Discourse of English Poetrie* (London: Imprinted by John Charlewood for Robert Walley, 1586), sig. D2.
5. Marston, *What You Will*, Induction.
6. Prynne, *Histrio-Mastix*, p. 289.
7. Ibid., pp. 273–74.
8. Webbe, *Discourse of English Poetrie*, sig. D2; and Gosson, *Playes Confuted*, sig. F6.
9. Thomas Rymer, *The Tragedies of the Last Age* (London: Printed for Richard Jonson, 1678), p. 6. The very incongruities between the pleasures of musical spectacle and the harsh realities of tragedy led some of the more daring young playwrights to introduce music at unexpected points in their tragedies shortly after 1600; see Linda Phyllis Austern, "Sweet Meats with Sour Sauce: The Genesis of Musical Irony in the English Private Theater after 1600," *The Journal of Musicology* 4 (1985–1986): 486–88.
10. See, in particular, Martin Butler, *Theatre and Crisis 1632–1642* (Cambridge: Cambridge University Press, 1984), pp. 293–306; Charney, "The Children's Plays in Performance," p. 19; Ann Jennalie Cook, *The Privileged Playgoers of Shakespeare's London 1576–1642* (Princeton: Princeton University Press, 1981), pp. 8–9, 212–14; Andrew Gurr, *Playgoing in Shakespeare's London* (Cambridge: Cambridge University Press, 1987), pp. 72–79; and Michael Hattaway, *Elizabethan Popular Theatre: Plays in Performance* (London: Routledge and Kegan Paul, 1982), pp. 44–50. The classic articulation of the older view that there were two completely distinct audiences and types of drama is Alfred Harbage, *Shakespeare and the Rival Traditions* (New York: Macmillan and Co., 1952), which is cited frequently in works on public and private theater in Shakespeare's day.
11. Cook, *Privileged Playgoers*, p. 3. See also Hattaway, *Elizabethan Popular Theater*, p. 47.
12. See Charney, "Children's Plays in Performance," p. 19; and Cook, *Privileged Playgoers*, p. 9.
13. See Butler, *Theatre and Crisis*, pp. 302–6; and Gurr, *Playgoing in Shakespeare's London*, pp. 72–79.
14. William Shakespeare, *The Tragicall Historie of Hamlet, Prince of Denmark* ([London:] N. L. a J. Trundell, 1603), sig. E2ᵛ.
15. Michael Shapiro, "Audience vs. Dramatist in Jonson's *Epicoene* and Other Plays of the Children's Troupes," *ELR* 3 (1973): 401.
16. Cook, *Privileged Playgoers*, pp. 213–14. See also Shapiro, "Audience vs. Dramatist," p. 401.
17. Joel Hurstfield and Alan G. R. Smith, eds., *Elizabethan People* (London: Edward Arnold, 1972), p. 24.
18. Raphaell Holinshed, William Harrison, and Others, *The First and Second Volumes of Chronicles*. Now newlie augmented and continued . . . to the yeare 1586 (London: at the expenses of J. Harison, G. Bishop, R. Newberie, H. Denam, à T. Woodcocke, 1587), p. 162.

19. See Cook, *Privileged Playgoers*, pp. 8–9; Christopher Hill, *The Century of Revolution* (London: Thomas Nelson, 1961), p. 16; Holinshed et al., *First and Second Volumes of Chronicles*, pp. 162–163; Joel Hurstfield, "The Politics of Corruption in Shakespeare's England," *Shakespeare Survey* 28 (1975): 17; Hurstfield and Smith, eds., *Elizabethan People*, pp. 2, 24; and Louis B. Wright, *Middle-Class Culture in Elizabethan England* (Ithaca: Cornell University Press, 1958), p. 2.

20. From a report by Venetian diplomat Michael Soriano to the Signory, as quoted in Hurstfield and Smith, eds., *Elizabethan People*, p. 33.

21. Harbage, *Shakespeare and the Rival Traditions*, p. 76.

22. For a concise summary of the sorts of plays presented by the children's companies before 1590, see Shapiro, *Children of the Revels*, pp. 136–78.

23. Gosson, *Playes Confuted*, sig. F6.

24. Harbage, *Shakespeare and the Rival Traditions*, p. 71. Harbage considers this preoccupation with sex and lust to "reveal inadvertently the latitudes of conduct among leisured people for whom a cultivated sensuality has become and escape from boredom," p. 190.

25. See Brian Gibbons, *Jacobean City Comedy*, p. 50; Neil Rhodes, *Elizabethan Grotesque* (London: Routledge and Kegan Paul, 1980), pp. 3–5; and Don E. Wayne, *"Drama and Society in the Age of Jonson*: An Alternative View," *RenD*, n.s., 13 (1982): 105–6.

26. For further information on this trend in music and literature, see Lillian M. Ruff and D. Arnold Wilson, "The Madrigal, the Lute Song, and Elizabethan Politics," *Past and Present* 44 (August 1969): 51.

27. As Irwin Smith has pointed out, the greater the risks the children took, the greater the notoriety and the greater the flocks of people who came to see them, *Shakespeare's Blackfriars Playhouse*, p. 191.

28. Thomas Heywood, *An Apology for Actors* (London: Printed by Nicholas Okes, 1612), sig. G3ᵛ.

29. Dekker, *The Guls Horne-Booke*, p. 31. The statement about drawing troops from the stage refers to the private theater custom of gallants sitting at the edge of the stage, the best seats in the house.

30. See, in particular, Foakes, "Tragedy at the Children's Theatres after 1600," pp. 38–39; and Shapiro, *Children of the Revels*, pp. 179–180, 227–28.

31. There is a certain amount of overlap between plays, but the principal characteristics of each of these categories are quite distinctive. Shapiro names each play that is included in each category or that includes any of the defining traits, *Children of the Revels*, pp. 180–227.

32. Ben Jonson, *The Fountaine of Selfe-Love, or Cynthia's Revels* (London Imprinted for Walter Burre, 1601), Induction.

33. Shapiro, *Children of the Revels*, p. 189.

34. The term "city comedy" (or "citizen comedy") is the modern critical designation for a group of early seventeenth-century English plays with strong stylistic similarities and common sources. However, scholars disagree as to precisely which plays belong fully to the genre and which absorbed only certain characteristic elements. See Arthur Brown, "Citizen Comedy and Domestic Drama," *Stratford-upon-Avon Studies I: Jacobean Theatre* (1960): 63–64; Gibbons, *Jacobean City Comedy*, pp. 1–2; and Alexander Leggatt *Citizen Comedy in the Age of Shakespeare* (Toronto: University of Toronto Press, 1973), pp. 3–5. The most inclusive list of city comedies to date, which shows their relationship to all other contemporary plays, is Gibbons, *Jacobean City Comedy*, first edition only (1968), Appendix B.

35. See Gibbons, *Jacobean City Comedy*, p. 62.

36. L. C. Knights, *Drama and Society in the Age of Jonson* (London: Chatto and Windus, 1937), p. 141.

37. Hurstfield and Smith, eds., *Elizabethan People*, pp. 32–35.

38. Ben Jonson, *The Alchemist* (London: Printed by Thomas Snodham for Walter Burre, 1612), Prologue.

39. Harbage, *Shakespeare and the Rival Traditions*, pp. 76–77.

40. The only work to date that deals with any aspect of music in these plays is Austern, "Musical Parody in the Jacobean City Comedy." A great deal more remains to be done.
41. Gosson, *Playes Confuted*, sig. C5.
42. Shapiro, *Children of the Revels*, pp. 104–5.
43. Foakes, "Tragedy at the Children's Theatres," p. 43.
44 See Juliet Dusinberre, *Shakespeare and the Nature of Women* (London: Macmillan Press, 1975), p. 270; and Foakes, "Tragedy at the Children's Theatres," p. 59.
45. Ibid.
46. See Gerald Eades Bentley, *The Profession of Dramatist in Shakespeare's Time* (Princeton: Princeton University Press, 1971), pp. 38–61.
47. Harbage, *Shakespeare and the Rival Traditions*, pp. 70–71.
48. David G. O'Neill, "The Influence of Music in the Works of John Marston," *ML* 53 (1972): 125; and Bruce Pattison, "Literature and Music in the Age of Shakespeare," *PRMA* 60 (1933–34): 71.
49. Stone, *Crisis of the Aristocracy*, p. 706.
50. Meres, *Palladis Tamia*, p. 283.
51. The classic pro-and anti-Marston essays are, respectively, T. S. Eliot, "John Marston," in Eliot, *Elizabethan Dramatists* (London: Faber and Faber Ltd., 1962), pp. 152–66; and Samuel Schoenbaum, "The Precarious Balance of John Marston," *PMLA* 67 (1952): 1069–78. In addition, Harbage has said that "any of Marston's plays may be defined as a five-act lapse in taste," *Shakespeare and the Rival Traditions*, p. 244; and Foakes has called him the presiding genius of the Children of Paul's in their final phase, "Tragedy at the Children's Theatres," p. 42. Recent critics have tended to be rather favorably inclined toward him.
52. O'Neill, "The Influence of Music in the Works of John Marston," pp. 125–126.
53. See Ingram, "Operatic Tendencies in Stuart Drama," p. 490; and O'Neill, "The Influence of Music in the Works of John Marston," pp. 408–9.
54. See Richard Dutton, *Ben Jonson: To the First Folio* (Cambridge, London and New York: Cambridge University Press, 1983), pp. 23–26; and W. David Kay, "The Shaping of Ben Jonson's Career: A Reexamination of Facts and Problems," *MP* 67 (1969–70): 224–37.
55. See Chan, *Music in the Theatre of Jonson*, pp. 45–46.
56. See ibid., p. 4; Willa McClung Evans, *Ben Jonson and Elizabethan Music*, (Lancaster, PA: Lancaster Press, 1929; New York: Da Capo Press, 1965), p. 14; and Knights, *Drama and Society in the Age of Jonson*, p. 179. Those of Jonson's books that survived a fire of 1623 are listed in C. H. Herford and Percy Simpson, eds., Ben Jonson, vol. 1 (Oxford: Clarendon Press, 1925), pp. 262–71.
57. Evans, *Ben Jonson and Elizabethan Music*, p. 44.
58. William W. Appleton, *Beaumont and Fletcher* (London: George Allen and Unwin, 1956), pp. 10–11; and Lawrence Bergman Wallis, *Fletcher, Beaumont and Company* (Morningside Heights, NY: King's Crown Press, 1947), p. 3. Beaumont's earliest known play was written for the Children of Paul's but all other children's plays by these two men were written for the Children of the Chapel.
59. Meres, *Palladis Tamia*, p. 283.

CHAPTER 4. PRACTICAL MUSIC AND THE DRAMATIC TEXT

1. See M. C. Bradbrook, "The Triple Bond: Audience, Actors, Authors in the Elizabethan Playhouse," in *The Triple Bond*, ed. Joseph G. Price (University Park: Pennsylvania State University Press, 1975), pp. 53–54.
2. *The Arte of English Poesie* (London: Printed by Richard Field, 1589), pp. 5–6. This work is most often attributed to Richard Puttenham.
3. Francis Bacon, *Sylvania Sylvarum: or a Naturall Historie*, 4th ed. (London: Printed by John Haviland for William Lee, 1635), p. 38. See also Robert Burton, *The Anatomy of Melancholy*, 4th ed. (Oxford: John Lichfield, 1632), p. 297; John Dee, Preface to [Euclid,] *The*

Elements of Geometrie of the most auncient Philosopher Euclid of Megara, translated into the Englishe toung by H. Billingsley (London: John Daye, 1570), sig. B2^v; and Sir Philip Sidney, *The Defence of Poesie* (London: Printed for William Ponsonby, 1595), sig. F3^v.

4. The most recent, most comprehensive books on this enormous topic are Elise Bickford Jorgens, *The Well-Tun'd Word: Musical Interpretations of English Poetry 1597–1651* (Minneapolis: University of Minnesota Press, 1982); Winifred Maynard, *Elizabethan Lyric Poetry and its Music* (Oxford: Clarendon Press, 1986); and Louise Schleiner, *The Living Lyre in English Verse from Elizabeth through the Restoration* (Columbia: University of Missouri Press, 1984). For further bibliographical information, see Louise Schleiner, "Recent Studies in Poetry and Music in the English Renaissance," *English Literary Renaissance* 16 (1986): 253–68.

5. Sidney, *Defence of Poesie*, sigs. E^v–E2.

6. Ravenscroft, *Briefe Discourse*, sig. C3^v.

7. See, for example, Edward Doughtie, "Words for Music: Simplicity and Complexity in the Elizabethan Air," *Rice University Studies* 51 (1965): 2, 11; R. W. Ingram, "Words and Music," in *Stratford-upon-Avon Studies* 2: *Elizabethan Poetry* (London: Edward Arnold, 1960), pp. 133–34; and Patricia Samson, "Words for Music," *SoRA* 1 (1963): 46.

8. Bertrand H. Bronson, "Literature and Music," in *Relations of Literary Study*, ed. James Thorpe (New York: Modern Language Association, 1967), p. 134.

9. Prynne, *Histrio-Maxtix*, p. 261.

10. Ibid., p. 263.

11. See, for example, Chan, *Music in the Theatre of Ben Jonson*, p. 30; Edward J. Dent, *The Foundations of English Opera* (Cambridge: Cambridge University Press, 1928), p. 6; Long, *Shakespeare's Use of Music*, vol. 1, pp. 3–6; Andrew J. Sabol, "Two Songs with Accompaniment for an Elizabethan Choirboy Play," *Studies in the Renaissance* 5 (1958): 153; Sabol, "Two Unpublished Stage Songs for the 'Aery of Children'," *Renaissance News* 13 (1960): 224; and Shapiro, *Children of the Revels*, p. 237.

12. See Frank J. Fabry, "Sidney's Poetry and Italian Song-Form," *ELR* 3 (1973): 234.

13. Richard Mulcaster, *The First Part of the Elementarie* (London: Thomas Vautroullier, 1582), p. 254.

14. Robert L. Weaver, "Sixteenth-Century Instrumentation," *MQ* 47 (1961): 370–71.

15. *The Praise of Musicke* (Oxenford: Joseph Barnes, 1586), p. 12. This work is sometimes attributed to John Case.

16. Michael Drayton, *Poly-Olbion or a Chorographicall Description of Great Britain* (London: F. M. Lownes, J. Browne, J. Helme, a J. Busbie, 1612), p. 63.

17. Claude Desainliens [Claudius Hollyband], *A Dictionarie of French and English* (London: Imprinted by T. O. for Thomas Woodcocke, 1593), sigs. H6^v, Hh7, and Ii6.

18. Marin Mersenne, *Harmonie Universelle (Paris, 1636)*, edition facsimile de l'examplaire conserve à la Bibliotheque des Arts et Metiers et annote par l'Auteur (Paris: Editions du centre national de la recherche scientifique, 1965), tome 3, p. 274. Translation: *As to the quality of sound that it [the cornett] makes, it is like the brilliance of a sunbeam that appears in shadow or in gloom, when one swells amidst voices in cathedral churches, or in chapels.*

19. Anthony Baines, *Woodwind Instruments and their History* (New York: W. W. Norton and Co., 1957), p. 260.

20. Michael Praetorius, *Syntagma Musicum*, band 2: *De Orqanographia* (Wolfenbuttel, 1619), Faksimilie Nachdruk (Basel: Barenreiter Kassel, 1958), s. 36. Translation: But because the the tone [of the bass cornett] is unpleasant and horn-like, I consider it better to use a trombone instead.

21. See, for instance, Long, *Shakespeare's Use of Music*, vol. 1, pp. 32–34, where it is claimed that young boys could not possibly have had strong enough lungs or the precision of lip control to play the cornett.

22. Praetorius, *Syntagma Musicum*, bd. 2, s. 36.

23. Baines, *Woodwind Instruments*, p. 272.

24. See Francis W. Galpin, *Old English Instruments of Music: Their History and Character*, 4th ed., revised (London: Methuen and Co., 1965), p. 137; John S. Manifold, *The Music in English Drama from Shakespeare to Purcell* (London: Rockliff Publishing Corp., 1956), pp. 42–43; and Mary Remnant, *Musical Instruments of the West* (London: B. T. Batsford, 1978), pp. 142–44.

25. The only play presented by the Children of Paul's that requires the trumpet is one of those few acted by both children and adults. It is printed as acted by both: "as it hath bin presented publikely, by the Right Honorable, the Lord Chamberlain his servants; and privately, by the Children of Paules," and therefore the use of the trumpet cannot be taken as definite. It is indeed possible that the trumpet was actually replaced by the customary cornett of the Paul's playhouse; Thomas Dekker [and John Marston], *Satiro-Mastix, or the Untrussing of the Humorous Poet* (London: Edward White, 1602).

26. Thomas Godwin, *Romanae Historiae Anthologie* (Oxford: Joseph Barnes, 1614), p. 92; and *The Praise of Musicke*, p. 87.

27. Rudolf Felber, "Music and Superstition," trans. Theodore Baker, *MG* 17 (1931): 238.

28. Drayton, *Poly-Olbion*, p. 55.

29. Christopher Welch, *Lectures on the Recorder in Relation to Literature* (London: Oxford University Press, 1961), p. 131 n. 2.

30. Praetorius, *Syntagma Musicum*, bd. 2, s. 35. Translation: *Transverse flutes . . . have six holes in front and none in back, producing 15 natural playing tones . . . .*
    The situation is the same for still flutes (which are also called transverse flutes) except that they are tuned and voiced like recorders.

31. For further information, see David Lasocki, "Professional Recorder Playing in England 1500–1700, Part I: 1500–1640," *Early Music* 10 (1982): 27–28; Manifold, *Music in English Drama*, pp. 68–69; and Welch, *Lectures on the Recorder*, pp. 130–31.

32. See Godwin, *Romanae Historiae Anthologia*, p. 66.

33. Lasocki, "Professional Recorder Playing," p. 23.

34. *The Praise of Musicke*, To the Reader. F. W. Sternfeld cites the ancient tradition of the rivalry between the heavenly strings of Apollo and the earthly pipes of Pan as being responsible for the relative disuse of the latter in stage plays, "The Dramatic and Allegorical Function of Music in Shakespeare's Tragedies," *Annales Musicologiques* 3 (1955): 269–73; see also Sternfeld, *Music in Shakespearean Tragedy*, pp. 226–35.

35. Randle Cotgrave, *A Dictionarie of the French and English Tongues* (London: Printed by Adam Islip, 1611), sig. Mmmm.

36. Curtis A. Price, "Restoration Stage Fiddlers and Their Music," *Early Music* 7 (1979): 315.

37. For further information, see Tobias Hume, *The First Part of Ayres (1605) and Captain Humes Poeticall Musicke (1607)*, ed. Sterling Jones (Winterthur: Amadeus Verlag, 1980), pp. 17–18; Jerome LeJeune, "The Lyra-Viol: An Instrument or a Technique?" *The Consort* 31 (1975): 125–31; Sibyl Marcuse, *A Survey of Musical Instruments* (London: David and Charles, 1976), pp. 15–16; Frank Traficante, "Lyra Viol Tunings: 'All Ways have been Tryed to do it'," *AcM* 42 (1970): 183–205; and J. Traficante, "Music for Lyra Viol: Manuscript Sources," *Chelys* 8 (1978–79):4.

38. Hume, *First Part of Ayres*, p. 21.

39. Mary Joiner Chan, "*Cynthia's Revels* and Music for a Choir School: Christ Church Manuscript Mus 439," *Studies in the Renaissance* 18 (1971): 140. See also Bacon, *Sylva Sylvarum*, p. 72; LeJeune, "The Lyra-Viol," pp. 128–30; and Praetorius, *Syntagma Musicum*, bd. 2, s. 47.

40. Robert Jones, *The Second Booke of Songs and Ayres* (London: Printed by P. S. for Mathew Selman by the assent of Thomas Morley, 1601).

41. Chan, "*Cynthia's Revels* and Music for a Choir School," p. 140.

42. Mersenne, *Harmonie Universelle*, tome 3, p. 204. Translation: *Now the sound of the lira is most melancholy and suitable for arousing devotional feelings, and for restoring the soul.*

43. Lennam, *Westcott*, p. 34.

44. Bacon, *Sylva Sylvarum*, p. 72. There is no evidence that any other sort of harp in use during the later Renaissance was known in England; see Robert Hadaway, "The Recreation of an Italian Renaissance Harp," *Early Music* 8 (1980): 59.
45. See ibid., p. 60; Marcuse, *Survey of Musical Instruments*, p. 390; and Remnant, *Musical Instruments of the West*, p. 23.
46. Marcuse, *Survey of Musical Instruments*, pp. 396–98; Remnant, *Musical Instruments of the West*, p. 23; and Joan Rimmer, "The Morphology of the Irish Harp," *GSJ* 17 (February 1964): 39.
47. Joan Rimmer, "Harps in the Baroque Era," *PRMA* 90 (1963–64): 61.
48. Douglas Alton Smith, "On the Origin of the Chitarrone," *JAMS* 32 (1979): 457.
49. See Nigel Fortune, "Continuo Instruments in the Italian Monodies," *GSJ* 6 (1953): 11; Thomas Mace, *Musick's Monument* (London: Printed by T. Ratcliffe and N. Thompson for the Author, 1676), p. 207; Praetorius, *Syntagma Musicum*, bd. 2, s. 52; and Smith, "On the Origin of the Chitarrone," p. 475. This courtly instrument is not to be confused with the hurdy-gurdy of the same name, described under "tiorba" in John Florio, *Queen Anna's New World of Words, or a Dictionarie of the Italian and English Tongues* (London: Printed by Melch, Bradwood for Edw. Blount, 1598), p. 421. See also Smith, "On the Origin of the Chitarrone," pp. 458–59.
50. Robert Spenser, "Chitarrone, Theorbo, and Archlute," *Early Music* 4 (1976): 411–12.
51. Charles Butler, *The Principles of Musik, in Singing and Setting* (London: Printed by John Haviland, 1636), p. 94.
52. Mace, *Musick's Monument*, p. 242.
53. Butler, *Principles of Musik*, p. 94.
54. Bacon, *Sylva Sylvarum*, p. 72.
55. Philip Rosseter, *Lessons for Consort* (London: Printed by Tho[mas] Este alias Snodham, for John Browne, 1609). This work is dedicated to Sir William Gascoyne of Sedbury, addressed by Rosseter in the Dedication as " . . . you, who maintain in your house such as may lively express" the arrangements included in the collection.
56. Bacon, *Sylva Sylvarum.*, pp. 35, 51.
57. Thomas Middleton, *Your Five Gallants* (London: Imprinted for Richard Bonlan, n. d.), Act V.

CHAPTER 5. PRELIMINARY, INTER-ACT AND FINALE MUSIC

1. See Chambers, *Elizabethan Stage*, vol. 2, pp. 556–57; Chan, *Music in the Theatre of Jonson*, p. 15; Curtis A. Price, *Music in the Restoration Theatre* (Ann Arbor: UMI Research Press, 1979), pp. 54–65; Shapiro, *Children of the Revels*, p. 250; Smith, *Shakespeare's Blackfriars Playhouse*, pp. 220–39; and Wallace, *Children of the Chapel*, pp. 9–10.
2. John Marston, *The Malcontent*, with the additions played by the Kings Majesties servants written by Jhon [sic] Webster (London: Printed by V. S. for William Aspley, 1604), Induction. The "[H]ieronimo" referred to may possibly by Thomas Kyd's *Spanish Tragedy* which the Children of the Chapel may have stolen from the adult company around the time of its revival.
3. Marston, *The Malcontent*. The play is unusually musical by the standards of any contemporary company, for it includes five songs, a complete masque with an extended dance sequence, and a number of instrumental pieces. Almost all of these are absolutely vital to the play.
4. John Marston, *The Wonder of Women or the Tragedy of Sophonisba* (London: Printed by John Windet), sig. G3ᵛ.
5. R. W. Ingram, *John Marston* (Boston: Twayne Publishers, 1978), p. 145.
6. See G. H. Cowling, *Music in the Shakespearean Stage* (Cambridge: Cambridge University Press, 1913), p. 66.
7. Wil[liam] Rankins, *A Mirrour of Monsters* (London: Printed by J. C. for T. H., 1587), p. 5.
8. Dekker, *The Guls Horne-Booke*, p. 30.

9. Ibid., p. 31.
10. Dekker [and Marston], *Satiro-Maxtix*, sig. A4^v.
11. Act I, scene i. Translation: A chorus of youths sings and dances. Exit dancing. Meanwhile, enter Lorenzo, papers in his hand.
12. Sternfeld, *Music in Shakespearean Tragedy*, p. 3.
13. See Hattaway, *Elizabethan Popular Theatre*, p. 63.
14. John Dryden, *Works*, ed., Sir Walter Scott, revised and corrected by George Saintsbury, "An Essay of Dramatic Poesy" (1668), vol. 15 (London: Printed for William Paterson and Co., 1892), p. 322.
15. *The Arte of English Poesie*, p. 29.
16. Marston, *Sophonisba*, "To the generall Reader," sig. A2.
17. See Smith, *Shakespeare's Blackfriars Playhouse*, p. 225.
18. John Fletcher, *The Faithful Shepheardesse* (London: Printed for R. Bonlan and H. Walley, n. d.), sig q3^v.
19. Dieter Mehl, *The Elizabethan Dumb Show* (Cambridge: Harvard University Press, 1966), p. xii.
20. See Hattaway, *Elizabethan Popular Theater*, p. 65; and W. J. Lawrence, *The Elizabethan Playhouse and Other Studies* (Philadelphia: J. B. Lipincott Co., 1912), pp. 76–77.
21. George R. Kernodle, *From Art to Theatre: Form and Convention in the Renaissance* (Chicago: University of Chicago Press, 1944), p. 145.
22. See Lawrence, *Elizabethan Playhouse*, pp. 76–77; Sternfeld, *Music in Shakespearean Tragedy*, pp. 2–3; and Enid Welsford, *The Court Masque* (New York: Russell and Russell, 1962), p. 292. However Mehl has shown that a major distinction between the English dumb-show and the Italian intermedio is the dumb-show's almost exclusive association with serious drama, *The Elizabethan Dumb Show*, p. XII.
23. Chan, *Music in the Theatre of Ben Jonson*, p. 11.
24. See William R. Bowden, *The English Dramatic Lyric, 1603–42* (New Haven: Yale University Press, 1951), p. 188; Shapiro, *Children of the Revels*, p. 250; and Sternfeld, *Music in Shakespearean Tragedy*, p. 3.

CHAPTER 6. MUSIC FOR CEREMONY, SPECTACLE AND SOCIAL OCCASION

1. Bevington, *Action is Eloquence*, p. 135.
2. Kernodle, *From Art to Theatre*, p. 151.
3. Thomas Heywood, *The English Traveller* (London: Printed by Robert Raworth, 1633), Prologue.
4. Ian Spink, *English Song from Dowland to Purcell* (London: B. T. Batsford, 1974), pp. 53–54.
5. Sarah P. Sutherland, *Masques in Jacobean Tragedy* (New York: AMS Press, 1983), p. 23.
6. The question of terminology and intention in plays which include masques or similar musical-dramatic insertions has arisen many times and has never been answered satisfactorily. Sutherland points out that there have been almost as many definitions of inserted masques as there have been studies of the device, ibid., p. x. Inga-Stina Ewbank demonstrates that part of the problem lies in imprecise modern critical use of such terms as "masquelike" and masque elements," "'These Pretty Devices': A Study of Masques in Plays," *A Book of Masques in Honor of Allardyce Nicoll* (Cambridge: Cambridge University Press, 1967), pp. 408–409. Suzanne Gossett has pointed out that William Shakespeare has a tendency to couple the term "masque" with "revel" or "dance" in a general allusion to festivity, which destroys any particularity in the concept of a masque, "The Term 'Masque' in Shakespeare and Fletcher, and *The Coxcomb*," *SEL* 14 (1974): 290.
7. See Northrop Frye, *Anatomy of Criticism* (Princeton: Princeton University Press, 1957), p. 287; and Suzanne Gossett, "Masque Influence on the Dramaturgy of Beaumont and Fletcher," *MP* 69 (1971–72): 200.

8. Curtis A. Price, "Restoration Theatre Music Restored," *MT* 124 (June 1983): 344.
9. Sir John Davies, *Orchestra or a Poem of Dauncing* (London: Printed by J. Robarts for N. Ling, 1596), sig. B6.
10. See Andrew J. Sabol, ed., *Four Hundred Songs and Dances from the Stuart Masques* (Providence: Brown University Press, 1978), p. 16; Sternfeld, *Music in Shakespearean Tragedy*, p. 252; and John Ward, "The English Measure," *Early Music* 14 (1986): 18–19, 20. There has been a great deal of confusion over the use of the term "measure," which had diverse contemporary meanings both general and specific. Ward, in the above article, has taken decisive steps toward sorting out the confusion. But see also Otto Gombosi, "Some Musical Aspects of the English Court Masque," *JAMS* 1 (Fall 1948): 12–15; and Sabol, *Four Hundred Songs and Dances*, p. 16.
11. Burton, *Anatomy of Melancholy*, p. 498.
12. See Alan Brissenden, *Shakespeare and the Dance* (Atlantic Highlands, NJ: Humanities Press, 1981), p. 3.
13. Agrippa, *Vanitie and Uncertaintie*, fol. 31^v.
14. *The Praise of Musicke*, p. 79.
15. Davies, Orchestra, sig. C2.
16. Burton, *Anatomy of Melancholy*, p. 499. See also Jehan Tabourot [Thoinot Arbeau], *Orchesography*, trans. Mary Stewart Evans (New York: Kamin Dance Publishers, 1948), p. 12.
17. Davies, *Orchestra*, sig. B7^v.
18. Godwin, *Romanae Historiae Anthologia*, p. 41.
19. Stephan Batman, *The Golden Booke of the Leaden Goddes* (London: Imprinted by Thomas Marshe, 1577), fol. 16^v.
20. Cecil J. Sharp and Herbert C. Macilwaine, *The Morris Book*, pt. 1, 2d ed., rev. (London: Novello and Co., 1912), pp. 21–22.
21. Frances Rust, *Dance in Society* (London: Routledge and Kegan Paul, 1969), p. 47.
22. Lawrence Stone, *The Family, Sex and Marriage in England 1500–1800* (New York: Harper and Row, 1977), p. 30.
23. Ibid., p. 31.
24. See Sydney Beck, ed., *The First Book of Consort Lessons Collected by Thomas Morley*, p. 17; and Walter L. Woodfill, *Musicians in English Society from Elizabeth to Charles I* (Princeton: Princeton University Press, 1953), p. 234.
25. Burton, *Anatomy of Melancholy*, p. 541.
26. Davies, *Orchestra*, sig. A5^v.
27. Stubbes, *Anatomy of Abuses*, sig. D^v. See also Burton, *Anatomy of Melancholy*, p. 540.
28. Robert Allott, *Wits Theater of the Little World* (London: Printed by J. R. for N. L., 1599), p. 106.
29. *The Arte of English Poesie*, pp. 41–42.
30. *The Praise of Musicke*, pp. 81–82.
31. Butler, Principles of Musik, p. 124
32. Gosson, *Schoole of Abuse*, sig. A7^v.
33. Burton, *Anatomy of Melancholy*, p. 296.
34. Records of some actual contemporary examples of this sort of affair are extant and help to illustrate the tradition that is imitated on the stage; see Woodfill, *Musicians in English Society*, pp. 234–35.
35. Bishop John Earle, *Microcosmographie, or, a Piece of the World Discovered: in Essays and Characters* (London: W. S. for E. Blount, 1628), sig. C11.
36. G[eorge] S[andys], *Ovids Metamorphosis Englished, Mythologiz'd and Presented in Figures* (Oxford: Imprinted by John Lickfield, 1632), p. 356.
37. Butler, *Principles of Musik*, p. 98. See also pp. 41, 105, 119.
38. Peacham, *The Compleat Gentleman*, p. 104.
39. *The Praise of Musicke*, p. 80.
40. Stone, *Family, Sex and Marriage*, p. 207.
41. Ibid., pp. 207–8.

42. Ibid.
43. Butler, *Principles of Musik*, p. 125.
44. See *The Praise of Musicke*, p. 86.
45. For an outline and description of the standard parts of a contemporary funeral, see Stone, *Family, Sex and Marriage*, pp. 207–8.
46. See Mehl, *Elizabethan Dumb Show*, p. 126.
47. Shakespeare, *Henry V*, Act I, scene i, in *Comedies, Histories, and Tragedies*.
48. Gosson, *Schoole of Abuse*, sig. A7ᵛ.
49. [Jacopo di Porcia,] *The Preceptes of Warre*, set forth by James the Erle of Purlilia, and tra[n]slated into Englysh by Peter Betham (n. p.: 1544), sig. B7ᵛ.
50. Burton, *Anatomy of Melancholy*, p. 540.
51. [Baldessar Castiglione,] *The Courtyer of Count Baldessar Castilio*, done into Englyshe by Thomas Hoby (London: William Seres, 1561), sig. I2.
52. Gosson, *Schoole of Abuse*, sigs. F4–F4ᵛ.

CHAPTER 7. MUSIC FOR CHARACTER

1. For example, see Bowden, *The English Dramatic Lyric*; Long, *Shakespeare's Use of Music*, volumes 1, 2, and 3; Manifold, *Music in English Drama*; J. T. McCullen, "The Functions of Songs Aroused by Madness in Elizabethan Drama," *A Tribute to George Coffin Taylor*, ed., Arnold Williams (Chapel Hill: University of North Carolina Press, 1952): 185–96; John Robert Moore, "The Function of Songs in Shakespeare's Plays," *Shakespeare Studies* by members of the Department of English of the University of Wisconsin (Madison: University of Wisconsin, 1916): 78–102; Peter J. Seng, *The Vocal Songs in the Plays of Shakespeare* (Cambridge: Harvard University Press, 1967); Sternfeld, "The Dramatic and Allegorical Function of Music in Shakespeare's Tragedies," 265–82; and Sternfeld, *Music in Shakespearean Tragedy*, all of which express these ideas repeatedly.
2. Peacham, *Compleat Gentleman*, p. 96.
3. Bowden, *The English Dramatic Lyric*, p. 42.
4. Burton, *Anatomy of Melancholy*, p. 295.
5. *The Praise of Musicke*, p. 44; see also Butler, *Principles of Musik*, pp. 122, 123.
6. Thomas Deloney, *The Gentle Craft; a Discourse containing Many Matters of Delight, Very Pleasant to be Read: Shewing What Famous Men Have Beene Shoomakers in Time Past in this Land*, [4th ed.] (London: Printed for Robert Bird, 1637), sig. F2.
7. Sir Thomas Overbury, *New and Choise Characters of Several Authors*, 6th impression (London: T. Creede for L. L'Isle, 1615), sig. G8.
8. Burton, *Anatomy of Melancholy*, p. 294.
9. Meres, *Palladis Tamia*, fol. 288.
10. Frank Aydclotte, *Elizabethan Rogues and Vagabonds* (New York: Barnes and Noble, 1967), p. 76.
11. Nicholas Breton, *The Court and Country, or a Briefe Discourse Betweene the Courtier and the Country-Man* (London: Printed by G. Eld for John Wright, 1618), sig. B2.
12. Rowdy, dishonest apprentices were featured in a great deal of contemporary literature; see Steven R. Smith, "The London Apprentices as Seventeenth-Century Adolescents," *Past and Present* 61 (November 1973): 153–54.
13. Burton, *Anatomy of Melancholy*, p. 490. See also p. 295.
14. Francis Lenton, *Characterismi: or Lentons Leasures* (London: J. B. for R. Michell, 1631), sigs. D8ᵛ–D9.
15. "A Woeful Ballad made by M. George Mannyngton, an Hour Before He Suffered at Cambridge Castell" was entered in the Stationers Register on 7 November 1576, the year in which Mannington was executed for unknown crimes. The earliest extant imprint appears in Clement Robinson et al., *A Handefull of Pleasant Delites* (London: Printed by Richard Jhones, 1584) as "A Sorrowfull Sonet made by M. George Mannington at Cambridge Castle. To the tune of Labandala Shot," sigs. C–C2ᵛ. The ballad remained quite

popular for many years after it was written; see Austern "Musical Parody in the Jacobean City Comedy," p. 361.

16. Peacham, *Compleat Gentleman*, p. 100.
17. Stubbes, *Anatomy of Abuses*, sig. D5; see also Prynne, Histrio-Maxtix, p. 277.
18. Ravenscroft, *A Briefe Discourse*, sig. A^v.
19. See Aydelotte, *Elizabethan Rogues and Vagabonds*, pp. 44–45.
20. Gosson, *Schoole of Abuse*, sig. B.
21. Overbury, *New and Choise Characters*, sig. D4.
22. Castiglione, *The Courtyer*, sig. I2.
23. Ravenscroft, *A Briefe Discourse*, sig. A.
24. Agrippa, *Vanitie and Uncertaintie*, fol. 29^v.
25. Peacham, *Compleat Gentleman*, p. 100. See also Castiglione, *The Courtyer*, sig. N1. For a modern description of the musical education and performance habits of contemporary English gentlemen, see Woodfill, *Musicians in English Society*, pp. 211–30.
26. Castiglione, *The Courtyer*, sig. N^v.
27. Lenton, *Characterismi*, sig. B4.
28. Overbury, *New and Choise Characters*, sig. C3. See also Edward Guilpin, *Skialethia, or, a Shadowe of Truth* (London: J. R. for Nicholas Ling, 1598) sig. B.
29. See Chan, *Music in the Theatre of Ben Jonson*, p. 57.
30. Anthony Gibson, *A Womans Woorth, Defended Against All the Men in the World* (London: John Wolfe, 1599), fol. 24.
31. Ibid., fol. 24^v.
32. Thomas Shater, *The Mirrhor of Modestie* (London: Edward White [1579]), sig. C6.
33. Castiglione, *The Courtyer*, sig. I3.
34. Pierre Erondelle, *The French Garden: for English Ladyes and Gentlewomen to Walke in* (London: Edward White, 1601), sigs. F3^v–F4^v.
35. See Linda Phyllis Austern, "'Sing Againe Syren': The Female Musician and Sexual Enchantment in Elizabethan Life and Literature," *RQ* 42 (1989): 420–448; Carroll Camden, *The Elizabethan Woman* (Houston: The Elsevier Press, 1952), p. 54; and Ruth Kelso, *Doctrine for the Lady of the Renaissance* (Urbana: University of Illinois Press, 1956), p. 53.
36. Allott, *Wits Theater of the Little World*, fol 98.
37. Stubbes, *Anatomy of Abuses*, sigs. O3^v–O4.
38. Ibid., sigs. D5–D5^v.
39. Burton, *Anatomy of Melancholy*, p. 488.
40. J. H., *The House of Correction: or Certayne Satyricall Epigrams* (London: Printed by Bernard Alsop for Richard Redmer, 1619), sigs. D2–D2^v.
41. See, for instance, Lenton, *Characterismi*, sigs. C3–C4^v; and Overbury, *New and Choise Characters*, sigs. E2–E3^v. See also Paul V. Kreider, *Elizabethan Comic Character Conventions* (Ann Arbor: University of Michigan Press, 1935), pp. 51–52, n. 2; and Leggatt, *Citizen Comedy in the Age of Shakespeare*, pp. 99–124.
42. Frances A. Yates, *The Occult Philosophy in the Elizabethan Age* (London: Routledge and Kegan Paul, 1979), p. 75.
43. See Linda Phyllis Austern, "'Art to Enchant': Musical Magic and its Practitioners in English Renaissance Drama," *Journal of the Royal Musical Association* 115 (1990): 191–206.
44. See Katharine M. Briggs, *The Anatomy of Puck: An Examination of Fairy Beliefs Among Shakespeare's Contemporaries and Successors* (London: Routledge and Kegan Paul, 1959), pp. 44–70; and Robert Rentoul Reed, Jr., *The Occult on the Tudor and Stuart Stage* (Boston: Christopher Publishing House, 1965), p. 93.
45. Ludwig Lavater [Lewes Lavaterus], *Of Ghostes and Spirites Walking by Nyght*, translated into Englyshe by R. H. (London: Printed by Henry Benneyman for Richard Watkyns, 1572), p. 93.
46. See Keith Thomas, *Religion and the Decline of Magic* (New York: Charles Scribner's Sons, 1971), pp. 607–8. However, Reed has pointed out that the first pronounced skepticism about fairies does not appear in drama until the end of the Jacobean era, *The Occult on the Tudor and Stuart Stage*, p. 208.

47. See ibid., pp. 24–28; and John Dover Wilson and May Yardley, eds., *Lewes Lavater, of Ghostes and Spirites Walking by Nyght 1572* (Oxford: Oxford University Press, 1929), p. xi.

48. Thomas Campion, *The Description of a Maske: resented in the banquetting roome at Whitehall, on Saint Stephens Night last, at the mariage of the Right Honourable the Earle of Somerset: and the Right Noble the Lady Frances Howard* (London: Printed by E. A. for Laurence Lisle, 1614), sig. A2.

CHAPTER 8. MUSIC TO MOVE THE AFFECTIONS

1. Gosson, *Plays Confuted*, sig. F.
2. Henry Peacham, minister, *The Garden of Eloquence, conteyning the figures of Grammar and Rhetorick* (London: H. Jackson, 1577), sig. A3.
3. Bacon, *Sylva Sylvarum*, p. 38.
4. Pyrnne, *Historio-Mastix*, p. 274.
5. Francis Meres, *witts Academy: A Treasurie of Goulden Sentences, Similes, and Examples* (London: Printed for Richard Royston, 1635), p. 288.
6. Thomas Morley, *A Plaine and Easie Introduction to Practicall Musicke* (London: Imprinted by Peter Short, 1597), pp. 195–96.
7. Shapiro, *Children of the Revels*, p. 231.
8. *The Praise of Musicke*, p. 2.
9. William Ingpen, *The Secrets of Numbers* (London: Printed by Humphrey Lowns for John Parker, 1624), p. 94.
10. A representative sample of views may be found in Bowden, *English Dramatic Lyric*, p. 4; Chan, *Music in the Theatre of Ben Jonson*, pp. 9–10; Dent, *The Foundations of English Opera*, p. 2; Gretchen L. Finney, *Musical Backgrounds for English Literature, 1850–1650* (New Brunswick: Rutgers University Press, 1962), introduction; John Hollander, *The Untuning of the Sky: Ideas of Music in English Poetry 1500–1700* (Princeton: Princeton University Press, 1961), pp. 162–180; Christian Kiefer, "Music and Marston's *The Malcontent*," *Studies in Philology* 51 (1954): Long, *Shakespeare's Use of Music*, vol. 2, pp. 25–34; Wilfred Mellers, *Harmoneous Meeting* (London: Dennis Dobson, 1965), pp. 135–137; A. D. Nuttall, *Two Concepts of Allegory* (New York: Barnes and Noble, 1967), p. 77; O'Neill, "The Influence of Music in the Works of Marston," pp. 122–24; Bruce Pattison, *Music and Poetry of the English Renaissance* (New York: Da Capo Press, 1971), p. 1; Lawrence J. Ross, "Shakespeare's 'Dull Clown' and Symbolic Music," *SQ* 27 (1966): 107–8; and Frederick W. Sternfeld, "Le symbolisme musical dans quelques pièces de Shakespeare," in *Les fêtes de la Renaissance* (Paris: Editions du centre de la recherche scientifique, 1956), pp. 320–33.
11. Gosson, *Schoole of Abuse*, sigs. A8–A8ᵛ.
12. Gastiglione, *The Courtyer*, sig. I2.
13. Burton, *Anatomy of Melancholy*, p. 15.
14. Theories concerning the substantive relationship between the human soul, music, and the auditory pathway to spiritual ecstasy were widely discussed by Renaissance neo-Platonists, most notably Marsilio Ficino and Pico della Mirandola, long before they were adopted by the English writers of the sixteenth and seventeenth centuries; see Gretchen L. Finney, "Ecstasy and Music in Seventeenth-Century England," *JHI* 8 (1947): 154, 176–86; Finney, *Musical Backgrounds for English Literature*, pp. 102–3, 109; and D. P. Walker, *Spiritual and Demonic Magic from Ficino to Campanella* (London: The Warburg Institute, 1958), pp. 8–9. The most comprehensive discussion of music, the soul, and related airy entities published in Elizabethan England is found in Agrippa, *Vanitie and Uncertaintie*, fols. 66ᵛ–70.
15. Burton, *Anatomy of Melancholy*, p. 295.
16. Sandys, *Ovids Metamorphosis Englished*, p. 356.

17. Thomas Wright, *The Passions of the Minde in Generall*, corrected, enlarged and with sundry new discourses added (London: Printed by Valentine Simmes for Walter Burre, 1604), pp. 170–71.
18. Meres, *Palladis Tamia*, fol. 53.
19. *The Praise of Musicke*, p. 61.
20. Burton, *Anatomy of Melancholy*, p. 295.
21. Bacon, *Sylva Sylvarum*, p. 38.
22. *The Art of English Poesie*, p. 36.
23. Ravenscroft, *A Briefe Discourse*, sig. A3ᵛ.
24. Burton, *Anatomy of Melancholy*, p. 540.
25. Davies, *Orchestra*, sig. C4ᵛ.
26. Ibid., sig. A5ᵛ.
27. The most comprehensive contemporary discussion of the dance as a discordant seed of lust, lewdness, voluptousness, and as "the instrument of lechery" is Stubbes, *Anatomy of Abuses*, sigs. M7ᵛ–03ᵛ.
28. Ravenscroft, *A Briefe Discourse*, sig. A3ᵛ.
29. Burton, *Anatomy of Melancholy*, p. 489.
30. George Chapman, *Ovid's Banquet of Sence* (London: Printed by J. R. for Richard Smith, 1595), sig. B3ᵛ.
31. Morley, *Plaine and Easie Introduction*, p. 195.
32. Ravenscroft, *A Briefe Discourse*, sig. A3ᵛ.
33. Detractors from the theater repeatedly condemned "the effeminate, delicate, lust-provoking musicke" of stage plays because it was capable of moral corruption and caused all voluptuousness, uncleanness, and wantonness; in particular, see Gosson, *Schoole of Abuse*, sigs. A8ᵛ–B3; Prynne, *Historio-Maxtix*, pp. 273–90; and Stubbes, *Anatomy of Abuses*, sigs. 03ᵛ–06.
34. Davies, *Orchestra*, sig. B6.
35. Burton, *Anatomy of Melancholy*, pp. 296–297.
36. Gibson, *A Womans Woorth*, fol. 26.
37. The extant quarto (1602) prints "Phoebe heere one night did lye," which makes no sense in the context of the rest of the song. The line substituted here is that of the setting of the song given in Thomas Ravenscroft's *Briefe Discourse* and transcribed in chapter 10.
38. Batman, *The Golden Booke of the Leaden Goddes*, fol. 20ᵛ.
39. Anthony Essler, *The Aspiring Mind of the Elizabethan Younger Generation* (Durham, NC: Duke University Press, 1966), pp. 231–232. See also Michael MacDonald, *Mystical Bedlam* (Cambridge: Cambridge University Press, 1981), p. 151.
40. Ibid., p. 150.
41. Bridget Gellert Lyons, *Voices of Melancholy: Studies in Literary Treatment of Melancholy in Renaissance England* (New York: Barnes and Noble, 1971), preface.
42. Essler, *The Aspiring Mind*, pp. 230–231.
43. MacDonald, *Mystical Bedlam*, p. 151.
44. William Barley, *A New Booke of Tabliture* (London: William Barley, 1596), sig. A2ᵛ.
45. Burton, *Anatomy of Melancholy*, p. 294.
46. Ibid., p. 297.
47. Barten Holyday, *Technogamia: or the Marriages of the Arts* (London: Printed by William Stansby for John Parker, 1618).
48. Thomas Nabbes, *Microcosmus, A Morrall Maske*. (London: Printed by Richard Oulton for Charles Greene, 1637), sig. B.
49. See Bowden, *English Dramatic Lyric*, pp. 38–39; Lyons, *Voices of Melancholy*, preface; and Anthony Rooley, "New Light on John Dowland's Songs of Darkness," *Early Music* 11 (1983): 12.
50. See Kathi Meyer-Baer, *Music of the Spheres and the Dance of Death: Studies of Musical Iconography* (Princeton: Princeton University Press, 1970), pp. 219–23.
51. See Philip Brett, "The English Consort, 1570–1625," *PRMA* 88 (1961–62): 78–80.
52. Ingpen, *Secrets of Numbers*, p. 94.

53. See Finney, *Musical Backgrounds for English Literature*, pp. 105–6.
54. Henry Reynolds, *Mythomystes* (London: Printed for Henry Seyle [1632]), p. 52.
55. Ibid., p. 53.
56. See, for instance, Bowden, *English Dramatic Lyric*, p. 11; and Long, *Shakespeare's Use of Music*, vol. 2, pp. 96–97.
57. Sandys, *Ovids Metamorphosis*, p. 390.
58. John Dee, Preface to [Euclid,] *The Elements of Geometrie of the most Auncient Philosopher Euclide of Megara*, trans. H. Billingsley (London: John Daye, 1570), sig. B2ᵛ.
59. See Sandys, *Ovids Metamorphosis*, p. 195.
60. Rudolf Felber, "Music and Superstition," trans. Theodore Baker, *MQ* 17 (1931): 245.
61. Mulcaster, *Positions*, p. 38.
62. Sandys, *Ovids Metamorphosis*, p. 195.

CHAPTER 9. THE SOURCES OF THE MUSIC

1. See Diana Poulton, *John Dowland* (London: Faber and Faber, 1972; rev. ed., 1982), p. 191; and Ian Spink, *English Song from Dowland to Purcell*, p. 15.
2. See Ruff and Wilson, "The Madrigal, the Lute Song, and Elizabethan Politics," p. 28.
3. See Thurston Dart, "Role de la danse dans "l'ayre" Anglais," in *Musique et poesie au XVIᵉ siècle* (Paris: Editions du centre national de la recherche scientifique, 1954), p. 207; Poulton, *John Dowland*, pp. 142, 194; and Claude Simpson, *the British Broadside Ballad and its Music* (New Brunswick: Rutgers University Press, 1966), pp. 242–44.
4. The work was long presumed to be a play, but John Cutts has shown that it was probably a pastoral poem, "Peele's *Hunting of Cupid*," *Studies in the Renaissance* 5 (1958): 121–24. For further information on the poem, see W. W. Greg, "The Hunting of Cupid," Malone Society *Collections* vol. I, parts 4 and 5 (1911), pp. 307–14; and David Horne, *The Life and Minor Works of George Peele* (New Haven: Yale University Press, 1952), pp. 153–54.
5. As given in Greg, "Hunting of Cupid," p. 130; and Horne, *Life and Minor Works of George Peele*, pp. 207–208.
6. As given in Greg, "Hunting of Cupid," p. 313.
7. Mary Joiner Chan, "*Cynthia's Revels* and Music for a Choir School," pp. 141–42.
8. David Fuller, "Ben Jonson's Plays and their Contemporary Music," *ML* 58 (1977): 61–62.
9. The concordances for most of these tunes are numerous and widespread. A complete study of the contemporary sources of popular music is well beyond the scope of the current study. But comprehensive listings of the extant musical sources for the popular tunes used in children's drama are included by title in Simpson, *British Broadside Ballad*, supplemented by John M. Ward, "Apropros *The British Broadside Ballad and its Music*," *JAMS* 20 (1967): 28–86.
10. Anthony Holborne, *The Cittharn Schoole* (London: Printed by Peter Short, 1597), the Preface to the Reader.
11. See R. Thurston Dart, "Morley's Consort Lessons of 1599," *PRMA* 74 (1947–48): 6–7.
12. Thomas Morley, *The First Booke of Consort Lessons, made by Divers Exquisite Authors* (London: Printed by William Barley, the assigne of Thomas Morley, 1599), Dedication.
13. Morley's remarkable sense of business has not gone unnoticed; see Beck, *First Book of Consort Lessons*, introduction; and Dart, "Morley's Consort Lessons," p. 7.
14. "The Spanish Pavin" was one of the most widely circulating tunes of the day and is found in a wide variety of contemporary printed and manuscript sources in numerous arrangements. For further information, see Diana Poulton, "Notes on the Spanish Pavin," *LSJ* 3 (1961): 5–16; Simpson, *The British Broadside Ballad*, pp. 678–81; and Ward, "Apropros *The British Broadside Ballad*," p. 75.
15. See Austern, "Thomas Ravenscroft," pp. 238–40.
16. Ravenscroft, *Pammelia*, sig. A2ᵛ.
17. Ibid., sig. A2.

18. This manuscript is described in Jill Vlasto, "An Elizabethan Anthology of Rounds," *MQ* 40 (1954): 222–34.

19. The manuscript is available in modern edition with an extensive introduction as Granville Bantock and H. Orsmond Anderton, ed., *The Melvill Book of Roundels* (London: Privately Printed for Presentation to members of the Roxburghe club, 1916; reprint ed., New York: B. Franklin, 1972). It is also available in microfilm copy under the Library of Congress microfilm shelf number 4083.

20. Thomas Ravenscroft, *Melismata. Musicall Phansies Fitting the Court. Citie, and Countrey Humours* (London: Printed by William Stansby for Thomas Adams, 1611), sig. A4.

21. Sabol, "Ravenscroft's *Melismata*, pp. 4–9.

22. Ravenscroft, *A Briefe Discourse*, sig. qq2ᵛ.

23. See Philip Brett, ed., *Consort Songs, Musica Britannica* vol. 22 (London: Stainer and Bell, 1967), p. 174; and Chan, "*Cynthia's Revels* and Music for a Choir School," p. 134.

24. See Ibid., pp. 137–40; and Andrew J. Sabol, "Two Unpublished Stage Songs," pp. 225–26.

25. Ian Spink, "Sources of English Song, 1620–1660: A Survey," *Miscellanea Musicologica* 1 (1966): 117–136.

26. Andrew J. Sabol, "A Newly-Discovered Contemporary Song Setting for Jonson's 'Cynthia's Revels'," *N&Q 203* (1958): 384–85.

27. See Chan, "*Cynthia's Revels* and Music for a Choir School," p. 137; Fuller, "Jonson's Plays and their Contemporary Music," pp. 62–63; Sabol, "A Newly-Discovered Contemporary Song Setting," p. 385; and Sabol, "Two Unpublished Stage Songs," pp. 225–226.

28. Augustus Hughes-Hughes, *Catalogue of Manuscript Music in the British Museum*, 3 vols., vol. 2: *Secular Vocal Music* (1908), p. 468.

29. Fuller, "Jonson's Plays and their Contemporary Music," p. 64, n. 11. See also Sabol, "Two Unpublished Stage Songs," p. 230.

30. Brett, *Consort Songs*, p. 175.

31. This setting has been transcribed and edited independently by Philip Brett, in *Consort Songs*, pp. 92–93; and Andrew J. Sabol, "Two Songs with Accompaniment," pp. 155–57. A transcription credited to Sabol is also included in Chan, *Music in the Theatre of Ben Jonson*, pp. 26–29.

32. This setting has been transcribed and edited in Linda Phyllis Austern, "Sweet Meats with Sour Sauce," pp. 479–81.

33. For further information on this small book of songs and music for the lyra viol, see Mary Cyr, "A Seventeenth-Century Source of Ornamentation for Voice and Viol: British Museum MS Egerton 2971," *RMARC* (n.d.): 53–72; and Thurston Dart, "Ornament Signs in Jacobean Music for Lute and Viol," *GSJ* 14 (1961): 31.

34. For further information on this sizeable collection of sacred and secular works arranged for voice and unfigured bass, see Mary Joiner [Chan], "British Museum Add. Manuscript 15117: A Commentary, Index, and Bibliography," *RMARC* 7 (n.d.): 52–75; Fuller, "Jonson's Plays and their Contemporary Music," pp. 66–67; and Hughes-Hughes, *Catalogue of Manuscript Music*, vol. 2, p. 225.

35. For further information on this mixed collection of lute-songs and music for instrumental consort, solo lute, and lyra viol, see Hughes-Hughes, *Catalogue of Manuscript Music*, vol. 2, p. 470.

36. For further information on this mixed manuscript and its connection with the repertoire of the adult company of the King's Men, see John P. Cutts, "Two Jacobean Theatre Songs," *ML* 33 (1952): 333–34; and Hughes-Hughes, *Catalogue of Manuscript Music*, vol. 2, p. 471.

37. For further information on this manuscript and its connection with plays acted by the King's Men in the Blackfriars theatre between 1608 and 1617, see John P. Cutts, "'Songs Unto the Violl and Lute'—Drexel MS 4175," *Musica Disciplina* 16 (1962): 73–92; Cutts, "An Unpublished Contemporary Setting of a Shakespeare Song," *ShS* 9 (1956): 86; and Spink, "Sources of English Song," p. 135.

38. The same song, with slightly different lyrics, is used in Act II, scene ii of Beaumont and Fletcher's *The Captain*, acted by the King's Men about four years after *The Knight of the Burning Pestle* was presented by the Children of the Chapel. John P. Cutts feels strongly that the song originated in *The Captain* and was only added to *The Knight of the Burning Pestle* when the latter was first published in 1613, a year after the first performance of *the Captain, La musique de scene de la troupe de Shakespeare* (Paris: Editions du centre national de la recherche scientifique, 1959), pp. 134–35. He feels that the textual variants in *The Knight of the Burning Pestle* are more imitative than original and that the song does not belong with the dominant musical style of the play, most of whose other music is popular and pre-existent. This argument is not entirely convincing. First of all, one of the two singers, Luce, is assigned another song whose setting is no longer extant but whose text is far from popular in style, in Act IV, scene iv. Second a love song such as "Tell Me Dearest" is quite appropriate dramatically at this point in the play, for it is the first time that we see the young lovers, Luce and Jasper, alone. Third, the popular songs in the play are sung exclusively by the parodic characters: the Merchant, Old Merrythought, Mistress Merrythought, and son Michael Merrythought. Luce and Jasper are far more "serious" characters to whom more "serious" music would be appropriate. Furthermore, the major textual variation between the two versions of the song is that *The Captain's* has three stanzas and *The Knight of the Burning Pestle's* two. It is difficult to determine whether one is a lengthened version or an abbreviated version of the other. Furthermore, the other variations show no clear evidence of being original or imitative versions. The song itself was evidently quite popular in later years, for it is included in a number of seventeenth-century manuscripts.

39. John Playford *The English Dancing Master: or, Plaine and Easie Rules for the Dancing of Country Dances, with a Tune to each Dance* (London: Printed by Thomas Harper for John Playford, 1651). For bibliographic and descriptive information about all editions of the work, see Margaret Dean-Smith, ed., *Playford's English Dancing Master 1651: A Facsimile Reprint with an introduction, bibliography, and notes* (London: Schott and Co., 1957), pp. xxi–xxxi; and Margaret Dean-Smith and E. J. Nichol, "'The Dancing Master': 1651–1728," *JEFDSS* 4 (1940–41): 132–44.

40. Ibid., p. 133.

41. Playford, *English Dancing Master*, Preface.

42. Dean-Smith and Nichol, "'The Dancing Master'," p. 131.

43. Spink, "Sources of English Song," p. 122.

44. Wilson includes the same piece in his own *Cheerful Ayres or Ballads first composed for one single voice and since set for three voices* (Oxford: Printed by W. Hall for Ric. Davis, 1660), whose contents were, as the subtitle proclaims, originally for solo voice. The same song is also given as an accompanied solo in Edinburgh University Library Library MS Dc.1.69, fol. 155. The melody is identical in all versions, and all are by John Wilson.

45. J. St. Loe Strachy, ed., *Beaumont and Fletcher*, 3 vols. (London: Vizetelley and co., 1887), vol. 2, p. 316.

46. Willa McClung Evans, *Ben Jonson and Elizabethan Music*, p. 114, n. 8.

47. John P. Cutts, "Drexel Manuscript 4041: '. . . Earl Ferrers' MS—a Treasure-House of Early Seventeenth-Century Song and Dramatic Lyric," *Musica Disciplina* 18 (1964): 151.

48. Ibid., pp. 153–154; and Spink, "Sources of English Song," p. 135.

49. Ibid.; and Cutts, "Drexel Manuscript 4041," pp. 153–54.

50. Pamela J. Willets, *The Henry Lawes Manuscript* (London: Published by the Trustees of the British Museum, 1969), p. 2. See also Joan Strait Applegate, "The Henry Lawes Autograph Manuscript: A Critical Edition of British Museum Loan MS 35" (Ph.D. diss. Eastman School of Music, 1966); Eric Ford Hart, "Introduction to Henry Lawes," *ML* 32 (1951): 219–21; and Spink, "Sources of English Song," p. 130. There are no dates in the manuscript except for a few songs from 1634–36.

51. Willa McClung Evans, *Henry Lawes: Musician and Friend of Poets* (New York: Modern Language Association of America, 1941), p. 28; and Fuller, "Jonson's Plays and their Contemporary Music," p. 62.

52. Willets, *The Henry Lawes Manuscript*, p. 2.
53. For further information on this manuscript, see M. C. Crum, "Notes on the Texts of William Lawes' Songs in B. M. MS Add. 31432," *The Library*, 5th ser. 9 (1954): 122–27; Murray Lefkowitz, *William Lawes* (London: Routledge and Kegan Paul, 1960), pp. 199–200; and Spink, "Sources of English Song," p. 130.
54. For further information on this manuscript, see John P. Cutts, "Seventeenth-Century Songs and Lyrics in Edinburgh University Library MS Dc. 1. 69," *MD* 12 (1959): 169–94; and Spink, "Sources of English Song," p. 132.
55. For more information about this important manuscript, at one time owned by seventeenth-century English musician and composer John Gamble, see Vincent Duckles, "The Gamble Manuscript as a Source of Continuo Song in England," *JAMS* 1 (1948): 23–40; Duckles, "John Gamble's Commonplace Book: A Critical Edition of New York Public Library MS Drexel 4257" (Ph.D. diss., University of California at Berkeley, 1953); Charles W. Hughes, "John Gamble's Commonplace Book," *ML* 25 (1945): 215–29; and Spink, "Sources of English Song," p. 135.
56. See Simpson, *British Broadside Ballad*, p. ix.
57. See William Chappell, ed., *The Roxburghe Ballads*, 2 vols. (vol. 1, London: Printed for the Ballad Society by Taylor and Co., 1871; vol. 2, Hertford: Printed for the Ballad Society by Stephen Austin and Sons, 1872); Francis James Child, ed., *The English and Scottish Popular Ballads*, 5 vols. (London: Houghton Mifflin, 1882–98; New York: Dover Books, 1965); Andrew Clark, ed., *The Shirburn Ballads. 1585–1616* (Oxford: Clarendon Press, 1907), introduction; John W. Hales and Frederick J. Furnivall, eds., *Bishop Percy's Folio Manuscript* (London: N. Trubner and Co., 1867); Thomas Percy, ed. *Reliques of Ancient English Poetry*, 3 vols. (London: Swan, Sonnenschein, Lebas, and Lowry, 1886; New York: Dover Books, 1966); Joseph Ritson, *Ancient Songs and Ballads* (London: Reeves and Turner, 1877); and Ritson, *A Select Collection of English Songs*, 3 vols. (London: Printed for J. Johnson, 1783).
58. The most comprehensive work on the topic to date is Simpson, *British Broadside Ballad*, supplemented by Ward, "Apropros *The British Broadside Ballad.*" supplemented by Ward, "Apropros *The British Broadside Ballad.*" Good, brief intrtoductions to the topic and its problems are Diana Poulton, "The Black-Letter Broadside Ballad and its Music," *Early Music* 9 (1981): 427–36; and Hyder E. Rollins, "The Black-Letter Broadside Ballad," *PLMA* 34 (1919): 258–339. For a study of the use of broadside ballads and other popular tunes on the English stage, see Andrew Jackson Walker, "Popular Songs and Broadside Ballads in the English Drama 1559–1642" (Ph.D. diss., Harvard University, 1934).
59. Simpson, *British Broadside Ballad*; and Ward, "Apropros *The British Broadside Ballad.*"
60. Simpson, *British Broadside Ballad*, pp. ix–x.
61. Butler, *Principles of Musik*, p. 8.
62. Guilpin, Skialethia, sigs. A4–A4^v.
63. Reynolds, Mythomystes, pp. 44–45.
64. Simpson, British Broadside Ballad, pp. ix–x.
65. Ibid., p. xi.
66. The musical relationship between England and the continent was a two-way street during this era. England borrowed such tunes as "The Spanish Pavin," but loaned such others as "Fortune My Foe." See Alan Curtis, ed., *Dutch Keyboard Music of the Sixteenth and Seventeenth Centuries, Monumenta Musica Neerlandica* (Amsterdam: Vereniging voor Nederlandaise Muziekgescheidenis, 1961), vol. 3, pp. XL–XLI; Simpson, *British Broadside Ballad*, p. xiii; Ward, "Apropros *The British Broadside Ballad*," p. 75; and Ward, "Music for *A Handefull of Pleasant Delites*," *JAMS* 10 (1957): 166, 175.
67. For example, see Clark, *The Shirburn Ballads;* Herbert L. Coleman, ed., *Ballads and Broadsides Chiefly of the Elizabethan Period* (Oxford: Oxford University Press, 1912); J. Payne Collier, *Broadside Black-Letter Ballads Printed in the Sixteenth and Seventeenth Centuries. Chiefly in the Possession of J. Payne Collier* (New York: Burt Franklin, 1969; reprint ed., 1968); Thomas Deloney, *The Garland of Good Will* (London: Robert Bird,

1631); Deloney, *Strange Histories of Kings [,] Princes, Dukes [,] Earles, Lords, Ladies, Knights, and Gentlemen* (London: printed by William Barley, the assigne of T. M., 1602); Henry Huth, ed., *Ancient Ballads and Broadsides* (London: Whittingham and Wilkins, 1867); Robinson et al., *A Handefull of Pleasant Delites*; and Hyder Rollins, comp., *An Analytical Index to the Ballad Entries (1557–1709) in the Registers of the Company of Stationers of London* (Hatboro, PA: Tradition Press, 1967). Many broadside ballads are also listed in Pollard and Redgrave, comps., *Short-Title Catalogue*, under their titles, and are thus available in microfilm as part of the STC series.

CHAPTER 10. THE MUSICAL STYLES

1. Sidney, *Defense of Poesie*, sig. F3^v.
2. Brett, "The English Consort Song," pp. 78–80.
3. Castiglione, *The Courtyer*, sig. M4.
4. Peacham, *The Compleat Gentleman*, p. 96.
5. See William Byrd, *Psalmes, Songs, and Sonnets* (London: Printed by Thomas Snodham, the asigne of W. Barley, 1611), whose title page advertises the contents to be "framed to the life of the Words;" and Morley, *a Plaine and Easie Introduction*, which states, under "Rules to be Observed in Dittying," that "It followeth to show you how to dispose your musick according to the nature of the words which you are therein to expresse, as whatsoever matter it be which you have in hand such a kind of musicke must you frame to it," p. 177.
6. Thomas Nashe, *The Terrors of the Night, or a Discourse of Apparitions* (London: John Danter for William Jones, 1594), sig. B2^v.
7. James I, *Daemonologie* (London: Arnold Hatfield for Robert Wald-Grave, 1603), pp. 72–73. For further information on contemporary associations between Olympian dieties and English fairies, see Briggs, *Anatomy of Puck*, p. 44; and Margaret Lucy, *Shakespeare and the Supernatural* (Liverpool: Shakespeare Press, 1906), pp. 20–21.
8. Florio, *Queen Anna's New World of Words*, p. 332.
9. See Joseph Kerman, *The Elizabethan Madrigal: A Comparative Study* (New York: American Musicological Society, 1962), pp. 17–18.
10. Ruff and Wilson, "The Madrigal, the Lute-Song, and Elizabethan Politics," p. 50.
11. Boyd, *Elizabethan Music and Musical Criticism*, p. 92.
12. Ruff and Wilson, "The Magrigal, the Lute-Song, and Elizabethan Politics," p. 50.
13. Kerman, *The Elizabethan Madrigal*, pp. 158–59.
14. Morley, *A Plaine and Easie Introduction*, p. 180.
15. Gio[vanni] Giacomo Gastoldi da Caravaggio, *Balletti a cinque voci. con li suoi versi per cantare, sonare, & ballare*, quinta impressione (Venice: Amadino, 1593), facsimile ed., Corpus of Early Music 30 (Brussels, 1970). See Denis Arnold, "Gastoldi and the English Ballett, " *MMR* 86 (1956): 44–45, 51–52; Kerman, *The Elizabethan Madrigal*, pp. 136, 145; and *The New Grove Dictionary of Music and Musicians*, 1980 ed., s.v. "Balletto," by Suzanne G. Cusick.
16. Gastildi's *Balletti a cinque voci* were probably performed in costume before an audience; see Arnold, "Gastoldi and the English Ballett," pp. 44–45; and Kerman, "The Elizabethan Madrigal," p. 138. In addition, Gastoldi's collections appears to be arranged programmatically, and Alfred Eistein considers it to be the most important forerunner of the madrigal comedies of Vecchi and Banchieri, *The Italian Madrigal*, trans. Alexander H. Krappe, Roger H. Sessions, and Oliver Strunk (Princeton: Princeton University Press, 1949), p.605.
17. Printed as "friske" in the Ravenscroft collection.
18. Bacon, *Sylva Sylvarum*, p. 38.
19. Edmund H. Fellowes, *The English Madrigal* (London: Oxford University Press, 1925), p. 83. Fellowes neither associates the piece with the play nor presents a transcription.
20. Ravenscroft, *A Briefe Discourse*, sig. A2^v.

21. Morley, *A Plaine and Easie Introduction*, p. 180.
22. Butler *Principles of Musik*, p. 8.
23. Byrd, *Psalmes, Sonets & Songs*, Epistle to the Reader.
24. Brett, "The English Consort Song," p. 73; see also Thurston Dart, "Role de la danse," p. 205.
25. See Brett, "The English Consort Song," pp. 74–75, 79.
26. Sabol, "Two Songs with Accompaniment," p. 147.
27. See Brett, "The English Consort Song," pp. 79–80; and Chan, *Music in the Theatre of Jonson*, pp. 15–21.
28. Morley, *A Plaine and Easie Introduction*, p. 178.
29. Butler, *Principles of Musik*, p. 96.
30. Bacon, *Sylva Sylvarum*, p. 38.
31. For descriptions of various stylistic influences on the English ayre, see Morrison Comegys Boyd, *Elizabethan Music and Musical Criticism*, 2d ed. (Philadelphia: University of Pennsylvania Press, 1962), p. 127; Dart, "Role de la danse," pp. 203–9; duckles, "The Gamble Manuscript," pp. 25–27; Kerman, *The Elizabethan Madrigal*, pp. 104–5; Poulton, *John Dowland*, pp. 191–192; and Ian Spink, *English Song from Dowland to Purcell* (London: B. T. Batsford, 1974), pp. 16–17, 62–63.
32. Poulton, *John Dowland*, pp. 182–89.
33. Duckles, "The Gamble Manscript," p. 25; McDonald Emslie, "Nicholas Lanier's Innovations in English Song," *ML* 41 (1960): 13–14, 21–25; Hart, "Introduction to Henry Lawes," p. 329; and Spink, *English Song*, pp. 38–71.
34. Kerman, *The Elizabethan Madrigal*, p. 137; and Bruce Pattison, "Literature and Music in the Age of Shakespeare," *PRMA* 60 (1933–34): 79.
35. Kerman, *The Elizabethan Madrigal*, pp. 34–35.
36. Philip Rosseter, *A Booke of Ayres* (London: Printed by Peter Short by the assent of Thomas Morley, 1601), Address to the Reader.
37. Butler, *Principles of Musik*, p. 98.
38. Ibid., p. 95.
39. Ibid., p. 98.
40. Thomas Campion, *Observatons on the Art of English Poesie* (London: Printed by Richard Field for Andrew Wise, 1602), p. 2.
41. Andrew Sabol transcribed the backward cut-C mensuration sign in the bass part of the version in British Library MS Add. 24665 as a flat sign. Consequently, his transcription, given in "Two Songs with Accompaniment, " has a misleading g-minor tonality.
42. Butler, *Principles of Musik*, p. 45.
43. Morley, *A Plaine and Easie Introduction*, p. 180.
44. See Spink, *English Song*, p. 135.
45. Webbe, *Discourse of English Poetrie*, sig. D.
46. R. M., *A President for Young Pen-Men* (London: Printed by G. Eld for Robert Wilson, 1615), sig. A1.
47. Simpson, *British Broadside Ballad and its Music*, p. 680. For concise information on the Spanish Pavan and its use as an English ballad tune, see Poulton, "Notes on the Spanish Pavin," pp. 5–16; and Simpson, *British Broadside Ballad and its Music*, pp. 678–81.

APPENDIX A. EXTANT PLAYS PRESENTED BY THE CHILDREN'S COMPANIES. C. 1597–1613

1. Harbage, *Annals of English Drama 975–1700*, revised by S. Schoenbaum; 3rd ed. revised by Sylvia Stoler Wagonheim (London: Routledge, 1989), pp. 66–106; Braunmuller and Hattaway, *Cambridge Companion to English Renaissance Drama*, pp. 419–46; and Shapiro, *Children of the Revels*, pp. 261–68.

SELECT BIBLIOGRAPHY*

MANUSCRIPTS

Bodleian Library, Oxford

MS Tenbury 786.
MS Tenbury 1009.
MS Tenbury 1018.
MS Tenbury 1019.
MSS Tenbury 1162-1167.

British Library

MS Add. 6274 (Statuta Paulinae Scholar. . . MCCCCCXVIII).
MS Add. 10337 (Elizabeth Rogers's Virginal Book).
MS Add. 11402 (Abstracts of the Registers of the Privy Council [Elizabeth I]).
MS Add. 11608.
MS Add. 15117.
MS Add. 15118.
MSS Add. 17786-91.
MS Add. 19758 (Thomas Ravenscroft, "A Treatise of Musick").
MS Add. 24665 (Giles Earle His Booke).
MS Add. 27879 (Bishop Percy's Folio Manuscript).

---

*Abbreviations are the standard ones used in the *MLA International Bibliography* and the *New Grove Dictionary of Music and Musicians*.

MS Add. 29481.
MS Add. 31432 (William Lawes's autograph manuscript).
MS Add. 53723 (Henry Lawes's autograph manuscript).
MS Add. 56279 (Sylvanus Stirrops Book).
MS Add. 59869.
MS Egerton 2971.
MS Harl. 6959 (Excerpta e regist. in Tur. Lond.).
MS RM.24.d.3 (Forster Virginal Book).
MS Sloane 2035B (Commission To Take Up Singing Children).

Christ Church Library, Oxford

MSS Mus 56-60.
MS Mus 87.
MS Mus 439.

Edinburgh University Library

MS Dc.1.69

Guildhall Library, London

MS 9531/13 (The Bishop of London's Register, 1559-1627).
MS 9537/9 (The Visitation Report of Bishop Robert Bancroft for the London
    Diocese, 1598).

King's College, Cambridge

MS KC1 (The Thomas Lant Collection of Rounds and Canons).
MS Rowe 2 (The Turpyn Book of Lute Songs).

Lambeth Palace Library, London

Bishop Bancroft's Register.
Archbishop Whitgift's Register.

Library of Congress

MS M1490.M535A5 (The Melvill Book of Roundells).

New York Public Library

MS Drexel 4041.
MS Drexel 4175 (Ann Twice her Book).

MSS Drexel 4180-85.
MS Drexel 4257 (John Gamble's Commonplace Book).

Public Record Office, London

Patent Roll 4 Eliz. pt. 6 (C.66/981).
Patent Roll 39 Eliz. pt. 9 (C66/1466).
Patent Roll 1 James I, pt. 8 (C.66/1614).
Patent Roll 4 James I, pt. 18 (C.66/1708).
Patent Roll 7 James I, pt. 13 (C.66/1801).
Star Chamber Proceedings, Elizabeth I, STAC 5 C.46/39.

Royal College of Music, London

MS 2049.

Trinity College, Dublin

MS.F.5.13.

ITEMS PUBLISHED TO 1700

Agrippa von Nettesheim, Henry Cornelius. *Of the Vanitie and Uncertaintie of Artes and Sciences.* Englished by Ja. San[ford]. London: Imprinted by Henry Wykes, 1569.

Allott, Robert. *Wits Theater of the Little World.* London: Printed by J.R. for N.L., 1599.

Armin, Robert. *The History of the Two Maids of More-Clacke.* London: Printed by N.O. for Thomas Archer, 1609.

The Arte of English Poesie [often attributed to George and/or Richard Puttenham]. London: Printed by Richard Field, 1589.

Ascham, Roger. *The Scholemaster.* London: Printed by John Daye, 1570.

Bacon, Francis. *Sylva Sylvarum: Or a Naturall Historie.* 4th ed. London: Printed by John Haviland for William Lee, 1635.

Baker, Sir Richard. *Theatrum Redivivum, or the Theatre Vindicated.* London: Printed by T.R. for Francis Eglesfield, 1662.

Barkstead, William. *Mirrha the Mother of Adonis: or, Lustes Prodegies.* London: Printed by E.A. for John Bache, 1607.

_____. *Hiren: or the Faire Greeke.* London: Printed for Roger Barnes, 1611.

Barley, William. *A New Booke of Tabliture.* London: William Barley, 1596.

Barnfield, Richard. *Poems: In Divers Humors.* London: Printed by G.S. for John Jaggard, 1598.

Barry, Lording. *Ram Alley: or Merrie-Trickes.* London: Printed by G. Eld for Robert Wilson, 1611.

_____. *Ram-Alley or. Merry-Trickes.* London: Printed by John Norton for Robert Wilson, 1636.

Bartlet, John. *A Book of Ayres.* London: Printed by John Windet for John Browne, 1606.

Bateson, Thomas. *The First Set of English Madrigales*. London: Printed by Thomas Este, 1604.

Batman, Stephan. *The Golden Booke of the Leaden Goddes*. London: Imprinted by Thomas Marshe, 1577.

Beaumont, Francis. *The Knight of the Burning Pestle*. London: Printed for Walter Burre, 1613.

Beaumont, Francis and John Fletcher. *Comedies and Tragedies, never printed before, and new published by the authors originall copies*. London: Printed by Humphrey Robinson for Humphrey Mosley, 1647.

———. *Cupids Revenge*. London: Printed by Thomas Creede for Josias Harrison, 1615.

———. *Cupids Revenge*. 2nd ed. London: Printed for Thomas Jones, 1630.

———. *The Scornefull Ladie*. London: Printed for M P[artriche], 1616.

———. *The Scornefull Ladie*. 2nd ed. London: Printed for M.P., 1625.

———. *The Scornfull Ladie. A Comedie*. 3d ed. London: T. Jones, 1630.

———. *The Scornfull Ladie*. 4th ed. London: Printed by A.M., 1635.

———. *The Woman Hater*. London: Printed by John Hodgets, 1607.

Bevin, Elway. *A Briefe and Short Instruction on the Art of Musick*. London: Printed by R. Young, 1631.

Blurt, Master-Constable or the Spainiards Night-Walke. London: Printed for Henry Rockytt, 1602.

Bodenham, John. *Bel-Vedere or the Garden of the Muses*. London: P.K. for Hugh Astley, 1600.

Breton, Nicholas. *Melancholike Humours*. London: Printed by Richard Bradocke, 1600.

———. *The Soules Harmony*. London: Imprinted by S. Stafford for Randoll Bearkes, 1602.

Bright, T[imothy], Doctor of Physicke. *A Treatise of Melancholie*. London: Imprinted by Thomas Vautrollier, 1586.

B[ullokar], J[ohn]. *An English Expositor: Teaching the Interpretation of the Hardest Words Used in our Language*. London: Printed by John Legatt, 1616.

Burton, Robert. *The Anatomy of Melancholy*. Oxford: Printed by John Lichfield and James Short for Henry Cripps, 1621.

———. *The Anatomy of Melancholy*. 2d ed., corrected and augmented by the Authtor. Oxford: Printed by John Lichfield and James Short for Henry Cripps, 1624.

———. *The Anatomy of Melancholy*. 4th ed., corrected and augmented by the Author. Oxford: Printed for Henry Cripps, 1632.

Butler, Charles. *The Principles of Musik, in Singing and Setting*. London: Printed by John Haviland, 1636.

Byrd, William. *Psalmes, Sonets & Songs of Sadnes and Pietie*. London: Printed by Thomas East, the asigne of W. Bird, 1588.

———. *Psalmes, Songs and Sonnets*. London: Printed by Thomas Snodham, the asigne of W. Barley, 1611.

Byrd, William; John Bull; and Orlando Gibbons. *Parthenia or the Maydenhead*. London: Printed for Mris: Dor: Evans, n.d. [1612-13].

Campion, Thomas. *The Description of a Maske: presented in the banqueting roome at Whitehall, on Saint Stephens night last, at the mariage of the Right Honour-*

able the Earle of Somerset: and the Right Noble the Lady Frances Howard. London: Printed by E.A. for Laurence Lisle, 1614.

_____. *The Description of a Maske, presented before the Kings Majestie at White-Hall, on Twelfth Night last, in honour of the Lord Hayes and his Bride.* London: Imprinted by John Windet for John Brown, 1607.

_____. *A New Way of Making Fowre Parts in Counterpoint.* London: Printed by T.S. for John Browne, [1610].

_____. *Observations on the Art of English Poesie.* London: Printed by Richard Field for Andrew Wise, 1602.

_____. *A Relation of the late Royall Entertainment given by the Right Honorable the Lord Knowles . . . whereunto is annexed the description, speeches, and song of the Lords Maske.* London: Printed for John Budge, 1613.

[Castiglione, Baldesar.] *The Courtyer of Count Baldessar Castilio.* Done into Englyshe by Thomas Hoby. London: Imprinted by William Seres, 1561.

Cawdrey, Robert. *A Table Alphabeticall, conteyning and teaching the True Writing, and Understanding of Hard Usuall English Wordes.* London: Printed by J.R. for Edmund Weaver, 1604.

Chapman, George. *Al Fooles.* London: Printed for Thomas Thorpe, 1605.

_____. *Bussy D'Ambois: A Tragedie.* Being much corrected and amended by the author before his death. London: Printed by A.N. for Robert Lunne, 1641.

_____. *The Conspiracie and Tragedy of Charles Duke of Byron, Marshall of France.* London: Printed by N.O. for Thomas Thorp, 1625.

_____. *The Gentleman Usher.* London: Printed by V.S. for Thomas Thorppe, 1606.

_____. *May Day.* London: Printed for John Browne, 1611.

_____. *Monsieur D'Olive.* London: Printed by T.C. for William Holmes, 1606.

_____. *Ovids Banquet of Sence: A Coronet for his Mistresse Philosophie, and his Amorous Zodiacke.* London: Printed by J.R. for Richard Smith, 1595.

_____. *The Revenge of Bussy D'Ambois.* London: Printed by T.S. for John Helme, 1613.

_____. *Sir Gyles Goosecappe Knight.* London: Printed by John Windet for Edward Blunt, 1606.

_____. *The Widdowes Teares.* London: Printed for John Browne, 1612.

Chapman, George, Ben Jonson, and John Marston. *Eastward Hoe.* London: Printed for William Aspley, 1605.

C[ockeram], H[enry]. *The English Dictionarie: or, an Interpreter of Hard English Words.* London: Printed for Nathaniell Butter, 1623.

The Contention Between Liberalitie and Prodigalitie. London: Printed by Simon Stafford for George Vincent, 1602.

Cotgrave, Randle. *A Dictionarie of the French and English Tongues.* London: Printed by Adam Islip, 1611.

Cyvile and Uncyvile Life. London: Printed by Richard Jones, 1579.

Daniel, Samuel. *The Whole Workes.* London: Printed by Nicholas Okes for Simon Waterson, 1623.

Davies, John. *The Scourge of Folly, consisting of satyricall Epigrams, and others in honour of many noble persons and worthy friends.* London: Printed by E.A. for Richard Redmer, 1610.

Davies, Sir John. *Humours Heav'n on Earth.* London: Printed by A.I., 1609.

_____. *Orchestra or a Poem of Dauncing.* London: Printed by J. Robarts for N. Ling, 1596.

Day, John. *Humour Out of Breath*. London: J. Helmes, 1608.
_____. *The Ile of Gulls*. London: John Hodgets, 1606.
_____. *The Ile of Gulls*. London: William Sheares, 1633.
_____. *Law-Trickes or, Who Would Have Thought It*. London: Printed for Richard More, 1608.
Dekker, Thomas [T. Deckar]. *The Guls Horne-Booke*. London: Imprinted for R.S., 1609.
_____. *Satiro-Mastix. or the Untrussing of the Humorous Poet*. London: Edward White, 1602.
_____. *The Seven Deadlie Sinns of London*. London: Printed by E.A. for Nathaniell Butter, 1606.
Dekker, Thomas, and John Webster. *Northward Hoe*. London: G. Eld, 1607.
_____. *Westward Ho*. London: John Hodgets, 1607.
Deloney, Thomas. *The Garland of Good Will*. London: Robert Bird, 1631.
_____. *The Gentle Craft: A Discourse Containing Many Matters of Delight, Very Pleasant to be Read: Shewing What Famous Men Have Beene Shoomakers in Time Past in this Land*. [4th ed.] London: Printed for Robert Bird, 1637.
_____. *The Gentle Craft. The Second Part*. London: Imprinted by Elizabeth Purslow, 1639.
_____. *Strange Histories of Kings, Princes, Dukes, Earles, Lords, Ladies, Knights, and Gentlemen*. London: Printed by William Barley, the asigne of of T.M., 1602.
Desainliens, Claude [Claudius Hollyband]. *A Dictionarie of French and English*. London: Imprinted by T.O. for Thomas Woodcock, 1593.
_____. *The French Littleton*. London: thomas Vautroullier, 1566.
_____. *The French Schoolemaister*. London: Imprinted by William Howe for Abraham Veale, 1573.
Dowland, John. *The First Booke of Songes or Ayres*. London: Printed by Peter Short, 1597.
_____. *The First Booke of Songes or Ayres*. Newly corrected and amended. [2d ed.] London: Printed by Peter Short the asigne of Th. Morley, 1600.
_____. *The First Book of Songes or Aires*. Newly corrected and amemded. [3d ed.] London: Printed by E. Short, 1603.
_____. *The First Booke of Songs or Aires*. Newly corrected and amended. [4th ed.] London: Humphrey Lownes, 1606.
_____. *The First Booke of Songs or Ayres*. Newly corrected and amended. [6th ed.] London: Humphrey Lownes, 1613.
_____. *Lachrimae, or Seaven Teares Figured in Seaven Passionate Pavans*. London: Printed by John Windet, n.d.
_____. *The Second Booke of Songs or Ayres*. London: Printed by Thomas Easte, the asigne of Thomas Morley, 1600.
_____. *The Third and Last Booke of Songs or Aires*. London: Printed by P.S. for Thomas Adams, 1603.
Drayton, Michael. *Poly-Olbion, or a Chorographicall Description of Great Britain*. London: F.M. Lownes, J. Browne, J. Helme, à J. Busbie, 1612.
Earle, Bishop John. *Micro-Cosmographie. or, a Peece of the World Discovered: in Essayes and Characters*. London: Printed by William Stansby for Robert Allot, 1628.

Elyot, Sir Thomas. *The Boke named the Governour.* London: Thomas Bertheleti, 1531.

The English Courtier, and the Cu[n]trey-Gentleman. London: Imprinted by Richard Jones, 1586.

Erondelle, Pierre. *The French Garden: for English Ladyes and Gentlewomen to walke in. or a Sommer dayes labour.* London: Printed for Edward White, 1605.

[Euclid.] *The Elements of Geometrie of the Most Auncient Philosopher Euclide of Megara.* Translated by H. Billingsley. Preface by John Dee. London: John Daye, 1570.

Everie Woman in Her Humour. London: Printed by Edward Allde for Thomas Archer, 1609.

Field, John. *A Godly Exhortation, by Occasion of the Late Judgement of God, Shewed at Paris-Garden.* London: Printed by Robert Waldgrave for Henry Carre, 1583.

Field, Nathan. *Amends for Ladies. With the Merry Prankes of Moll Cutpurse: or the Humour of Roaring.* London: Printed by Jo. Okes, for Math. Walbanke, 1639.

_____. *A Woman is a Weather-Cocke.* London: John Budge, 1612.

Flecknoe, Richard. *Loves Kingdom, a Pastorall Trage-Comedy. . . with a short Treatise of the English Stage &c.* London: Printed by R. Wood for the Author, 1664.

Fletcher, John. *The Faithfull Sheapherdesse.* London: Printed for R. Bonian and H. Walley, n.d. [c. 1610].

_____. *The Faithfull Sheapherdesse.* 3rd ed., with additions. London: Printed by A.M. for Richard Meighan, 1634.

Florio, John. *Queen Anna's New World of Words, or a Dictionarie of the Italian and English Tongues.* London: Printed by Melch. Bradwood, for Edw. Blount and William Barret, 1611.

_____. *A Worlde of Wordes, or the Most Copious and Exact Dictionarie in Italian and English.* London: Printed by Arnold Hatfield for Edw. Blount, 1598.

Fraunce, Abraham. *The Arcadian Rhetoricke.* London: Printed by Thomas Orwin, [1588].

Fuller, Thomas. *The History of the Worthies of England.* London: Printed by J.G.[,] W.L. and W.G. for Thomas Williams. 1662.

Fulwell, Ulpian. *The First parte of the Eyghth Liberall Science: entituled, Ars Adulandi, the Arte of Flatterie.* London: Imprinted by Richarde Jones, 1579.

Gainesford, Thomas. *The Rich Cabinet.* London: Printed by I.B. for Roger Jackson, 1616.

Gibson, Anthony. *A Womans Woorth, Defended Against All the Men in the World.* London: John Wolfe, 1599.

Godwin, Thomas. *Romanae Historiae Anthologia. And English Exposition of the Romane Antiquities, wherein many Romane and English Offices are Paralleled and Divers Obscure Phrases Explained.* Oxford: Joseph Barnes, 1614.

Gosson, Stephen. *Playes Confuted in Five Actions.* London: Imprinted for Thomas Gosson [1582].

_____. [Stephan Gosson]. *The S[c]hoole of Abuse.* London: Printed for Thomas Woodcocke, 1579.

Guilpin, Edward. *Skialethia, or, A Shadowe of Truth.* London: Printed by J.R. for Nicholas Ling, 1598.

H., J. *The House of Correction: or, Certayne Satyricall Epigrams*. London: Printed by Bernard Alsop for Richard Redmer, 1619.

Heywood, Thomas. *An Apology for Actors*. London: Printed by Nicholas Okes, 1612.

_____. *The English Traveller*. London: Printed by Robert Raworth, 1633.

Holborne, Anthony. *The Cittharn Schoole*. London: Printed by Peter Short, 1597.

Holinshed, Raphaell, William Harrison, and Others. *The First and Second Volumes of Chronicles*. Now newlie augmented and continued... to the yeare 1586. London: at the expenses of J. Harison, G. Bishop, R. Newberie, H. Denham à T. Woodcocke, 1587.

Holyday, Barten. *Technogamia: or the Marriages of the Arts*. London: Printed by William Stansby for John Parker, 1618.

Ingpen, William. *The Secrets of Numbers; According to their Theologicall, Arithmeticall, Geometricall, and Harmonicall Computation*. London: Printed by Humphrey Lowns for John Parker, 1624.

James, I. *Daemonologie, in forme of a Dialogue*. London: Printed by Arnold Hatfield for Robert Wald-grave, 1603.

Jones, Robert. *The First Booke of Songs or Ayres*. London: Printed by Peter Short with the asent of Thomas Morley, 1600.

_____. *The Muses Gardin for Delights, or the Fift Booke of Ayres*. London: Printed by the Asignes of William Barley, 1610.

_____. *A Musicall Dreame. Or the Fourth Booke of Ayres*. London: Imprinted by the Assignes of William Barley, 1609.

_____. *The Second Booke of Songs and Ayres*. London: Printed by P.S. for Mathew Selman by the assent of Thomas Morley, 1601.

_____. *Ultimum Vale*. London: Printed by John Windet, 1605.

Jonson, Ben. *[Epicoene or] The Silent Woman*. London: Printed by William Stansby, 1620.

_____. *The Fountaine of Self-Love. or Cynthia's Revels*. London: Imprinted for Walter Burre, 1601.

_____. *His Case is Altered*. London: Printed for Bartholomew Sutton, 1609.

_____. *The Workes of Benjamin Jonson*. London: Printed by William Stansby, 1616.

[Kyd, Thomas?] *The First Part of [H]ieronimo*. London: Thomas Pavyer, 1605.

Lavater, Ludwig [Lewes Lavaterus]. *Of Ghostes and Spirites Walking by Nyght*. Translated into Englyshe by R.H. London: Printed by Henry Benneyman for Richard Waykyns, 1572.

Lawes, Henry, and William Lawes. *Choice Psalmes put into Musicke, for Three Voices*. London: Printed by James Young, for Humphrey Mosley and for Richard Wodenothe, 1648.

Lenton, Francis. *Characterismi: or, Lentons Leasures*. London: Printed by J.B. for Roger Michell, 1631.

Lyly, John. *Alexander, Campaspe, and Diogenes, A Most Excellent Comedie of*. London: Imprinted for Thomas Cadman, 1584.

_____. *Endimion, the Man in the Moone*. London: Printed by J. Charlewood, for the Widdowe Broome, 1591.

_____. *Loves Metamorphosis*. London: Printed for William Wood, 1601.

_____. *Sapho and Phao*. Imprinted for Thomas Cadman, 1584.

_____. *Sixe Court Comedies*. London: Printed by William Stansby for Edward Blount, 1632.

M., R. *A president for Young Pen-Men.* London: Printed by G. Eld for Robert Wilson, 1615.

Mace, Thomas. *Musick's Monument.* London: Printed by T. Ratcliffe, and N. Thompson, for the Author, 1676.

Markham, Gervase, and Lewis Machin. *The Dumbe Knight.* London: Printed by A.M. for William Sheares, 1633.

Marprelate, Martin [pseud.]. *Mar-Martin.* N.p., n.d.

Marston, John. *Antonio and Mellida, The History of.* The First Part. London: Printed for Mathewe Lownes, and Thomas Fisher, 1602.

_____. *Antonios Revenge.* The Second Part of the History of Antonio and Mellida. London: Printed for Thomas Fisher, 1603.

_____. *The Dutch Courtesan.* London: Printed by T.P. for John Hodgets, 1605.

_____. *Histrio-Mastix, or The Player Whipt.* London: Printed for Th. Thorpe, 1610.

_____. *Jacke Drums Entertainment: or the Comedy of Pasquill & Katherine.* London: Richard Olive, 1601.

_____. *The Malcontent.* London: Printed by V.S. for William Aspley, 1604.

_____. *Parasitaster, or the Fawne.* London: Printed by T.P. for W.C., 1606.

_____. *Parasitaster, or the Fawne.* [2nd ed.] And now corrected of the many faults, which by reason of the authors absence, were let slip in the first edition. London: Printed by T.P. for W.C., 1606.

_____. *What You Will.* London: Imprinted by G. Eld for Thomas Thorppe, 1607.

_____. *The Wonder of Women or the Tragedie of Sophonisba.* London: Printed by John Windet, 1606.

_____. *The Works of Mr. John Marston, being Tragedies and Comedies Collected into One Volume.* London: Printed for William Sheares, 1633.

[Marston, John and William Barkstead.] *The Insatiate Countesse.* London: Printed for Thomas Archer, 1613.

_____. *The Insatiate Countesse.* London: Printed by I.N. for Hugh Perrie, 1631.

Marston, John and John Webster. *The Malcontent.* Augmented by Marston. With the additions played by the Kings Majesties Servants written by Jhon [sic] Webster. London: Printed by V.S. for William Aspley, 1604.

Mason, John. *Mulleasses the Turke, and Borgias Governour of Florence, An Excellent Tragedy of.* London: Printed by T.P. for Francis Falkner, 1632.

M[assinger], P[hilip], and N[athan] F[ield]. *The Fatall Dowry.* London: J. Norton for F. Constable, 1632.

The Maydes Metamorphosis. London: Printed by Thomas Creede, for Richard Olive, 1600.

Meres, Francis. *Palladis Tamia.* London: Printed by P. Short for Cuthbert Burbie, 1598.

_____. *Witts Academy: A Treasurie of Goulden Sentences, Similes, and Examples.* London: Printed for Richard Royston, 1635.

Middleton, Thomas. *The Famelie of Love.* London: Printed for John Helmes, 1608.

_____. *Father Hubburds Tales: Or the Ant, and the Nightingale.* London: Printed by T.C. for William Cotton, 1604.

_____. *A Mad World, My Masters.* London: Printed by H.B. for Walter Burre, 1608.

_____. *A Mad World, My Masters.* London: Printed by J.S. for James Becket, 1640.

_____. *Michaelman Terme.* London: Printed for A.I., 1607.

_____. *Michaelman Terme.* Newly Corrected. London: Printed by T.H. for R. Meighan, 1630.

_____. *The Phoenix*. London: Printed by E.A. for A.I., 1607.

_____. *The Phoenix*. London: Printed by T.H. for R. Meighan, 1630.

_____. *A Trick to Catch the Old-One*. London: George Eld, 1608.

_____. *Women Beware Women*. London: Printed for Humphrey Moseley, 1657.

_____. *Your Five Gallants*. London: Imprinted for Richard Bonlan, n.d.

Morley, Thomas. *Canzonets or Little Short Songs to Three Voyces*. London: Imprinted by Tho: Est, 1593.

_____. *The First Booke of Ayres*. London: Imprinted by William Barley, the asigne of Thomas Morley.

_____. *The First Booke of Balletts to Five Voyces*. London: Printed by Thomas Este, 1595.

_____. *The First Booke of Consort Lessons, made by divers exquisite authors, for six instruments to play together*. London: Printed by William Barley, the asigne of Thomas Morley, 1599. [cittern part only]

_____. *The First Part of the Elementarie Which Entreateth Chefelie of the Right Writing of our English Tung*. London: Imprinted by Thomas Vautroullier, 1582.

_____. *A Plaine and Easie Introduction to Practicall Musicke*. London: Imprinted by Peter Short, 1597.

Mulcaster, Richard. *Positions wherein those primitive circumstances be examined, which are necessarie for the training up of children*. London: Imprinted by Thomas Vautrollier for Thomas Chare, 1581.

Munday, Anthony. *A Second and Third Blast of Retrait from Plaies and Theaters*. London: Allowed by Auctoritie, 1586.

Nabbes, Thomas. *Microcosmus. A Morall Maske*. London: Printed by Richard Oulton for Charles Greene, 1637.

Nashe, Thomas. *The Terrors of the Night, or a Discourse of Apparitions*. London: John Danter for William Jones, 1594.

Norden, John. *Speculum Britanniae. The First Part*. N.p.: 1593.

Northbrooke, John. *A treatise wherein Dicing, Dauncing, Vaine playes or Enterluds with other idle pastimes commonly used on the Sabboth day, are reproved by the authoritie of the word of God and auntient writers*. London: Imprinted by H. Bynneman for George Byshop, [1577].

Ornithoparcus, Andreas. *Andreas Ornithoparcus His Micrologus or Introduction: Containing the Art of Singing*. Translated by John Dowland. London: Printed for Thomas Adams, 1609.

Overbury, Sir Thomas. *New and Choise Characters of Several Authors, together with The Wife written by Syr T. Overburie*. 6th impression. London: T. Creede for L. L'Isle, 1615.

[Ovid.] *The XV. Bookes of P. Ovidus Naso, entytled Metamorphosis*. Translated oute of Latin into English Meeter, by Arthur Golding. London: Imprynted by William Seres, 1567.

Peacham, Henry [minister]. *The Garden of Eloquence, conteyning the figures of grammar and rhetorick*. London: Imprinted by H. Jackson, 1577.

Peacham, Henry [the younger]. *The Compleat Gentleman*. London: Francis Constable, 1622.

_____. *The Compleat Gentleman*. 2nd impression much enlarged. London: Imprinted for Francis Constable, 1634.

Playford, Henry. *Wit and Mirth: or Pills to Purge Melancholy: Being a Collection of the Best Merry Ballads and Songs, Old and New.* London: Printed by Will. Pearson for Henry Playford, 1699.

_____. *Wit and Mirth: or Pills to Purge Melancholy: Being a Collection of the Best Merry Ballads and Songs, Old and New.* The Second Part. London: Printed by William Pearson for Henry Playford, 1700.

Playford, John. *The Dancing Master.* 2nd ed. London: Printed for John Playford, 1652.

_____. *The Dancing Master.* 5th ed. with additions. London: Printed by W. Godbid for John Playford, 1675.

_____. *The English Dancing Master: or, Plaine and Easie Rules for the Dancing of Country Dances, with a Tune to each Dance.* London: Printed by Thomas Harper for John Playford, 1651.

_____. *A Musicall Banquet.* London: Printed by T.H. for John Benson and John Playford, 1651.

_____. *Musicks Hand-Maide. . . presenting New and Pleasant Lessons for the Virginalls or Harpsychon.* London: Printed for John Playford, 1663.

_____. *The Treasury of Musick: Containing Ayres and Dialogues to sing to the Theorbo-Lute or Bass-Viol.* Composed by Mr. Henry Lawes. . . and other excellent masters. In three books. London: Printed by William Godbid for John Playford, 1669.

[Porcia, Jacopo di.] *The Preceptes of Warre, set forth by James the Erle of Purlilia.* Tra[n]slated into Englysh by Peter Betham. N.p.: 1544.

The Praise of Musicke. Oxenford: Joseph Barnes, 1586.

Prynne, William. *Histrio-Mastix: The Players Scourge, or Actors Tragedie*, divided into two parts. London: Printed by E.A. and W.I. for Michael Spark, 1633.

The Puritaine or the Widdow of Watling-Streete. London: Imprinted by G. Eld, 1607.

Rankins, Wil[liam]. *A Mirrour of Monsters.* London: Printed by J.C. for T.H., 1587.

Ravenscroft, Thomas. *A Briefe Discourse of the True (but neglected) Use of Charact'ring the Degrees by their Perfection, Imperfection, and Diminution in Measurable Musicke, Against the Common Practice and Custome of These Times.* London: Printed by Edw: Allde for Tho. Adams, 1614.

_____. *Deuteromelia: or the Second Part of Musicks Melodie, or Melodius Musicke.* London: Printed for Thomas Adams, 1609.

_____. *Melismata. Musicall Phansies Fitting the Court, Citie, and Countrey Humours.* London: Printed by William Stansby for Thomas Adams, 1611.

_____. *Pammelia. Musicks Miscellanie.* London: Printed by William Barley, 1609.

_____. *The Whole Booke of Psalmes: With the Hymnes Evangelicall, and Songs Spirituall.* Newly corrected and enlarged. London: n.p., 1621.

Reynolds, Henry. *Mythomystes.* London: Printed for Henry Seyle [1632].

Robinson, Clement, and Divers Others. *A Handefull of Pleasant Delites, containing sundrie new Sonets and delectable Histories, in divers kindes of Meeter.* London: Printed by Richard Jhones, 1584.

Robinson, Thomas. *New Citharen Lessons.* London: Printed by William Barley, 1609.

_____. *The Schoole of Musicke.* London: Printed by Tho. Este for Simon Waterson, 1603.

Roscio, I.L. *Brief Conclusions of Dancers and Dancing.* London: John Orphinstrange, 1609.

Rosseter, Philip. *A Booke of Ayres*. London: Printed by Peter Short, by the assent of Thomas Morley, 1601.

_____. *Lessons for Consort*. London: Printed by Tho. Este alias Snodham, for John Browne, 1609. [citterne part only]

Rowley, William. *A Match at Mid-Night*. London: Printed by Aug. Mathewes, for William Sheares, 1633.

Rymer, Thomas. *The Tragedies of the Last Age*. London: Printed for Richard Tonson, 1678.

Salter, Thomas. *A Mirrhor mete for all Mothers, Matrones, and Maidens, intituled the Mirrhor of Modestie, no lesse profitable and pleasant, then necessary to be read and practised*. London: Edward White [1579].

S[andys], G[eorge]. *Ovids Metamorphosis Englished. Mythologiz'd and Represented in Figures*. Oxford: Imprinted by John Lichfield, 1632.

Shakespeare, William. *Comedies, Histories, & Tragedies*. London: Printed by Isaac Jaggard, and Ed. Blount, 1623.

_____. *Hamlet, Prince of Denmark. The Tragicall Historie of*. [London:] N.L. à J. Trundell, 1603.

_____. *The Merchant of Venice, The Most Excellent Historie of*. London: Printed by J.R. for Thomas Heyes, 1600.

Sharpham, Edward. *Cupids Whirligig*. London: Imprinted by T.C., 1611.

_____. *The Fleire*. London: Printed for Nathaniell Butter, 1610.

Sidney, Sir Phillip. *The Defence of Poesie*. London: Printed for William Ponsonby, 1595.

Stubbes, Phillip. *The Anatomy of Abuses*. London: Richard Jones, 1583.

Webbe, William. *A Discourse of English Poetrie*. London: Imprinted by John Charlewood for Robert Walley, 1586.

Wilson, John. *Cheerful Ayres or Ballads first Composed for one single Voice and since set for three Voices*. Oxford: Printed by W. Hall, for Ric. Davis, 1660.

Wily Beguilde. London: Printed by H.L. for Clement Knight, 1606.

The Wisdom of Dr. Dodypoll. London: Printed by Thomas Creede for Richard Olive, 1600.

Wright, Thomas. *The Passions of the Minde in Generall*. Corrected, enlarged and with sundry new discourses added. London: Printed by Valentine Simmes for Walter Burre, 1604.

Youll, Henry. *Canzonets to Three Voyces*. London: Printed by Thomas Este, the asigne of William Barley, 1608.

ITEMS PUBLISHED FROM 1701 ONWARD

Adams, Joseph Quincy. *Shakespearean Playhouses*. Boston: Houghton Mifflin Co., 1917.

Albright, Evelyn May. *Dramatic Publication in England. 1580-1640*. New York: D.C. Heath and Co., 1927.

Appleton, William W. *Beaumont and Fletcher*. London: George Allen and Unwin, 1956.

Arkwright, G.E.P. *Catalogue of Music in the Library of Christ Church Oxford*. London: Oxford University Press, 1915.

_____. "Elizabethan Choirboy Plays and their Music." *PRMA* 40 (1913-14): 117-38.

Arnold, Denis. "Gastoldi and the English Ballett." *MMR* 86 (1956): 44-52.

Attridge, Derek. *Well-Weighed Syllables: English Verse in Classical Metres*. London: Cambridge University Press, 1974.

Auden, W.H. *The Dyer's Hand and Other Essays*. New York: Random House, 1962.

Austern, Linda Phyllis. "'Art to Enchant' Musical Magic and its Practitioners in English Renaissance Drama." *Journal of the Royal Musical Association* 115 (1990): 191-206.

_____. "Musical Parody in the Jacobean City Comedy." *ML* 66 (1985): 355-66.

_____. "'Sing Againe Syren:' The Female Musician and Sexual Enchantment in Elizabethan Life and Literature." *RQ* 42 (1989): 420-48.

_____. "Sweet Meats with Sour Sauce: The Genesis of Musical Irony in the English Private Theater after 1600." *The Journal of Musicology* 4 (1985-86): 472-90.

_____. "Thomas Ravenscroft: Musical Chronicler of an Elizabethan Theater Company." *JAMS* 38 (1985): 238-63.

Aydelotte, Frank. *Elizabethan Rogues and Vagabonds*. New York: Barnes and Noble, 1967.

Baines, Anthony. *Woodwind Instruments and their History*. New York: W.W Norton and Co., 1957.

Baker, Roger. *Drag: A History of Female Impersonation on the Stage*. London: McDonald and Co., 1968.

Ball, Roma. "The Choirboy Actors of St. Paul's Cathedral." *Emporia State Research Studies* 10 (June 1962): 5-16.

Bantock, Granville and H. Orsmond Anderton, ed. *The Melvill Book of Roundels*. London: Privately Printed for. . . the members of the Roxburghe Club, 1916; reprint ed., New York: Burt Franklin, 1972.

Barton, Anne. *Ben Jonson, Dramatist*. Cambridge: Cambridge University Press, 1984.

Baskerville, Charles Read. *The Elizabethan Jig and Related Song Drama*. Chicago: University of Chicago Press, 1929; reprint ed., New York: Dover Books, 1965.

Beck, Sydney, ed. *The First Book of Consort Lessons, Collected by Thomas Morley, 1599 and 1611*. New York: Published for the New York Public Library by C.F. Peters Corp. 1959.

Bedford, Jessie [Elizabeth Godfrey]. *Home Life Under the Stuarts 1603-1649*. London: Stanley Pauland Co., 1925.

Bentley, Gerald Eades. *The Jacobean and Caroline Stage*. Oxford: Clarendon Press, 1941-1956. Vol. 1 (1941): *Dramatic Companies and Players*. Vols. 3-5 (1956): *Plays and Playwrights*.

_____. *The Profession of Dramatist in Shakespeare's Time*. Princeton: Princeton University Press, 1971.

_____. *The Profession of Player in Shakespeare's Time, 1590-1642*. Princeton: Princeton University Press, 1984.

_____, ed. *The Seventeenth-Century Stage*. Chicago: University of Chicago Press, 1968.

Berger, Thomas Leland, ed. *A Critical Old-Spelling Edition of Thomas Dekker's Blurt, Master-Constable*. Salzburg, Austria: Institut fur Anglistik und Amerikanistik Universitat Salzburg, 1979.

Bergeron, David M. *English Civic Pageantry 1558-1642*. Columbia: University of South Carolina Press, 1971.

Berry, Herbert. "The Stage and Boxes at Blackfriars." *SP* 63 (1966): 163-86.

Bevington, David. *Action is Eloquence: Shakespeare's Language of Gesture*. Cambridge: Cambridge University Press, 1984.

Bontoux, Germaine. *La chanson en Angleterre au temps d'Elisabeth*. Oxford: Oxford University Press, 1936.

Bowers, Fredson, gen. ed. *The Dramatic Works of the Beaumont and Fletcher Canon*. 5 vols. Cambridge: Cambridge University Press, 1966-82.

Bowden, William R. *The English Dramatic Lyric, 1603-42*. New Haven: Yale University Press, 1951.

Boyd, Morrison Comegys. *Elizabethan Music and Musical Criticism*. 2d ed. Philadelphia: University of Pennsylvania Press, 1962.

Bradbrook, M.C. *The Growth and Structure of Elizabethan Comedy*. London: Chatto and Windus, 1973.

_____. "'Silk? Satin? Kersey? Rags?' The Choristers' Theater under Elizabeth and James." *SEL* 1 (Spring 1961): 53-64.

_____. "The Triple Bond: Audience, Actors, Author in the Elizabethan Playhouse." In *The Triple Bond*, edited by Joseph G. Price. University Park and London: Pennsylvania State University Press, 1975.

Braunmuller, A.R. and Michale Hattaway, eds. *The Cambridge Companion to English Reniassance Drama*. Cambridge: Cambridge University Press, 1990.

Brett, Philip. "The English Consort Song, 1570-1625." *PRMA* 88 (1961-62): 73-88.

_____, ed. *Consort Songs. Musica Britannica*, vol 22. London: Stainer and Bell, 1967.

A Brief Account of Cathedral and Collegiate Schools. London: J.B. Nichols, 1827.

Briggs, Julia. *This Stage-Play World: English Literature and its Background 1580-1625*. Oxford: Oxford University Press, 1983.

Briggs, Katharine M. *The Anatomy of Puck: An Examination of Fairy Beliefs Among Shakespeare's Contemporaries and Successors*. London: Routledge and Kegan Paul, 1959.

Brissenden, Alan. *Shakespeare and the Dance*. Atlantic Heights, NJ: Humanities Press, 1981.

Brock, D. Heywood. *A Ben Jonson Companion*. Bloomington: Indiana University Press, 1983.

Bronson, Bertrand H. "Literature and Music." In *Relations of Literary Study*, edited by James Thorpe. New York: Modern Language Association, 1967.

Britten, Norman A. *Thomas Middleton*. New York: Twayne Publishers, Inc., 1972.

Bry, Andre. "Middleton et le public des 'city comedies.'" In *Dramturgie et société*. Paris: Editions du centre national de la recherche scientifique, 1968.

Bryant, J.A., Jr. *The Compassionate Satirist: Ben Jonson and his Imperfect World*. Athens, GA: University of Georgia Press, 1972.

Bulliet, C.J. *Venus Castina: Famous Female Impersonators, Celestial and Human*. New York: Bonanza Books, 1956.

Butler, Gregory G. "Music and Rhetoric in Early Seventeenth-Century English Sources." *MQ* 66 (1980): 53-64.

Butler, Martin. *Theatre and Crisis 1632-1642*. Cambridge: Cambridge University Press, 1984.

Camden, Caroll. *The Elizabethan Woman*. Houston: The Elsevier Press, 1952.

Caputi, Anthony. *John Marston, Satirist*. Ithaca, NY: Cornell University Press, 1961.

Carpenter, Nan Cooke. *Music in the Medieval and Renaissance Universities*. Norman: University of Oklahoma Press, 1958.

Chalfant, Fran. *Ben Jonson's London: A Jacobean Placename Dictionary*. Athens: University of Georgia Press, 1978.

Chambers, E.K. *The Elizabethan Stage*. Vols. 2 and 3. Oxford: Clarendon Press, 1923.

[Chan,] Mary Joiner. "British Museum Add. MS 15117: A Commentary, Index, and Bibliography." *RMARC* 7 (n.d.): 51-75.

_____. *"Cynthia's Revels* and Music for a Choir School: Christ Church Manuscript Mus 439." *Studies in the Renaissance* 18 (1971): 134-69.

_____. *Music in the Theatre of Ben Jonson*. Oxford: Clarendon Press, 1980.

Chappell, William. *The Ballad Literature and Popular Music of the Olden Time*. 2 vols. London: 1855-59; reprint ed., New York: Dover Books, 1965.

_____, ed. *The Roxburghe Ballads*. 2 vols. Vol. 1 London: Printed for the Ballad Society by Taylor and Co., 1871. Vol. 2 Hertford: Printed for the Ballad Society by Stephen Austin & Sons, 1872.

Charney, Maurice. "The Children's Plays In Performance." *RORD* 18 (1975): 19-23.

Child, Francis James, ed. *The English and Scottish Popular Ballads*. 5 vols. London: Houghton Mifflin, 1882-98; reprint ed., New York: Dover Books, 1965.

Clark, Andrew, ed. *The Shirburn Ballads, 1585-1616*. Oxford: Clarendon Press, 1907.

Colley, John Scott. *John Marston's Theatrical Drama*. Salzburg, Austria: Institut fur Englische Sprache und Literatur Universitat Salzburg, 1974.

_____. "Music in the Elizabethan Private Theatres." *YES* 4 (1974): 62-69.

Collier, J. Payne. *Broadside Black-Letter Ballads, Printed in the Sixteenth and Seventeenth Centuries, chiefly in the possession of J. Payne Collier*. New York: Burt Franklin, 1968.

Collman, Herbert L. *Ballads and Broadsides Chiefly of the Elizabethan Period*. Oxford: Oxford University Press, 1912.

Cook, Ann Jennalie. *The Privileged Playgoers of Shakespeare's London, 1576-1642*. Princeton: Princeton University Press, 1981.

Cope, Jackson I. *Dramaturgy of the Daemonic*. Baltimore: Johns Hopkins University Press, 1984.

_____. *The Theater and the Dream: From Metaphor to Form in Renaissance Drama*. Baltimore: Johns Hopkins University Press, 1973.

Correspondence and Evidence Respecting the Ancient Collegiate School Attached to St. Paul's Cathedral. London: J.B. Nichols, 1832.

Cowling, G.H. *Music on the Shakespearean Stage*. Cambridge: Cambridge University Press, 1913.

Craig, Hardin. *The Enchanted Glass: the Elizabethan Mind In Literature*. New York: Oxford University Press, 1936.

Crum, M.C. "Notes on the Texts of William Lawes' Songs in B.M. MS Add. 31432." *The Library*, 5th series, 9 (1954): 122-27.

Cutts, John P. "A Bodleian Song-Book: Don.C.57." *ML* 34 (1953): 192-211.

_____. "British Museum Additional MS 31432: William Lawes' Writing for the Theatre and the Court." *The Library*, 5th series, 7 (1952): 225-34.

_____. "Drexel Manuscript 4041: '... Earl Ferrers' MS—A Treasure-House of Early Seventeenth-Century Song and Dramatic Lyric." *MD* 18 (1964): 151-202.

_____. "Early Seventeenth-Century Lyrics at St. Michael's College." *ML* 37 (1956): 221-33.

_____. *"Everie Woman in Her Humor."* *Renaissance News* 18 (1965): 209-13.

_____. *La musique de scène de la troupe de Shakespeare.* Paris: Editions du centre national de la recherche scientifique, 1959.

_____. "Peele's *Hunting of Cupid.*" *Studies in the Renaissance* 5 (1958): 121- 32.

_____. "A Reconsideration of the *Willow Song.*" *JAMS* 10 (1957): 14-24.

_____. "Robert Johnson and the Court Masque." *ML* 41 (1960): 111-26.

_____. "Robert Johnson: King's Musician in His Majesty's Public Entertainment." *ML* 36 (1955): 110-125.

_____. "La rôle de la musique dans les masques de Ben Jonson." In *Les fêtes de la Renaissance.* Paris: Editions du centre national de la recherche scientifique, 1956.

_____. "Seventeenth-Century Lyrics: Oxford, Bodelian, MS Mus.b.1." *MD* 10 (1956): 142-209.

_____. *Seventeenth-Century Songs and Lyrics.* Columbia, MO: University of Missouri Press, 1959.

_____. "Seventeenth-Century Songs and Lyrics in Edinburgh University Library MS Dc.1.69" *MD* 12 (1959): 169-94.

_____. "Seventeenth-Century Songs and Lyrics in Paris Conservatoire MS Res. 2489." *MD* 23 (1969): 117-39.

_____. "'Songs Unto the Violl and Lute'—Drexel MS 4175." *MD* 16 (1962): 73-92.

_____. "Two Jacobean Theatre Songs." *MS* 33 (1952): 333-34.

_____. "An Unpublished Contemporary Setting of a Shakespeare Song." *ShS* 9 (1956): 86-89.

_____. "William Lawes' Writing for the Theater and Court." *JAMS* 16 (1963): 243-53.

Cyr, Mary. "A Seventeenth-Century Source of Ornamentation for Voice and Viol: British Museum MS Egerton 2971." *RMARC* 9 (n.d.): 53-72.

Dart, R. Thurston. "Morley's Consort Lessons of 1599." *PRMA* 74 (1947-48): 1- 9.

_____. "Music and Musical Instruments in Cotgrave's *Dictionarie* (1611)." *GSJ* 21 (March 1968): 70-80.

_____. "Ornament Signs in Jacobean Music for Lute and Viol." *GSJ* 14 (1961): 30-33.

_____. "Role de la danse dans l"ayre' Anglais." In *Musique et poesie au XVIᵉ siècle.* Paris: Editions du centre national de la recherche scientifique, 1954.

Davies, W. Robertson. *Shakespeare's Boy Actors.* London: J.M. Dent and Sons, 1939.

Day, Cyrus Lawrence, and Eleanore Boswell Murrie. *English Song-Books 1651-1702: A Bibliography with a First-Line Index of Songs.* London: Printed for the Bibliographical Society, 1940.

Dean-Smith, Margaret, ed. *Playford's English Dancing Master 1651: A Facsimile Reprint with an Introduction, Bibliography, and Notes.* London: Schott & Co., 1957.

Dean-Smith, Margaret, and E.J. Nichol. "'The Dancing Master': 1651-1728." *JEFDSS* 4 (1940-41): 131-45 and 167-79.

De Lafontaine, Henry Cart. *The King's Musick.* London: Novello and Co., 1909.

Deloney, Thomas. *Works.* Edited by Francis Oscar Mann. Oxford: Clarendon Press, 1912.

Dent, Edward J. *The Foundations of English Opera*. Cambridge: Cambridge University Press, 1928.

Doughtie, Edward. "Words for Music: Simplicity and Complexity in the Elizabethan Air." *Rice University Studies* 51 (1965): 1-12.

_____, ed. *Lyrics from English Airs, 1596-1622*. Cambridge: Harvard University Press, 1970.

Dryden, John. *Works*. Edited by Sir Walter Scott. Revised and corrected by George Saintsbury. Vol. 15. London: Printed for William Paterson & Co., 1892.

Duckles, Vincent. "English Song and the Challenge of Italian Monody." In *Words to Music: Papers on English Seventeenth-Century Song*. Los Angeles: The William Andrews Clark Memorial Library of the University of California at Los Angeles, 1967. Pp 3-23.

_____. "The Gamble Manuscript as a Source of Continuo Song in England." *JAMS* 1 (1948): 23-40.

_____. "The Music for the Lyrics in Early Seventeenth-Century English Drama: A Bibliography of the Primary Sources." In *Music in English Renaissance Drama*, edited by John H. Long. Lexington: University of Kentucky Press, 1968.

Dusinberre, Juliet. *Shakespeare and the Nature of Women*. London: Macmillan Press, 1975.

Dutton, Richard. *Ben Jonson: To the First Folio*. Cambridge: Cambridge University Press, 1983.

Eccles, Mark. "Martin Peerson and the Blackfriars." *ShS* 11 (1958): 100-106.

Edwards, Warwick. "The Walsingham Consort Books." *ML* 55 (1974): 209-14.

_____, ed. *Music for Mixed Consort*. *Musica Britannica*, vol. 40. London: Stainer and Bell, 1977.

Eggar, Katharine E. "The Blackfriars Plays and Their Music: 1576-1600." *PRMA* 87 (1960-61): 57-68.

Einstein, Alfred. *The Italian Madrigal*. Translated by Alexander H. Krappe, Roger H. Sessions, and Oliver Strunk. Vols. 1 and 2. Princeton: Princeton University Press, 1949.

Eliot, T.S. *Elizabethan Dramatists*. London: Faber and Faber, 1962.

Emslie, McDonald. "Dowland, Ornithoparcus, and Musica Mundana." *Notes and Queries* 199 (September 1954): 372-74.

_____. "Nicholas Lanier's Innovations in English Song." *ML* 41 (1960): 13- 27.

Esler, Anthony. *The Aspiring Mind of the Elizabethan Younger Generation*. Durham: Duke University Press, 1966.

Evans, Willa McClung. *Ben Jonson and Elizabethan Music*. Lancaster, PA: Lancaster Press, 1929; reprint ed., New York: Da Capo Press, 1965.

_____. *Henry Lawes: Musician and Friend of Poets*. New York: Modern Language Association of America, 1941.

Ewbank, Inga-Stina. "'These Pretty Devices': A Study of Masques in Plays." In *A Book of Masques in Honor of Allardyce Nicoll*. Cambridge: Cambridge University Press, 1967.

Fabry, Frank J. "Sidney's Poetry and Italian Song-Form." *ELR* 3 (1973): 232- 48.

Farr, Dorothy M. *Thomas Middleton and the Drama of Realism*. Edinburgh: Oliver and Boyd, 1973.

Felber, Rudolf. "Music and Superstition." Translated by Theodore Baker. *MQ* 17 (1931): 234-47.

Fellowes, Edmund H. *The Catalogue of Manuscripts in the Library of St. Michael's College, Tenbury.* Paris: Editions de l'oiseau lyre, 1934.
_____. *The English Madrigal.* London: Oxford University Press, 1925.
_____. "The Texts of the Song-Books of Robert Jones." *ML* 8 (1927): 25-37.
Finkelpearl, Philip J. *John Marston of the Middle Temple: An Elizabethan Dramatist in his Social Setting.* Cambridge: Harvard University Press, 1969.
Finney, Gretchen L. "Ecstasy and Music in Seventeenth-Century England." *JHI* 8 (1947): 153-88.
_____. *Musical Backgrounds for English Literature: 1580-1650.* New Brunswick: Rutgers University Press, 1962.
_____. "A World of Instruments." *ELH* 20 (1953): 87-120.
Fitzgibbon, H. Macaulay. "Instruments and their Music In Elizabethan Drama." *MQ* 17 (1931): 319-29.
_____. "The Lute Books of Ballett and Dallis." *ML* 11 (1930): 71-77.
Fleay, Frederick Gard. *A Chronicle History of the London Stage, 1559-1642.* London: Reeves and Turner, 1890.
Foakes, R.A. *Illustrations of the English Stage, 1580-1642.* London: Scolar Press, 1985.
_____. "Playhouses and Players." *The Cambridge Companion to English Renaissance Drama.* Edited by A.R. Braunmuller and Michael Hattaway. Cambridge: Cambridge University Press, 1990.
_____. "Tragedy at the Children's Theatres After 1600: A Challenge to the Adult Stage." *The Elizabethan Theatre* II (1970): 37-59.
Foakes, R.A., and R.T. Rickert, eds. *Henslowe's Diary.* Cambridge: Cambridge University Press, 1961.
Folger Shakespeare Library. *Catalogue of Manuscripts of the Folger Shakespeare Library, Washington DC.* 3 vols. Boston: G.K. Hall and Co., 1971.
Fortune, Nigel. "Continuo Instruments in Italian Monodies." *GSJ* 6 (1953): 10- 13.
_____. "Giustiniani on Instruments." *GSJ* 5 (1952): 48-54.
_____. "Philip Rosseter and his Songs." *LSJ* 7 (1965): 7-14.
Frye, Northrop. *Anatomy of Criticism.* Princeton: Princeton University Press, 1957.
_____. "The Argument of Comedy." In *English Institute Essays, 1948*, edited by D.A. Robertson, Jr. New York: Columbia University Press, 1948.
_____. *A Natural Perspective: The Development of Shakespearean Comedy and Romance.* New York: Columbia University Press, 1965.
Fuller, David. "Ben Jonson's Plays and their Contemporary Music." *ML* 58 (1977): 60-75.
_____. "The Jonsonian Masque and its Music." *ML* 54 (1973): 440-52.
Gair, W. Reavley. *The Children of Paul's: The Story of a Theatre Company, 1553-1608.* Cambridge: Cambridge University Press, 1982.
_____. "The Presentation of Plays at Second Paul's: The Early Phase (1599- 1602)." *The Elizabethan Theatre* 6 (1975): 21-47.
_____. "Second Paul's: Its Theatre and Personnel: Its Later Repertoire and Audience (1602-6)." *The Elizabethan Theatre* 7 (1977): 21-43.
Galpin, Francis W. *Old English Instruments of Music: Their History and Character.* 4th ed., revised. London: Methuen & Co., 1965.
Geckle, George. *John Marston's Drama: Themes, Images, Sources.* London: Associated University Presses, 1980.

Gibbons, Brian. *Jacobean City Comedy: A Study of Satiric Plays by Jonson, Marston, and Middleton*. Cambridge: Harvard University Press, 1968.

_____. *Jacobean City Comedy*. 2d ed. London: Methuen and Co., 1980.

Gilbert, Allan H. "The Function of the Masques in *Cynthia's Revels*." *PQ* 22 (1943): 211-30.

Gilchrist, Anne G. "Some Additional Notes on the Traditional History of Certain Ballad-Tunes in the *Dancing Master* (1650) [sic]." *JEFDSS* 3 (1936-37): 274-80.

Godwin, Joscelyn. "The Renaissance Flute." *The Consort* 28 (1972): 70-81.

Gombosi, Otto. "Some Musical Aspects of the English Court Masque." *JAMS* 1 (Fall, 1948): 3-19.

Gossett, Suzanne. "Masque Influence in the Dramaturgy of Beaumont and Fletcher." *MP* 69 (1971-72): 199-208.

_____. "The Term 'Masque' in Shakespeare and Fletcher and *The Coxcomb*." *SEL* 14 (1974): 285-95.

Graves, R.B. "Daylight in the Elizabethan Private Theatres." *SQ* 33 (1982): 80-92.

Greenstreet, James. "Blackfriars Theatre in the Time of Shakespeare." *The Athenaeum* 3224 (August 10, 1889): 203-4.

Greer, David. "'What If A Day'—An Examination of the Words and Music." *ML* 43 (1962): 304-19.

Greg, W[alter] W[ilson]. *A Bibliography of the English Printed Drama to the Restoration*. London: Printed for the Bibiographical Society at the University Press, Oxford. Vol. 1 (1939): *Stationers Records Plays to 1616*. Vol. 3 (1957): *Collections, Appendix, Reference Lists*.

_____, ed. *Dramatic Documents from the Elizabethan Playhouses*. Oxford: Clarendon Press, 1931.

_____. *Pastoral Poetry and Pastoral Drama*. London: A.H. Bullen, 1906.

Grew, Eva Mary. "Music and Morality." *MR* 1 (1940): 159–76.

Gurr, Andrew. *Playgoing in Shakespeare's London*. Cambridge and New York: Cambridge University Press, 1987.

_____. *The Shakespearean Stage, 1574-1642*. Cambridge: Cambridge University Press, 1970.

Hadaway, Robert. "The Re-Creation of an Italian Renaissance Harp." *Early Music* 8 (1980): 59-62.

Hales, John W. and Furnivall, Frederick J., eds. *Bishop Percy's Folio Manuscript*. 3 vols. London: N. Trubner & Co., 1868.

Harbage, Alfred. *Annals of English Drama*. Revised by S. Schoenbaum. 3rd ed., revised by Sylvia Stoler Wagonheim. London and New York: Routledge, 1989.

_____. *Annals of English Drama*. Revised by S. Schoenbaum. 2nd ed., revised. Philadelphia: University of Pennsylvania Press, 1964.

_____. *Shakespeare and the Rival Traditions*. New York: Macmillan and Co., 1952.

Harris, Anthony. *Night's Black Agents*. Manchester: Manchester University Press, 1980.

Harris, David G.T. "Musical Education in Tudor Times." *PRMA* 65 (1938-39): 109-39.

Harrison, G.B. *Elizabethan Plays and Players*. Ann Arbor: University of Michigan Press, 1956.

Hart, Eric Ford. "Introduction to Henry Lawes." *ML* 32 (1951): 217-25 and 328-44.

Hartnoll, Phyllis, ed. *Shakespeare in Music*. London: Macmillan and Co., 1964.

Hattaway, Michael. *Elizabethan Popular Theatre: Plays in Performance*. London: Routledge and Kegan Paul, 1982.

Hendrick, Donald K. "The Masquing Principle in Marston's *The Malcontent*." *English Literary Renaissance* 8 (1978): 24-42.

Henning, Rudolf. "A Possible Source of Lachrimae?" Translated by Uta Henning and John E. Hancock. *LSJ* 16 (1974): 67-67.

Herford, C.H., and Percy Simpson, eds. *Ben Jonson*. 11 vols. Oxford: Clarendon Press, 1925-52.

Heseltine, Philip [Peter Warlock]. *The English Ayre*. London: Oxford University Press, 1926.

_____, ed. *Giles Earle His Booke*. London: The Houghton Publishing Co., 1932.

Hill, Christopher. *The Century of Revolution*. London: Thomas Nelson, 1961.

Hillebrand, Harold Newcomb. *The Child Actors*. Urbana: University of Illinois Studies in Language and Literature, vol. 11, nos. 1 and 2, 1926.

Hollander, John. *The Untuning of the Sky: Ideas of Music in English Poetry, 1500-1700*. Princeton: Princeton University Press,1961.

Holmes, David M. *The Art of Thomas Middleton*. Oxford: Clarendon Press, 1970.

Horne, David. *The Life and Minor Works of George Peele*. New Haven: Yale University Press, 1952.

Hosley, Richard. "The Playhouses and the Stage." In *A New Companion to Shakespeare Studies*, edited by Kenneth Muir and S. Schoenbaum. Cambridge: Cambridge University Press, 1971.

_____. "A Reconstruction of the Second Blackfriars." *The Elizabethan Theatre* 1 (1969): 74-88.

Hughes, Charles W. "John Gamble's Commonplace Book." *ML* 26 (1945): 215-29.

Hughes-Hughes, Augustus. *Catalogue of Manuscript Music in the British Museum*. 3 vols. London: Published by the Trustees of the British Museum, 1906-1911. Vol. 1 (1906): *Sacred Vocal Music*. Vol. 2 (1908): *Secular Vocal Music*. Vol. 3 (1911): *Instrumental Music, Treatises, Etc.*

Hume, Tobias. *The First Part of Ayres (1605) and Captaine Humes Poeticall Musicke (1607)*. Edited by Sterling Jones. Introduction by Veronika Gutmann. Winterthur: Amadeus Verlag, 1980.

Hunter, G.K. "English Folly and Italian Vice: The Moral Landscape of John Marston." In *Stratford-upon-Avon Studies 1: Jacobean Theatre*. New York: St. Martin's Press, 1960.

Hurstfield, Joel. "The Politics of Corruption in Shakespeare's England." *ShS* 28 (1975): 15-28.

_____, and Alan G.R. Smith, eds. *Elizabethan People: State and Society*. London: Edward Arnold, 1972.

Huth, Henry, ed. *Ancient Ballads and Broadside*. London: Whittingham and Wilkins, 1867.

Hutton, James. "Some English Poems in Praise of Music." In *English Miscellany* 2, edited by Mario Praz. Rome: Published for the British Council by Edizioni di storia e letteratura, 1951.

Ing, Catherine. *Elizabethan Lyrics: A Study in the Development of English Metres and Their Relation to Poetic Effect*. London: Chatto and Windus, 1968.

Ingram, R.W. *John Marston*. Boston: Twayne Publishers, 1978.

_____. "Operatic Tendencies in Stuart Drama." *MQ* 44 (1958): 489-502.

_____. "Patterns of Music and Action in Fletcherian Drama." In *Music in English Renaissance Drama*, edited by John H. Long. Lexington: University of Kentucky Press, 1968.

_____. "The Use of Music in the Plays of Marston." *ML* 37 (1956): 154-164.

_____. "Words and Music." *Stratford-upon-Avon Studies 2: Elizabethan Poetry*. London: Edward Arnold, Ltd., 1960. Pp. 131-149.

Isaacs, J. *Production and Stage Management at the Blackriars Theatre*. London: Oxford University Press, 1933.

Jacquot, Jean. "Le Repertoire des compagnies d'enfants à Londres (1600-1610): Essai d'interpretation socio-dramaturgique." *Dramaturgie et société*. Paris: Editions du centre national de la recherche scientifique, 1968. Pp. 731-82.

Jensen, Ejner J. "The Boy Actors: Plays and Playing." *RORD* 28 (1975): 5-11.

_____. *John Marston, Dramatist: Themes and Imagery in the Plays*. Salzburg, Austria: Institut fur Anglistik und Amerikanistik Universitat Salzburg, 1979.

Jewkes, Wilfred T. *Act Division in Elizabethan and Jacobean Plays*. Hamden, CT: Shoe String Press, 1958.

Johnson, Paula. *Form and Transformation in Music and Poetry of the English Renaissance*. New Haven: Yale University Press, 1972.

Jorgens, Elise Bickford. "On Matters of Manner and Music in Jacobean and Caroline Song." *ELR* 10 (1980): 239-64.

_____. *The Well-Tun'd Word: Musical Interpretations of English Poetry, 1597-1651*. Minneapolis: University of Minnesota Press, 1982.

Kay, W. David. The Shaping of Ben Jonson's Career: A Re-Examination of Facts and Problems." *MP* 67 (1969-70): 224-37.

Kelso, Ruth. *Doctrine for the Lady of the Renaissance*. Urbana: University of Illinois Press, 1956.

Kemp, William, ed. *John Marston's The Wonder of Women or the Tragedy of Sophonisba: A Critical Edition*. New York: Garland Publishing Inc., 1979.

Kerman, Joseph. *The Elizabethan Madrigal: A Comparative Study*. New York: American Musicological Society, 1962.

Kernodle, George R. *From Art to Theatre: Form and Convention in the Renaissance*. Chicago: University of Chicago Press, 1944.

Kiefer, Christian. "Music and Marston's *The Malcontent*." *SP* 51 (1954): 163- 71.

King, A. Hyatt. *Some British Collectors of Music, c. 1600-1960*. Cambridge: Cambridge University Press, 1963.

Kirk, Florence Ada, ed. *The Faithful Shepherdess by John Fletcher: A Critical Edition*. New York and London: Garland Publishing, Inc., 1980.

Knights, L.C. *Drama and Society in the Age of Jonson*. London: Chatto and Windus, 1937.

Kolin, Philip C. "An Annotated Bibliography of Scholarship on the Children's Companies and their Theatres." *RORD* 19 (1976): 57-82.

_____, and R.O. Wyatt, II. "A Bibliography of Scholarship on the Elizabethan Stage since Chambers." *RORD* 15 (1972): 33-59.

Kreider, Paul V. *Elizabethan Comic Character Conventions as Revealed in the Comedies of George Chapman*. Ann Arbor: University of Michigan Press, 1935.

Lawrence. W.J. *The Elizabethan Playhouse and Other Studies*. Philadelphia: J.B. Lipincott Co., 1912.

_____. "The English Theatre Orchestra: Its Rise and Early Characteristics." *MQ* 3 (1917): 9-27.

_____. "Music in the Elizabethan Theatre." *MQ* 6 (1920): 192-205.

_____. *Pre-Restoration Stage Studies*. Cambridge: Harvard University Press, 1927; reprint ed., New York: Benjamin Blom, 1967.

_____. "Thomas Ravenscroft's Theatrical Associations." *MLR* 29 (1924): 418- 23.

Lasocki, David. "Professional Recorder Playing in England 1500-1740. Part I: 1500-1640." *Early Music* 10 (1982): 23-29.

LeCocq, Louis. "Le Theatre de Blackfriars de 1596 à 1606." In *Dramaturgie et Société*. Paris: Editions du centre national de la recherche scientifique, 1968.

Lefkowitz, Murray. *William Lawes*. London: Routledge and Kegan Paul, 1960.

Leggatt, Alexander. *Ben Jonson: His Vision and His Art*. London: Meuthen, 1981.

_____. *Citizen Comedy in the Age of Shakespeare*. Toronto: University of Toronto Press, 1973.

Lell, Gordon. "'Ganymede' on the Elizabethan Stage: Homosexual Implications of the Use of Boy Actors." *Aegis* 1 (Spring 1973): 5-15.

LeJeune, Jerome. "The Lyra-Viol: An Instrument or a Technique?" *The Consort* 31 (1975): 125-31.

Lennam, Trevor. "The Children of Paul's, 1551-1582." *The Elizabethan Theatre* 2 (1970): 20-36.

_____. *Sebastian Westcott, The Children of Paul's, and "The Marriage of Wit and Science."* Toronto: University of Toronto Press, 1975.

Lilly, Joseph, ed. *A Collection of Seventy-Nine Black-Letter Ballads and Broadsides, Printed in the Reign of Queen Elizabeth, Between 1559 and 1597*. London: Joseph Lilly, 1867.

Lindley, David., ed. *The Court Masque*. Manchester: Manchester University Press, 1984.

Lindsey, Edwin S. "The Music of the Songs in Fletcher's Plays." *SP* 21 (1924): 325-55.

_____. "The Original Music for Beaumont's Play *The Knight of the Burning Pestle*." *SP* 26 (1929): 425-43.

Lippman, Edward Arthur. "Symbolism in Music." *MQ* 39 (1953): 554-75.

Long, John H. *Shakespeare's Use of Music*. 3 vols. Gainesville: University of Florida Press, 1955-71. Vol. 1 (1955): *A Study of the Music and Its Performance in the Original Production of Seven Comedies*. Vol. 2 (1961): *The Final Comedies*. Vol. 3 (1971): *The Histories and Tragedies*.

_____. "Sneak's 'Noyse' Heard Again?" *MQ* 44 (1958): 76-81.

_____, ed. *Music in English Renaissance Drama*. Lexington: University of Kentucky Press, 1968.

Love, Harold. "The Fiddlers on the Restoration Stage." *Early Music* 6 (1978): 391-99.

Lumsden, David. "The Sources of English Lute Music (1540-1620)." *GSJ* 6 (1953): 14-19.

Lyons, Bridget Gellert. *Voices of Melancholy: Studies in Literary Treatment of Melancholy in Renaissance England*. New York: Barnes and Noble, 1971.

MacDonald, Michael. *Mystical Bedlam: Madness, Anxiety and Healing in Seventeenth-Century England*. Cambridge: Cambridge University Press, 1981.

Mackerness, E.D. *A Social History of English Music*. Toronto: University of Toronto Press, 1964.

MacLean, Ian. *The Renaissance Notion of Woman*. Cambridge, London, and New York: Cambridge University Press, 1980.

The Malone Society. W.W. Greg, gen. ed. *Collections*. London: Oxford University Press, 1907.

Manifold, John S. *The Music in English Drama from Shakespeare to Purcell*. London: Rockliff Publishing Corp., 1956.

_____. "Theatre Music in the Sixteenth and Seventeenth Centuries." *ML* 29 (1948): 366-97.

Mann, Francis Oscar, ed. *The Works of Thomas Deloney*. Oxford: Clarendon Press, 1912.

Marcuse, Sibyl. *A Survey of Musical Instruments*. New York: Harper and Row, 1975.

Maynard, Winifred. *Elizabethan Lyric Poetry and its Music*. Oxford: Clarendon Press, 1986.

Mazzaro, Jerome. *Transformations in the Renaissance English Lyric*. Ithaca: Cornell University Press, 1970.

McCullen, J.T. "The Functions of Songs Aroused by Madness in Elizabethan Drama." In *A Tribute to George Coffin Taylor*. Edited by Arnold Williams. Chapel Hill: University of North Carolina Press, 1952.

McDonnel, Michael F. *A History of St. Paul's School*. London: Chapman and Hall, 1909.

Mehl, Dieter. *The Elizabethan Dumb Show*. Cambridge: Harvard University Press, 1966.

Mellers, Wilfrid. *Harmonious Meeting: A Study of the Relationship Between English Music, Poetry, and Theatre, c. 1600-1900*. London: Dennis Dobson, 1965.

_____. "La Melancholie au debut du XVIIe siècle et la madrigal Anglais." In *Musique et poesie au XVIe siècle*. Paris: Editions du centre national de la recherche scientifique, 1954.

Mersenne, Marin. *Harmonie Universelle (Paris, 1636)*. Edition facsimile de l'exemplaire conserve a la Bibliothèque de Arts et Metiers et annote par l'Auteur. Paris: Editions du centre national de la recherche scientifique, 1965.

Meyer, Ernst H. *English Chamber Music*. London: Lawrence and Wishart, 1946.

Meyer-Baer, Kathl. *Music of the Spheres and the Dance of Death: Studies in Musical Iconography*. Princeton: Princeton University Press, 1970.

Mies, Otto Heinrich. "Dowland's Lachrimae Tune." *MD* 4 (1950): 59-64.

Monson, Craig. "Thomas Myriell's Manuscript Collection: One View of Musical Taste in Jacobean London." *JAMS* 30 (1977): 419-65.

_____. *Voices and Viols in England, 1600-1650: The Sources and the Nusic*. Ann Arbor: University Microforms International Research Press, 1982.

Montagu, Jeremy. *The World of Baroque and Classical Musical Instruments*. London: David and Charles, 1979.

_____. *The World of Medieval and Renaissance Musical Instruments*. London: David and Charles, 1976.

Moore, John Robert. "The Function of Songs in Shakespeare's Plays." In *Shakespeare Studies*. By members of the department of English at the University of Wisconsin to commemorate the 300th anniversary of the death of William Shakespeare, April 23, 1616. Madison: University of Wisconsin, 1916.

Moss, Harold Gene. "Popular Music and the Ballad Opera." *JAMS* 26 (1973): 365-82.

Muir, Kenneth and S. Schoenbaum, eds. *A New Companion to Shakespeare Studies*. Cambridge: Cambridge University Press, 1971.

Murray, John Tucker. *English Dramatic Companies, 1558-1642*. Boston: Houghton Mifflin Co., 1910. Vol. 1: *London Companies, 1558-1642*.

Naylor, Edward W. *Shakespeare and Music*. New York: Da Capo Press, 1965.

Newcomb, Wilburn W., ed. *Lute Music of Shakespeare's Time*. University Park: Pennsylvania State University Press, 1966.

Newton, Richard. "English Lute Music of the Olden Age." *PRMA* 6 (1939): 63-90.

Nicoll, Allardyce. *Stuart Masques and the Renaissance Stage*. New York: Benjamin Blom. 1938.

Nuttall, A.D. *Two Concepts of Allegory*. New York: Barnes and Noble, 1967.

Obertello, Alfredo. *Madrigali Italiani in Inghilterra*. Milano: Valentino Bompiani, 1949.

Oboussier, Philippe. "Turpyn's Book of Lute-Songs." *ML* 34 (1953): 145-49.

O'Neill, Davis G. "The Influence of Music in the Works of Marston." *ML* 53 (1972): 122-33, 239-308, and 400-410.

Orgel, Stephen. *The Illusion of Power*. Berkeley: University of California Press, 1975.

_____. "Nobody's Perfect: Or Why Did the English Stage Take Boys for Women?" *The South Atlantic Quarterly* 88 (1989): 7-30.

Orgel, Stephen and Roy Strong. *Indigo Jones: The Theatre of the Stuart Court*. 2 vols. London: Sotheby Parke Bernet, and Berkeley and Los Angeles: University of California Press, 1973.

Pallis, Marco. "The Instrumentation of English Viol Consort Music." *Chelys* 1 (1970): 27-35.

Parrot, Thomas Marc, ed. *The Plays of George Chapman: The Tragedies*. 2 vol. New York: Russell and Russell, 1961.

Pattison, Bruce. "Literature and Music in the Age of Shakespeare." *PRMA* 60 (1933-34): 67-86.

_____. *Music and Poetry of the English Renaissance*. New York: Da Capo Press, 1971.

Payne, Ian. "The Sacred Music of Thomas Ravenscroft." *Early Music* 10 (1982): 309-14.

Peery, William. *The Plays of Nathan Field*. Austin: University of Texas Press, 1950.

Percy, Thomas. *Reliques of Ancient English Poetry*. 3 vols. London: Swan, Sonnenschein, Lebas, & Lowry, 1886; reprint ed., New York: Dover Books, 1966.

Phillips, James E., and Bertrand H. Bronson. *Music and Literature in England in the Seventeenth and Eighteenth Centuries*. Los Angeles: William Andrews Clark Memorial Library of the University of California at Los Angeles, 1953.

Pollard, A.W. and G.R. Redgrave, comps. *A Short-Title Catalogue of Books Printed in England, Scotland, and Ireland, 1475-1640*. London: Bibliographical Society, 1969.

Poulton, Diana. "The Black-Letter Broadside Ballad and its Music." *Early Music* 9 (1981): 427-36.

_____. *John Dowland*. London: Faber and Faber, 1972; rev. ed., 1982.

_____. "Notes on the Spanish Pavin." *LSJ* 3 (1961): 5-16.

Praetorius, Michael. *Syntagma Musicum*. Band 2: *De Organographia* (Wolfenbuttel 1619). Faksimile-Nachdruk. Basel: Barenreiter Kassel, 1958.

Price, Curtis A. *Music in the Restoration Theatre*. Ann Arbor: University Microfilms International Research Press, 1979.

_____. "Restoration Stage Fiddlers and Their Music." *Early Music* 7 (1979): 315-21.

_____. "Restoration Theatre Music Restored." *MT* 124 (June 1983): 344-47.

Price, Joseph G., ed. *The Triple Bond: Plays, Mainly Shakespearean, in Performance*. University Park: Pennsylvania State University Press, 1975.

Rastall, Richard. "Female Roles in All-Male Casts." *Medieval English Theatre* 7 (1985): 25-50.

Ratcliffe, Stephen. *Campion: On Song*. London: Routledge and Kegan Paul, 1981.

Raynor, Henry. "Framed to the Life of the Words." *MR* 19 (1958): 261-72.

_____. "Words for Music." *MMR* 88 (1958): 174-82.

Reed, D.G. "Italian and Italiante Poetry." *Stratford-upon-Avon Studies 2: Elizabethan Poetry*. London: Edward Arnold, 1960. Pp. 53-69.

Reed, Robert Rentoul, Jr. *The Occult on the Tudor and Stuart Stage*. Boston: Christopher Publishing House, 1965.

Remnant, Mary. *Musical Instruments of the West*. London: B.T. Batsford, 1978.

Rhodes, Neil. *Elizabethan Grotesque*. London: Routledge and Kegan Paul, 1980.

Ribner, Irving, and Clifford Chalmers Huffman. *Tudor and Stuart Drama*. Second Edition. Arlington Heights, IL: AHM Publishing Corporation, 1978.

Riddell, James A. "Some Actors in Ben Jonson's Plays." *Shakespeare Studies* 5 (1969): 285-98.

Rimbault, Edward F. *Bibliotheca Madrigaliana: A Bibliographical Account of the Musical and Poetical Works Published in England During the Sixteenth and Seventeenth Centuries*. London: John Russell Smith, 1847.

_____, ed. *The Old Cheque-Book, or Book of Remembrance of the Chapel Royal from 1561 to 1744*. Westminster: J.B. Nichols & Sons, 1872.

Rimmer, Joan. "Harps in the Baroque Era." *PRMA* 90 (1963-64): 59-75.

_____. "James Talbot's Manuscript (Christ Church Library Music MS 1187)— VI. Harps." *GSJ* 16 (May 1963): 63-72.

_____. "The Morphology of the Irish Harp." *GSJ* 17 (February 1964): 39-49.

Ritson, Joseph. *Ancient Songs and Ballads*. London: Reeves and Turner, 1877. 3d ed., revised by W. Carew Hazlitt. Detroit: Singing Tree Press, 1968.

_____. *A Select Collection of English Songs*. 3 vols. London: Printed for J. Johnson, 1783.

Roche, Jerome. *The Madrigal*. New York: Charles Scribner's Sons, 1972.

Rollins, Hyder E. "The Black-Letter Broadside Ballad." *PMLA* 34 (1919): 258- 339.

_____, comp. *An Analytical Index to the Ballad Entries (1557-1709) in the Registers of the Company of Stationers of London*. Hatboro, PA: Tradition Press, 1967.

_____, ed. *A Handfull of Pleasant Delights (1584) by Clement Robinson and Divers Others*. Cambridge, MA: Harvard University Press, 1924.

Rooley, Anthony. "New Light on John Dowland's Songs of Darkness." *Early Music* 11 (1983): 6-21.

Ross, Lawrence J. "Shakespeare's 'Dull Clown' and Symbolic Music." *SQ* 27 (1966): 107-28.

Rowan, D.F. "The English Playhouse: 1595-1630." *RenD*, New Series 4 (1971): 37-51.

Ruff, Lillian M. "The Social Significance of the Seventeenth Century English Musical Treatises." *The Consort* 26 (1970): 412-22.

Ruff, Lillian M. and D. Arnold Wilson. "The Madrigal, the Lute Song, and Elizabethan Politics." *Past and Present* 44 (August 1969): 3-51.

Rust, Frances. *Dance in Society*. London: Routledge and Kegan Paul, 1969.

Sabol, Andrew J. "A Newly Discovered Contemporary Song Setting for Jonson's
'Cynthia's Revels.'" *N&Q* 203 (1958): 384-85.

_____. "Ravenscroft's *Melismata* and the Children of Paul's." *Renaissance News*
12 (1959): 3-9.

_____. "Recent Studies in Music and English Renaissance Drama." *Shakespearean
Research Opportunities* 4 (1968-69): 1-14.

_____. "Two Songs with Accompaniment for an Elizabethan Choirboy Play." *Stud-
ies in Renaissance* 5 (1958): 145-59.

_____. "Two Unpublished Stage Songs for the 'Aery of Children.'" *Renaissance
News* 13 (1960): 222-32.

_____, ed. *Four Hundred Songs and Dances from the Stuart Masques*. Providence:
Brown University Press, 1978.

Samson, Patricia. "Words for Music." *SORA* 1 (1963): 46-52.

Schleiner, Louise. *The Living Lyre in English Verse from Elizabeth Through the Restoration*. Columbia: University of Missouri Press, 1984.

Schoenbaum, Samuel. "The Precarious Balance of John Marston." *PMLA* 67 (1952):
1069-78.

Scholes, Percy A. *The Puritans and Music in England and New England*. New York:
Russell and Russell, 1962.

Scott, Michael. *John Marston's Plays: Theme, Structure and Performance*. London:
Macmillan Press, 1978.

Seng, Peter J. *The Vocal Songs in the Plays of Shakespeare*. Cambridge: Harvard University Press, 1967.

Shapiro, Michael. "Audience vs. Dramatist in Jonson's *Epicoene* and Other Plays of
the Children's Troupes." *ELR* 3 (1973): 400-417.

_____. "The Children of Paul's and their Playhouse." *TN* 36 (1982): 3-13.

_____. *Children of the Revels: The Boy Companies of Shakespeare's Time and their
Plays*. New York: Columbia University Press, 1977.

_____. "Music and Song in Plays Acted by Children's Companies During the Eng-
lish Renaissance." *CMc* 7 (1968): 97-100.

Shumaker, Wayne. *The Occult Sciences in the Renaissance: A Study in Intellectual
Patterns*: University of California Press, 1972.

Simpson, Claude. *The British Broadside Ballad and Its Music*. New Brunswick: Rutgers University Press, 1966.

Smith, Alan. "The Cultivation of Music in English Cathedrals in the Reign of Elizabeth I." *PRMA* 94 (1967-68): 34-49.

_____. "The Gentlemen and Children of the Chapel Royal of Elizabeth I: An Anno-
tated Register." *RMARC* 5 (1965): 13-46.

Smith, David M. *Guide to Bishop's Registers of England and Wales*. London: Offices
of the Royal Historical Society, 1981.

Smith, Douglas Alton. "On the Origin of Chitarrone." *JAMS* 32 (1979): 440-62.

Smith, Hallett. *Elizabethan Poetry: A Study in Conventions, Meaning, and Expression*. Cambridge: Harvard University Press, 1952.

Smith, Irwin. *Shakespeare's Blackfriars Playhouse*. New York: New York University
Press, 1964.

Smith, Steven R. "The London Apprentices as Seventeenth-Century Adolescents." *Past and Present* 61 (November 1973): 149-61.

Spencer, Robert, "Chitarrone, Theorbo and Archlute." *Early Music* 4 (1976): 407-22.

_____. "The Tollmache Lute Manuscript." *LSJ* 7 (1965): 38-39.

Spink, Ian. *English Song from Dowland to Purcell*. London: B.T. Batsford, 1974.

_____. "Sources of English Song, 1620-1660: A Survey." *MMA* 1 (1966): 117- 36.

Starnes, DeWitt T., and Gertrude Noyes. *The English Dictionary from Cawdrey to Johnson, 1604-1755*. Chapel Hill: University of North Carolina Press, 1946.

Steele, Mary Susan. *Plays and Masques at Court*. New Haven: Yale University Press, 1926.

Steele, Robert. *The Earliest English Music Printing: A Description and Bibliography of English Printed Music to the Close of the Sixteenth Century*. London: Printed for the Bibliographical Society at the Chiswick Press, 1903.

Steen, Sara Jayne. *Thomas Middleton: A Reference Guide*. Boston: G.K. Hall and Co., 1984.

Sternfeld, Frederick W. "The Dramatic and Allegorical Function of Music in Shakespeare's Tragedies." *AnnM* 3 (1955): 265-82.

_____. *Music in Shakespearean Tragedy*. London: Routledge and Kegan Paul, 1963.

_____. "La musique dans les tragedies Elizabethaines inspirees de Senèque." In *Les tragedies de Senèque et le theatre de la Renaissance*. Paris: Editions du centre national de la recherche scientifique, 1964.

_____. "Shakespeare's Use of Popular Song." In *Elizabethan and Jacobean Studies Presented to Frank Percy Wilson*, edited by H.J. Davis and H.L. Gardner. Oxford: Clarendon Press, 1959.

_____. "Le symbolisme musical dans quelques pièces de Shakespeare." In *Les fêtes de la Renaissance*. Paris: Editions du centre national de la recherche scientifique, 1956.

_____. "The Use of Song in Shakespeare's Tragedies." *PRMA* 86 (1959-60): 45-49.

Stevens, David. *English Renaissance Theatre History: A Reference Guide*. Boston: G.K. Hall and Co., 1982.

Stevens, Denis. "Pièces de theatre et 'pageants' a l'epoque des Tudor." In *Les fêtes de la Renaissance*. Paris: Editions du centre national de la recherche scientifique, 1956.

_____. *Thomas Tompkins*. London: Macmillan and Co., 1957.

Stevens, John E. *Music and Poetry In the Early Tudor Court*. London: Methuen and Co., 1961.

Stone, Lawrence. *The Crisis of the Aristocracy, 1558-1641*. Oxford: Clarendon Press, 1965.

_____. "The Educational Revolution in England, 1560-1640." *Past and Present* 28 (July 1964): 41-80.

_____. *The Family, Sex and Marriage in England, 1500-1800*. New York: Harper and Row, 1977.

Sutherland, Sara P. *Masques in Jacobean Tragedy*. New York: AMS Press, 1983.

Tabourot, Jehan [Thoinot Arbeau]. *Orchesography*. Translated by Mary Stewart Evans. New York: Kamin Dance Publishers, 1948.

Teague, Frances. "Ben Jonson's Stagecraft in *Epicoene*." *RenD*, n.s. 9 (1978): 75-192.

Thomas, Keith. *Religion and the Decline of Magic*. New York: Charles Scribner's Sons, 1971.

Tilley, Morris Palmer. *A Dictionary of Proverbs in England in the Sixteenth and Seventeenth Centuries*. Ann Arbor: University of Michigan Press, 1950.

Tillyard, E.M.W. *The Elizabethan World Picture*. London: Chatto and Windus, 1950.

Tovey, Donald Francis. "Words and Music: Some *Obiter Dicta*." In *Seventeenth Century Studies Presented to Sir Herbert Grierson*. Oxford: Clarendon Press, 1938.

Traficante, Frank. "Lyra Viol Tunings: 'All Ways have been Tryed to do it.'" *AcM* 42 (1970): 183-205.

_____. "Music for Lyra Viol: Manuscript Sources." *Chelys* 8 (1978-79): 4- 6.

Tuve, Rosemond. *Elizabethan and Metaphysical Imagery*. Chicago: University of Chicago Press, 1947.

Tyson, Archie Mervin. *Every Woman in Her Humor: A Critical Edition*. New York: Garland Publishing, Inc., 1980.

Ure, Peter. "Chapman's Tragedies." In *Elizabethan and Jacobean Drama: Critical Essays by Peter Ure*. Edited by J.C. Maxwell. Liverpool: Liverpool University Press, 1974.

Vlasto, Jill. "An Elizabethan Anthology of Rounds." *MQ* 40 (1954): 222-34.

Waith, Eugene M. "The English Masque and the Functions of Comedy." *The Elizabethan Theatre* 8 (1979): 144-63.

Walker, Andrew Jackson. "Popular Songs and Broadside Ballads in the English Drama, 1559-1642." Ph.D. diss., Harvard University, 1934.

Walker, D.P. "Musical Humanism in the Sixteenth and Early Seventeenth Centuries." *MR* 2 (1941): 1-13, 111-21, 220-27, and 228-308; and *MR* 3 (1942): 55-71.

_____. *Spiritual and Demonic Magic from Ficino to Campanella*. London: The Warburg Institute, 1958.

Wallace, Charles William. "The Children of the Chapel at Blackfriars, 1597- 1603." *University Studies* 8 (April-July 1908); reprinted as *The Children of the Chapel at Blackfriars*. New York: AMS Press, 1970.

Wallis, Lawrence Bergman. *Fletcher, Beaumont, and Company*. Morningside Heights, NY: King's Crown Press, 1947.

Ward, John M. "Apropros *The British Broadside Ballad and its Music*." *JAMS* 20 (1967): 28-86.

_____. "The English Measure." *Early Music* 14 (1986): 15-21.

_____. "Music for *A Handefull of Pleasant Delites*." *JAMS* 10 (1957): 151- 80.

_____. "The So-Called 'Dowland Lute Book' in the Folger Shakespeare Library." *Lute Society of America Journal* 9 (1976): 5-29.

Wayne, Don E. "*Drama and Society in the Age of Johnson*: An Alternative View." *RenD*, n.s. 13 (1982): 103-29.

Weaver, Robert L. "The Orchestra in Early Italian Opera." *JAMS* 17 (1964): 83- 89.

_____. "Sixteenth-Century Instrumentation." *MQ* 47 (1961): 363-78.

Welch, Christopher. *Lectures on the Recorder in Relation to Literature*. London: Oxford University Press, 1961.

Wells, Evelyn K. "Playford Tunes and Broadside Ballads." *JEFDSS* 3 (1936-37): 81-92, 195-202, and 259-73.

Wells, Robin Headlam. "John Dowland and Elizabethan Melancholy." *Early Music* 13 (1985): 514-28.

Welsford, Enid. *The Court Masque*. New York: Russell and Russell, Inc., 1962.

Westrup, J.A. "Domestic Music Under the Stuarts." *PRMA* 68 (1941-42): 19-53.

White, Eric Walter. *A History of English Opera*. London: Faber and Faber, 1983.

_____. *The Rise of English Opera*. New York: Philosophical Library, 1951.

Wickham, Glynne. *Early English Stages, 1300 to 1660*. London: Routledge and Kegan Paul, 1972. Vol. 2: *1576-1660*, pt. 2.

Wilets, Pamela J. *The Henry Lawes Manuscript*. London: Published by the Trustees of the British Museum, 1969.

Willets, Pamela J. "A Neglected Source of Monody and Madrigal." *ML* 43 (1962): 329-39.

_____. "Silvanus Stirrop's Book." *RMARC* 10 (n.d.): 101-07.

Wilson, John Dover, comp. *Life in Shakespeare's England*. Cambridge: Cambridge University Press, 1920.

Wilson, John Dover and May Yardley, eds. *Lewes Lavater Of Ghostes and Spirites Walking by Nyght 1572*. Oxford: Oxford University Press, 1929.

Wing, Donald, comp. *Short-Title Catalogue of Books Printed in England, Scotland, Ireland, Wales, and British America, 1641-1700*. 3 vols. New York: Printed for the Index Society by Columbia University Press, 1945-51.

Woodfill, Walter L. *Musicians in English Society from Elizabeth to Charles I*. Princeton: Princeton University Press, 1953.

Woodman, David. *White Magic and English Renaissance Drama*. Rutherford: Farleigh Dickinson University Press, 1973.

Wright, Louis B. *Middle-Class Culture in Elizabethan England*. Ithaca: Cornell University Press, 1958.

Yates, Frances A. *The Occult Philosophy in the Elizabethan Age*. London: Routledge and Kegan Paul, 1979.

_____. *Theatre of the World*. Chicago: University of Chicago Press, 1969.

Young, Alan R. "Henry Peacham, Ben Jonson, and the Cult of Elizabeth-Oriana." *ML* 60 (1979): 305-11.

INDEX

For Product Safety Concerns and Information please contact our EU
representative GPSR@taylorandfrancis.com
Taylor & Francis Verlag GmbH, Kaufingerstraße 24, 80331 München, Germany